THE
TOP
10
OF EVERYTHING
1997

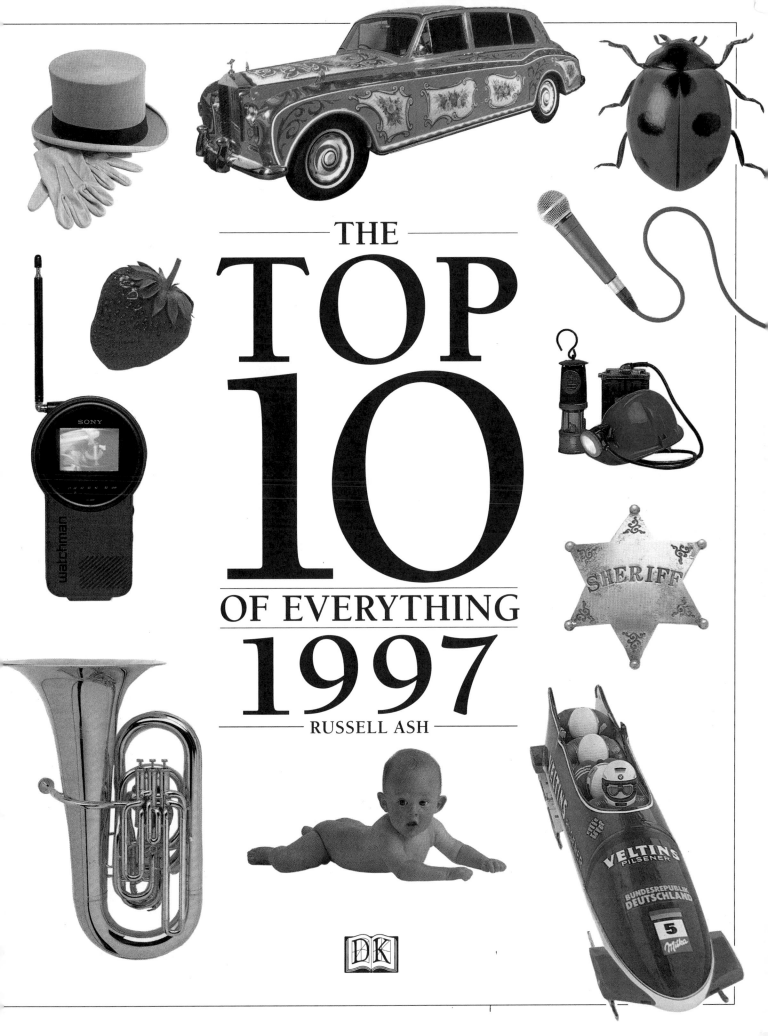

THE
TOP
10
OF EVERYTHING
1997

RUSSELL ASH

A DK PUBLISHING BOOK

Project Editor Adèle Hayward
US Editor Michael Wise
Managing Editor Stephanie Jackson
Managing Art Editor Nigel Duffield
Senior Managing Editor Krystyna Mayer
Senior Managing Art Editor Lynne Brown
Production Controller Louise Daly

Designed and Typeset by Blackjacks Limited
Designer Jonathan Baker
Project Editor Helen Freeman
Senior Editor Jack Buchan
Editors Krystyna Green, Casey Horton

First American Edition, 1996
2 4 6 8 10 9 7 5 3 1

Published in the United States by
DK Publishing, Inc.
95 Madison Avenue
New York, New York 10016

Copyright © 1996
Dorling Kindersley Limited, London
Text copyright © 1996 Russell Ash

Visit us on the World Wide Web at
http://www.dk.com

Library of Congress Cataloging-in-Publication Data
Ash, Russell.
The top ten of everything, 1997 / by Russell Ash. – 1st
American ed.
p. cm.
ISBN 0-7894-1264-0 (pbk.)
ISBN 0-7894-1083-4 (cloth)
1. Curiosities and wonders. 2. World records–Miscellanea.
I. Title.
AG243.A712 1996
031.02–dc20
96-14203
CIP

Reproduction by HBM Print Ltd, Singapore.
Printed and bound in the United States by
R.R. Donnelley & Sons Company.

CONTENTS

INTRODUCTION

Welcome to the 8th annual edition of *The Top 10 of Everything*. If this is your first edition, it is worth knowing that this is not a book of "bests," but of Top 10s that can be measured in some way. The only "bests" you will find here are bestsellers, because their sales can be quantified, and "worsts" are generally those incidents in which the most people were killed. The lists therefore represent no one's opinions, least of all my own, in any area other than my personal choice of what I include and what I omit. There are also some firsts and, just occasionally, unquantifiable lists of 10 prominent but not definitively "Top" examples in certain categories.

THE WORLD OF TOP 10

The Top 10 of Everything has its roots in the UK, but editions have also been published in countries as diverse as France, Italy, Australia, Finland, Canada, Japan, and the US. In this, the 8th annual edition, we have introduced a selection of lists from each side of the Atlantic. Both Oscar Wilde and George Bernard Shaw coined phrases to the effect that Britain and America were divided by their common language (but then, they were both Irish...). However, the similarities and the differences between two cultures that overlap in so many ways, as revealed by these lists, are fascinating. Cinema, literature, and music are the most notable areas, and yet – as our Top 10s reveal – Beatles records achieved different levels of success in their homeland and in the US, and while our surnames may be similar, the names we give to our pets are not. There are convergences in certain sporting enthusiasms, such as golf and tennis, and yet we remain worlds apart in others (such as the passions of each nation for cricket and baseball). The US is, statistically speaking, a dangerous country in terms of violent crime and motor-vehicle accidents, but it records few major railroad accidents, and so on.

WHAT'S NEW?

Although it is no easy task, it has always been my aim to make each new edition of the book as different as possible from its predecessor, while retaining its overall formula and mixture of trivia and hard facts, old favorites, and debut Top 10s. There are some list subjects that appear annually, but which are updated as new data comes in (even long-standing, "all-time" lists can change). Others retain the same title from year to year but the contents change completely (the 10 most-watched films of one year are quite different from those of the previous year), while a proportion of the lists are entirely new to this edition. As we approach the millennium, there are more lists summarizing the events of the 20th Century, and there are many new "Did You Know?" features throughout.

WHO SAYS SO?

Where does all this information come from? As well as published information and, increasingly, material accessed electronically, I make use of specialty organizations, research bodies, and experts. There is often a time-lag in the compilation of statistics – especially government figures – sometimes of several years, but you should assume that those I have presented are the latest available.

FACT OR FICTION?

Mark Twain remarked, "There are three kinds of lies: lies, damned lies, and statistics." As a major consumer of reference books, I can tell you that few are free of mistakes, and some are worse than others. It is no easy task to keep up to date with changes and to ensure a high level of accuracy, and mistakes do occasionally creep in: the subway in Washington, DC turns out to be shorter than this and other reference books have previously quoted; a major national museum "forgot" to tell us about some of its best-attended exhibitions; and a distinguished consultant provided an erroneous figure for the size of a kiwi, thereby conjuring up an image of a monster bird. Some questions have no definitive answer: debate even rages over such issues as the identity of the world's tallest building, the height of Everest, and the lengths of the longest rivers. Some of these disagreements derive from varying methods of measurement and definitions (do you include or exclude a building's spires? what are the precise boundaries of a city?); others from the immense difficulty of calculating certain statistics (how many Christians are there in the world? how many people in the US are called Smith?). Figures for country and city populations are based on the latest available census, with estimates for increases where officially available, and in most instances "countries" should be taken as meaning "countries, colonies, and dependent territories."

ENTRY LEVELS

As the years go by, the minimum qualification for entry to élite Top 10 lists becomes ever more demanding: it is distressing that this is so with accidents and disasters, and numbers of murder victims, but it is equally true with escalating prices paid for works of art and achievements in the realms of sports and entertainment. For example, if you want to take your chances with a long-staying chart CD, you now have to remain there for more than five years even to qualify to 10th position, and you now need to be at least 72 years old to be numbered among the 10 oldest Oscar winners, and not a day over 13 to be one of the 10 youngest. Good luck!

SUGGESTIONS OR CORRECTIONS

For either, you can contact me on our World Wide Web site at http://www.dk.com (where you will find more Top 10 lists and information about other DK books), e-mail me direct at ash@pavilion.co.uk, or write to me in care of the publishers.

8

THE UNIVERSE & EARTH

20TH CENTURY

The 20th century has witnessed immense advances in the study of space. The birth of space travel and the use of manned and robotic space probes, combined with extraordinary progress in such areas as optical and radio telescopes and computer science, have vastly enhanced our knowledge and understanding of the universe and revealed worlds and galaxies far beyond our own.

SCANNING THE SKY
Discoveries by both amateur astronomers and the world's great observatories – as well as recent revelations by space telescopes – have revolutionized our understanding of space in the 20th century.

TOP 10

LARGEST REFLECTING TELESCOPES IN THE WORLD

	Telescope name	Location	Opened*	Aperture (m)
1	Keck I & II Telescopes	Mauna Kea Observatory, Hawaii	1992/96	10.82
2	Bolshoi Teleskop Azimutal'ny	Special Astrophysical Observatory of the Russian Academy of Sciences, Mount Pastukhov, Russia	1976	6.0
3	Hale Telescope	Palomar Observatory, California	1948	5.0
4	William Herschel Telescope	Observatorio del Roque de los Muchachos, La Palma, Canary Islands	1987	4.2
5=	Mayall Telescope#	Kitt Peak National Observatory, Arizona	1973	4.0
5=	Four-meter Telescope#	Cerro Tololo Inter-American Observatory, Chile	1976	4.0
7	Anglo–Australian Telescope	Siding Spring Observatory, New South Wales, Australia	1974	3.9
8=	ESO 3.6-meter Telescope	European Southern Observatory, La Silla, Chile	1975	3.6
8=	Canada–France–Hawaii Telescope	Mauna Kea Observatory, Hawaii	1970	3.6
8=	United Kingdom Infrared Telescope	Mauna Kea Observatory, Hawaii	1979	3.6

* Dedicated or regular use commenced
 # Northern/Southern Hemisphere "twin" telescopes

If the Keck I & II (identical twin telescopes) at No. 1 are discounted because their "mirrors" are not in one piece (they comprise 36 hexagonal segments slotted together) then the joint-10th entries in the list become the 3.5-m New Technology Telescope at the European Observatory, Chile, which started operations in 1990, and the 3.5-m WIYN (Wisconsin, Indiana, and Yale Universities and the National Optical Astronomy Observatories) Telescope, which joined the Mayall at Kitt Peak National Observatory, Arizona, in October 1994.

REACHING FOR THE STARS

TOP 10

LARGEST ASTEROIDS DISCOVERED IN THE 20TH CENTURY

	Name/no.	Year	Discoverer	Diameter km	miles
1	Hektor (624)	1907	A. Kopff	440	273
2	Davida (511)	1903	R.S. Dugan	326	203
3	Interamnia (704)	1910	V. Cerulli	317	197
4	Herculina (532)	1904	M. Wolf	222	138
5	Alauda (702)	1910	J. Helffrich	195	121
6	Winchester (747)	1913	J.H. Metcalf	172	107
7	Pretoria (790)	1912	H.E. Wood	170	106
8	Stereoskopia (566)	1905	P. Gotz	168	104
9	Agamemnon (911)	1919	K. Reinmuth	167	104
10	Diomedes (1437)	1937	K. Reinmuth	164	102

TOP 10

ASTEROID DISCOVERERS

	Astronomer	Period	Observatory	Asteroids discovered
1	K. Reinmuth	1914–57	Heidelberg	375
2	N.S. Chernykh	1966–89	Nauchnyj	335
3	E. Bowell	1977–88	Palomar/Flagstaff	334
4	Maximilian Wolf	1891–1932	Heidelberg	246
5	C.S. Shoemaker	1980–91	Palomar	149
6	L. Chernykh	1966–87	Nauchnyj	148
7	S.J. Bus	1975–89	Palomar/Siding Spring/Cerro Tololo	137
8	Y. Vaisala	1935–44	Turku	126
9	H. Debehogne	1978–90	La Silla	123
10	J. Palisa	1874–1923	Pola/Vienna	121

From January 1, 1801, when Ceres became the first asteroid to be discovered, up to 1900, a total of 452 had been identified, named, and numbered. No. 453 was found on February 22, 1900 by A. Charlois of Nice, and given the name Tea – not after the drink but in honor of an Irish goddess. Since then, the catalogue has risen to more than 5,000, with smaller and smaller examples being discovered as astronomical techniques constantly improve.

ECLIPSE OF THE SUN

TOP 10

FIRST PLANETARY PROBES

	Probe/country/planet	Arrival*
1	*Venera 4*, USSR, Venus	Oct 18, 1967
2	*Venera 5*, USSR, Venus	May 16, 1969
3	*Venera 6*, USSR, Venus	May 17, 1969
4	*Venera 7*, USSR, Venus	Dec 15, 1970
5	*Mariner 9*, US, Mars	Nov 13, 1971
6	*Mars 2*, USSR, Mars	Nov 27, 1971
7	*Mars 3*, USSR, Mars	Dec 2, 1971
8	*Venera 8*, USSR, Venus	Jul 22, 1972
9	*Venera 9*, USSR, Venus	Oct 22, 1975
10	*Venera 10*, USSR, Venus	Oct 25, 1975

* Successfully entered orbit or landed

This list excludes "fly-bys" – probes that passed by but did not land on the surface of another planet. The US's *Pioneer 10*, for example, launched on March 2, 1972, flew past Jupiter on December 4, 1973 but did not land. *Venera 4* was the first unmanned probe to land on a planet, and *Venera 9* the first to transmit pictures from a planet's surface. *Mariner 9* was the first to orbit another planet; earlier and later *Mariners* were not designed to land and are now either in orbit around the Sun or have traveled beyond the Solar System.

TOP 10

LARGEST MOONS IN THE SOLAR SYSTEM DISCOVERED IN THE 20TH CENTURY

	Moon	Planet	Year	Discoverer	Diameter km	miles
1	Charon	Pluto	1978	James Christy	1,240	771
2	Miranda	Uranus	1948	Gerard Kuiper	472	293
3	Proteus	Neptune	1989	*Voyager 2*	403	250
4	Nereid	Neptune	1949	Gerard Kuiper	340	211
5	Larissa	Neptune	1989	*Voyager 2*	192	119
6	Janus	Saturn	1966	Audouin Dollfus	190	118
7	Himalia	Jupiter	1904	Charles Perrine	184	114
8	Puck	Uranus	1985	*Voyager 2*	170	106
9	Galatea	Neptune	1989	*Voyager 2*	158	98
10	Despina	Neptune	1989	*Voyager 2*	148	92

10

NATURAL DISASTERS

20TH CENTURY

Natural disasters have affected the human race for thousands of years. As the 20th century has progressed, such catastrophes have, if anything, become worse: population increases, especially in cities, and the growth of high rise buildings, mean that earthquakes that might once have affected a handful of people, now kill thousands and cause disruption on a massive scale. Modern advances in the provision of food aid and medical supplies have alleviated, but not conquered, such long-established scourges as famines and plagues.

THE WRATH OF THE VOLCANO
There are perhaps more than 500 currently active volcanoes in the world, with as many as 2,500 that have been active in recorded history. Fortunately, most do not endanger human life, but the attractions of farming on rich volcanic soil means that settlements have sometimes fallen victim to major eruptions.

THE 10

WORST AVALANCHES AND LANDSLIDES OF THE 20th CENTURY*

	Location	Incident	Date	Estimated no. killed
1	Yungay, Peru	Landslide	May 31, 1970	17,500
2	Italian Alps	Avalanche	December 13, 1916	10,000
3	Huarás, Peru	Avalanche	December 13, 1941	5,000
4	Nevada Huascaran, Peru	Avalanche	January 10, 1962	3,500
5	Medellin, Colombia	Landslide	September 27, 1987	683
6	Chungar, Peru	Avalanche	March 19, 1971	600
7	Rio de Janeiro, Brazil	Landslide	January 11, 1966	550
8=	Northern Assam, India	Landslide	February 15, 1949	500
8=	Grand Riviere du Nord, Haiti	Landslide	November 13–14, 1963	500
10	Blons, Austria	Avalanche	January 11, 1954	411

* Excluding those where most deaths resulted from flooding, earthquakes, etc., associated with landslides

The worst incident of all, the destruction of Yungay, Peru, in May 1970, was only part of a much larger cataclysm that left a total of up to 70,000 dead. Following an earthquake and flooding, the town was wiped out by an avalanche that left just 2,500 survivors out of a population of 20,000. Similar incidents, in which the avalanche was a contributor in a series of disasters, include that at Khansou, China, on December 16, 1920, when a total of 180,000 were killed from the combined effects of earthquake, a massive landslide, and winter weather after their homes were destroyed. In Italy on October 9, 1963, 1,190 people were killed when a landslide fell into the reservoir of the Vaiont Dam causing it to overflow and flood. Among the most tragic of such disasters in this century was that at Aberfan, Wales, UK, on October 20, 1966. Waste from a coal mine had been building up for many years to become a heap some 800 ft/244 m in height. Weakened by the presence of a spring, a huge volume of slurry suddenly flowed down and engulfed the local school, killing 144, of whom 116 were children.

THE 10

WORST FLOODS AND STORMS OF THE 20th CENTURY

	Location	Date	Estimated no. killed
1	Huang He River, China	Aug 1931	3,700,000
2	Pakistan (now Bangladesh)	Nov 13, 1970	300–500,000
3	Henan, China	1939	more than 200,000
4	Chang Jiang River, China	Sep 1911	100,000
5	Bengal, India	Nov 15–16, 1942	40,000
6	Pakistan (now Bangladesh)	Jun 1–2, 1965	30,000
7	Pakistan (now Bangladesh)	May 28–29, 1963	22,000
8	Pakistan	May 11–12, 1965	17,000
9	Morvi, India	Aug 11, 1979	5,000–15,000
10	Hong Kong	Sep 18, 1906	10,000

THE AFTERMATH OF AN EARTHQUAKE IN ALASKA

THE 10

WORST EARTHQUAKES OF THE 20th CENTURY

	Location	Date	Estimated no. killed
1	Tang-shan, China	July 28, 1976	242,419
2	Nanshan, China	May 22, 1927	200,000
3	Kansu, China	December 16, 1920	180,000
4	Messina, Italy	December 28, 1908	160,000
5	Tokyo/Yokohama, Japan	September 1, 1923	142,807
6	Kansu, China	December 25, 1932	70,000
7	Callejon de Huaylas, Peru	May 31, 1970	66,800
8	Quetta, India*	May 30, 1935	50–60,000
9	Armenia	December 7, 1988	over 55,000
10	Iran	June 21, 1990	over 40,000

* Now Pakistan

There are some discrepancies between the "official" death tolls in many of the world's worst earthquakes and the estimates of other authorities: a figure of 750,000 is sometimes quoted for the Tang-shan earthquake of 1976, for example, and totals ranging from 58,000 to 250,000 are given for the quake that devastated Messina in 1908. Several other earthquakes in China and Turkey have resulted in deaths of 100,000 or more. In recent times, the Armenian earthquake of December 7, 1988, and that which struck northwest Iran on June 21, 1990, resulted in the deaths of more than 55,000 (official estimate 28,854) and 50,000 respectively. One of the most famous earthquakes, the one that destroyed San Francisco on April 18, 1906, killed only between 500 and 1,000 – mostly in the fires that followed the shock.

THE 10

WORST VOLCANIC ERUPTIONS OF THE 20th CENTURY

	Location/date	Estimated no. killed
1	Mt. Pelée, Martinique, May 8, 1902	up to 40,000

After lying dormant for centuries, Mt. Pelée began to erupt in April 1902. Assured that there was no danger, the 30,000 residents of the main city, St. Pierre, stayed in their homes and were there on May 8, when the volcano burst apart at 7:30 am and showered the port with molten lava, ash, and gas, destroying all life and property. The official death toll was 29,025. One of the bizarre, but horrific, side effects was that some 50 people were killed by deadly fer-de-lance snakes that had been disturbed by the eruption.

2	Nevado del Ruiz, Colombia, November 13, 1985	22,940

The Andean volcano gave warning signs of erupting, but by the time it was decided to evacuate the local inhabitants, it was too late. The hot steam, rocks, and ash ejected from Nevado del Ruiz melted its icecap, resulting in a mudslide that completely engulfed the town of Armero.

3	Santa Maria, Guatemala, October 24, 1902	6,000
4	Keluit, Java, 1919	5,110
5	Mt. Lamington, New Guinea, January 21, 1951	2,942

Mt. Lamington erupted with hardly any warning, with a huge explosion that was heard up to 200 miles/320 km away.

6	Lake Nyos, Cameroon, August 21, 1986	more than 1,700

A volcano erupted beneath the lake, and deadly gases asphyxiated sleeping villagers.

7	La Soufrière, St. Vincent, May 7–8, 1902	1,565

The day before the cataclysmic eruption of Mt. Pelée (No. 1 in this list), 90 miles/145 km to the south, La Soufrière erupted and engulfed the local inhabitants in ash flows.

8	Taal, Philippines, January 30, 1911	1,335

Taal, a volcano in the lake of the same name to the south of Manila, has erupted frequently, with the 1911 incident the worst of several during this century (200 people were killed as recently as 1965).

9	Merapi, Java, December 13–28, 1931	more than 1,300
10	Mt. Agung, Indonesia, January–May 1963	1,184

SPITTING FIRE AND BRIMSTONE
Red hot lava (liquid rock) shoots out of a volcano in a curtain of fire. Severe volcanic eruptions in the past have destroyed entire communities and killed thousands of people.

THE PLANETS

TOP 10

LARGEST PLANETARY MOONS

	Moon	Planet	Diameter km	miles
1	Ganymede	Jupiter	5,269	3,274

Discovered by Galileo in 1609–10 and believed to be the largest moon in the Solar System, Ganymede – one of Jupiter's 16 satellites – is thought to have a surface of ice about 60 miles/97 km thick. The 1979 Voyager 1 and 2 space probes failed to detect evidence of an atmosphere. Launched in 1989, NASA's aptly named Galileo probe reached Ganymede in June 1996.

	Moon	Planet	Diameter km	miles
2	Titan	Saturn	5,150	3,200

Titan, the largest of Saturn's 18 confirmed moons, is actually larger than Mercury and Pluto. It was discovered by the Dutch astronomer Christian Huygens in 1655. We have no idea what its surface looks like because it has a dense atmosphere, containing nitrogen, ethane, and other gases, that shrouds its surface, but data sent back by Voyager 1 in 1980 and recent radio telescope observations suggest that it may have ethane "oceans" and "continents" of ice. NASA and the European Space Agency have announced plans to send a space probe to Titan as part of the Cassini mission. It should touch down on Titan's surface in October 2002.

	Moon	Planet	Diameter km	miles
3	Callisto	Jupiter	4,820	2,995

Possessing a similar composition to Ganymede, Callisto is heavily pitted with craters, perhaps more so than any other body in the Solar System.

	Moon	Planet	Diameter km	miles
4	Io	Jupiter	3,632	2,257

Most of what we know about Io was reported by the 1979 Voyager probe, which revealed a crust of solid sulfur, with massive volcanic eruptions hurling sulfurous material 186 miles/300 km into space.

INHOSPITABLE
The surface of Venus is extremely hot, with high atmospheric pressure and clouds of sulfuric acid.

	Moon	Planet	Diameter km	miles
5	Moon	Earth	3,475	2,159

Our own satellite is a quarter of the size of the Earth, the 5th largest in the Solar System, and the only moon explored by humans.

	Moon	Planet	Diameter km	miles
6	Europa	Jupiter	3,126	1,942

Although Europa's ice-covered surface is apparently smooth and crater-free, it is covered with mysterious black lines, some of them 40 miles/64 km wide, resembling canals.

	Moon	Planet	Diameter km	miles
7	Triton	Neptune	2,750	1,708

This moon was discovered on October 10, 1846 by British brewer and amateur astronomer William Lassell 17 days after German astronomer Galle discovered Neptune itself. Triton is the only known satellite in the Solar System that revolves around its planet in the opposite direction to the planet's rotation. It is moving progressively closer to Neptune, and it is believed that in several million years the force of the planet's gravity may pull Triton apart, scattering it into a form like the rings of Saturn. Information sent back to Earth by Voyager 2 during August 1989 revealed the presence of three or four rings and "ring arcs," as well as six previously undiscovered moons, which were given the temporary names of 1989N1–1989N6. The average surface temperature of Triton was calculated to reach as low as –391°F/–235°C, but the ice layer actually shifts from one pole to the other and back again once every 165 years, the length of time it takes for Neptune to orbit the Sun. Photographs transmitted back to Earth also showed dark streaks shooting 5 miles/8 km into the atmosphere. These have been explained as resulting from seasonal temperature changes, which cause methane in the moon's crust to heat up and break through nitrogen ice layers as geysers, or they may be dust storms similar to those observed on Mars.

	Moon	Planet	Diameter km	miles
8	Titania	Uranus	1,580	982

The largest of Uranus's 15 moons, Titania was discovered by William Herschel in 1787 and has a snowball-like surface of ice. Data obtained from Voyager 2 led to a revision in the estimate of Titania's size.

	Moon	Planet	Diameter km	miles
9	Rhea	Saturn	1,530	951

Saturn's second largest moon was discovered by 17th-century, Italian-born French astronomer Giovanni Cassini. Voyager 1, which flew past Rhea in November 1980, confirmed that its icy surface is pitted with craters.

	Moon	Planet	Diameter km	miles
10	Oberon	Uranus	1,516	942

Oberon, also discovered by Herschel, was given the name of the fairy-king husband of Queen Titania, both characters in Shakespeare's A Midsummer Night's Dream.

TOP 10

LONGEST YEARS IN THE SOLAR SYSTEM

	Body	Length of year* years	days
1	Pluto	247	256
2	Neptune	164	298
3	Uranus	84	4
4	Saturn	29	168
5	Jupiter	11	314
6	Mars	1	322
7	Earth		365
8	Venus		225
9	Mercury		88
10	Sun		0

* *Period of orbit around the Sun, in Earth years and days*

TOP 10

COLDEST BODIES IN THE SOLAR SYSTEM*

	Body	Lowest temperature (°F)	(°C)
1	Pluto	–382	–230
2	Uranus	–369	–223
3	Neptune	–364	–220
4	Mercury	–328	–200
5	Saturn	–256	–160
6	Jupiter	–229	–145
7	Mars	–220	–140
8	Earth	–128	–89
9	Venus	+867	+464
10	Sun	+9,932	+5,500

* *Excluding satellites and asteroids*

BODIES FARTHEST FROM THE SUN

(In the Solar System, excluding satellites)

	Body	Average distance from the Sun km	miles
1	Pluto	5,914,000,000	3,675,000,000
2	Neptune	4,497,000,000	2,794,000,000
3	Uranus	2,871,000,000	1,784,000,000
4	Chiron	2,800,000,000	1,740,000,000
5	Saturn	1,427,000,000	887,000,000
6	Jupiter	778,300,000	483,600,000
7	Mars	227,900,000	141,600,000
8	Earth	149,600,000	92,900,000
9	Venus	108,200,000	67,200,000
10	Mercury	57,900,000	36,000,000

THE MYSTERIOUS GAS GIANT
Jupiter, seen here with two of its moons, is composed almost entirely of hydrogen and helium.

TOP 10

LARGEST ASTEROIDS

	Name	Year discovered	Diameter km	miles
1	Ceres	1801	936	582
2	Pallas	1802	607	377
3	Vesta	1807	519	322
4	Hygeia	1849	450	279
5	Euphrosyne	1854	370	229
6	Interamnia	1910	349	217
7	Davida	1903	322	200
8	Cybele	1861	308	192
9	Europa	1858	288	179
10	Patienta	1899	275	171

Asteroids, sometimes referred to as "minor planets," are fragments of rock orbiting between Mars and Jupiter. There are perhaps 45,000 of them, but fewer than 10 percent have been named. The first (and largest) to be discovered was Ceres, which was found by Giuseppe Piazzi (1746–1826), director of the Palermo observatory in Sicily, on New Year's Day, 1801. All have been numbered according to the order in which they were discovered. Some have only code numbers, but most also have names: women's names, including Hilda and Bertha, are especially popular.

TOP 10

LARGEST BODIES IN THE SOLAR SYSTEM

	Body	Maximum diameter km	miles
1	Sun	1,392,140	865,036
2	Jupiter	142,984	88,846
3	Saturn	120,536	74,898
4	Uranus	51,118	31,763
5	Neptune	49,532	30,778
6	Earth	12,756	7,926
7	Venus	12,103	7,520
8	Mars	6,794	4,222
9	Ganymede	5,269	3,274
10	Titan	5,150	3,200

Most of the planets are visible with the naked eye and have been observed since ancient times. The exceptions are Uranus, discovered on March 13, 1781, by the British astronomer Sir William Herschel; Neptune, found by German astronomer Johann Galle on September 23, 1846 (Galle was led to his discovery by the independent calculations of the French astronomer Urbain Leverrier and the British mathematician John Adams); and, outside this Top 10, Pluto, located using photographic techniques by American astronomer Clyde Tombaugh. The announcement of its discovery came on March 13, 1930. Its diameter is not precisely known, but it is thought to be approximately 1,430 miles/2,302 km.

DID YOU KNOW

ROCK STARS

Among astronomical features named after 20th-century characters are Gabi, an asteroid named in 1970 after the East German women's ice-skating champion Gabriele Seyfert, who had been placed second in the 1968 Olympic figure-skating competition. Nata, an asteroid discovered by Russian astronomer S.I. Belyavasky in 1927, was named after Russian female parachutist Natalya Babushkina, and two other asteroids, Lyuba and Tamariva, after other women parachutists, all of whom had been killed in parachuting accidents. A rock known as a planetesimal in the Kuiper Belt, beyond Pluto's orbit, was named George Smiley by its discoverers David Jewitt and Jane Luu after the character in John Le Carré's novels; they also named a 1993 discovery Karla, after Smiley's opponent.

DARK AND LIGHT
The carbon-rich rock of Ceres's surface reflects little light, while the highly reflective surface of Vesta makes it just visible to the naked eye.

STARS & COMETS

14

STARS NEAREST THE EARTH

(*Excluding the Sun*)

	Star	Light years*	Distance km	miles
1	Proxima Centauri	4.22	39,923,310,000,000	24,792,500,000,000
2	Alpha Centauri	4.35	41,153,175,000,000	25,556,250,000,000
3	Barnard's Star	5.98	56,573,790,000,000	35,132,500,000,000
4	Wolf 359	7.75	73,318,875,000,000	45,531,250,000,000
5	Lalande 21185	8.22	77,765,310,000,000	48,292,500,000,000
6	Luyten 726-8	8.43	79,752,015,000,000	49,526,250,000,000
7	Sirius	8.64	81,833,325,000,000	50,818,750,000,000
8	Ross 154	9.45	89,401,725,000,000	55,518,750,000,000
9	Ross 248	10.40	98,389,200,000,000	61,100,000,000,000
10	Epsilon Eridani	10.80	102,173,400,000,000	63,450,000,000,000

* *One light year =5,878,812,000 miles / 9,460,528,404,000 km*

A spaceship traveling at 25,000mph/ 40,237 km/h – which is faster than any speed yet achieved in space – would take more than 113,200 years to reach Earth's closest star, Proxima Centauri.

THE MILKY WAY
The Milky Way galaxy, made up of about 200 billion stars, is as much as 100,000 light years across. Although the Milky Way is considered a close neighbor of Earth, our Solar System lies 26,100 light years from its center.

GALAXIES NEAREST THE EARTH

Galaxy	Diameter (light years)	Distance (light years)
1 Large Cloud of Magellan	30	169,000
2 Small Cloud of Magellan	16	190,000
3 Ursa Minor dwarf	2	250,000
4 Draco dwarf	3	260,000
5 Sculptor dwarf	5	280,000
6 Fornax dwarf	7	420,000
7= Leo I dwarf	2	750,000
7= Leo II dwarf	3	750,000
9 Barnard's Galaxy	5	1,700,000
10 Andromeda Spiral	130	2,200,000

BRIGHTEST STARS

	Star	Constellation	Distance*	Apparent magnitude
1	Sun	Solar System	92,952,665,590 miles	−26.8
2	Sirius	Canis Major	8.64	−1.46
3	Canopus	Carina	1,200	−0.73
4	Alpha Centauri	Centaurus	4.35	−0.27
5	Arcturus	Boötes	34	−0.04
6	Vega	Lyra	26	+0.03
7	Capella	Auriga	45	+0.08
8	Rigel	Orion	900	+0.12
9	Procyon	Canis Minor	11.4	+0.38
10	Achernar	Eridanus	85	+0.46

* *From Earth in light years, unless otherwise stated*

MOST RECENT OBSERVATIONS OF HALLEY'S COMET

1 1986

Japanese, Soviet, and European probes were all sent to investigate the comet. All were heavily battered by dust particles, and it was concluded that Halley's comet is composed of dust bonded by water and carbon dioxide ice.

2 1910

Predictions of disaster were widely published in the media, with many people convinced that the world would come to an end.

3 1835

Although dim, the comet was widely observed.

4 1759

The comet's first return, as predicted by Halley, proved his calculations to be correct.

5 1682

It was observed in Africa, China, and Europe between September 5 and 19. Edmond Halley studied it during this period, successfully calculating its orbit and predicting its return.

6 1607

Seen extensively in China, Japan, Korea, and Europe, it was described by German astronomer Johannes Kepler. Its position was accurately measured by Welshman and amateur astronomer Thomas Harriot.

7 1531

It was observed in China, Japan, Korea, and Europe, where Peter Appian, a German geographer and astronomer, noted that comets' tails point away from the Sun.

8 1456

Papal forces saw the comet as a portent of their victory over the invading Turks.

9 1378

The comet was widely observed in China, Japan, Korea, and Europe.

10 1301

Halley's comet was seen in Iceland and parts of Europe, China, Japan, and Korea.

TYPES OF STAR

| Type | Maxmimum surface temp. | |
	°F	°C
1 W	144,000	80,000
2 O	72,000	40,000
3 B	45,000	25,000
4 A	18,000	10,000
5 F	14,000	7,500
6 G	11,000	6,000
7 K	9,000	5,000
8 M	6,000	3,400
9= C	5,000	2,600
9= S	5,000	2,600

Stars are classified by type according to their spectra – the colors by which they appear when viewed with a spectroscope. These vary according to the star's surface temperature. A letter is assigned to each type. (There are some variations; For example, Type C may be divided into R and N.) Using this code, one mnemonic for remembering the sequence in the correct order takes the initial letters of the words in the phrase "Wow! O Be A Fine Girl Kiss Me Right Now Sweetie." Most stars fall in the mid-range (B to M), with those at the extreme ends being comparatively rare.

MOST FREQUENTLY SEEN COMETS

	Comet	Orbit period (years)
1	Encke	3.302
2	Grigg–Skjellerup	4.908
3	Honda–Mrkós–Pajdusáková	5.210
4	Tempel 2	5.259
5	Neujmin 2	5.437
6	Brorsen	5.463
7	Tuttle–Giacobini–Kresák	5.489
8	Tempel–L. Swift	5.681
9	Tempel 1	5.982
10	Pons–Winnecke	6.125

COMETS COMING CLOSEST TO THE EARTH

	Comet	Date*	Distance (AU)#
1	Lexell	Jul 1, 1770	2.3
2	Tempel–Tuttle	Oct 26, 1366	3.4
3	Halley	Apr 10, 837	5.0
4	Biela	Dec 9, 1805	5.5
5	Grischow	Feb 8, 1743	5.8
6	Pons–Winnecke	Jun 26, 1927	5.9
7	La Hire	Apr 20, 1702	6.6
8	Schwassmann–Wachmann	May 31, 1930	9.3
9	Cassini	Jan 8, 1760	10.2
10	Schweizer	Apr 29, 1853	12.6

* *Of closest approach to Earth*
# *Astronomical units: 1AU = mean distance from Earth to the Sun (92,955,900 miles/149,598,200 km)*

THE FAMOUS HALLEY'S COMET
Halley's comet is named after the first person to make an in-depth study of the comet, the English astronomer Edmond Halley.

REACHING FOR THE MOON

THE 10

FIRST WOMEN IN SPACE

Name/nationality/mission	Date
1 Valentina Vladimirovna Tereshkova, USSR, *Vostok VI*	Jun 16–19, 1963

Tereshkova (b. March 6, 1937) was the first and youngest woman in space. She was only 26 years old at the time.

2 Svetlana Savitskaya, USSR, *Soyuz T7*	Aug 19, 1982

On July 25, 1984 Savitskaya (b. August 4, 1948) also walked in space (from Soyuz T12).

3 Sally K. Ride, US, *STS-7 Challenger*	Jun 18–24, 1983

Ride (b. May 26, 1951) was the first American woman and, at age 32, the youngest American astronaut in space.

4 Judith A. Resnik, US, *STS-41-D Discovery*	Aug 30–Sep 5, 1984

Resnik (b. April 5, 1949) was later killed in the STS-51-L Challenger Shuttle *disaster.*

5 Kathryn D. Sullivan, US, *STS-41-G Challenger*	Oct 5–13, 1984

Sullivan (b. October 3, 1951) was the first American woman to walk in space.

6 Anna L. Fisher, US, *STS-51-A Discovery*	Nov 8–16, 1984

Fisher (b. August 24, 1949) was the first American mother in space.

7 Margaret Rhea Seddon, US, *STS-51-D Discovery*	Apr 12–19, 1985

Seddon (b. November 8, 1947) flew again in STS-40 Columbia (June 5–14, 1991) and STS-58 Columbia (October 18–November 1, 1993).

8 Shannon W. Lucid, US, *STS-51-G Discovery*	Jun 17–24, 1985

Lucid (b. January 14, 1943) also flew in STS-34 Atlantis (October 18–23, 1989), STS-43 Atlantis (August 2–11, 1991), and STS-58 Atlantis (October 18–November 1, 1993).

9 Bonnie J. Dunbar, US, *STS-61-A Challenger*	Oct 30–Nov 6, 1985

Dunbar (b. March 3, 1949) also flew in STS-32 Columbia (January 9–20, 1990), STS-50 Columbia (June 25–July 9, 1992), and STS-71 Atlantis (June 27–July 7, 1995).

10 Mary L. Cleave, US, *STS-61-B Atlantis*	Nov 26–Dec 3, 1985

Cleave (b. February 5, 1947) also flew in STS-30 Atlantis (May 4–8, 1989).

THE 10

FIRST UNMANNED MOON LANDINGS

Name	Country of origin	Date (launch/impact)
1 *Lunik 2*	USSR	Sep 12/14, 1959
2 *Ranger 4**	US	Apr 23/26, 1962
3 *Ranger 6*	US	Jan 30/Feb 2, 1964
4 *Ranger 7*	US	July 28/31, 1964
5 *Ranger 8*	US	Feb 17/20, 1965
6 *Ranger 9*	US	Mar 21/24, 1965
7 *Luna 5**	USSR	May 9/12, 1965
8 *Luna 7**	USSR	Oct 4/8, 1965
9 *Luna 8**	USSR	Dec 3/7, 1965
10 *Luna 9*	USSR	Jan 31/Feb 3, 1966

* Crash-landing

In addition to these 10 craft, debris left on the Moon includes the remains of several further *Luna* craft, unmanned sample-collectors, and *Lunakhod 1* and *2* (1966–71; all Soviet), as well as seven *Surveyors* (1966–68) and five *Lunar Orbiters* (1966–67) (all US). Before crashing onto the Moon, the 830-lb/380-kg *Lunar Orbiters* relayed detailed photographic images of the surface, mapping suitable sites for the manned *Apollo* landings that followed. The descent stages of six *Apollo* modules and three of the world's most expensive used cars (the *Lunar Rovers* used on *Apollo* missions Nos. 15 to 17) were all later added to the Lunar junkyard.

THE 10

FIRST PEOPLE IN SPACE

Name	Orbits	Duration hr:min	Spacecraft/ country of origin	Date
1 Yuri Alekseyivich Gagarin	1	1:48	*Vostok I* USSR	April 12, 1961
2 Gherman Stepanovich Titov	17	25:18	*Vostok II* USSR	August 6–7, 1961
3 John Herschel Glenn	3	4:56	*Friendship 7* US	February 20, 1962
4 Malcolm Scott Carpenter	3	4:56	*Aurora 7* US	May 24, 1962
5 Andrian Grigoryevich Nikolayev	64	94:22	*Vostok III* USSR	August 11–15, 1962
6 Pavel Romanovich Popovich	48	70:57	*Vostok IV* USSR	August 12–15, 1962
7 Walter Marty Schirra	6	9:13	*Sigma 7* US	October 3, 1962
8 Leroy Gordon Cooper	22	34:19	*Faith 7* US	May 15–16, 1963
9 Valeri Fyodorovich Bykovsky	81	119:60	*Vostok* USSR	June 14–19, 1963
10 Valentina Vladimirovna Tereshkova	48	70:50	*Vostok VI* USSR	June 16–19, 1963

No. 2 was the youngest-ever astronaut, age 25 years 329 days, and No. 10 was the first woman in space. Among early pioneering flights, neither Alan Shepard (May 5, 1961: *Freedom 7*) nor Gus Grissom (July 21, 1961: *Liberty Bell 7*) actually entered space, achieving altitudes of only 115 miles/185 km and 118 miles/190 km respectively, and neither flight lasted more than 15 minutes. John Glenn was the first American to orbit the Earth.

APOLLO COMMAND AND
SERVICE MODULE

T H E   1 0

FIRST ARTIFICIAL SATELLITES

	Satellite	Country of origin	Launch date
1	*Sputnik 1*	USSR	Oct 4, 1957
2	*Sputnik 2*	USSR	Nov 3, 1957
3	*Explorer 1*	US	Feb 1, 1958
4	*Vanguard 1*	US	Mar 17, 1958
5	*Explorer 3*	US	Mar 26, 1958
6	*Sputnik 3*	USSR	May 15, 1958
7	*Explorer 4*	US	July 26, 1958
8	*SCORE*	US	Dec 18, 1958
9	*Vanguard 2*	US	Feb 17, 1959
10	*Discoverer 1*	US	Feb 28, 1959

Artificial satellites for use as radio relay stations were first proposed by the British science fiction writer Arthur C. Clarke in the October 1945 issue of *Wireless World*, but it was 12 years before his fantasy became reality with the launch of the satellite *Sputnik 1*, the first-ever artificial satellite to enter the Earth's orbit. An 184 lb/83.6 kg metal sphere, it transmitted signals back to the Earth for three weeks before its batteries failed. However, it continued to be tracked until it fell back to the Earth and burned up on January 4, 1958. Most of its early successors were similarly short-lived, or were destroyed on reentering the atmosphere. In contrast, *Vanguard 1* is destined to remain in orbit for the next 274 years, and *Vanguard 2* for 124 years. *Sputnik 2* carried the first animal into space, and *Explorer 1* first detected the radiation zone known as the Van Allen belts. *Explorer 2* failed to enter the Earth's orbit. *SCORE* (the Signal Communications Orbit Relay Experiment) transmitted a prerecorded Christmas message from President Eisenhower. *Discoverer 1*, the first to be launched in a polar orbit, was a military satellite.

T H E   1 0

FIRST MOONWALKERS

	Astronaut	Spacecraft	Total EVA* hr:min	Mission dates
1	Neil A. Armstrong	*Apollo 11*	2:32	July 16–24, 1969
2	Edwin E. ("Buzz") Aldrin	*Apollo 11*	2:15	July 16–24, 1969
3	Charles Conrad, Jr.	*Apollo 12*	7:45	Nov 14–24, 1969
4	Alan L. Bean	*Apollo 12*	7:45	Nov 14–24, 1969
5	Alan B. Shepard	*Apollo 14*	9:23	Jan 31–Feb 9, 1971
6	Edgar D. Mitchell	*Apollo 14*	9:23	Jan 31–Feb 9, 1971
7	David R. Scott	*Apollo 15*	19:08	Jul 26–Aug 7, 1971
8	James B. Irwin	*Apollo 15*	18:35	Jul 26–Aug 7, 1971
9	John W. Young	*Apollo 16*	20:14	Apr 16–27, 1972
10	Charles M. Duke	*Apollo 16*	20:14	Apr 16–27, 1972

* Extra-vehicular Activity (time spent out of the lunar module on the Moon's surface)

Six US *Apollo* missions resulted in successful Moon landings (*Apollo 13*, April 11–17, 1970, was aborted after an oxygen tank exploded). During the last of these (*Apollo 17*, December 7–19, 1972), Eugene A. Cernan (b. March 14, 1934) and Harrison H. Schmitt (b. July 3, 1935) became the only other astronauts to date who have walked on the surface of the Moon. Although Russian scientists recently proposed sending a series of unmanned probes to land on Mars, which could lead to a follow-up manned mission between 2005 and 2010, the entire Russian space program is suffering from such severe financial problems that its current missions appear to be in jeopardy.

FLY ME TO THE MOON
The launch vehicle Saturn V was built to send US astronauts to the Moon. Fifteen vehicles were built and launched between 1967 and 1973.

T H E   1 0

FIRST SPACEWALKERS

	Astronaut	Spacecraft	EVA* hr:min	Launch Date
1	Alexei Leonov	*Voskhod 2*	0.12	Mar 18, 1965
2	Edward H. White	*Gemini 4*	0:23	June 3, 1965
3	Eugene A. Cernan	*Gemini 9*	2:08	June 3, 1966
4	Michael Collins	*Gemini 10*	1:30	July 18, 1966
5	Richard F. Gordon	*Gemini 11*	1:57	Sep 12, 1966
6	Edwin E. ("Buzz") Aldrin	*Gemini 12*	5:37	Nov 11, 1966
7	Alexei Yeleseyev	*Soyuz 5*	#	Jan 15, 1969
8	Yevgeny Khrunov	*Soyuz 5*	#	Jan 15, 1969
9	David R. Scott	*Apollo 9*	1:01	Mar 3, 1969
10	Russell L. Schweickart	*Apollo 9*	1:07	Mar 3, 1969

* Extra-vehicular Activity # Short-duration transfer to Soyuz 4

ASTRONAUTS & COSMONAUTS

TOP 10
MOST EXPERIENCED SPACEWOMEN*

	Name#	Missions	Total duration of missions days	hr	min	sec
1	Tamara Kondakova	1	169	05	22	00
2	Bonnie J. Dunbar	4	41	12	37	47
3	Kathryn C. Thornton	4	40	15	16	31
4	Tamara E. Jernigan	3	35	14	19	33
5	Shannon W. Lucid	4	34	22	53	14
6	Marsha S. Ivins	3	31	07	32	40
7	Margaret Rhea Seddon	3	30	02	23	09
8	Kathryn D. Sullivan	3	22	04	48	39
9	Ellen Ochoa	2	20	04	43	10
10	Svetlana Savitskaya	2	19	17	07	00

* To January 1, 1996
# All US citizens except 1 and 10 (citizens of the former USSR)

TOP 10
LONGEST SPACE SHUTTLE FLIGHTS*

	Flight	Dates	Duration hr	min	sec
1	STS-67 Endeavour	Mar 2–18, 1995	399	09	46
2	STS-73 Columbia	Oct 20–Nov 5, 1995	381	53	16
3	STS-65 Columbia	Jul 8–23, 1994	353	55	00
4	STS-58 Columbia	Oct 18–Nov 1, 1993	336	12	32
5	STS-62 Columbia	Mar 9–18, 1994	335	16	41
6	STS-50 Columbia	Jun 25–Jul 9, 1992	331	30	04
7	STS-59 Endeavour	Apr 9–20, 1994	269	49	30
8	STS-68 Endeavour	Sep 30–Oct 11, 1994	269	46	08
9	STS-64 Discovery	Sep 9–20, 1994	262	49	57
10	STS-66 Discovery	Nov 3–14, 1994	262	32	02

* To January 1, 1996

TOP 10
COUNTRIES WITH MOST SPACEFLIGHT EXPERIENCE*

	Country	Missions	Total duration of missions day	hr	min	sec
1	USSR	72	3,835	08	16	44
2	US	89	738	03	57	18
3	Russia#	4	710	06	23	05
4	France	5	74	04	43	36
5	Germany	5	41	04	33	03
6	Canada	3	26	03	34	31
7	Japan	2	15	20	26	11
8	Bulgaria	2	11	19	11	06
9	Belgium	1	08	22	09	25
10	Afghanistan	1	08	20	27	00

* To January 14, 1994 (date of the return of the Russian TM17)
# Russia became a separate independent state from the USSR on December 25, 1991

UNTETHERED SPACE WALK
On an eight-day US space mission in 1984, astronauts made their first untethered space walks, using their hands as instruments in guiding a nitrogen-propelled maneuvering unit.

THE 10

FIRST IN-FLIGHT SPACE FATALITIES

1 Vladimir M. Komarov (1927–67)

Launched on April 24, 1967, Soviet spaceship Soyuz 1 *experienced various technical problems during its 18th orbit. After a successful reentry, the capsule parachute was deployed at 23,000 ft/7,010 m, but its lines became tangled, and it crash-landed near Orsk in the Urals. Komarov (the survivor of a previous one-day flight on October 12, 1964) was killed as a result.*

2= Georgi T. Dobrovolsky (1928–71)
2= Viktor I. Patsayev (1933–71)
2= Vladislav N. Volkov (1933–71)

After a (for then) record 23 days in space and a link-up with the Salyut *space station, the Soviet* Soyuz 9 *mission ended in disaster on June 29, 1971, when the capsule depressurized during reentry. Although it landed intact, all three cosmonauts – who were not wearing spacesuits – were found dead. The ashes of the three men were buried, along with those of Yuri Gagarin and Vladimir Komarov, at the Kremlin, Moscow.*

5= Gregory B. Jarvis (1944–86)
5= Sharon C. McAuliffe (1948–86)
5= Ronald E. McNair (1950–86)
5= Ellison S. Onizuka (1946–86)
5= Judith A. Resnik (1949–86)
5= Francis R. Scobee (1939–86)
5= Michael J. Smith (1945–86)

Challenger STS-51-L, the 25th Space Shuttle mission, exploded on take-off from Cape Canaveral, Florida, on January 28, 1986. The cause was determined to have been leakage of seals in the joint between rocket sections. The disaster, watched by thousands on the ground and millions on worldwide television, halted the US space program until a comprehensive review of the engineering problems and review of the safety methods had been undertaken. It was not until September 29, 1988 that the next Space Shuttle, Discovery STS-26, *was successfully launched.*

The 11 cosmonauts and astronauts in this list are, to date, the only in-flight space fatalities. They are not, however, the only victims of accidents during the space programs of the former USSR and the US. On October 24, 1960, Field Marshal Mitrofan Nedelin, the commander of the Soviet Strategic Rocket Forces, and an unknown number of other personnel (a total of 165 according to some authorities), were killed in the launchpad explosion of an unmanned space rocket at the Baikonur cosmodrome. Another explosion, during the refueling of a Vostok rocket at the Plesetsk Space Center on March 18, 1980, left some 50 dead. During a test countdown of *Apollo 1* on January 27, 1967, Roger B. Chaffee, Virgil I. "Gus" Grissom, veteran of the second and seventh US space missions, and Edward H. White (who flew in the eighth US mission) were killed in a fire, probably caused by an electrical fault.

SPACE SALVAGE OPERATION
Photographed on November 14, 1984, Discovery *Space Shuttle 51-A astronaut Dale A. Gardner uses his MMU (Manned Maneuvering Unit) to recover the malfunctioning* Weststar VI *communications satellite, which had failed to enter its correct orbit after its launch earlier that year. During over 12 hours of EVA (Extra-Vehicular Activity), Gardner used a special device to stabilize its spin, returning the expensive malfunctioning satellite to the cargo bay of the Shuttle for repair back on Earth.*

TOP 10

OLDEST US ASTRONAUTS

	Astronaut	Born	Last flight	Age*
1	Vance D. Brand	May 9, 1931	Dec 10, 1990	59
2	Karl G. Henize	Oct 17, 1926	Aug 6, 1985	58
3	F. Story Musgrave	Aug 19, 1935	Dec 12, 1993	58
4	William E. Thornton	Apr 14, 1929	May 6, 1985	56
5	Henry W. Hartsfield	Nov 21, 1933	Nov 6, 1988	54
6	Don L. Lind	May 18, 1930	May 6, 1985	54
7	John W. Young	Sep 24, 1930	Dec 8, 1983	53
8	Owen K. Garriott	Nov 22, 1930	Dec 8, 1983	53
9	Joe H. Engle	Aug 26, 1932	Sep 3, 1985	53
10	Donald K. Slayton#	Mar 1, 1924	Jul 15, 1975	51

* Those of apparently identical age have been ranked according to their precise age in days at the time of their last flight
\# Deceased June 13, 1993

TOP 10

YOUNGEST US ASTRONAUTS

	Astronaut	Born	First flight	Age*
1	Kenneth D. Bowersox	Nov 14, 1955	Jun 25, 1984	28
2	Sally K. Ride	May 26, 1951	Jun 18, 1983	32
3	Eugene A. Cernan	Mar 14, 1934	Jun 3, 1966	32
4	Steven A. Hawley	Dec 12, 1951	Aug 30, 1984	32
5	Kathryn D. Sullivan	Oct 3, 1951	Oct 5, 1984	33
6	Ronald E. McNair#	Oct 21, 1950	Feb 3, 1984	33
7	George D. Nelson	Jul 13, 1950	Apr 6, 1984	33
8	David R. Scott	Jun 6, 1932	Mar 16, 1966	33
9	Russell L. Schweickart	Oct 25, 1935	Mar 3, 1969	34
10	Edward H. White	Nov 14, 1930	Jun 3, 1965	34

* Those of apparently identical age have been ranked according to their precise age in days at the time of their first flight
\# Killed in Challenger *disaster, January 28, 1986*

THE FACE OF THE EARTH

TOP 10

MOST COMMON ELEMENTS IN THE EARTH'S CRUST

	Element	Percentage*
1	Oxygen	45.6
2	Silicon	27.3
3	Aluminum	8.4
4	Iron	6.2
5	Calcium	4.7
6	Magnesium	2.8
7	Sodium	2.3
8	Potassium	1.8
9	Hydrogen	1.5
10	Titanium	0.6

Totals more than 100% due to rounding

This is based on the average percentages of the elements in igneous rock. At an atomic level, out of every million atoms, some 205,000 are silicon, 62,600 are aluminum, and 29,000 are hydrogen. However, in the universe as a whole, hydrogen is by far the most common element, comprising some 927,000 out of every million atoms, followed by helium at 72,000 per million.

DEATH VALLEY, CALIFORNIA
The lowest-lying place in the western hemisphere, and one of the hottest with a US record 134°F/57°C, California's Death Valley is almost rainless. It contains fascinating desert plants and animals and since 1933 has been a US National Monument.

TOP 10

DEEPEST DEPRESSIONS IN THE WORLD

	Depression/location	Maximum depth below sea level m	ft
1	Dead Sea, Israel/Jordan	400	1,312
2	Turfan Depression, China	154	505
3	Qattâra Depression, Egypt	133	436
4	Poluostrov Mangyshlak, Kazakhstan	132	433
5	Danakil Depression, Ethiopia	117	383
6	Death Valley, US	86	282
7	Salton Sink, US	72	235
8	Zapadny Chink Ustyurta, Kazakhstan	70	230
9	Prikaspiyskaya Nizmennost', Kazakhstan/Russia	67	220
10	Ozera Sarykamysh, Turkmenistan/Uzbekistan	45	148

The shore of the Dead Sea is the lowest exposed ground below sea level. However, its bed, at 2,388 ft/728 m below sea level, is only half as deep as that of Lake Baikal, Russia, which is 4,872 ft/1,485 m below sea level. A great deal of Antarctica is also below sea level (at 8,326 ft/2,538 m), but the land there is covered by an ice cap.

TOP 10

LONGEST CAVES IN THE WORLD

	Cave	Location	Total known length km	miles
1	Mammoth Cave system	Kentucky	567	350
2	Optimisticeskaja	Ukraine	183	114
3	Hölloch	Switzerland	166	104
4	Jewel Cave	South Dakota	162	103.2
5	Lechuguilla Cave	New Mexico	142	89
6	Siebenhengsteholensystem	Switzerland	135	84
7	Fisher Ridge cave system	Kentucky	126	79
8	Wind Cave	South Dakota	121	76.9
9	Ozernaya	Ukraine	111	69
10	Gua Air Jernih	Malaysia	106	66

DID YOU KNOW

THE DEEPEST CAVE

As revealed by the list of the world's longest caves, there are many very extensive cave systems in the world. However, none goes as deep as the Réseau Jean Bernard in the French Alps to the north of Mont Blanc. Extensive explorations since the 1960s have penetrated deeper and deeper into the system, reaching a world record depth of 5,256 ft/ 1,602 m, which was attained by a French caving team in 1989.

AS HARD AS ROCK

The Mohs Scale, named after Friedrich Mohs (1773–1839), is used for comparing the relative hardness of minerals. Each mineral, shown below with its Mohs Scale number, can be scratched by all those below it on the scale.

1	Talc	6	Orthoclase
2	Gypsum	7	Quartz
3	Calcite	8	Topaz
4	Fluorite	9	Corundum
5	Apatite	10	Diamond

TOP 10

LARGEST METEORITE CRATERS IN THE WORLD

	Crater/location	Diameter km	miles
1=	Sudbury, Canada	140	87
1=	Vredefort Ring, South Africa	140	87
3=	Manicouagan, Canada	100	62
3=	Popigai, Russia	100	62
5	Puchezh-Katunki, Russia	80	50
6	Kara, Russia	60	37
7	Siljan, Sweden	52	32
8	Charlevoix, Canada	46	29
9	Araguainha Dome, Brazil	40	25
10	Carswell, Canada	37	23

Unlike on the Solar System's other planets and moons, many astroblemes (collision sites) on the Earth have been weathered and obscured over time. One of the ongoing debates in geology is whether or not certain craterlike structures are of meteoric origin or are the remnants of long-extinct volcanoes. The Vredefort Ring, long thought to be meteoric, was declared in 1963 to be volcanic, but has since been claimed as a definite meteor crater, as are all the giant meteorite craters in this Top 10.

TOP 10

LARGEST ISLANDS IN THE WORLD

	Island	Location	Approx. area* sq km	sq miles
1	Greenland (Kalaatdlit Nunaat)	Arctic Ocean	2,175,590	840,000
2	New Guinea	West Pacific	789,900	304,982
3	Borneo	Indian Ocean	751,000	289,961
4	Madagascar (Malagasy Republic)	Indian Ocean	587,041	226,657
5	Baffin Island, Canada	Arctic Ocean	507,451	195,926
6	Sumatra, Indonesia	Indian Ocean	422,200	163,011
7	Honshu, Japan	Northwest Pacific	230,092	88,839
8	Great Britain	North Atlantic	218,041	84,186
9	Victoria Island, Canada	Arctic Ocean	217,290	83,896
10	Ellesmere Island, Canada	Arctic Ocean	196,236	75,767

Mainlands, including areas of inland water, but excluding offshore islands

Australia is regarded as a continental landmass rather than an island; otherwise it would rank 1st, at 2,941,517 sq miles/7,618,493 sq km, over three times the size of Greenland. The smallest island with country status is Pitcairn, at just 1¾ sq miles/4.53 sq km.

TOP 10

LARGEST DESERTS IN THE WORLD

	Desert	Location	Approx. area sq km	sq miles
1	Sahara	North Africa	9,000,000	3,500,000
2	Australian	Australia	3,800,000	1,470,000
3	Arabian	Southwest Asia	1,300,000	502,000
4	Gobi	Central Asia	1,040,000	401,500
5	Kalahari	Southern Africa	520,000	201,000
6	Turkestan	Central Asia	450,000	174,000
7	Takla Makan	China	327,000	125,000
8=	Namib	Southwest Africa	310,000	120,000
8=	Sonoran	US/Mexico	310,000	120,000
10=	Somali	Somalia	260,000	100,000
10=	Thar	India/Pakistan	260,000	100,000

This Top 10 presents the approximate areas and ranking of the world's great deserts. These are often broken down into smaller desert regions – the Australian Desert into the Gibson, Simpson, and Great Sandy Desert, for example. Of the total land surface of the Earth, as much as one-quarter may be considered "desert," or land where more water is lost through evaporation than is acquired through precipitation. However, deserts may range from the extremely arid and barren sandy desert, through arid, to semiarid, and most exhibit features that encompass all these degrees of aridity without a precise line of demarcation.

ON TOP OF THE WORLD

T O P 1 0

HIGHEST MOUNTAINS IN THE WORLD

(Height of principal peak; lower peaks of the same mountain are excluded)

	Mountain	Location	m	ft
1	Everest	Nepal/Tibet	8,846	29,022
2	K2	Kashmir/China	8,611	28,250
3	Kanchenjunga	Nepal/Sikkim	8,598	28,208
4	Lhotse	Nepal/Tibet	8,501	27,890
5	Makalu I	Nepal/Tibet	8,470	27,790
6	Dhaulagiri I	Nepal	8,172	26,810
7	Manaslu I	Nepal	8,156	26,760
8	Cho Oyu	Nepal	8,153	26,750
9	Nanga Parbat	Kashmir	8,126	26,660
10	Annapurna I	Nepal	8,078	26,504

The height of Everest was estimated in the 19th century as 29,002 ft/8,840 m. This was later revised to 29,029 ft/8,848 m, but on April 20, 1993, using the latest measuring techniques, this was revised to the current "official" figure. Many of the 10 highest mountains have alternative names: in Tibetan, Everest is known as *Chomolungma* ("Goddess Mother of the World"). K2 (so called because it was the second mountain in the Karakoram range counting from the Kashmir end) is also referred to by the local name *Chogori* and sometimes as Godwin-Austen, after Lieutenant Henry Haversham Godwin-Austen (1834–1923), who first surveyed it in 1865.

T O P 1 0

HIGHEST MOUNTAINS IN NORTH AMERICA

	Mountain/location	m	ft
1	McKinley, US	6,194	20,320
2	Logan, Canada	6,050	19,850
3	Citlaltépetl (Orizaba), Mexico	5,700	18,700
4	St. Elias, US/Canada	5,489	18,008
5	Popocatépetl, Mexico	5,452	17,887
6	Foraker, US	5,304	17,400
7	Ixtaccihuatl, Mexico	5,286	17,343
8	Lucania, Canada	5,226	17,147
9	King, Canada	5,173	16,971
10	Steele, Canada	5,073	16,644

T O P 1 0

HIGHEST MOUNTAINS IN OCEANIA

	Mountain/location	m	ft
1	Jaya, Indonesia	5,030	16,500
2	Daam, Indonesia	4,920	16,150
3	Pilimsit, Indonesia	4,800	15,750
4	Trikora, Indonesia	4,750	15,580
5	Mandala, Indonesia	4,700	15,420
6	Wilhelm, Papua New Guinea	4,690	15,400
7	Wisnumurti, Indonesia	4,590	15,080
8	Yamin, Papua New Guinea	4,530	14,860
9	Kubor, Papua New Guinea	4,360	14,300
10	Herbert, Papua New Guinea	4,270	14,000

T O P 1 0

HIGHEST ACTIVE VOLCANOES IN THE WORLD

	Volcano	Location	Latest activity	m	ft
1	Guallatiri	Chile	1987	6,060	19,882
2	Lááscar	Chile	1991	5,990	19,652
3	Cotopaxi	Ecuador	1975	5,897	19,347
4	Tupungatito	Chile	1986	5,640	18,504
5	Popocatépetl	Mexico	1995	5,452	17,887
6	Ruiz	Colombia	1992	5,400	17,716
7	Sangay	Ecuador	1988	5,230	17,159
8	Guagua Pichincha	Ecuador	1988	4,784	15,696
9	Purace	Colombia	1977	4,755	15,601
10	Kliuchevskoi	Russia	1995	4,750	15,584

This list includes all volcanoes that have been active at some time during the 20th century. Although it does not qualify for the list above, the highest currently active volcano in Europe is Mt. Etna in Italy (10,855 ft/3,311 m), which was responsible for many deaths in earlier times. Etna is still active – there was a 4-month eruption in 1983 – but its last major eruption took place on March 11, 1669 when the lava flow engulfed the town of Catania, killing at least 20,000. In 1169 more than 15,000 died in Catania cathedral where they had taken shelter, and more were killed when a tidal wave caused by the eruption hit the port of Messina.

T O P   1 0

HIGHEST MOUNTAINS IN SOUTH AMERICA

	Mountain/location	m	ft
1	Cerro Aconcagua, Argentina	6,960	22,834
2	Ojos del Salado, Argentina/Chile	6,885	22,588
3	Bonete, Argentina	6,873	22,550
4	Pissis, Argentina/Chile	6,780	22,244
5	Huascarán, Peru	6,768	22,205
6	Llullaillaco, Argentina/Chile	6,723	22,057
7	Libertador, Argentina	6,721	22,050
8	Mercadario, Argentina/Chile	6,670	21,884
9	Yerupajá, Peru	6,634	21,765
10	Tres Cruces, Argentina/Chile	6,620	21,720

T O P   1 0

HIGHEST MOUNTAINS IN AFRICA

	Mountain/location	m	ft
1	Kibo (Kilimanjaro), Tanzania	5,895	19,340
2	Batian (Kenya), Kenya	5,199	17,058
3	Ngaliema, Uganda/Zaïre	5,109	16,763
4	Duwoni, Uganda	4,896	16,062
5	Baker, Uganda	4,843	15,889
6	Emin, Zaïre	4,798	15,741
7	Gessi, Uganda	4,715	15,470
8	Sella, Uganda	4,627	15,179
9	Ras Dashen, Ethiopia	4,620	15,158
10	Wasuwameso, Zaïre	4,581	15,030

T O P   1 0

HIGHEST MOUNTAINS IN EUROPE

	Mountain/location	m	ft
1	Mont Blanc, France/Italy	4,807	15,771
2	Monte Rosa, Italy/Switzerland	4,634	15,203
3	Dom, Switzerland	4,545	14,911
4	Liskamm, Italy/Switzerland	4,527	14,853
5	Weisshorn, Switzerland	4,505	14,780
6	Täschorn, Switzerland	4,491	14,734
7	Matterhorn, Italy/Switzerland	4,477	14,688
8	La Dent Blanche, Switzerland	4,357	14,293
9	Nadelhorn, Switzerland	4,327	14,196
10	Le Grand Combin, Switzerland	4,314	14,153

All 10 of Europe's highest mountains are in the Alps; there are, however, at least 15 mountains in the Caucasus (the mountain range that straddles Europe and Asia) that are taller than Mont Blanc. The highest of them, the west peak of Mt. Elbrus, is 18,481 ft/5,633 m and was climbed in 1963 by 107-year-old mountaineer Tschokka Zalichanov.

T O P   1 0

HIGHEST DORMANT VOLCANOES IN THE WORLD

	Volcano	Location	Latest activity	m	ft
1	Llullaillaco	Argentina/Chile	1877	6,723	22,057
2	El Misti	Peru	c.1870	5,822	19,101
3	Orizaba	Mexico	1687	5,610	18,405
4	Rainier	US	c.1894	4,392	14,410
5	Shasta	US	1786	4,317	14,162
6	Fuji	Japan	1708	3,776	12,388
7	Tolbachik	Russia	1876	3,682	12,080
8	Turrialba	Costa Rica	1866	3,246	10,650
9	Baitoushan	China/Korea	1702	2,774	9,003
10	Bandai	Japan	1888	1,819	5,968

This list comprises the world's tallest volcanoes that are known to have been active at some time before the 20th century, but that now appear to be dormant – although some, including Mount Rainier in Washington, Mount Shasta in California, and Fuji, still emit steam. Rainier and Fuji are both classic examples of "composite cones" or "strato-volcanoes" – volcanoes that have been built up by the depositing of layer after layer of lava, volcanic ash, and cinders during sequential eruptions over many thousands of years.

RIVERS & WATERFALLS

GREATEST WATERFALLS IN THE WORLD

(*Based on volume of water*)

	Waterfall	Location	Average flow (m³/sec)
1	Boyoma (Stanley)	Zaïre	17,000
2	Khône	Laos	11,610
3	Niagara (Horseshoe)	Canada/US	5,830
4	Grande	Uruguay	4,500
5	Paulo Afonso	Brazil	2,890
6	Urubupungá	Brazil	2,750
7	Iguaçu	Argentina/ Brazil	1,700
8	Maribondo	Brazil	1,500
9	Churchill (Grand)	Canada	1,390
10	Kabalega (Murchison)	Uganda	1,200

FALL AND ANGEL

In 1933, while prospecting for gold in Venezuela, American adventurer James Angel landed his monoplane, *El Rio Caroní*, on the plateau above a waterfall. The waterfall had been spotted by early explorers – perhaps including Sir Walter Raleigh as early as 1594 – but had never been mapped. Angel's plane became bogged down, making it impossible for him to take off. However, after trudging back to civilization, he did at least have the consolation of announcing that he had discovered what turned out to be the world's tallest waterfall – some 15 times as high as Niagara Falls. Subsequently, the Angel Falls were named after him. Angel died in 1956, but somewhat remarkably, his aircraft remained stranded until 1970, when it was recovered and put on public display at Ciudad Bolivar airport.

GREATEST RIVERS IN THE WORLD

(*Based on rate of discharge at mouth*)

	River	Outflow	Average flow (m³/sec)
1	Amazon	South Atlantic	175,000
2	Congo	South Atlantic	39,000
3	Negro	South Atlantic	35,000
4	Yangtze–Kiang	Yellow Sea	32,190
5	Orinoco	South Atlantic	25,200
6	Plata–Paraná–Grande	South Atlantic	22,900
7	Madeira–Mamoré–Grande	South Atlantic	21,800
8	Yenisey–Angara–Selenga	Kara Sea	18,000
9	Brahmaputra	Bay of Bengal	16,290
10	Lena–Kirenga	Arctic Ocean	16,100

HIGHEST WATERFALLS IN THE WORLD

1 Angel, Carrao River, Venezuela 3,212 ft/979 m (Longest single drop 2,648 ft/807 m)

2 Tugela, Tugela River, South Africa 3,110 ft/948 m

3 Utigård, Jostedal Glacier, Nesdale, Norway 2,625 ft/800 m

4 Mongefossen, Monge River, Mongebekk, Norway 2,540 ft/774 m

5 Yosemite, Yosemite Creek, California, 2,425 ft/739 m

6 Østre Mardøla Foss, Mardals River, Eikisdal, Norway 2,154 ft/657 m

7 Tyssestrengane, Tysso River, Hardanger, Norway 2,120 ft/646 m

8 Cuquenán, Arabopo River, Venezuela 2,000 ft/610 m

9 Sutherland, Arthur River, South Island, New Zealand 1,904 ft/580 m

10 Kjellfossen, Naero River, Gudvangen, Norway 1,841 ft/561 m

THE RIVER RHINE AT ST. GOAR
The Rhine, the longest river in Western Europe, is easily navigable. As a consequence it is the busiest waterway on the continent.

T O P   1 0

LONGEST RIVERS IN NORTH AMERICA

	River	Location	km	miles
1	Mackenzie–Peace	Canada	4,241	2,635
2	Missouri–Red	US	4,088	2,540
3	Mississippi	US	3,779	2,348
4	Missouri	US	3,726	2,315
5	Yukon	US	3,185	1,979
6	St. Lawrence	Canada	3,130	1,945
7	Rio Grande	US	2,832	1,760
8	Nelson	Canada	2,575	1,600
9	Arkansas	US	2,348	1,459
10	Colorado	US	2,334	1,450

The principal reaches of the Mississippi, Missouri, and Red rivers are often combined, thus becoming the 4th longest river in the world at 3,710 miles/5,971 km.

T O P   1 0

LONGEST GLACIERS IN THE WORLD

	Name	km	miles
1	Lambert–Fisher	515	320
2	Novaya Zemlya	418	260
3	Arctic Institute	362	225
4	Nimrod–Lennox–King	290	180
5	Denman	241	150
6=	Beardmore	225	140
6=	Recovery	225	140
8	Petermanns	200	124
9	Unnamed	193	120
10	Slessor	185	115

Though the longest in the world, the Lambert–Fisher Glacier was discovered as recently as 1956; it is as much as 2.2 miles/3.5 km deep and 40 miles/64 km wide.

T O P   1 0

LONGEST RIVERS IN THE WORLD

	River	Location	km	miles
1	Nile	Tanzania/Uganda/Sudan/Egypt	6,670	4,145
2	Amazon	Peru/Brazil	6,448	4,007
3	Yangtze–Kiang	China	6,300	3,915
4	Mississippi–Missouri–Red	US	5,971	3,710
5	Yenisey–Angara–Selenga	Mongolia/Russia	5,540	3,442
6	Huang Ho (Yellow River)	China	5,464	3,395
7	Ob'–Irtysh	Mongolia/Kazakhstan/Russia	5,410	3,362
8	Congo (Zaïre)	Angola/Zaïre	4,700	2,920
9	Lena–Kirenga	Russia	4,400	2,734
10	Mekong	Tibet/China/Myanmar (Burma)/Laos/Cambodia/Vietnam	4,350	2,703

T O P   1 0

LONGEST RIVERS IN EUROPE
(Excluding former USSR)

	River	Location	km	miles
1	Danube	Germany/Austria/Slovakia/Hungary/Serbia/Romania/Bulgaria	2,842	1,766
2	Rhine	Switzerland/Germany/Holland	1,368	850
3	Elbe	Czech Republic/Slovakia/Germany	1,167	725
4	Loire	France	1,014	630
5	Tagus	Portugal	1,009	627
6	Meuse	France/Belgium/Holland	950	590
7	Ebro	Spain	933	580
8	Rhône	Switzerland/France	813	505
9	Guadiana	Spain/Portugal	805	500
10	Seine	France	776	482

SEAS & LAKES

LARGEST OCEANS AND SEAS IN THE WORLD

	Ocean/sea	Approx. area sq km	sq miles
1	Pacific Ocean	165,241,000	63,800,000
2	Atlantic Ocean	82,439,000	31,830,000
3	Indian Ocean	73,452,000	28,360,000
4	Arctic Ocean	13,986,000	5,400,000
5	Arabian Sea	3,864,000	1,492,000
6	South China Sea	3,447,000	1,331,000
7	Caribbean Sea	2,753,000	1,063,000
8	Mediterranean Sea	2,505,000	967,000
9	Bering Sea	2,269,000	876,000
10	Bay of Bengal	2,173,000	839,000

Geographers hold differing opinions as to whether certain bodies of water are regarded as seas in their own right or as parts of larger oceans – the Coral, Weddell, and Tasman Seas would be eligible for this list, but most authorities consider them part of the Pacific Ocean.

THE GREAT LAKES OF NORTH AMERICA
The vast expanse of the Great Lakes is impressive even when viewed from space. Superior and Huron are partly within Canada, making Michigan the largest lake wholly situated within the US.

COUNTRIES WITH THE GREATEST AREA OF INLAND WATER

	Country	Percentage of total area	Water area sq km	sq miles
1	Canada	7.60	755,170	291,573
2	India	9.56	314,400	121,391
3	China	2.82	270,550	104,460
4	US	2.20	206,010	79,541
5	Ethiopia	9.89	120,900	46,680
6	Colombia	8.80	100,210	38,691
7	Indonesia	4.88	93,000	35,908
8	Russia	0.47	79,400	30,657
9	Australia	0.90	68,920	26,610
10	Tanzania	6.25	59,050	22,799

Large areas of some countries are occupied by major rivers and lakes. Lake Victoria, for example, raises the water area of Uganda to 15.39 percent of its total. In Europe, three Scandinavian countries have considerable areas of water: Sweden has 15,072 sq miles/ 39,036 sq km (8.68 percent), Finland has 12,185 sq miles/ 31,560 sq km (9.36 percent), and Norway has 6,317 sq miles/ 16,360 sq km (5.05 percent). The UK has 1,247 sq miles/ 3,230 sq km, which is 1.32 percent of the total area of the country.

TOP 10

DEEPEST OCEANS AND SEAS IN THE WORLD

	Ocean/sea	Average depth m	ft
1	Pacific Ocean	4,028	13,215
2	Indian Ocean	3,963	13,002
3	Atlantic Ocean	3,926	12,880
4	Caribbean Sea	2,647	8,685
5	South China Sea	1,652	5,419
6	Bering Sea	1,547	5,075
7	Gulf of Mexico	1,486	4,874
8	Mediterranean Sea	1,429	4,688
9	Sea of Japan	1,350	4,429
10	Arctic Ocean	1,205	3,953

The deepest point in the deepest ocean is the Marianas Trench in the Pacific with a depth of 35,837 ft/10,924 m, according to a recent hydrographic survey, although a depth of 35,814 ft/10,916 m was recorded by Jacques Piccard and Donald Walsh in the 58 ft- /17.7 m-long bathyscaphe *Trieste 2* during their descent of January 23, 1960. Whichever is correct, it is close to seven miles down, or almost 29 times the height of the Empire State Building.

TOP 10

DEEPEST OCEAN TRENCHES

	Trench	Ocean	Deepest point m	ft
1	Marianas	Pacific	10,924	35,837
2	Tonga*	Pacific	10,800	35,430
3	Philippine	Pacific	10,497	34,436
4	Kermadec*	Pacific	10,047	32,960
5	Bonin	Pacific	9,994	32,786
6	New Britain	Pacific	9,940	32,609
7	Kuril	Pacific	9,750	31,985
8	Izu	Pacific	9,695	31,805
9	Puerto Rico	Atlantic	8,605	28,229
10	Yap	Pacific	8,527	27,973

* Some authorities consider these parts of the same ocean-bed geological feature

TOP 10

LARGEST LAKES IN THE WORLD

	Lake	Location	Approx. area sq km	sq miles
1	Caspian Sea	Azerbaijan/Iran/Kazakhstan/ Russia/Turkmenistan	378,400	146,101
2	Superior	Canada/US	82,100	31,699
3	Victoria	Kenya/Tanzania/Uganda	62,940	24,301
4	Huron	Canada/US	59,580	23,004
5	Michigan	US	57,700	22,278
6	Aral Sea	Kazakhstan/Uzbekistan	40,000	15,444
7	Tanganyika	Burundi/Tanzania/Zaïre/Zambia	31,987	12,350
8	Baikal	Russia	31,494	12,160
9	Great Bear	Canada	31,153	12,028
10	Great Slave	Canada	28,570	11,031

TOP 10

DEEPEST FRESHWATER LAKES IN THE WORLD

	Lake	Location	Greatest depth m	ft
1	Baikal	Russia	1,637	5,371
2	Tanganyika	Burundi/Tanzania/Zaïre/Zambia	1,471	4,825
3	Malawi	Malawi/Mozambique/Tanzania	706	2,316
4	Great Slave	Canada	614	2,015
5	Matana	Celebes, Indonesia	590	1,936
6	Crater	Oregon, US	589	1,932
7	Toba	Sumatra, Indonesia	529	1,736
8	Hornindals	Norway	514	1,686
9	Sarez	Tajikistan	505	1,657
10	Tahoe	California/Nevada	501	1,645

DID YOU KNOW

TALLER THAN EVEREST?

Mountains are conventionally measured from sea level. Thus Everest, at 29,022 ft/ 8,846 m above sea level, is the world's tallest mountain. However, the bases of some mountains lie far below the sea. The Hawaiian volcano Mauna Kea is 13,796 ft/ 4,206 m tall but has even greater height below sea level, some 19,683 ft/6,000 m, bringing its total height to 33,481 ft/10,206 m, or 4,461 ft/1,360 m taller than Everest. Its neighbor, Mauna Loa, 13,681 ft/4,171 m tall with a further 18,043 ft/5,500 m below sea level, is also taller than Everest and is reckoned to be the world's most voluminous mountain at 10,076 mi^3/42,000 km^3. The tallest mountain wholly beneath the sea is in the Pacific Ocean's Tonga Trench, rising 28,510 ft/8,690 m.

WORLD WEATHER

TOP 10

COLDEST INHABITED PLACES IN THE WORLD

	Location	Average temperature °C	°F
1	Norlísk, Russia	−10.9	12.4
2	Yakutsk, Russia	−10.1	13.8
3	Yellowknife, Canada	−5.4	22.3
4	Ulaanbator, Mongolia	−4.5	23.9
5	Fairbanks, Alaska	−3.4	25.9
6	Surgut, Russia	−3.1	26.4
7	Chita, Russia	−2.7	27.1
8	Nizhnevartosvsk, Russia	−2.6	27.3
9	Hailar, Mongolia	−2.4	27.7
10	Bratsk, Russia	−2.2	28.0

TOP 10

DRIEST CITIES IN THE US

	City	Mean annual precipitation mm	in
1	Yuma, Arizona	67	2.65
2	Las Vegas, Nevada	106	4.19
3	Bishop, California	142	5.61
4	Bakersfield, California	145	5.72
5	Phoenix, Arizona	180	7.11
6	Alamosa, Colorado	181	7.13
7	Reno, Nevada	190	7.49
8	Winslow, Arizona	194	7.64
9	El Paso, Texas	199	7.82
10	Winnemucca, Nevada	200	7.87

TOP 10

WETTEST CITIES IN THE US

	City	Mean annual precipitation mm	in
1	Quillayute, Washington	2,672	105.18
2	Astoria, Oregon	1,687	66.40
3	Tallahassee, Florida	1,669	65.71
4	Mobile, Alaska	1,625	63.96
5	Pensacola, Florida	1,581	62.25
6	New Orleans, Louisiana	1,572	61.88
7	Baton Rouge, Louisiana	1,547	60.89
8	West Palm Beach, Florida	1,543	60.75
9	Meridian, Mississippi	1,440	56.71
10	Tupelo, Mississippi	1,419	55.87

TOP 10

HOTTEST INHABITED PLACES IN THE WORLD

	Location	Average temperature °C	°F
1	Djibouti, Djibouti	30.0	86.0
2=	Timbuktu, Mali	29.3	84.7
2=	Tirunelveli, India	29.3	84.7
2=	Tuticorin, India	29.3	84.7
5=	Nellore, India	29.2	84.6
5=	Santa Marta, Colombia	29.2	84.6
7=	Aden, South Yemen	28.9	84.0
7=	Madurai, India	28.9	84.0
7=	Niamey, Niger	28.9	84.0
10=	Hudaydah, North Yemen	28.8	83.8
10=	Ouagadougou, Burkina Faso	28.8	83.8
10=	Thanjāvūr, India	28.8	83.8
10=	Tiruchchlrāppalli, India	28.8	83.8

TOP 10

DRIEST INHABITED PLACES IN THE WORLD

	Location	Average annual rainfall mm	in
1	Aswan, Egypt	0.5	0.02
2	Luxor, Egypt	0.7	0.03
3	Arica, Chile	1.1	0.04
4	Ica, Peru	2.3	0.09
5	Antofagasta, Chile	4.9	0.19

	Location	Average annual rainfall mm	in
6	Minya el Qamn, Egypt	5.1	0.20
7	Asyût, Egypt	5.2	0.20
8	Callao, Peru	12.0	0.47
9	Trujillo, Peru	14.0	0.54
10	Fayyum, Egypt	19.0	0.75

LAS VEGAS – 2ND DRIEST CITY IN THE US

SEASON OF DOWNPOURS
In tropical and semitropical regions of the world, most of the rainfall for the year occurs in prolonged bursts during the monsoon period, which can last several months. Following months of high temperatures and dryness, the inhabitants look forward to the rainy season.

TOP 10

WETTEST INHABITED PLACES IN THE WORLD

	Location	Average annual rainfall mm	in
1	Buenaventura, Colombia	6,743	265.47
2	Monrovia, Liberia	5,131	202.01
3	Pago Pago, American Samoa	4,990	196.46
4	Moulmein, Myanmar (Burma)	4,852	191.02
5	Lae, Papua New Guinea	4,645	182.87
6	Baguio, Luzon Island, Philippines	4,573	180.04
7	Sylhet, Bangladesh	4,457	175.47
8	Conakry, Guinea	4,341	170.91
9=	Bogor, Java, Indonesia	4,225	166.34
9=	Padang, Sumatra Island, Indonesia	4,225	166.34

TOP 10

SNOWIEST CITIES IN THE US

	City	Mean annual snowfall mm	in
1	Blue Canyon, California	6,116	240.8
2	Marquette, Michigan	3,282	129.2
3	Sault Ste. Marie, Michigan	2,949	116.1
4	Syracuse, New York	2,896	114.0
5	Caribou, Maine	2,794	110.0
6	Mount Shasta, California	2,664	104.9
7	Lander, Wyoming	2,596	102.2
8	Flagstaff, Arizona	2,560	100.8
9	Sexton Summit, Oregon	2,484	97.8
10	Muskegon, Michigan	2,466	97.1

TOP 10

COLDEST CITIES IN THE US

	Location	Average temperature °C	°F
1	International Falls, MN	2.4	36.4
2	Duluth, MN	3.4	38.2
3	Caribou, ME	3.8	38.9
4	Marquette, MI	4.0	39.2
5	Sault Ste. Marie, MI	4.3	39.7
6	Fargo, ND	4.7	40.5
7	Williston, ND	4.9	40.8
8	Alamosa, CO	5.1	41.2
9	Bismarck, ND	5.2	41.3
10	Saint Cloud, MN	5.2	41.4

TOP 10

HOTTEST CITIES IN THE US

	Location	Average temperature °C	°F
1	Key West, Florida	25.4	77.7
2	Miami, Florida	24.2	75.6
3	West Palm Beach, Florida	23.7	74.6
4=	Fort Myers, Florida	23.3	73.9
4=	Yuma, Arizona	23.3	73.9
6	Brownsville, Texas	23.1	73.6
7=	Orlando, Florida	22.4	72.4
7=	Vero Beach, Florida	22.4	72.4
9	Corpus Christi, Texas	22.3	72.1
10	Tampa, Florida	22.2	72.0

TOP 10

WINDIEST PLACES IN THE US

	City	Mean wind speed km/h	mph
1	Blue Hill, Maine	24.8	15.4
2	Dodge City, Kansas	22.5	14.0
3	Amarillo, Texas	21.7	13.5
4	Rochester, Minnesota	21.1	13.1
5=	Casper, Wyoming	20.8	12.9
5=	Cheyenne, Wyoming	20.8	12.9
7	Great Falls, Montana	20.4	12.7
8	Goodland, Kansas	20.3	12.6
9	Boston, Massachusetts	20.1	12.5
10	Lubbock, Texas	20.0	12.4

Source: National Climatic Data Center

LIFE ON EARTH

20TH CENTURY

As the dinosaur lists on this spread remind us, cataclysmic extinctions have occurred. In our own time, numerous species of birds and mammals have been hunted to extinction, and the process continues today with widespread pollution and the destruction of habitats accelerating the process. There are success stories of animals saved and reintroduced to the wild, but lists of endangered and vanished animals are a salutary indication of just how fragile the balance of life on earth remains.

AMAZING ARMORED MAMMAL
The once prolific rhinoceros now has only five different species, all of which are threatened with extinction.

10 ANIMALS THAT HAVE DISAPPEARED IN THE 20TH CENTURY

	Animal	Last seen alive
1	Guam flying fox	1968

This rare bat finally disappeared from its native Pacific island of Guam.

	Animal	Last seen alive
2	Crescent nailtail wallaby	1964

Along with other wallabies and bandicoots, this is one of several species of marsupial to have vanished during the 20th century.

3	Eskimo curlew	1963

The last known specimen was shot by a hunter on Barbados during September 1963.

4	Euler's flycatcher	1955

The last two of this species were killed by Hurricane Janet when it struck Jamaica on September 26, 1955.

5	Arabian ostrich	1941

The Chinese ostrich became extinct around the turn of the century, leaving only the large African variety and the smaller, but equally beautifully feathered, Arabian type. Hunted for its plumage, the last specimen is believed to have been killed in Bahrain during World War II.

6	Heath hen	1933

The grouselike prairie chicken known as the heath hen was extensively hunted in the New England states until only a few specimens survived, all on the island of Martha's Vineyard, Massachusetts. Despite measures to protect them, many were killed in a forest fire in 1916, and by 1933 the bird was no more.

7	Carolina parakeet	1918

On February 21, 1918, like Martha the Passenger pigeon, the last of this colorful species died at the Cincinnati Zoo.

8	Passenger pigeon	1914

This is an example of a creature whose final moment can be stated very precisely, when, at 1:00 pm on September 1, 1914, at the Cincinnati Zoo, a 29-year-old bird named Martha expired; her stuffed body is displayed by the Smithsonian Institution, Washington, DC. Once there had been vast flocks of passenger pigeons, with estimated totals running to a staggering five to nine billion in the 19th century. Unfortunately they were remorselessly killed for food and to protect farm crops in the US, and – since each bird laid only one egg each season – its decline was almost inevitable. By March 24, 1900 (when the last one in the wild was shot), it was virtually extinct, with only a few specimens, such as Martha, in zoos.

9	Japanese gray wolf	1905

One of the smallest known wolves, it was finally hunted to extinction in the early years of the century. The last one was seen alive in 1905.

10	Pilori muskrat	1902

This species became extinct following the May 1902 eruption of Mont Pelée, Martinique.

LOST & FOUND

T O P   1 0

LARGEST DINOSAURS DISCOVERED IN THE 20TH CENTURY

1 Seismosaurus
Length: 98–119 ft/30–36 m
Estimated weight: 50–80 tons

A skeleton of this colossal plant-eater was excavated in 1985 near Albuquerque, New Mexico, by US paleontologist David Gillette and given a name that means "earth-shaking lizard." It is being studied by the New Mexico Museum of Natural History, which may confirm its position as the largest dinosaur, with some claiming a length of up to 170 ft/52 m.

2 Supersaurus
Length: 80–100 ft/24–30 m
Estimated weight: 50 tons

The remains of Supersaurus were found in Colorado in 1972. Some scientists have suggested a length of up to 138 ft/42 m and a weight of 75–100 tons.

3 Antarctosaurus
Length: 60–98 ft/18–30 m
Estimated weight: 40–50 tons

Named Antarctosaurus ("southern lizard") by German paleontologist Friedrich von Huene in 1929, this creature's thigh bone alone measures 7 ft 6 in/2.3 m. Some authorities have put its weight as high as 80 tons.

4 Mamenchisaurus
Length: 89 ft/27 m
Weight uncertain

An almost complete skeleton discovered in 1972 showed it had the longest neck of any known animal, comprising more than half its total body length. It was named by Chinese paleontologist Yang Zhong-Jian (known in paleontological circles as "C.C. Young") after the place in China where it was found.

5 Ultrasauros
Length: Over 82 ft/25 m
Estimated weight: 50 tons

Ultrasauros was discovered by US paleontologist James A. Jensen in Colorado in 1979 but has not yet been fully studied. Some authorities have claimed its weight as an unlikely 100–140 tons. It was originally called "Ultrasaurus" ("ultra lizard"), which, it turned out, was a name also given to another, smaller dinosaur. To avoid confusion, its spelling was altered.

6 Brachiosaurus
Length: 82 ft/25 m
Estimated weight: 50 tons

Its name means "arm lizard." Some paleontologists have put the weight of Brachiosaurus as high as 190 tons, but this seems improbable (if not impossible, in the light of theories of the maximum possible weight of terrestrial animals).

7 Alamosaurus
Length: 69 ft/21 m
Estimated weight: 30 tons

So named by American paleontologist Charles W. Gilmore in 1922 from finds in the Alamo region of Texas, this large plant-eating sauropod ("lizard feet") lived during the late Cretaceous period.

8 Euhelopus
Length: 49 ft/15 m
Estimated weight: 24 tons

Another sauropod, Euhelopus was a late Jurassic dinosaur found in China.

9= Spinosaurus
Length: 39 ft/12 m
Estimated weight: 6.4 tons

German paleontologist Ernst Stromer von Reichenbach named Spinosaurus ("thorn lizard") from finds in Africa in 1915.

9= Tyrannosaurus
Length: 39 ft/12 m
Estimated weight: 6.4 tons

Henry F. Osborn, an American scientist, named everyone's favourite dinosaur, Tyrannosaurus ("tyrant lizard"), in 1905. Although it was one of the fiercest flesh-eating dinosaurs, it was not as large as many of the herbivorous ones. However, measuring a probable 39 ft/12 m and weighing more than six tons, it certainly ranks as one of the largest flesh-eating animals yet discovered. Bones of an earlier dinosaur called Epanterias were found in Colorado in 1877 and 1934, but were incorrectly identified until recently, when studies suggested that this creature was possibly larger than Tyrannosaurus, but its precedence has yet to be firmly established.

Although several large dinosaurs were found in the 19th century (most notably Barosaurus, Diplodocus, Pelorosaurus, and Apatosaurus), excavations during the 20th century have revealed some similarly large specimens, and this Top 10 is based on the most reliable recent evidence of their lengths and indicates the probable ranges; as more and more information is assembled, these are undergoing constant revision.

T O P   1 0

DINOSAUR DISCOVERERS OF THE 20TH CENTURY

	Name	Period	Dinosaurs named*
1	Friedrich von Huene	1902–61	45
2	Dong Zhiming	1973–93	24
3	José F. Bonaparte	1969–95	20
4=	Henry F. Osborn	1902–24	17
4=	Yang Zhong-Jian ("C.C. Young")	1937–82	17
6=	Robert Broom	1904–16	14
6=	Peter M. Galton	1971–95	14
6=	Lawrence M. Lambe	1902–19	14
9	Charles W. Gilmore	1913–45	11
10	Franz Nopsca	1900–29	10

* 20th-century only, including joint namings

STYRACOSAURUS

COMMON & RARE

MOST ENDANGERED MAMMALS IN THE WORLD

Mammal	Number
1= Tasmanian wolf	?
1= Halcon fruit bat	?
1= Ghana fat mouse	?
4 Kouprey	10
5 Javan rhinoceros	50
6 Iriomote cat	60
7 Black lion tamarin	130
8 Pygmy hog	150
9 Tamaraw	200
10 Indus dolphin	400

The first three mammals on the list have not been seen for many years and may well be extinct. However, zoologists are hopeful of the possibility of their survival. The Tasmanian wolf, for example, has been technically extinct since the last specimen died in a zoo in 1936, but occasional unconfirmed sightings suggest that there may still be animals in the wild, and a 1,601,240 acre nature preserve has been set aside for it in Tasmania in the expectation that the wolf will be found again. The only Halcon fruit bat that has ever been seen is one that was discovered in the Philippines in 1937.

JUMBO SIZE

In 1882 the American showman Phineas T. Barnum bought London Zoo's gigantic African elephant, Jumbo. Despite an outcry from the public, Jumbo was shipped to New York before going on show as "The Biggest Elephant in the World." On September 15, 1885, while he was being led across railroad tracks at St. Thomas, Ontario, Canada, he was struck by a freight train and died. His stuffed body was exhibited at Tufts University, near Boston, until 1975 when it was destroyed in a fire, but his skeleton survives. His name is still used today to mean "huge" in such expressions as "jumbo jet."

RAREST MARINE MAMMALS

Mammal	Estimated no.
1 Caribbean monk seal	200
2 Mediterranean monk seal	400
3 Juan Fernandez fur seal	750
4 West Indian manatee	1,000
5 Guadeloupe fur seal	1,600
6 New Zealand fur seal	2,000
7= Hooker's sea lion	4,000
7= Right whale	4,000
9 Fraser's dolphin	7,800
10 Amazon manatee	8,000

The hunting of seals for their fur and of whales for oil and other products, combined in many instances with the depletion of their natural food resources by the fishing industry, has resulted in a sharp decline in the populations of many marine mammals. Populations of some species of seal formerly numbering millions have shrunk to a few thousand, and it has been estimated that the world population of humpback whales has dwindled from 100,000 to 10,000.

COUNTRIES WITH THE MOST ELEPHANTS

Country	Elephants
1 Zaïre	195,000
2 Tanzania	100,000
3 Gabon	76,000
4 Congo	61,000
5 Botswana	51,000
6 Zimbabwe	43,000
7 Zambia	41,000
8 Sudan	40,000
9 Kenya	35,000
10 Cameroon	21,000

All the countries in this Top 10 are in Africa, which in 1987 was reckoned to have a total elephant population of 764,410. India's 20,000 Asian elephants just fail to enter the list, and the entire surviving population of wild Asian elephants in the world is only a fraction of that of Africa at between 30,000 and 55,000. In addition, about 16,000 tame elephants are found in Myanmar (Burma), India, Thailand, Vietnam, and Cambodia. Estimates of populations of Asian elephants are notoriously unreliable since this species is exclusively a forest animal, and its numbers cannot be sampled using aerial survey techniques. The same is true of the forest variety of African elephant, distributed in heavily wooded countries such as Gabon and Zaïre, as distinct from the savannah elephant found in the wide open spaces of scantily wooded countries including Tanzania and Zimbabwe. This problem may account for widely varying estimates of elephant populations in such countries.

JUNGLE JUGGERNAUT
Asian elephants are smaller than their African cousins. Because they live in forests, they are less easy to survey accurately.

T O P 1 0

MOST ABUNDANT TYPES OF ANIMAL

1 Insects and spiders

Of animals that can readily be seen without a microscope, insects unquestionably top the numbers league: there are at least 1,000,000 insects for each of the Earth's 5,292,000,000 humans. Among the most common insects are ants, fleas, flies, and the little-known springtails, which inhabit moist topsoil the world over. The latter alone probably outnumber the human race.

2 Crustaceans

Besides crabs, woodlice, and so on, this class also includes krill and other tiny, shrimplike creatures that form a major ingredient of plankton, the mainstay of life in the oceans.

3 Worms

Earthworms and other tubelike animals, including parasitic worms, occur in great numbers in some habitats: more than 1,000,000 earthworms were counted in 1 acre of British farmland. But their distribution is variable compared with the teeming arthropods higher up the list.

4 Fish

The total fish population of the world's oceans has been estimated at around 760,000,000 tons – at least 100,000,000,000,000 individuals.

5 Mollusks

This list includes snails, slugs, most shellfish, squids, and octopus, and many tiny animals that make up the plankton horde.

6 Amphibians

Frogs, toads, newts, and the like make a group of an estimated one trillion (1,000,000,000,000) creatures.

7 Birds

Many birds share human habitats yet avoid conflict with humans, so they have the edge in numbers over most other larger wildlife outside the oceans. There are probably about 100,000,000,000 birds in the world, and the most common must include poultry species and specialist townies such as the sparrows.

8 Mammals (excluding humans)

Despite exploding human numbers and heavy pressures on many rare mammal species in the wild, other mammals probably still outnumber humans by at least four to one, boosted by the huge numbers of herd animals, pets, and "commensal" or scavenging animals such as rats and mice that share our habitats.

9 Humans

The baby that pushed the world's human population meter past the 5,000,000,000 mark was in all probability born in 1987.

10 Reptiles

Reptiles never recovered from the unknown cataclysm that finished off the dinosaurs well before humans arrived on the scene. Now, largely through conflict and competition with humans, the world's snakes, lizards, turtles, crocodiles, and other scaly skinned beasts are once more in decline and may number fewer than 2,000,000,000 individuals at present.

Microbes exist in staggering numbers: some nine trillion (9,000,000,000,000) of medium size could be packed into a cube with equal sides of 1 inch/2.5 cm. The four trillion trillion trillion world population claimed by some for nematodes (microscopic wormlike parasites) is a dubious sum based on birthrate, without proper adjustments for survival rate or gaps in distribution. Estimates of the populations of other classes are at best "guesstimates," and this Top 10 should be viewed as a general picture of the relative numbers of each type of animal.

T O P 1 0

GROUPS WITH MOST KNOWN SPECIES

	Group	Approx. no. of known species
1	Insects	1,000,000
2	Other arthropods*	500,000
3	Higher plants	248,000
4	Mollusks	100,000
5	Fungi	69,000
6	Worms	25,000
7	Fish#	13,000
8	Birds#	9,000
9	Reptiles#	7,000
10	Mammals#	4,500

* Spiders, shrimps, crabs, etc.
 # Vertebrates

OUR FAVORITE FEATHERED FRIENDS
Birds rank seventh in the most abundant classes of animal. Chickens are the most popular among the few breeds of birds that have been domesticated.

T O P 1 0

ANIMALS MOST MENTIONED IN THE BIBLE

	Animal	OT*	NT*	Total
1	Sheep	155	45	200
2	Lamb	153	35	188
3	Lion	167	9	176
4	Ox	156	10	166
5	Ram	165	0	165
6	Horse	137	27	164
7	Bullock	152	0	152
8	Ass	142	8	150
9	Goat	131	7	138
10	Camel	56	6	62

* Occurrences in verses in the King James Bible (Old and New Testaments), including plurals

The sheep are sorted from the goats (itself a biblical expression – "a shepherd divideth his sheep from the goats," in Matthew 25:32) in this Top 10, in a list of the animals regarded as most significant in biblical times, either economically or symbolically.

CREATURES GREAT & SMALL

Diversity is one of the most impressive features of the animal kingdom, and even within a single species huge variations can be encountered. There are practical problems that make measurement difficult – it is virtually impossible to weigh an elephant in the wild or to estimate a bird's air speed minus the wind factor, for example. Most of the lists, therefore, represent "likely averages" based on the informed observations of expert researchers, rather than individual assessments or rare and extreme record-breaking cases.

T O P 1 0

HEAVIEST PRIMATES

	Primate	Length* cm	in	Weight kg	lb
1	Gorilla	200	79	220	485
2	Human	177	70	77	170
3	Orangutan	137	54	75	165
4	Chimpanzee	92	36	50	110
5=	Baboon	100	39	45	99
5=	Mandrill	95	37	45	99
7	Gelada baboon	75	30	25	55
8	Proboscis monkey	76	30	24	53
9	Hanuman langur	107	42	20	44
10	Siamang gibbon	90	35	13	29

* Excluding tail

The largest primates (including humans) and all the apes are rooted in the Old World (Africa, Asia, and Europe): only one member of a New World species of monkey (the Guatemalan howler at 36 in/91 cm; 20 lb/9 kg) is a close contender for this Top 10. The difference between the prosimians (primitive primates), great apes, lesser apes, and monkeys has more to do with shape than size, although the great apes mostly top the table anyway. Lower down the list, the longer, skinnier, and lighter forms of the lemurs, langurs, gibbons, and monkeys, designed for life among the trees, send the length column haywire.

T O P 1 0

LARGEST CARNIVORES

	Carnivore	Length m	ft	in	Weight kg	lb
1	Southern elephant seal	6.5	21	4	3,500	7,716
2	Walrus	3.8	12	6	1,200	2,646
3	Steller sea lion	3.0	9	8	1,100	2,425
4	Grizzly bear	3.0	9	8	780	1,720
5	Polar bear	2.5	8	2	700	1,543
6	Tiger	2.8	9	2	300	661
7	Lion	1.9	6	3	250	551
8	American black bear	1.8	6	0	227	500
9	Giant panda	1.5	5	0	160	353
10	Spectacled bear	1.8	6	0	140	309

Of the 273 species in the mammalian order Carnivora, or meat-eaters, many (including its largest representatives on land, the bears) are in fact omnivorous (animals that eat both meat and plants), and around 40 species specialize in eating fish or insects. As this Top 10 would otherwise consist exclusively of seals and related marine carnivores, only three representatives have been included in order to enable the terrestrial heavyweight division to make an appearance. The polar bear is probably the tallest land carnivore if shoulder height (when the animal is on all fours) is taken into account: it tops an awesome 5 ft 3 in/1.60 m, compared with the 4 ft/1.20 m of its nearest rival, the grizzly bear. The common (or least) weasel is almost certainly the smallest carnivore: small individuals are less than 7 in/17 cm long, not counting the tail, and can weigh as little as 3 oz (less than 90 g).

T O P 1 0

HEAVIEST TERRESTRIAL MAMMALS

	Carnivore	Length m	ft	in	Weight kg	lb
1	African elephant	7.2	23	7	5,000	11,023
2	Great Indian rhinoceros	4.2	13	10	4,000	8,818
3	Hippopotamus	4.9	16	1	2,000	4,409
4	Giraffe	5.8	19	0	1,200	2,646
5	American bison	3.9	12	10	1,000	2,205
6	Grizzly bear	3.0	9	10	780	1,720
7	Arabian camel (dromedary)	3.0	9	10	600	1,323
8	Moose	3.0	9	10	595	1,312
9	Tiger	2.8	9	2	300	661
10	Gorilla	2.0	6	7	220	485

This list excludes domesticated cattle and horses. It also avoids comparing close kin such as the African and Indian elephants, highlighting instead the sumo stars within distinctive large mammal groups such as the bears, deer, big cats, primates, and bovines (oxlike mammals). Sizes are not necessarily the top of the known range: records exist, for instance, of African elephant individuals weighing in excess of 13,228 lb/6,000 kg.

TOP 10

LARGEST TURTLES AND TORTOISES

	Turtle/tortoise	Maximum weight kg	lb
1	Pacific leatherback turtle	865	1,908
2	Atlantic leatherback turtle	454	1,000
3=	Green sea turtle	408	900
3=	Aldabra giant tortoise	408	900
5	Loggerhead turtle	386	850
6	Galapagos giant or elephant tortoise	385	849
7	Alligator snapping turtle	183	403
8	Black sea turtle	126	278
9	Flatback turtle	84	185
10	Hawksbill turtle	68	150

Both the sizes and the longevity of turtles and tortoises remain hotly debated by zoologists, and although the weights on which this Top 10 are ranked are from corroborated sources, there are many claims of even larger specimens among the 265 species of *Chelonia* (turtles and tortoises). The largest are marine turtles, and the Aldabra giant tortoises, found on an island in the Seychelles, the largest land-dwellers – and probably the longest-lived land creatures of all, at more than 150 years.

TOP 10

SMALLEST MAMMALS

	Mammal	Weight g	oz	Length cm	in
1	Kitti's hognosed bat	2.0	0.07	2.9	1.1
2	Pygmy shrew	1.5	0.05	3.6	1.4
3	Pipistrelle bat	3.0	0.11	4.0	1.6
4	Little brown bat	8.0	0.28	4.0	1.6
5	Masked shrew	2.4	0.08	4.5	1.8
6	Southern blossom bat	12.0	0.42	5.0	2.0
7	Harvest mouse	5.0	0.18	5.8	2.3
8	Pygmy glider	12.0	0.42	6.0	2.4
9	House mouse	12.0	0.42	6.4	2.5
10	Common shrew	5.0	0.18	6.5	2.5

The pygmy glider and another that does not quite make this Top 10, the pygmy possum, are marsupials, more closely related to kangaroos than to anything else in this list. Some classifications exclude marsupials from the mammal class. Among other contenders for the small world are the water shrew (0.42 oz/12.0 g; 2.8 in/7.0 cm) and bank vole (0.53 oz/15.0 g; 3.2 in/8.0 cm). The Kitti's hognosed bat is represented only by a few specimens in museum collections, and larger examples may be discovered.

TOP 10

LONGEST SNAKES

	Snake	Maximum length m	ft
1	Reticulated python	10.7	35
2	Anaconda	8.5	28
3	Indian python	7.6	25
4	Diamond python	6.4	21
5	King cobra	5.8	19
6	Boa constrictor	4.9	16
7	Bushmaster	3.7	12
8	Giant brown snake	3.4	11
9	Diamondback rattlesnake	2.7	9
10	Indigo or gopher snake	2.4	8

Although the South American anaconda is sometimes claimed to be the longest snake, this has not been authenticated, and it seems that the python remains entitled to claim preeminence.

GIANT OF THE SEAS
Probably the largest animal that ever lived, the blue whale dwarfs all the other whales.

TOP 10

HEAVIEST MARINE MAMMALS

	Mammal	Length m	ft	in	Weight (tons)
1	Blue whale	33.5	110	0	130.0
2	Fin whale	25.0	82	0	45.0
3	Right whale	17.5	57	5	40.0
4	Sperm whale	18.0	59	0	36.0
5	Gray whale	14.0	46	0	32.7
6	Humpback whale	15.0	49	2	26.5
7	Baird's whale	5.5	18	0	11.0
8	Southern elephant seal	6.5	21	4	3.6
9	Northern elephant seal	5.8	19	0	3.4
10	Pilot whale	6.4	21	0	2.9

ANIMAL RECORD BREAKERS

T O P 1 0

LONGEST LIVED ANIMALS
(Excluding humans)

Animal	Maximum age (years)
1 Quahog (marine clam)	up to 200
2 Giant tortoise	150
3 Garden tortoise	110
4 Killer whale	90
5 European eel	88
6 Lake sturgeon	82
7 Sea anemone	80
8 Elephant	78
9 Freshwater mussel	75
10 Andean condor	70

The ages of animals in the wild are difficult to determine with accuracy because the precise birth and death dates of relatively few long-lived animals have ever been recorded. There are clues, such as annual growth of shells, teeth, and – in the case of whales – even ear wax. This Top 10 represents documented maximum ages of animals attained by more than one example – although there may well be extreme cases of animals exceeding these life spans.

T O P 1 0

MAMMALS WITH THE LARGEST LITTERS

Mammal	Average litter
1 Malagasy tenrec	25.0
2 Virginian opossum	22.0
3 Golden hamster	11.0
4 Ermine	10.0
5 Prairie vole	9.0
6 Coypu	8.5
7= European hedgehog	7.0
7= African hunting dog	7.0
9= Meadow vole	6.5
9= Wild boar	6.5

The prairie vole probably holds the world record for most offspring produced in a season. It has up to 17 litters in rapid succession, bringing up to 150 young into the world. All the numbers in this list are averages: the tiny tenrec can produce as many as 31 in a single litter, and instances of domestic pigs producing 30 or more piglets at one time are not uncommon. Despite these prodigious reproductive peaks, mammalian litter sizes appear minute when compared with those of other animal groups. Many fish, for instance, can lay more than 10,000 eggs at a time, and many amphibians more than 1,000.

T O P 1 0

DEADLIEST SNAKES IN THE WORLD

Species	Native region
1= Taipan	Australia and New Guinea

Mortality is practically 100 percent unless antivenin is administered immediately. Taipans have very long fangs and are able to deliver a large quantity of venom.

1= Black mamba	Southern and Central Africa

Mortality nearly 100 percent without antivenin.

3 Tiger snake	Australia

Very high mortality without antivenin.

4 Common krait	South Asia

Up to 50 percent mortality even with antivenin.

5 Death adder	Australia

Over 50 percent mortality without antivenin.

6 Yellow or Cape cobra	Southern Africa

The most dangerous type of cobra in the world, with high mortality.

7 King cobra	India and Southeast Asia

At 16 ft/4.9 m long, the king cobra is the largest poisonous snake in the world. It also injects the most venom into its victims.

8= Bushmaster	Central and South America
8= Green mamba	Africa
10 Coral snake	North, Central, and South America

Most people fear snakes, but only a few dozen of the 3,500-odd snake species that exist cause serious harm, and many more are beneficial because they prey on vermin and other snake species of worse repute. Measuring the strength of the venom of snakes is technically possible, but this factor does not indicate how dangerous they may be: the Australian smooth- or small-scaled snake, for example, is believed to be the most venomous land snake in the world, but no human victims have ever been recorded. This Top 10 takes account of the degree of threat posed by those snakes that have a record of causing fatalities.

VERMILLION FLYCATCHER

GIANT TORTOISE

TOP 10

LAZIEST ANIMALS IN THE WORLD

	Animal	Average hours of sleep
1	Koala	22
2	Sloth	20
3=	Armadillo	19
3=	Opossum	19
5	Lemur	16
6=	Hamster	14
6=	Squirrel	14
8=	Cat	13
8=	Pig	13
10	Spiny anteater	12

This list excludes periods of hibernation, which can last up to several months among creatures such as the ground squirrel, marmot, and brown bear. At the other end of the scale comes the frantic shrew, which has to hunt and eat constantly or perish: it literally has no time for sleep. The incredible swift contrives to sleep on the wing, "turning off" alternate halves of its brain for shifts of two hours or more. Flight control is entrusted to whichever hemisphere is on duty at the time.

SLOTH

TOP 10

MOST INTELLIGENT MAMMALS

1	Human
2	Chimpanzee
3	Gorilla
4	Orangutan
5	Baboon
6	Gibbon
7	Monkey
8	Smaller toothed whale
9	Dolphin
10	Elephant

This list is based on research conducted by Edward O. Wilson, Professor of Zoology at Harvard University, who defined intelligence as speed and extent of learning performance over a wide range of tasks, also taking account of the ratio of an animal's brain size to its body bulk. It may come as a surprise that the dog does not make the Top 10, and that if humans are excluded No. 10 becomes the pig.

TOP 10

MAMMALS WITH THE LONGEST GESTATION PERIODS

	Mammal	Average gestation (days)
1	African elephant	660
2	Asiatic elephant	600
3	Baird's beaked whale	520
4	White rhinoceros	490
5	Walrus	480
6	Giraffe	460
7	Tapir	400
8	Arabian camel (dromedary)	390
9	Fin whale	370
10	Llama	360

The 480-day gestation of the walrus includes a delay of up to five months while the fertilized embryo is held as a blastocyst (a sphere of cells) but is not implanted until later in the wall of the uterus. This option enables offspring to be produced at the most favorable time of the year. Human gestation (ranging from 253 to 303 days) is exceeded not only by the Top 10 mammals but also by others including the porpoise, the horse, and the water buffalo.

TOP 10

FASTEST FISH IN THE WORLD

	Fish	Maximum recorded speed km/h	mph
1	Sailfish	110	68
2	Marlin	80	50
3	Bluefin tuna	74	46
4	Yellowfin tuna	70	44
5	Blue shark	69	43
6	Wahoo	66	41
7=	Bonefish	64	40
7=	Swordfish	64	40
9	Tarpon	56	35
10	Tiger shark	53	33

THE 10

FASTEST MAMMALS IN THE WORLD

	Mammal	Maximum recorded speed km/h	mph
1	Cheetah	105	65
2	Pronghorn antelope	89	55
3=	Mongolian gazelle	80	50
3=	Springbok	80	50
5=	Grant's gazelle	76	47
5=	Thomson's gazelle	76	47
7	Brown hare	72	45
8	Horse	69	43
9=	Greyhound	68	42
9=	Red deer	68	42

BIRDS OF A FEATHER

LARGEST LIVING BIRD
The ostrich, a flightless bird, is capable of running at speeds of up to 45 mph/72 km/h over short distances.

FLIGHTLESS KIWI
The virtually wingless and tailless kiwi is incapable of flight.

DID YOU KNOW

GROUNDED

The ostrich was very likely outweighed by such extinct flightless birds as the emu-like *Dromornis stirtoni* of Australia, which stood perhaps 9 ft 9 in/3 m in height and weighed as much as 1,102 lb/500 kg. The "Elephant bird," *Aepyornis maximus*, of Madagascar, which became extinct in 1649, weighed an estimated 966 lb/438 kg. The New Zealand moa, *Dinornis maximus*, was taller than the *Aepyornis* but was less heavily-built.

TOP 10

LARGEST FLIGHTLESS BIRDS

	Bird	Weight			Height	
		kg	lb	oz	cm	in
1	Ostrich	156.5	345	0	274.3	108
2	Emu	40.0	88	3	152.4	60
3	Cassowary	33.5	73	14	152.4	60
4	Rhea	25.0	55	2	137.1	54
5	Emperor penguin	29.4	64	13	114.0	45
6	Flightless cormorant	4.5	9	15	95.0	37⅓
7	Flightless steamer	5.5	12	2	84.0	33
8	Kakapo	2.5	5	8	66.0	26
9	Kagu	5.0	11	0	59.9	23⅗
10	Kiwi	3.5	7	12	55.9	22

TOP 10

LARGEST FLIGHTED BIRDS

	Bird	Weight				Bird	Weight		
		kg	lb	oz			kg	lb	oz
1	Great bustard	20.9	46	1	**6**	Manchurian crane	14.9	32	14
2	Trumpeter swan	16.8	37	1	**7**	Kori bustard	13.6	30	0
3	Mute swan	16.3	35	15	**8**	Gray pelican	13.0	28	11
4=	Albatross	15.8	34	13	**9**	Black vulture	12.5	27	8
4=	Whooper swan	15.8	34	13	**10**	Griffon vulture	12.0	26	7

TOP 10

MOST COMMON BREEDING BIRDS IN THE US

1	Red-winged blackbird
2	House sparrow
3	Mourning dove
4	European starling
5	American robin
6	Horned lark
7	Common grackle
8	American crow
9	Western meadowlark
10	Brown-headed cowbird

This list, based on research carried out by the Breeding Bird Survey of the US Fish and Wildlife Service, ranks birds breeding in the US, with the red-winged blackbird (*Agelaius phoeniceus*) heading the list.

Wing size does not necessarily correspond to weight in flighted birds. The13-ft/4-m wingspan of the marabou stork beats all the birds listed here, yet its body weight is usually no heavier than any of these. When laden with a meal of carrion, however, the marabou doubles its weight and needs all the lift it can get to take off.

HOUSE SPARROW
This adaptable little bird is found worldwide, in urban as well as rural areas. Originally confined to Eurasia, it has been introduced to most other parts of the world.

T O P 1 0

FASTEST BIRDS IN THE WORLD

	Bird	Maximum recorded speed	
		km/h	mph
1	Spine-tailed swift	171	106
2	Frigate bird	153	95
3	Spur-winged goose	142	88
4	Red-breasted merganser	129	80
5	White-rumped swift	124	77
6	Canvasback duck	116	72
7	Eider duck	113	70
8	Teal	109	68
9=	Mallard	105	65
9=	Pintail	105	65

Until pilots cracked 190 mph/306 km/h in 1919, birds were the fastest creatures on the Earth: diving peregrine falcons clock up speeds approaching 185 mph/298 km/h. However, most comparisons of air speed of birds rule out diving or wind-assisted flight: most small birds on migration can manage a ground speed (speed relative to ground) of 60 mph/97 km/h to 70 mph/113 km/h. This list therefore picks out star performers among the medium- to large-sized birds that do not need help from wind or gravity to hit their top speed.

T O P 1 0

RAREST BIRDS IN THE WORLD

	Bird	Number*
1	Echo parakeet (Mauritius)	1
2	Mauritius parakeet	4
3	White-eyed river martin (Thailand)	5
4	Cuban ivory-billed woodpecker	8
5	Madagascar sea eagle	10
6	Pink pigeon (Mauritius)	11
7	Magpie robin (Seychelles)	12
8	Imperial Amazon parrot	15
9	Mauritius kestrel	16
10	Kakapo (New Zealand)	21

Of breeding pairs reported since 1986

T O P 1 0

BIRDS WITH THE LARGEST WINGSPANS

	Bird	Maximum wingspan	
		m	ft
1	Marabou stork	4.0	13
2	Albatross	3.7	12
3	Trumpeter swan	3.4	11
4=	Mute swan	3.1	10
4=	Whooper swan	3.1	10
4=	Gray pelican	3.1	10
4=	Californian condor	3.1	10
4=	Black vulture	3.1	10
9=	Great bustard	2.7	9
9=	Kori bustard	2.7	9

WINGED WONDER
The albatross is among the world's largest birds, with one of the most impressive wingspans.

T O P 1 0

LARGEST BIRDS OF PREY*

	Bird	Length	
		cm	in
1	Californian condor	124	49
2=	Steller's sea eagle	114	45
2=	Lammergeier	114	45
4	Bald eagle	109	43
5=	Andean condor	107	42
5=	European black vulture	107	42
5=	Ruppell's griffon	107	42
8	Griffon vulture	104	41
9	Wedge-tailed eagle	102	40
10	Lappet-faced vulture	100	39

Diurnal only – hence excluding owls

The entrants in this Top 10 all measure more than 39 in/1 m from beak to tail, but birds of prey generally have smaller body weights than those appearing in the list of 10 largest flighted birds. All these raptors, or aerial hunters, have remarkable eyesight and can spot their victims from great distances, but even if they kill animals heavier than themselves they are generally unable to take wing with them: stories of eagles carrying off lambs and small children are usually fictitious, although there are instances where this may have happened.

T O P 1 0

LONGEST AERIAL MIGRATIONS

	Bird	Maximum migration	
		km	miles
1	Arctic tern	20,117	12,500
2	Parasitic jaeger	16,093	10,000
3=	Baird's sandpiper	15,450	9,600
3=	Pectoral sandpiper	15,450	9,600
5=	Gray-headed albatross	14,967	9,300
5=	Hudsonian godwit	14,967	9,300
5=	Lesser yellowlegs	14,967	9,300
5=	Light-mantled sooty albatross	14,967	9,300
5=	Northern giant petrel	14,967	9,300
5=	Pomarine jaeger	14,967	9,300
5=	Red phalarope	14,967	9,300
5=	Royal albatross	14,967	9,300
5=	Ruddy turnstone	14,967	9,300
5=	Southern polar skua	14,967	9,300
5=	Surfbird	14,967	9,300
5=	Wandering tattler	14,967	9,300
5=	Whimbrel	14,967	9,300
5=	White-rumped sandpiper	14,967	9,300

CATS, DOGS, & OTHER PETS

TOP 10

TYPES OF PET IN THE US

	Pet	Estimated number
1	Cats	63,000,000
2	Dogs	54,200,000
3	Small animal pets*	12,200,000
4	Parakeets	11,000,000
5	Freshwater fish	9,400,000 #
6	Reptiles	7,300,000
7	Finches	5,700,000
8	Cockatiels	4,900,000
9	Canaries	2,000,000
10	Parrots	1,200,000

* Includes rabbits, ferrets, hamsters, guinea pigs, and gerbils.
\# Number of households owning, rather than individual specimens.

Source: Pet Industry Joint Advisory Council

TOP 10

CATS' NAMES IN THE US

1	Kitty	7	Missy
2	Smoky	8	Shadow
3	Tigger	9	Samantha
4	Tiger	10=	Baby
5	Max	10=	Callie
6	Patches	10=	Midnight

This Top 10 is based on a survey of the most popular name requests among 30,000 orders placed with Tags & Etc., a Sweet Home, Oregon Company.

TOP 10

TYPES OF PET IN THE UK

	Pet	Percentage of households
1	Dogs	26.9
2	Cats	21.5
3	Goldfish	9.1
4	Rabbits	4.5
5	Budgerigars	4.2
6	Tropical fish	2.9
7	Other caged bird(s)	2.8
8	Hamsters	2.3
9	Guinea pigs	1.5
10	Canaries	1.2

This Top 10 is based on the results of a national poll. If the miscellaneous category "Other caged bird(s)" is deleted, No. 10 becomes horse/pony/donkey (0.9 percent).

TOP 10

PEDIGREE CAT BREEDS IN THE UK

	Breed	No. registered 1994	1995
1	Persian Longhair	9,091	9,547
2	Siamese	4,728	4,939
3	British Shorthair	3,894	4,204
4	Burmese	3,590	3,571
5	Birman	1,982	2,173
6	Oriental Shorthair	1,186	1,336

	Breed	No. registered 1994	1995
7	Maine Coon	1,049	1,319
8	Exotic Shorthair	581	658
9	Tonkinese	370	559
10	Ragdoll	363	536

This list is based on a total of 32,646 cats registered with the Governing Council of the Cat Fancy in 1995 (1994: 30,013).

TOP 10

PEDIGREE CAT BREEDS IN THE US

	Breed	No. registered*
1	Persian	44,735
2	Maine Coon	4,332
3	Siamese	3,025
4	Abyssinian	2,469
5	Exotic Shorthair	1,610
6	Scottish Fold	1,327
7	Oriental Shorthair	1,191
8	American Shorthair	1,050
9	Birman	990
10	Burmese	896

Of the 39 different breeds of cats listed with the Cat Fancier's Association, these were the Top 10 registered in 1995 out of a total of 70,288. The biggest increase in popularity since the 1980s has been for the Exotic Shorthair, the rank of which has leaped from 14th in 1982. The Maine Coon has also consolidated its popularity. Many legends are attached to this breed – for instance, that it is so called because it resulted from cross-breeding a cat and a racoon, that it descends from the Angora cats that were owned by Marie Antoinette, and that these cats escaped to Maine during the French Revolution.

* To year ending December 31, 1995

TOP 10

CATS' NAMES IN THE UK

*(Based on an RSPCA survey
conducted during
National Pet Week, 1991)*

1	Sooty	**6**	Tom
2	Tigger	**7**	Fluffy
3	Tiger	**8**	Lucy
4	Smokey	**9**	Sam
5	Ginger	**10**	Lucky

TOP 10

DOGS' NAMES IN THE US

1	Max	**6=**	Buddy
2	Lady	**6=**	Ginger
3	Jake	**9=**	Casey
4=	Sam	**9=**	Sadie
4=	Molly	**9=**	Maggie
6=	Shadow	**9=**	Buster

TOP 10

GOLDFISH NAMES IN THE UK

*(Based on an RSPCA survey
conducted during
National Pet Week, 1991)*

1	Jaws	**6**	George
2	Goldie	**7**	Flipper
3	Fred	**8**	Ben
4	Tom	**9**	Jerry
5	Bubbles	**10**	Sam

TOP 10

DOGS' NAMES IN THE UK

Female		Male
Lucky	**1**	Ben
Tara	**2**	Lucky
Muffin	**3**	Sandy
Trixie	**4**	Patch
Lucy	**5**	Oscar
Bonnie	**6**	Teddy/Toby
Spot	**7**	Tramp
Lady	**8**	Beano
Pippa	**9**	Murphy
Suzie	**10**	Napoleon

As we have observed in previous editions of *The Top 10 of Everything*, a move away from traditional dogs' names occurred during the 1980s, with the demise of perennial (and specifically canine) names such as Shep, Brandy, Whisky, Rex, and Lassie, and an increasing tendency toward human first names. The latest research conducted by the British dog welfare organization, the National Canine Defence League, reveals the arrival of several new names, including Tara, Muffin, and Trixie for females, and Tramp, Beano, and Napoleon for males (for readers unfamiliar with British popular culture, *The Beano* is the title of a children's comic book that has been published since 1938). Though now out of fashion, Rover was once one of the top dog's names in both the US and the UK. It appears in a poem by 17th-century British poet Jonathan Swift and was popularized by the canine hero of the silent film, *Rescued by Rover* (1905).

TOP 10

DOG BREEDS IN THE US

	Breed	No. registered by American Kennel Club
1	Labrador Retriever	126,393
2	Rottweiler	102,596
3	German Shepherd (Alsatian)	78,999
4	Golden Retriever	64,322
5	Poodle	61,775
6	Cocker Spaniel	60,888
7	Beagle	59,215
8	Dachshund	46,129
9	Dalmatian	42,621
10	Pomeranian	39,947

TOP 10

DOG BREEDS IN THE UK

	Breed	No. registered by Kennel Club
1	Labrador Retriever	32,429
2	German Shepherd (Alsatian)	24,261
3	Golden Retriever	15,925
4	West Highland White Terrier	15,331
5	Cavalier King Charles Spaniel	14,449
6	Cocker Spaniel	14,437
7	English Springer Spaniel	12,768
8	Yorkshire Terrier	11,941
9	Boxer	9,406
10	Staffordshire Bull Terrier	7,053

42

PLANT LIFE

T O P 1 0

COUNTRIES WITH THE LARGEST AREAS OF FOREST

	Country	Forest area hectares	acres
1	Russia	778,500,000	1,923,712,000
2	Canada	494,000,000	1,220,699,000
3	Brazil	488,000,000	1,205,872,000
4	USA	286,200,000	707,215,000
5	Zaïre	173,800,000	429,468,000
6	Australia	145,000,000	358,302,000
7	China	130,496,000	322,462,000
8	Indonesia	111,774,000	276,199,000
9	Peru	84,800,000	209,545,000
10	India	68,500,000	169,267,000
	World total	*4,179,808,000*	*10,328,514,000*

THE HIGH AND MIGHTY REDWOOD
Originally there were 40 species of Redwood, but now there are only three – two in the US and one in China. Redwoods were widely harvested for their wood until their numbers dwindled. Today they are found mainly in protected areas.

T O P 1 0

TALLEST TREES IN THE UK*

(The tallest known example of each of the 10 tallest species)

	Tree	Location	m	ft
1	Douglas Fir	The Hermitage, Dunkeld, Tayside	64.5	212
2	Grand Fir	Strone House, Argyll, Strathclyde	63.0	207
3	Sitka Spruce	Private estate, Strathearn, Tayside	61.5	202
4=	Giant Sequoia	Castle Leod, Strathpeffer, Highland	53.0	174
4=	Low's Fir	Diana's Grove, Blair Castle, Strathclyde	53.0	174
6=	Noble Fir	Ardkinglas House, Argyll, Strathclyde	52.0	171
6=	Norway Spruce	Moniac Glenn, Highland	52.0	171
8	Western Hemlock	Benmore Younger Botanic Gardens, Argyll, Strathclyde	51.0	167
9	European Silver Fir	Armadale Castle, Skye, Highland	50.0	164
10	London Plane	Bryanstone School, Blandford, Dorset	48.0	157

* Based on data supplied by The Tree Register of the British Isles

T O P 1 0

TALLEST TREES IN THE US

(The tallest known example of each of the 10 tallest species)

	Tree	Location	m	ft
1	Coast Douglas Fir	Coos County, Oregon	100.3	329
2	Coast Redwood	Humboldt Redwoods State Park, California	95.4	313
3	General Sherman (Giant Sequoia)	Sequoia National Park, California	83.8	275
4	Noble Fir	Mount St. Helens National Monument, Washington	82.9	272
5	Grand Fir	Olympic National Park, Washington	76.5	251
6	Western Hemlock	Olympic National Park, Washington	73.5	241
7	Sugar Pine	Yosemite National Park, California	70.7	232
8	Ponderosa Pine	Plumas National Forest, California	68.0	223
9	Port-Orford Cedar	Siskiyou National Forest, Oregon	66.8	219
10	Pacific Silver Fir	Forks, Washington	66.1	217

A Coast Redwood known as the Dyerville Giant (from Dyerville, California), which stood 362 ft/110.3 m high, fell in a storm on March 27, 1991, and a slightly taller (363-ft/110.6-m) Coast Redwood, which formerly topped this list, fell during 1992. The "General Sherman" Giant Sequoia is thought to be the planet's most colossal living thing, weighing about 1,400 tons – as much as nine blue whales or 360 elephants.

TOP 10

MOST FORESTED COUNTRIES IN THE WORLD
(By percent forest cover)

	Country	Forest cover
1	Suriname	91
2	Solomon Islands	89
3	Papua New Guinea	83
4	French Guiana	81
5	Guyana	76
6=	Gabon	74
6=	North Korea	74
8	Finland	69
9	Japan	67
10	South Korea	65

TOP 10

WORLD VEGETABLE RECORDS
(As held by Bernard Lavery)

	Vegetable/ record year*	kg	lb	oz
1	Pumpkin (1989 – 3 days)	322.06	710	0
2	Cabbage (1989)	56.24	124	0
3	Vegetable marrow (1990)	49.04	108	2
4	Zucchini courgette (1990)	29.25	64	8
5	Kohl-rabi (1990)	28.18	62	2
6	Celery (1990)	20.89	46	1
7	Radish (1990)	12.73	28	1
8	Cucumber (1991)	9.10	20	1
9	Brussels sprout (1992)	8.25	18	3
10	Carrot (1996)	5.20	11	7½

* *Standing world record unless otherwise stated*

Bernard Lavery of Mid Glamorgan, UK, holds 19 world and 10 British records for his giant vegetables, and offers advice through books and a telephone hotline.

RAIN FOREST IN SOUTH AMERICA

TOP 10

FOOD CROPS IN THE WORLD

	Crop	Annual production (tons)
1	Sugar cane	1,075,893,000
2	Corn	569,557,000
3	Rice	534,701,000
4	Wheat	527,982,000
5	Potatoes	265,436,000
6	Sugar beets	259,335,000
7	Barley	160,810,000
8	Cassava	152,473,000
9	Soybeans	136,725,000
10	Sweet potatoes	124,339,000

DID YOU KNOW

YEW ARE OLD . . .

Sequoias and bristlecone pines found in the southwestern US are among the oldest trees in the world, some being as much as 6,000 or more years old. In the UK, yews are claimed by some authorities to have attained similar longevity, with one at Fortingall, Tayside, Scotland, said to be 6,000 years old. The oldest yew in Wales is a 5,000-year-old specimen in St. Digain's churchyard, Llangernyw, Clwyd. The reason that ancient yews are found in churchyards has been much debated, with explanations ranging from their being planted to provide wood for longbows, to isolate them from grazing cattle (because they are poisonous), to symbolize everlasting life, and, more mundanely, to provide shelter for pallbearers.

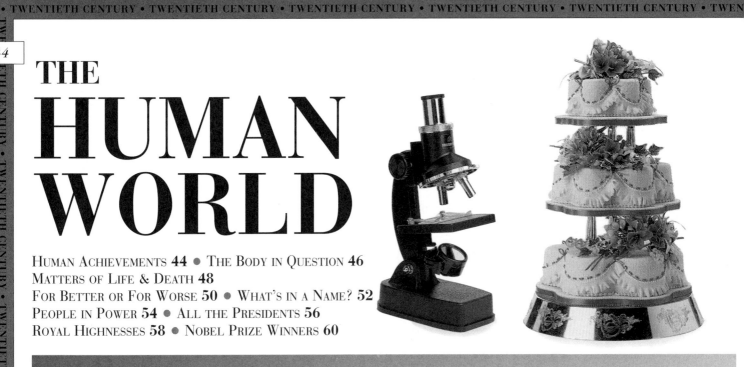

THE HUMAN WORLD

20TH CENTURY

As we approach the end of the 20th century, it is possible to begin to identify some of those whose contribution to world events and human progress has been most notable. These lists provide a flavor of this century's principal figures, as well as the technical achievements and daredevil enterprises that have taken place during its course.

CHARLES LINDBERGH – MAN OF THE YEAR
After his 1927 solo crossing of the Atlantic in his tiny Spirit of St. Louis, *25-year-old Charles Lindbergh became an international hero and was hailed as* Time *magazine's first "Man of the Year."*

THE 10 FIRST *TIME* MAGAZINE "MEN OF THE YEAR"

	Recipient	Year
1	Charles Lindbergh (1902–74), US aviator	1927
2	Walter P. Chrysler (1875–1940), US businessman	1928
3	Owen D. Young (1874–1962), US lawyer	1929
4	Mahatma Gandhi (1869–1948), Indian politician	1930
5	Pierre Laval (1883–1945), French President	1931
6	Franklin D. Roosevelt (1882–1945), US President	1932
7	Hugh S. Johnson (1882–1942), US soldier	1933
8	Franklin D. Roosevelt, US President	1934
9	Haile Salassie (1891–1975), Emperor of Ethiopia	1935
10	Wallis Simpson (1896–1986), Duchess of Windsor	1936

THE 10 LAST *TIME* MAGAZINE "MEN OF THE YEAR"

	Recipient	Year
1	Newt Gingrich (1943–), US politician	1995
2	Pope John Paul II (1920–)	1994
3	Yasser Arafat (1929–), F.W. de Klerk (1936–), Nelson Mandela (1918–), Yitzhak Rabin (1922–95), "Peacemakers"	1993
4	Bill Clinton (1946–), US President	1992
5	George Bush (1924–), US President	1991
6	Ted Turner (1938–), US businessman	1990
7	Mikhail Gorbachev (1931–), Soviet leader	1989
8	"Endangered Earth"	1988
9	Mikhail Gorbachev, Soviet leader	1987
10	Corazon Aquino (1933–), President of the Philippines	1986

The most newsworthy "Man of the Year" nominated annually by the editors of *Time* magazine may be one man, a group of men, a couple, a woman (as in Queen Elizabeth II in 1952), a group of women, a machine (in 1982 a computer), or even (as in 1988) "Endangered Earth."

HUMAN ACHIEVEMENTS

THE PROGRESSION OF SPEED OF THE X-15

X-15 Flt. No.	Pilot	Date	km/h	Speed mph	Mach
1	A. Scott Crossfield	June 8, 1959	840	522	0.79
2	A. Scott Crossfield	Sep 17, 1959	2,242	1,393	2.11
3	A. Scott Crossfield	Oct 17, 1959	2,284	1,419	2.15
6	A. Scott Crossfield	Feb 11, 1960	2,688	1,670	2.22
13	Joseph A. Walker	Apr 19, 1960	2,720	1,690	2.56
15	Joseph A. Walker	May 12, 1960	3,396	2,110	3.19
18	Joseph A. Walker	Aug 4, 1960	3,533	2,195	3.31
33	Robert M. White	Feb 7, 1961	3,661	2,275	3.50
34	Robert M. White	Mar 7, 1961	4,675	2,905	4.43
36	Robert M. White	Apr 21, 1961	4,949	3,075	4.62
37	Joseph A. Walker	May 25, 1961	5,322	3,307	4.95
38	Robert M. White	June 23, 1961	5,798	3,603	5.27
40	Joseph A. Walker	Sep 12, 1961	5,826	3,620	5.21
41	Forrest S. Petersen	Sep 28, 1961	5,794	3,600	5.30*
43	Robert M. White	Oct 11, 1961	5,864	3,644	5.21
44	Joseph A. Walker	Oct 17, 1961	6,276	3,900	5.74
45	Robert M. White	Nov 9, 1961	6,589	4,094	6.04
X-15A-2					
59	Joseph A. Walker	June 27, 1962	6,606	4,105	5.92
175	William J. Knight	Nov 18, 1966	6,857	4,261	6.33
188	William J. Knight	Oct 3, 1967	7,274	4,520	6.70

Slower actual speed, but higher Mach No.

Although achieved 30 or more years ago, the speeds attained by the rocket-powered X-15 and X-15A-2 aircraft are still the greatest ever attained by piloted vehicles within the Earth's atmosphere. They were air-launched by being released from B-52 bombers, and thus do not qualify for the official air speed record, for which aircraft must take off and land under their own power. These X-15 aircraft attained progressively greater speeds, and ultimately more than doubled that of the now long-standing conventional air speed record (2,193.17 mph/3,529.56 km/h by US pilots Eldon W. Joersz and George T. Morgan, Jr. in a Lockheed SR-71A over California on July 28, 1976), and set an unofficial altitude record (during Flight No. 91 on August 22, 1963, when Joseph A. Walker piloted an X-15 to 354,200 ft/ 107,960 m – some 67 miles/108 km high). The pioneering work of the pilots of the X-15 program laid the foundations of the US space program – indeed, prior to his spaceflights and moon landing, NASA astronaut Neil Armstrong had been an X-15 pilot.

THE 10

FIRST TO GO OVER NIAGARA FALLS
(AND SURVIVE)

	Name/date	Method
1	Annie Edison Taylor, October 24, 1901	Barrel
2	Bobby Leach, July 25, 1911	Steel barrel
3	Jean Lussier, July 4, 1928	Rubber ball fitted with oxygen cylinders
4	William Fitzgerald (aka Nathan Boya), July 15, 1961	Rubber ball
5	Karel Soucek, July 3, 1984	Barrel
6	Steven Trotter, August 18, 1985	Barrel
7	Dave Mundy, October 5, 1985	Barrel
8=	Peter deBernardi, September 28, 1989	Metal container
8=	Jeffrey Petkovich, September 28, 1989	Metal container
10	Dave Mundy, September 26, 1993	Diving bell

Source: Niagara Falls Museum

Captain Matthew Webb, the first person to swim the English Channel, was killed on July 24, 1883 attempting to swim the rapids beneath Niagara Falls, and many people have lost their lives attempting to go over the mighty falls. They include, in 1901, Maud Willard, who suffocated when her dog, whom she cajoled into performing the feat with her, retaliated by pressing its nose against the air vent, thus suffocating its owner. In the same year Annie Edison Taylor became the first to survive the drop, going over the Horseshoe Falls in a 4.5 x 3-ft/1.4 x 0.9-m barrel. Peter deBernardi and Jeffrey Petkovich traveled in the same container. Dave Mundy made a second trip in response to criticism that his original container, a 10-ft/3-m steel tube, was too sophisticated.

ROCKET POWER AND SUPER SPEED
An X-15 blasts off from beneath a B-52 bomber. Although unable to take off under their own power, the X-15 flights of the 1960s remain the fastest ever achieved.

THE BODY IN QUESTION

LONGEST BONES IN THE HUMAN BODY

	Bone	Average length cm	in
1	Femur (thighbone – upper leg)	50.50	19.88
2	Tibia (shinbone – inner lower leg)	43.03	16.94
3	Fibula (outer lower leg)	40.50	15.94
4	Humerus (upper arm)	36.46	14.35
5	Ulna (inner lower arm)	28.20	11.10
6	Radius (outer lower arm)	26.42	10.40
7	Seventh rib	24.00	9.45
8	Eighth rib	23.00	9.06
9	Innominate bone (hipbone – half pelvis)	18.50	7.28
10	Sternum (breastbone)	17.00	6.69

The above are average dimensions of the bones of an adult male measured from the extremities of each bone. (Ribs are curved, and the pelvis measurement is taken diagonally.) The same bones in an adult female are usually 6 to 13 percent smaller, with the exception of the sternum.

MOST COMMON COSMETIC SURGERY PROCEDURES

1 Body reshaping by liposuction/liposculpture
2 Nose reshaping (rhinoplasty)
3 Upper or lower eye bag removal (blepharoplasty)
4 Face lift
5 Breast augmentation
6 Breast reduction
7 Ear reshaping (otoplasty)
8 Laser treatment for the removal of lines and wrinkles
9 Laser treatment for snoring problems
10 Varicose veins/thread vein removal

Plastic surgery to rebuild damaged parts of the human body was performed in India in ancient times. It was developed to aid disfigured service personnel during World War I and in recent times has spawned cosmetic surgery techniques, whereby individuals elect to have various parts of their bodies reshaped in the interests of aesthetic appeal.

MOST COMMON ALLERGENS

(Substances that cause allergies)

Food allergen		Environmental allergen
Nuts	1	House dust mite (*Dermatophagoides pteronyssinus*)
Shellfish/seafood	2	Grass pollens
Milk	3	Tree pollens
Wheat	4	Cats
Eggs	5	Dogs
Fresh fruit (apples, oranges, strawberries, etc.)	6	Horses
Fresh vegetables (potatoes, cucumbers, etc.)	7	Molds (*Aspergillus fumigatus, Alternaria, Cladosporium*, etc.)
Cheese	8	Birch pollen
Yeast	9	Weed pollen
Soy protein	10	Wasp/bee venom

An allergy has been defined as "an unpleasant reaction to foreign matter, specific to that substance, which is altered from the normal response and peculiar to the individual concerned". Allergens, the substances that cause allergies, are usually foods but may also be environmental agents, such as pollen, which causes hay fever. Reactions can cause symptoms ranging from severe mental or physical disability to minor irritations such as a mild headache. "Elimination dieting" to pinpoint and avoid food allergens, and identifying and avoiding environmental, allergens, can result in the complete cures of many allergies.

ALLERGIC SUBSTANCES
An allergic reaction may be caused by a substance taken internally, such as a strawberry (left), or by something external, such as a dust mite (above). Symptoms vary from serious spasms to watery eyes and sneezing. The latter are often mistaken for the symptoms of a common cold.

TOP 10

LARGEST HUMAN ORGANS

	Organ		Average weight	
			g	oz
1	Liver		1,560	55.0
2	Brain	male	1,408	49.7
		female	1,263	44.6
3	Lungs	right	580	20.5
		left	510	18.0
		total	1,090	38.5
4	Heart	male	315	11.1
		female	265	9.3
5	Kidneys	left	150	5.3
		right	140	4.9
		total	290	10.2
6	Spleen		170	6.0
7	Pancreas		98	3.5
8	Thyroid		35	1.2
9	Prostate	male only	20	0.7
10	Adrenals	left	6	0.2
		right	6	0.2
		total	12	0.4

This list is based on average immediate postmortem weights from several hospitals over a 10-year period. If the skin were considered an organ, it would head the list by a long way because it can make up 16 percent of a body's weight (384 oz/ 10,886 g in a person weighing 150 lb/68 kg).

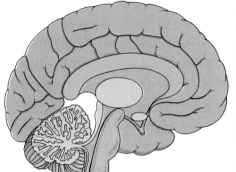

POWER OF THE BRAIN
The brain is the second-largest organ in the average person's body, but in some individuals it may actually be the biggest.

TOP 10

CAUSES OF STRESS-RELATED ILLNESSES

	Event	Value
1	Death of spouse	100
2	Divorce	73
3	Marital separation	65
4=	Detention in prison or other institution	63
4=	Death of close family member	63
6	Major personal injury or illness	53
7	Marriage	50
8	Losing one's job	47
9=	Marital reconciliation	45
9=	Retirement	45

Psychiatrists Dr. Thomas Holmes and Dr. Richard Rahe devised what they called the "Social Readjustment Rating Scale" to place a value on the likelihood of illness occurring as a result of stress caused by various "life events."

TOP 10

MOST COMMON PHOBIAS

	Object of phobia	Medical term
1	Spiders	Arachnephobia or arachnophobia
2	People and social situations	Anthropophobia or sociophobia
3	Flying	Aerophobia or aviatophobia
4	Open spaces	Agoraphobia, cenophobia, or kenophobia
5	Confined spaces	Claustrophobia, cleisiophobia, cleithrophobia, or clithrophobia
6	Vomiting	Emetophobia or emitophobia
7	Heights	Acrophobia, altophobia, hypsophobia, or hypsiphobia
8	Cancer	Carcinomaphobia, carcinophobia, carcinomatophobia, cancerphobia, or cancerophobia
9	Thunderstorms	Brontophobia or keraunophobia; related phobias are those associated with lightning (astraphobia), cyclones (anemophobia), and hurricanes and tornadoes (lilapsophobia)
10	Death	Necrophobia or thanatophobia

TOP 10

MOST COMMON ANIMAL PHOBIAS

	Animal	Medical term
1	Spiders	Arachnephobia or arachnophobia
2	Bees and wasps	Bees: Apiphobia, apiophobia, or melissophobia; wasps: spheksophobia
3	Reptiles	Batrachophobia
4	Snakes	Ophidiophobia, ophiophobia, ophiciophobia, herpetophobia
5	Mice	Musophobia or muriphobia
6	Dogs	Cynophobia or kynophobia
7	Birds	Ornithophobia
8	Frogs	Batrachophobia
9=	Ants	Myrmecophobia
9=	Horses	Hippophobia or equinophobia
9=	Rats	No medical term

Phobias directed at creatures that may bite, sting, or carry disease, such as rabid dogs and rats during the Plague, are understandable. Such fears are so widespread that they have been readily exploited in films including *Arachnophobia* (1990), *The Swarm* (1978), *Venom* (1982), and *The Birds* (1963).

MATTERS OF LIFE & DEATH

TOP 10

COUNTRIES WITH THE HIGHEST MALE LIFE EXPECTANCY

	Country	Life expectancy at birth (years)
1	Japan	76.1
2	Iceland	75.7
3	Costa Rica	75.6
4	Andorra	75.3
5=	Hong Kong	75.1
5=	Israel	75.1
7	Australia	75.0
8	Sweden	74.8
9=	Spain	74.6
9=	Greece	74.6
	US	*72.0*

The relatively high and generally increasing life expectancy for males in the Top 10 countries contrasts sharply with that in many underdeveloped countries, particularly most African countries, where it rarely exceeds 45 years. Sierra Leone is at the bottom of the league with an average life expectancy of 41.4 years.

TOP 10

COUNTRIES WITH THE HIGHEST FEMALE LIFE EXPECTANCY

	Country	Life expectancy at birth (years)
1	Japan	82.2
2	Andorra	81.3
3	France	81.1
4	Martinique	81.0
5=	Australia	80.9
5=	Iceland	80.9
5=	Switzerland	80.9
8	Hong Kong	80.7
9	Canada	80.6
10	Spain	80.5
	US	*78.9*

Female life expectancy in all the Top 10 countries – as well as for a further six – now exceeds 80 years. The comparative figure for such Third World countries as Sierra Leone, where the average life expectancy is 44.6 years for women, and other African countries, where it is less than 50 years makes for much less encouraging reading.

THE 10

COUNTRIES WITH THE MOST DEATHS CAUSED BY INFECTIOUS AND PARASITIC DISEASES

	Country	Death rate per 100,000*
1	Malawi	711.0
2	São Tomé and Príncipe	240.7
3	Guatemala	211.5
4	Philippines	179.8
5	Cape Verde	153.7
6	Marshall Islands	102.0
7	Nicaragua	100.0
8	Egypt	98.9
9	Peru	85.0
10	Tajikistan	81.2
	US	*27.5*

* In latest year for which figures are available

Although it is considered that infectious and parasitic diseases are the leading cause of mortality worldwide, those countries that have the highest rates of death are among the least efficient in reporting them.

THE 10

COUNTRIES WITH THE MOST DEATHS FROM HEART DISEASE

	Country	Death rate per 100,000
1	Czech Republic	314.4
2	Scotland	258.3
3	New Zealand	248.6
4	Finland	243.2
5	Hungary	240.0
6	Bulgaria	230.1
7	Denmark	211.1
8	England & Wales	210.0
9	Sweden	209.3
10	Australia	200.5
	US	*188.1*

TOP 10

COUNTRIES WITH THE LOWEST INFANT MORTALITY

	Country	Death rate per 1,000 live births
1	Japan	4.5
2	Hong Kong	4.7
3	Iceland	4.8
4	Singapore	5.0
5	Taiwan	5.2
6	Sweden	5.6
7	Gibraltar	5.7
8=	Finland	5.9
8=	Norway	5.9
10	Luxembourg	6.0
	US	*8.5*

THE 10

COUNTRIES WITH THE HIGHEST INFANT MORTALITY

	Country	Death rate per 1,000 live births
1	Central African Republic	219
2	Western Sahara	177
3	Afghanistan	161
4=	Guinea	147
4=	Mozambique	147
6	Malawi	142
7	Guinea-Bissau	140
8	Gambia	132
9	Angola	127
10	Liberia	126

THE 10

MOST COMMON CAUSES OF DEATH IN THE US

	Cause	Deaths
1	Diseases of the heart	739,580
2	Cancer and other neoplasms	530,870
3	Cerebrovascular diseases	149,740
4	Chronic obstructive pulmonary diseases and allied conditions	101,090
5	Accidents and adverse effects	88,630
6	Pneumonia and influenza	81,730
7	Diabetes	55,110
8	Human Immunodeficiency Virus infection	38,500
9	Suicide	31,230
10	Homicide and legal intervention	25,470

Source: National Center for Health Statistics
Figures are for 1993 based on a total number of 2,288,000 deaths estimated in the US for that year

THE 10

MOST COMMON CAUSES OF DEATH IN THE UK

	Cause	Deaths
1	Diseases of the circulatory system	295,202
2	Cancer and other neoplasms	161,770
3	Diseases of the respiratory system	102,035
4	Diseases of the digestive system	21,029
5	Injury and poisoning	19,809
6	Diseases of the nervous system and sense organs	10,188
7	Mental disorders	9,097
8	Endocrine, nutritional, and metabolic diseases, and immunity disorders	8,768
9	Diseases of the genito-urinary system	7,560
10	Infectious and parasitic diseases	3,801

Total annual deaths from all causes (including some that do not appear in this Top 10): **653,852**

The 10 principal causes of death remain the same and appear in approximately the same order from year to year, with only slight fluctuations in total numbers. Deaths resulting from injury and poisoning overtook diseases of the digestive system in 1990 after several years in 5th place, but subsequently reverted to their former position. Of deaths that resulted from accidents and violence, motor vehicle accidents accounted for most – 4,744 in total, 434 fewer than in 1991 – and represent the continuation of a downward trend.

THE 10

SHORTEST-LIVED PROFESSIONS

	Profession	SMR*
1	Deckhands, engine-room hands, bargemen, lightermen, boatmen	304
2	Hairdressers and barbers	263
3	General laborers	243
4	Foremen on ships and other vessels	236
5	Fishermen	234
6	Steel erectors, scaffolders, etc.	180
7	Foremen in product inspection and packaging	160
8	Chemical and petroleum processing-plant operators	154
9	Travel stewards and attendants, hospital and hotel porters	150
10	Foremen on production lines	149

* Standard Mortality Ratio

TOP 10

LONGEST-LIVED PROFESSIONS

	Profession	SMR*
1	Sales clerks	48
2=	Hairdressing supervisors	49
2=	Mechanical and aeronautical engineers	49
2=	Local government officers	49
5=	General administration, national government	52
5=	Maintenance workers	52
7	Teachers in higher education	54
8=	Forepersons	58
8=	Professionals in science, engineering, and other technologies	58
10	Laboratory and engineering technicians	59

* Standard Mortality Ratio

Standard Mortality Ratios are a commonly used method of comparing the risk of death in one group with that in another. If an SMR of 100 is the average, then one of 50 is low. Perhaps as a result of the small size of the sample, a somewhat bizarre differential arises between hairdressing supervisors (in the low-risk group) and hairdressers (in the high-risk group, above). As the list above indicates, workers on ships and those involved in the construction and chemical industries, with their exposure to hazardous conditions and materials, are as much as three times as likely to die prematurely.

FOR BETTER OR FOR WORSE

Marriage rates for most Western countries have been steadily declining: in the UK, despite population increases, there were 533,900 marriages in the country's peak year of 1940, but only 341,246 in 1993, more than one-third of which were remarriages. The UK's marriage rate is 5.9 per 1,000, but Sweden's is the lowest in Europe at just 3.9 per 1,000. In 1994 the 2,362,000 marriages that took place in the US represented a rate of 9.1 per 1,000. Conversely, the annual average rate for divorces has risen inexorably in most Western countries: the UK now has the highest divorce rate in the whole of Europe – at 3.1 per 1,000 it was almost twice the European average of 1.7. Divorce in the US hit an all-time high in 1992 with 1,215,000 divorces granted, and in 1994 it topped 1,191,000, a rate of 4.6 divorces per 1,000.

TOP 10
PROFESSIONS OF COMPUTER-DATING MEMBERS

MEN

	Profession	% of those registered
1	Accountants	9.7
2	Computer programmers	5.7
3	Teachers	4.6
4	Engineers	4.0
5	Company executives	3.8
6	Managers	2.6
7	Civil servants	2.2
8	Self-employed	2.0
9	Farmers	1.8
10	Students	1.6

WOMEN

	Profession	% of those registered
1	Teachers	10.4
2	Nurses	9.2
3	Women at home	8.3
4	Social workers	7.2
5	Secretaries	6.9
6	Civil servants	4.0
7	Receptionists	3.4
8	Sales staff	2.1
9	Clerks	1.1
10	Students	1.0

These Top 10s are based on figures supplied by Dateline, the UK's largest and oldest-established computer-dating agency, but evidence from other Western countries suggests the pattern is similar worldwide.

TOP 10
COUNTRIES WITH THE MOST MARRIAGES

	Country*	Marriages per annum
1	China	9,545,047
2	US	2,362,000
3	Russia	1,277,232
4	Indonesia	1,210,570
5	Bangladesh	1,130,000
6	Brazil	777,460
7	Japan	722,138
8	Mexico	667,598
9	Ukraine	489,330
10	Turkey	459,624

* *Excludes India, Nigeria, and Pakistan*

TOP 10
MONTHS FOR MARRIAGES IN ENGLAND AND WALES

	Month	Marriages
1	July	41,855
2	August	40,151
3	September	39,547
4	June	33,125
5	May	32,769
6	October	25,248
7	April	22,327
8	March	15,411
9	December	14,210
10	November	13,459

The figures are for 1993, when there were a total of 299,197 marriages in England and Wales – a drop of 13 percent on the 1983 figure of 344,334, and a fall of four percent on the previous year's 311,564. The popularity order of the months remains similar each year – although, with Saturday being the favored day for weddings, the number of Saturdays in a month can boost that month's apparent popularity.

TOP 10
MONTHS FOR MARRIAGES IN THE US

	Month	Marriages (1994)
1=	August	262,000
1=	June	262,000
3=	May	232,000
3=	October	232,000
5	September	224,000
6	July	222,000
7	April	175,000
8	December	173,000
9	November	171,000
10	February	156,000

THE 10
FIRST WEDDING ANNIVERSARY GIFTS

1 Cotton
2 Paper
3 Leather
4 Fruit and flowers
5 Wood
6 Sugar (or iron)
7 Wool or copper
8 Bronze (or electrical appliances)
9 Pottery (or willow)
10 Tin (or aluminum)

The custom of celebrating different wedding anniversaries by presenting specific types of gift has a long tradition. In the UK and US most of the earlier themes are generally disregarded in favor of the "milestone" anniversaries: the 25th (silver), 40th (ruby), 50th (gold), and 60th (diamond). Correctly, the 75th anniversary is the "diamond," but since Queen Victoria's so-called "Diamond Jubilee" was celebrated on the 60th anniversary of her succession to the throne it has usually been commemorated as the 60th.

TOP 10
US STATES WITH THE MOST MARRIAGES

	State	Marriages (1994)
1	California	202,827
2	Texas	190,272
3	New York	149,615
4	Florida	144,548
5	Nevada	140,325
6	Ohio	92,797
7	Illinois	92,719
8	Tennessee	80,030
9	Pennsylvania	75,512
10	Michigan	71,222

Source: National Center for Health Statistics

THE 10
MOST COMMON CAUSES OF MARITAL DISCORD AND BREAKDOWN

1 Lack of communication
2 Continual arguments
3 Infidelity
4 Sexual problems
5 Physical or verbal abuse
6 Financial problems, recession, and fears of losing job
7 Work (usually one partner devoting excessive time to work)
8 Children (whether to have them; attitudes towards their upbringing)
9 Addiction (to drinking, gambling, spending, etc.)
10 Step-parenting

This list is based on information supplied by Relate National Marriage Guidance, which counsels people with marriage problems. In recent years, Relate reports that money is an increasingly prominent feature among the difficulties faced by many married couples.

THE 10
US STATES WITH THE MOST DIVORCES

	State*	Divorces (1994)
1	Texas	99,073
2	Florida	82,963
3	New York	59,195
4	Ohio	49,968
5	Illinois	43,398
6	Pennsylvania	40,040
7	Michigan	38,727
8	Georgia	37,001
9	North Carolina	36,292
10	Tennessee	34,167

Source: National Center for Health Statistics

* Figures are not available for California, Indiana, and Louisiana

TOP 10
COUNTRIES WITH THE HIGHEST MARRIAGE RATE

	Country	Marriages per 1,000 p.a.*
1	Cuba	17.7
2	Bermuda	15.0
3	Benin	12.8
4	Bangladesh	11.3
5	Guam	10.6
6	Mauritius	10.4
7	Azerbaijan	10.1
8=	Kazakhstan	10.0
8=	Uzbekistan	10.0
10	Turkmenistan	9.8

* *During latest period for which figures are available*

THE 10
COUNTRIES WITH THE HIGHEST DIVORCE RATE

	Country	Divorces per 1,000 p.a.
1	Maldives	7.9
2	US	4.6
3	Cuba	4.2
4	Lithuania	4.1
5=	Russia	4.0
5=	Latvia	4.0
7	Ukraine	3.9
8	Puerto Rico	3.8
9	Estonia	3.7
10	Belarus	3.4

WHAT'S IN A NAME?

TOP 10

GIRLS' AND BOYS' NAMES IN THE US

Girls		Boys
Brittany	1	Michael
Ashley	2	Christopher
Jessica	3	Matthew
Amanda	4	Joshua
Sarah	5	Andrew
Megan	6	James
Caitlin	7	John
Samantha	8	Nicholas
Stephanie	9	Justin
Katherine	10	David

American name fashions are highly volatile and vary considerably according to a child's ethnic background and the influences of popular culture. Jennifer, for example, once rose to the No. 2 position because the heroine of the book and 1970 movie, *Love Story*, had this name, and Tiffany entered the Top 10 in 1980 in the wake of the TV series, *Charlie's Angels*, and its character Tiffany Welles. Ashley rose to prominence only in the 1980s: by 1984 it was already being noted as the girl's name of the year, (just as Angela had been 10 years earlier), and by 1990 it had reached the No. 1 position. This pattern has been mirrored in the 1990s with Brittany, a name that does not even make an appearance among the Top 100 of British girls' names; only Jessica appears in the Top 10s of both countries. In contrast, three of the Top 10 US boys' names (Matthew, Joshua, and James) also appear in the British Top 10. Michael has topped every US list for 30 years, while Joshua appeared in the Top 10 for the first time in 1983. Richard plummeted from the ranking after Richard Nixon's disgrace in the Watergate scandal, and it has never regained its former popularity.

TOP 10

GIRLS' AND BOYS' NAMES IN THE US 50 YEARS AGO

Girls		Boys
Mary	1	Robert
Patricia	2	James
Barbara	3	John
Judith	4	William
Carol/Carole	5	Richard
Sharon	6	Thomas
Nancy	7	David
Joan	8	Ronald
Sandra	9	Donald
Margaret	10	Michael

TOP 10

GIRLS' AND BOYS' NAMES IN THE UK

Girls		Boys
Jessica	1	Jack
Lauren	2	Daniel
Rebecca	3	Thomas
Sophie	4	James
Charlotte	5	Joshua
Hannah	6	Matthew
Amy	7	Ryan
Emily	8	Luke
Chloe	9	Samuel
Emma	10	Jordan

TOP 10

GIRLS' AND BOYS' NAMES 50 YEARS AGO IN THE UK

Girls		Boys
Margaret	1	John
Patricia	2	David
Christine	3	Michael
Mary	4	Peter
Jean	5	Robert
Ann	6	Anthony
Susan	7	Brian
Janet	8	Alan
Maureen	9	William
Barbara	10	James

TOP 10

GIRLS' AND BOYS' NAMES IN AUSTRALIA

Girls		Boys
Jessica	1	Matthew
Sarah	2	James
Emily	3	Thomas
Rebecca	4	Joshua
Emma	5	Benjamin
Hannah	6	Daniel
Stephanie	7	Samuel
Amy	8	Nicholas
Caitlin	9	Alexander
Lauren	10	Michael

TOP 10

MOST COMMON NAMES OF MOVIE CHARACTERS

	Name	Characters		Name	Characters
1	Jack	126	7=	Michael	59
2	John	104	7=	Tom	59
3	Frank	87	9	Mary	54
4	Harry	72	10	Paul	53
5	David	63			
6	George	62			

Based on Simon Rose's One FM Essential Film Guide *(1993) survey of feature films that were released in the period 1983–93*

TOP 10

MOST COMMON SURNAMES IN THE US

	Surname	Number
1	Smith	2,382,509
2	Johnson	1,807,263
3	Williams/Williamson	1,568,939
4	Brown	1,362,910
5	Jones	1,331,205
6	Miller	1,131,205
7	Davis	1,047,848
8	Martin/Martinez/ Martinson	1,046,297
9	Anderson/Andersen	825,648
10	Wilson	787,825

The United States Social Security Administration published its survey of the most common surnames over 20 years ago, based on the number of people for whom it had more than 10,000 files, which covered a total of 3,169 names. The SSA has not repeated the exercise, but it is probable that the ranking order has remained very similar.

TOP 10

MOST COMMON SURNAMES IN THE UK

1	Smith	6	Davies/Davis
2	Jones	7	Evans
3	Williams	8	Thomas
4	Brown	9	Roberts
5	Taylor	10	Johnson

The UK list of top 10 surnames has a number of entries in common with its US counterpart, reflecting the British ancestry of a high proportion of American citizens. Smith heads the list in both countries: it is reckoned that there are at least 800,000 in England and Wales alone – which means that one person in every 61 is called Smith.

TOP 10

MOST COMMON INITIAL LETTERS OF SURNAMES IN THE US

	Surname	Percentage
1	S	9.8
2	B	7.0
3	M	6.5
4	K	6.4
5	D	5.9
6=	C	5.5
6=	P	5.5
8	G	5.2
9	L	5.0
10	A	4.8

TOP 10

MOST COMMON PATRONYMS IN THE US

1	Johnson ("son of John")
2	Williams/Williamson ("son of William")
3	Jones ("son of John")
4	Davis ("son of Davie/David")
5	Martin/Martinez/Martinson ("son of Martin")
6	Anderson/Andersen ("son of Andrew")
7	Wilson ("son of Will")
8	Harris/Harrison ("son of Harry")
9	Thomas ("son of Thomas")
10	Thomson/Thompson ("son of Thomas")

TOP 10

MOST COMMON SURNAMES IN THE TELEPHONE DIRECTORY IN LONDON, UK

1	Smith	6	Harris/Harrison
2	Brown/Browne	7	Taylor
3	Jones	8	Roberts/ Robertson
4	Williams/ Williamson	9	Patel
5	Clark/Clarke	10	James

TOP 10

MOST COMMON DESCRIPTIVE SURNAMES IN THE US

1	Brown (brown-haired)
2	White (light-skinned, or white-haired)
3	Young (youthful, or a younger brother)
4	Gray (gray-haired)
5	Long (tall)
6	Russell (red-haired)
7	Black/Blake (black-haired, or dark-skinned)
8	Little (small)
9	Reid (red-haired)
10	Curtis (courteous, or well-educated)

As many as one in 10 of all US surnames may be derived from a physical description that was once applied to an ancestor. The list is headed by the Browns, whose role as laborers and pioneers was recognized by the 19th-century British author Thomas Hughes in his novel *Tom Brown's Schooldays* (1857), writing: "For centuries, in their quiet, dogged, homespun way, they have been subduing the earth in most English counties, and leaving their mark in American forests and Australian uplands."

TOP 10

MOST COMMON SURNAMES DERIVED FROM OCCUPATIONS IN THE US

1	Smith
2	Miller
3	Taylor
4	Clark (cleric)
5	Walker (cloth worker)
6	Wright (workman)
7	Baker
8	Carter (driver or maker of carts)
9	Stewart (steward)
10	Turner (woodworker)

PEOPLE IN POWER

54

VOTES FOR WOMEN

Although certain states of the US gave women the vote at early dates (Wyoming in 1869, Colorado in 1894, Utah in 1895, and Idaho in 1896), it was not granted nationally until 1920. The Isle of Man, though not a sovereign state, first granted women the vote in 1880. In 1893 New Zealand became the first country to enfranchise women, followed by South Australia in 1894, Western Australia in 1898, and Australia as a whole in 1902. As the women's suffrage movement gathered momentum in the early years of the 20th century, most European countries followed suit, with Great Britain and Ireland in 1918. A number of countries, such as France and Italy, did not permit women to vote until 1945. Switzerland did not allow women to vote in elections to the Federal Council until 1971, and Liechtenstein was one of the last to relent, in 1984.

TOP 10

LONGEST SERVING PRESIDENTS IN THE WORLD

	President	Country	Took office
1	Marshal Mobutu Sésé Séko	Zaïre	November 24, 1965
2	General Suharto	Indonesia	March 28, 1967
3	General Gnassingbé Eyadéma	Togo	April 14, 1967
4	El Hadj Omar Bongo	Gabon	December 2, 1967
5	Colonel Muammar Gadhafi	Libya	September 1, 1969
6	Lt. General Hafiz al-Asad	Syria	February 22, 1971
7	Fidel Castro	Cuba	December 2, 1976
8	France Albert René	Seychelles	June 5, 1977
9	Hassan Gouled Aptidon	Djibouti	September 30, 1977
10	Daniel Teroitich arap Moi	Kenya	October 14, 1978

Félix Houphouët-Boigny, President of the Côte d'Ivoire, died on December 7, 1993 after serving as leader of his country since November 27, 1960. Having been born on October 18, 1905, he was, at 88, the oldest president in the world. President Kim Il-song of North Korea was president from December 28, 1972 until his death on July 8, 1994. Alhaji Sir Dawda Kairaba Jawara, President of The Gambia from April 24, 1970, was ousted by a military coup on July 23, 1994.

FIDEL CASTRO
Revolutionary leader Fidel Castro became prime minister of Cuba in 1959 and has been president since 1976.

TOP 10

US PRESIDENTS WITH THE MOST ELECTORAL VOTES

	President	Year	Votes
1	Ronald Reagan	1984	525
2	Franklin D. Roosevelt	1936	523
3	Richard Nixon	1972	520
4	Ronald Reagan	1980	489
5	Lyndon B. Johnson	1964	486
6	Franklin D. Roosevelt	1932	472
7	Dwight Eisenhower	1956	457
8	Franklin D. Roosevelt	1940	449
9	Herbert Hoover	1928	444
10	Dwight Eisenhower	1952	442

TOP 10

MOST COMMON ZODIAC SIGNS OF US PRESIDENTS

	Zodiac sign	No. presidents
1	Aquarius (Jan 21–Feb 19)	6
2	Scorpio (Oct 24–Nov 22)	5
3=	Taurus (Apr 21–May 21)	4
3=	Cancer (Jun 23–Jul 23)	4
3=	Virgo (Aug 24–Sep 23)	4
3=	Capricorn (Dec 22–Jan 20)	4
7=	Pisces (Feb 20–Mar 20)	3
7=	Leo (Jul 24–Aug 23)	3
7=	Sagittarius (Nov 23–Dec 21)	3
10=	Aries (Mar 21–Apr 20)	2
10=	Libra (Sep 24–Oct 23)	2

Among the 42 US presidents, the only sign that fails to make this Top 10 is Gemini (May 22–June 22): its sole representative is George Bush. Few conclusions can be drawn from their respective political affiliations, other than that presidents born under Libra or Leo tend to be Republicans (with the exception of Jimmy Carter and Bill Clinton).

THE 10

FIRST FEMALE PRIME MINISTERS AND PRESIDENTS

	Name/office	Country	Period in office
1	Sirimavo Bandaranaike (PM)	Ceylon (Sri Lanka)	1960–64/1970–77
2	Indira Gandhi (PM)	India	1966–84
3	Golda Meir (PM)	Israel	1969–74
4	Maria Estela Perón (President)	Argentina	1974–75
5	Elisabeth Domitien (PM)	Central African Republic	1975
6	Margaret Thatcher (PM)	UK	1979–90
7	Dr. Maria Lurdes Pintasilgo (PM)	Portugal	1979
8	Vigdís Finnbogadóttir (President)	Iceland	1980–
9	Mary Eugenia Charles (PM)	Dominica	1980–95
10	Gro Harlem Brundtland (PM)	Norway	1981/1986–89

Mrs. Bandaranaike of Ceylon (Sri Lanka) became the world's first female prime minister on July 21, 1960. Mrs. Thatcher became Britain's first on May 4, 1979. The first 10 have been followed by Corazón Aquino, President of the Philippines (1986–92); Benazir Bhutto, Prime Minister of Pakistan (1988–90; 1993–); Violeta Barrios de Chamorro, President of Nicaragua (1990–); Ertha Pascal-Trouillot, President of Haiti (1990–95); and Mary Robinson, President of the Irish Republic (1990–). Since 1990 several other countries appointed female prime ministers who remained in office for only a brief period. They included France (Edith Cresson), Canada (Kim Campbell), Burundi (Sylvie Kinigi), and, for a relatively more sustained spell, Turkey (Tansu Çiller).

TOP 10

OLDEST SERVING BRITISH PRIME MINISTERS

	Name/party*	Born	Last year in office	Age at retirement
1	William E. Gladstone (Lib)	1809	1894	84
2=	Viscount Palmerston (Lib)	1784#	1865	80
2=	Winston S. Churchill (Con)	1874	1955	80
2=	Earl of Wilmington (W)	1663/64#	1743	79–80
5	Benjamin Disraeli (Con)	1804	1880	75
6	Earl Russell (Lib)	1792	1866	73
7	Marquess of Salisbury (Con)	1830	1902	72
8=	Duke of Portland (Co)	1738	1809	71
8=	Sir H. Campbell-Bannerman (Lib)	1836	1908	71
8=	Neville Chamberlain (Co)	1869	1940	71

*   Co = Coalition; Con = Conservative; Lib = Liberal; W = Whig
#   Exact birthdate unknown

Gladstone was 84 years and 64 days old when he left office. Viscount Palmerston has the distinction of being the oldest prime minister to take office for the first time, at the age of 70 in 1855. A matter of months separates the last three prime ministers in the Top 10.

THE 10

CATEGORIES OF PEOPLE WHO MAY NOT STAND FOR PARLIAMENT IN THE UK

1	Peers (unless they have renounced their peerages)
2	Priests and ministers of the Church of England
3	Priests and ministers of the Church of Scotland
4	Priests and ministers of the Roman Catholic Church
5	People who hold public offices (judges, civil servants, members of the armed forces, police)
6	People under 21 years of age
7	Non-British subjects
8	People with severe mental disorders
9	Bankrupts
10	People convicted of certain crimes

TOP 10

MOST COMMON ZODIAC SIGNS OF BRITISH PRIME MINISTERS

Zodiac sign	No. PMs
1= Pisces (Feb 20–Mar 20)	5
1= Aries (Mar 21–Apr 20)	5
1= Taurus (Apr 21–May 21)	5
1= Gemini (May 22–Jun 22)	5
1= Virgo (Aug 24–Sep 23)	5
6= Aquarius (Jan 21–Feb 19)	4
6= Libra (Sep 24–Oct 23)	4
6= Scorpio (Oct 24–Nov 22)	4
9= Cancer (Jun 23–Jul 23)	3
9= Leo (Jul 24–Aug 23)	3
9= Capricorn (Dec 22–Jan 20)	3

The birth pattern of British Prime Ministers shows a remarkably even spread across the 12 signs of the zodiac, and their representatives are similarly randomly distributed across the various political parties: Conservative leader John Major and former Labour leader James Callaghan, for example, were both born under Aries.

ALL THE PRESIDENTS

THE 10

FIRST PRESIDENTS OF THE US

President (dates)	Period of office
1 George Washington (1732–99)	1789–97
2 John Adams (1735–1826)	1797–1801
3 Thomas Jefferson (1743–1826)	1801–09
4 James Madison (1751–1836)	1809–17
5 James Monroe (1758–1831)	1817–25
6 John Quincy Adams (1767–1848)	1825–29
7 Andrew Jackson (1767–1845)	1829–37
8 Martin Van Buren (1782–1862)	1837–41
9 William H. Harrison (1773–1841)	1841
10 John Tyler (1790–1862)	1841–45

TOP 10

TALLEST US PRESIDENTS

President	Height m	ft in
1 Abraham Lincoln	1.93	6 4
2 Lyndon B. Johnson	1.91	6 3
3= Bill Clinton	1.89	6 2½
3= Thomas Jefferson	1.89	6 2½
5= Chester A. Arthur	1.88	6 2
5= George Bush	1.88	6 2
5= Franklin D. Roosevelt	1.88	6 2
5= George Washington	1.88	6 2
9= Andrew Jackson	1.85	6 1
9= Ronald Reagan	1.85	6 1

LONG AND LANKY PRESIDENT
It has been suggested that Abraham Lincoln, the tallest US President, suffered from an hereditary anomaly known as Marfan syndrome. Those affected tend to be lanky, have hands with extremely long fingers, and have large feet.

TOP 10

LONGEST-SERVING US PRESIDENTS

President	Years	Days
1 Franklin D. Roosevelt	12	39
2= Grover Cleveland	8*	
2= Dwight D. Eisenhower	8*	
2= Ulysses S. Grant	8*	
2= Andrew Jackson	8*	
2= Thomas Jefferson	8*	
2= James Madison	8*	
2= James Monroe	8*	
2= Ronald Reagan	8*	
2= Woodrow Wilson	8*	

* Two four-year terms – now the maximum any US President may remain in office

TOP 10

SHORTEST-SERVING US PRESIDENTS

President	Years	Days
1 William H. Harrison*		32
2 James A. Garfield		199
3 Zachary Taylor	1	128
4 Gerald R. Ford	2	150
5 Warren G. Harding	2	151
6 Millard Fillmore	2	236
7 John F. Kennedy	2	306
8 Chester A. Arthur	3	166
9 Andrew Johnson	3	323
10 John Tyler	3	332

* William H. Harrison died of pneumonia on April 4, 1841 and was the first US President to die in office

TOP 10

SHORTEST US PRESIDENTS

President	Height m	ft in
1 James Madison	1.63	5 4
2= Benjamin Harrison	1.68	5 6
2= Martin Van Buren	1.68	5 6
4= John Adams	1.70	5 7
4= John Quincy Adams	1.70	5 7
4= William McKinley	1.70	5 7
7= William H. Harrison	1.73	5 8
7= James K. Polk	1.73	5 8
7= Zachary Taylor	1.73	5 8
10= Ulysses S. Grant	1.74	5 8½
10= Rutherford B. Hayes	1.74	5 8½

PRESIDENT OF THE US, BILL CLINTON
Bill Clinton, the 42nd US President, features in lists of the youngest and the most popular US Presidents – as well as the tallest.

TOP 10

US PRESIDENTS WITH THE GREATEST NUMBER OF POPULAR VOTES

	President	Year	Votes
1	Ronald Reagan	1984	54,455,075
2	George Bush	1988	48,886,097
3	Richard Nixon	1972	47,169,911
4	Bill Clinton	1992	44,909,889
5	Ronald Reagan	1980	43,899,248
6	Lyndon B. Johnson	1964	43,129,484
7	Jimmy Carter	1976	40,830,763
8	Dwight D. Eisenhower	1956	35,590,472
9	John F. Kennedy	1960	34,226,731
10	Dwight D. Eisenhower	1952	33,936,234

TOP 10

YOUNGEST US PRESIDENTS

	President	Age on taking office Years	Days
1	Theodore Roosevelt	42	322
2	John F. Kennedy	43	236
3	Bill Clinton	46	154
4	Ulysses S. Grant	46	236
5	Grover Cleveland	47	351
6	Franklin Pierce	48	101
7	James A. Garfield	49	105
8	James K. Polk	49	122
9	Millard Fillmore	50	184
10	John Tyler	51	8

TOP 10

OLDEST US PRESIDENTS

	President	Age on taking office Years	Days
1	Ronald Reagan	69	349
2	William H. Harrison	68	23
3	James Buchanan	65	315
4	George Bush	64	223
5	Zachary Taylor	64	100
6	Dwight D. Eisenhower	62	98
7	Andrew Jackson	61	354
8	John Adams	61	125
9	Gerald R. Ford	61	26
10	Harry S Truman	60	339

THE 10

LAST US PRESIDENTS AND VICE PRESIDENTS TO DIE IN OFFICE

	Name/date of death	Office
1	John F. Kennedy* November 22, 1963	P
2	Franklin D. Roosevelt April 12, 1945	P
3	Warren G. Harding August 2, 1923	P
4	James S. Sherman October 30, 1912	VP
5	William McKinley* September 14, 1901	P
6	Garret A. Hobart November 21, 1899	VP
7	Thomas A. Hendricks November 25, 1885	VP
8	James A. Garfield* September 19, 1881	P
9	Henry Wilson November 10, 1875	VP
10	Abraham Lincoln* April 15, 1865	P

* *Assassinated*

DID YOU KNOW

THE FIRST PRESIDENT TO TAKE A BATH?

On December 28, 1917, in an article in the *New York Evening Mail*, American satirist Henry Louis Mencken (1880–1956) announced that it was exactly 75 years since the installation of the first plumbed bath in the US. The bath, Mencken wrote, was the brainchild of a wealthy Cincinnati cotton broker. Mencken packed his story with convincing facts: that various authorities had attempted to ban baths altogether, and that it was not until President Millard Fillmore had installed one in the White House that they had become acceptable. A few years later, Mencken confessed that the article was a total fabrication.

ROYAL HIGHNESSES

ROMAN RULER
Augustus was the first Caesar to rule under the title of "Emperor."

FIRST ROMAN EMPERORS

	Caesar	Born	Year of accession	Died	Fate
1	Julius Caesar	Jul 12, 100 BC	48 BC	Mar 15, 44 BC	Assassinated
2	Augustus	Sep 23, 63 BC	27 BC	Aug 19, AD 14	Died
3	Tiberius	Nov 16, 42 BC	AD 14	Mar 16, AD 37	Died
4	Caligula	Aug 31, AD 12	AD 37	Jan 24, AD 41	Assassinated
5	Claudius	Aug 1, AD 10	AD 41	Oct 13, AD 54	Assassinated
6	Nero	Dec 15, AD 37	AD 54	Jun 9, AD 68	Suicide
7	Galba	Dec 24, AD 3	AD 68	Jan 15, AD 69	Assassinated
8	Otho	Apr 28, AD 32	AD 69	Apr 16, AD 69	Suicide
9	Vitellius	Sep 24, AD 15	AD 69	Dec 22, AD 69	Assassinated
10	Vespasian	Nov 18, AD 9	AD 69	Jun 23, AD 79	Died

Although regarded as one of the "Twelve Caesars," the first, Julius Caesar, did not rule under this title. If he is excluded, Titus (born December 30, AD 40; ruled from AD 79; died September 13, AD 81) becomes the new No. 10.

LONGEST-REIGNING BRITISH MONARCHS

	Monarch	Reign	Age at accession	Age at death	Years reigned
1	Victoria	1837–1901	18	81	63
2	George III	1760–1820	22	81	59
3	Henry III	1216–72	9	64	56
4	Edward III	1327–77	14	64	50
5	Elizabeth II	1952–	25	–	44
6	Elizabeth I	1558–1603	25	69	44
7	Henry VI	1422–61 (deposed, d. 1471)	8 months	49	38
8	Henry VIII	1509–47	17	55	37
9	Charles II	1660–85	19	54	36
10	Henry I	1100–35	31–32*	66–67*	35

* *Henry I's birthdate is unknown, so his ages at accession and death are uncertain*

This list excludes the reigns of monarchs before 1066, so omits such rulers as Ethelred II who reigned for 37 years. Queen Elizabeth II overtook Henry VI's reign in August 1990, and that of Elizabeth I in June 1996. If she is still on the throne on September 11, 2015, she will have beaten Queen Victoria's record by one day.

LONGEST-REIGNING MONARCHS IN THE WORLD

	Monarch	Country	Reign	Age at accession	Years reigned
1	Louis XIV	France	1643–1715	5	72
2	John II	Liechtenstein	1858–1929	18	71
3	Franz-Josef	Austria–Hungary	1848–1916	18	67
4	Victoria	UK	1837–1901	18	63
5	Hirohito	Japan	1926–89	25	62
6	George III	UK	1760–1820	22	59
7	Louis XV	France	1715–74	5	59
8	Pedro II	Brazil	1831–89	6	58
9	Wilhelmina	Netherlands	1890–1948	10	58
10	Henry III	England	1216–72	9	56

Some authorities have claimed a 73-year reign for Alfonso I of Portugal, but his father, Henry of Burgundy, who conquered Portugal, ruled as Count, and it was this title that Alfonso inherited at the age of two on April 30, 1112. His mother, Theresa of Castile, ruled until he took power in 1128, but he did not assume the title of king until July 25, 1139, during the Battle of Ourique, at which he vanquished the Moors. Therefore, he ruled as king for 46 years until his death on December 6, 1185. More extravagant claims are made for long-reigning monarchs in the ancient world. One example is the alleged 94-year reign of Phiops II, a 6th Dynasty Egyptian pharaoh, but since his dates are uncertain, he has not been included in this Top 10.

T O P 1 0

CURRENT MONARCHIES* WITH MOST RULERS

	Monarchy	Line commenced	No. rulers#
1	Japan	40 BC	125
2	England	802	64
3	Sweden	980	59
4	Denmark	940	55
5	Norway	858	42
6	Monaco	1458	20
7	Spain	1516	18
8=	Netherlands	1572	14
8=	Liechtenstein	1699	14
10	Thailand	1782	9

* Including principalities
\# Monarchs deposed and later restored counted once only

Among the dwindling ranks of monarchies, these are the longest-established, at least according to the number of successive incumbents. There are many other countries that had innumerable monarchs, but which no longer have hereditary rulers, among them Ceylon, China, Egypt, France, Hungary, Portugal, Russia, and Turkey.

T O P 1 0

LONGEST-REIGNING QUEENS* IN THE WORLD

QUEEN VICTORIA
After the deaths of her uncles, George IV and William IV, Princess Alexandrina Victoria became Queen of Great Britain and Ireland, and later Empress of India.

	Queen	Country	Reign	Years reigned
1	Victoria	UK	1837–1901	63
2	Wilhelmina	Netherlands	1890–1948	58
3	Wu Chao	China	655–705	50
4	Salote Tubou	Tonga	1918–65	47
5	Elizabeth II	UK	1952–	44
6	Elizabeth I	UK	1558–1603	44
7	Maria Theresa	Hungary	1740–80	40
8	Maria I	Portugal	1777–1816	39
9	Joanna I	Italy	1343–81	38
10=	Suiko Tenno	Japan	593–628	35
10=	Isabella II	Spain	1833–68	35

* Queens and empresses who ruled in their own right, not as consorts of kings or emperors

As well as being the longest-reigning queen, Victoria is among the longest-reigning monarchs in the world. She also holds 1st place as the British monarch who occupied the throne for the longest time, beating her nearest rival, George III, by four years.

RULED OUT

Britain's rulers have included just three monarchs who have reigned for less than a year. Lady Jane Grey was queen for 14 days in 1553, from the time of the death of Edward VI on July 6, until July 19, when she was deposed by Mary I and executed. Edward V, one of the "Princes in the Tower," was king for 75 days in 1483 before being imprisoned and murdered. Edward VIII succeeded his father George V on January 20, 1936 but abdicated 325 days later, on December 11. The shortest reign was that of Luis Philippe of Portugal. Both he and his father, King Carlos I, were shot in Lisbon in February 1908. The king died instantly, and his son ruled for 20 minutes.

T O P 1 0

LONGEST-REIGNING LIVING MONARCHS IN THE WORLD
(Including hereditary rulers of principalities, dukedoms, etc.)

	Monarch	Country	Date of birth	Accession
1	Bhumibol Adulyadej	Thailand	December 5, 1927	June 9, 1946
2	Rainier III	Monaco	May 31, 1923	May 9, 1949
3	Elizabeth II	UK	April 21, 1926	February 6, 1952
4	Hussein	Jordan	November 14, 1935	August 11, 1952
5	Hassan II	Morocco	July 9, 1929	February 26, 1961
6	Isa bin Sulman al-Khalifa	Bahrain	July 3, 1933	November 2, 1961
7	Malietoa Tanumafili II	Western Samoa	January 4, 1913	January 1, 1962
8	Jean	Luxembourg	January 5, 1921	November 12, 1964
9	Taufa'ahau Tupou IV	Tonga	July 4, 1918	December 16, 1965
10	Qaboos bin Said	Oman	November 18, 1942	July 23, 1970

Following the independence of Western Samoa, Malietoa Tanumafili II, the oldest monarch in the world, held office jointly with another chief, but since the latter's death in 1963 has been sole ruler. Malaysia, uniquely, has an elected monarchy.

NOBEL PRIZE WINNERS

NOBEL PRIZE-WINNING COUNTRIES

	Country	Phy	Che	Ph/Med	Lit	Pce	Eco	Total
1	US	60	39	74	10	17	24	224
2	UK	20	23	24	8	11	6	92
3	Germany	19	27	15	6	4	1	72
4	France	11	7	7	12	9	1	47
5	Sweden	4	4	7	7	5	2	29
6	Switzerland	2	5	5	2	3	–	17
7	Former USSR	7	1	2	3	2	1	16
8	Stateless institutions	–	–	–	–	15	–	15
9=	Italy	3	1	3	5	1	–	13
9=	Netherlands	6	3	2	–	1	1	13

Phy – Physics; Che – Chemistry; Ph/Med – Physiology or Medicine; Lit – Literature; Pce – Peace; Eco – Economic Sciences. Germany includes the united country before 1948, West Germany to 1990, and the united country since 1990

THE NOBEL CENTURY

Alfred Nobel was born in Stockholm on October 21, 1833. His father was an engineer and inventor. Alfred studied widely in Europe and the US before perfecting a method of stabilizing nitroglycerine, a notoriously dangerous explosive (Nobel's brother Emil had been killed during an experiment). The result was dynamite, which Nobel patented in 1866. Used extensively in the construction of railroads and for quarrying, dynamite and 354 further patents granted to Alfred Nobel earned him a fortune. When Nobel died in 1896 he left a will establishing a trust fund, which is now estimated to be worth over $225,000,000/£150,000,000. Interest earned from this has enabled annual prizes to be awarded since 1901 to those who have achieved the greatest common good in the fields of Chemistry, Physiology or Medicine, Literature, Peace, Physics, and, since 1969, Economic Sciences. All the awards take place in Stockholm, Sweden, with the exception of the Peace Prize, which is awarded in Oslo, Norway.

LAST WINNERS OF THE NOBEL PRIZE FOR LITERATURE

	Winner/country/dates	Prize year
1	Seamus Heaney (Ireland, 1939–)	1995
2	Kenzaburo Oe (Japan, 1935–)	1994
3	Toni Morrison (US, 1931–)	1993
4	Derek Walcott (St. Lucia, 1930–)	1992
5	Nadine Gordimer (South Africa, 1923–)	1991
6	Octavio Paz (Mexico, 1914–)	1990
7	Camilo José Cela (Spain, 1916–)	1989
8	Naguib Mahfouz (Egypt, 1911–)	1988
9	Joseph Brodsky (Russia/US, 1940–96)	1987
10	Wole Soyinka (Nigeria, 1934–)	1986

LAST WINNERS OF THE NOBEL PRIZE FOR ECONOMIC SCIENCE

	Winner/country/dates	Prize year
1	Robert E. Lucas (US, 1937–)	1995

The hypothesis of rational expectations as an aid to macroeconomic analysis and economic policy.

2=	John C. Harsanyi (Hungary/US, 1920–)	
2=	Reinhard Selten (Germany, 1930–)	
2=	John F. Nash (US, 1928–)	1994

Analysis of equilibria in the theory of non-cooperative games.

5=	Robert W. Fogel (US, 1926–)	
5=	Douglass C. North (US, 1920–)	1993

The application of economic theory and quantitative methods to explain economic and institutional change.

7	Gary S. Becker (US, 1930–)	1992

Extending microeconomic analysis to a wide range of human behavior and interaction.

8	Ronald H. Coase (UK/US, 1910–)	1991

Discovery and clarification of the significance of transaction costs and property rights for the traditional structure and functioning of the economy.

9=	Harry M. Markowitz (US, 1927–)	1990

Theory of portfolio choice.

9=	Merton H. Miller (US, 1923–)	1990

The theory of corporate finance.

9=	William F. Sharpe (US, 1934–)	1990

Contributions to the theory of price formation for financial assets.

The Nobel Prize for Economic Science is a recent addition to the Nobel Prizes, first awarded in 1969. It is presented annually by the Royal Swedish Academy of Sciences and consists of a gold medal, a diploma, and a sum of money that increases each year and is now almost $1,000,000.

THE 10

LAST WINNERS OF THE NOBEL PEACE PRIZE

	Winner/country/dates	Prize year		Winner/country/dates	Prize year
1	Joseph Rotblat (UK, 1908–)	1995	**5=**	Frederik Willem de Klerk (South Africa, 1936–)	1993
2=	Yasir Arafat (Palestine, 1929–)	1994	**7**	Rigoberta Menchú (Guatemala, 1959–)	1992
2=	Shimon Peres (Israel, 1923–)	1994	**8**	Aung San Suu Kyi (Burma, 1945–)	1991
2=	Itzhak Rabin (Israel, 1922–1995)	1994	**9**	Mikhail Gorbachev (USSR, 1931–)	1990
5=	Nelson Rolihlahla Mandela (South Africa, 1918–)	1993	**10**	Dalai Lama (Tibet, 1935–)	1989

THE 10

LAST WINNERS OF THE NOBEL PRIZE FOR CHEMISTRY

	Winner/country/dates	Prize year
1=	Paul Crutzen (Netherlands, 1933–)	
1=	Mario Molina (Mexico, 1943–)	
1=	Frank Sherwood Rowland (US, 1927–)	1995

Work in atmospheric chemistry concerning the formation and decomposition of ozone.

4	George A. Olah (Hungary/US, 1927–)	1994

Carbocations.

5=	Michael Smith (UK/Canada, 1932–)	1993

Development of site-specific mutagenesis.

5=	Kary Banks Mullis (US, 1944–)	1993

Invention of the polymerase chain reaction.

7	Rudolph A. Marcus (US, 1923–)	1992

Theories of electron transfer.

8	Richard Robert Ernst (Switzerland, 1933–)	1991

Development of high resolution nuclear magnetic resonance (NMR) spectroscopy.

9	Elias James Corey (US, 1928–)	1990

Development of novel methods for the synthesis of complex natural compounds (retrosynthetic analysis).

10=	Sidney Altman (Canada, 1939–)	
10=	Thomas Robert Cech (US, 1947–)	1989

Discovery of the catalytic properties of ribonucleic acid (RNA).

THE 10

LAST WINNERS OF THE NOBEL PRIZE FOR PHYSIOLOGY OR MEDICINE

	Winner/country/dates	Prize year
1=	Christiane Nüsslein-Volhard (Germany, 1942–)	
1=	Eric F. Wieschaus (US, 1947–)	
1=	Edward B. Lewis (US, 1918–)	1995

Discoveries about the involvement of genes in the spatial organization of organisms.

4=	Alfred G. Gilman (US, 1941–)	
4=	Martin Rodbell (US, 1925–)	1994

Signal transfer within cells, and the discovery of G proteins.

6=	Richard J. Roberts (US, 1943–)	
6=	Phillip A. Sharp (US, 1944–)	1993

Discovery of mosaic genes.

8=	Edmond H. Fischer (US, 1920–)	
8=	Edwin G. Krebs (US, 1918–)	1992

Discovery of mechanisms for the regulation of proteins in the human body.

10=	Erwin Neher (Germany, 1944–)	
10=	Bert Sakmann (Germany, 1942–)	1991

Discovery of the function of the ion channels in the human cell and for the development of the patch-clamp technique.

THE 10

LAST WINNERS OF THE NOBEL PRIZE FOR PHYSICS

	Winner/country/dates	Prize year
1=	Martin L. Perl (US, 1927–)	1995

Discovery of the tau lepton.

1=	Frederick Reines (US, 1918–)	1995

Detection of the neutrino.

3=	Bertram Neville Brockhouse (Canada, 1918–)	
3=	Clifford G. Shull (US, 1915–)	1994

Studies of neutron beams.

5=	Russell A. Hulse (US, 1950–)	
5=	Joseph H. Taylor, Jr. (US, 1941–)	1993

Discovery of a new type of pulsar.

7	Georges Charpak (France, 1924–)	1992

Invention of devices for the detection of interactions of elementary particles.

8	Pierre-Gilles de Gennes (France, 1932–)	1991

Theoretical description of ordering phenomena of liquid crystals, polymers, magnets, and superconductors.

9=	Jerome I. Friedman (US, 1930–)	
9=	Henry W. Kendall (US, 1926–)	
9=	Richard E. Taylor (Canada, 1929–)	1990

Inelastic scattering of electrons by protons and bound neutrons, and for the development of the quark model.

62

THE GOOD & THE BAD

20TH CENTURY

The lists on the following pages provide a broad image of a lawless century in which property theft and drug-related crime have become commonplace, and every advance made by the police has seemingly been matched by the increasing ruthlessness and sophistication of criminals. Murder numbers, especially those perpetrated with firearms, have risen inexorably (although when population sizes are taken into account, the current rate for the US is no worse than in the 1930s), while the horrific murders by serial killers are now at such a level that the murderer of 50 people does not even qualify for a place in the world Top 10.

POLICE ON THE BEAT
At the turn of the century the London bobby faced criminals with little more than a truncheon for protection.

RIOT POLICE IN ACTION
As this century progresses, the police have found it increasingly necessary to arm and protect themselves.

TOP 10

COUNTRIES WITH THE LOWEST CRIME RATES

	Country	Reported crime rate per 100,000 population		Country	Reported crime rate per 100,000 population
1	Togo	11.0	6	Guinea	32.4
2	Bangladesh	16.8	7	Mali	33.0
3	Nepal	29.1	8	Burkina Faso	41.0
4=	Congo	32.0	9	Syria	73.0
4=	Niger	32.0	10	Burundi	87.0

CRITICAL: CRIME WATCH

THE 10

COUNTRIES WITH THE HIGHEST CRIME RATES

	Country	Reported crime rate per 100,000 population
1	Dominica	22,432
2	Suriname	17,819
3	St. Kitts and Nevis	15,468
4	Sweden	14,188
5	New Zealand	13,247
6	Canada	11,443
7	US Virgin Islands	10,441
8	Denmark	10,270
9	Guam	10,080
10	Gibraltar	10,039

These figures are based on reported crimes. The reporting of crimes is not just a response to lawlessness, but also relates to public confidence in the police. In many countries crime is so common and law enforcement so inefficient or corrupt that many crimes are unreported.

THE 10

COUNTRIES WITH MOST BURGLARIES

	Country	Annual burglaries per 100,000 population
1	US Virgin Islands	3,183.7
2	Netherlands	2,621.8
3	Israel	2,483.0
4	New Zealand	2,447.6
5	Denmark	2,382.9
6	Bermuda	2,092.3
7	England and Wales	1,991.2
8	Australia	1,962.8
9	Malta	1,907.1
10	Greenland	1,883.5
	US	*1,041.8*

Crime statistics issued by the international agency Interpol generally relate to the numbers of offenses reported to police, rather than those where suspects have been apprehended or convicted.

THE 10

WORST YEARS FOR CRIME IN THE US

	Year	Crimes per 100,000 of population
1	1980	5,950.0
2	1991	5,897.8
3	1981	5,858.2
4	1990	5,820.3
5	1989	5,741.0
6	1988	5,664.2
7	1992	5,660.2
8	1982	5,603.6
9	1979	5,565.4
10	1987	5,550.0

THE 10

COUNTRIES WITH MOST CAR THEFTS

	Country	Annual thefts per 100,000 population
1	Switzerland	1,504.6*
2	New Zealand	1,026.4
3	US Virgin Islands	954.0
4	Sweden	879.0
5	England and Wales	858.2
6	Australia	770.6
7	US	631.5
8	Denmark	575.9
9	Italy	546.0
10	Puerto Rico	526.9

* Including motorcycles and bicycles

TOP 10

FBI "MOST WANTED" CRIMINALS

Fugitive/crime

1   Arthur Lee Washington, Jr. (b. November 30, 1949)

Interstate flight, attempted murder.

2   Donald Eugene Webb (b. July 14, 1931)

Interstate flight, murder, attempted burglary.

3   Leslie Isben Rogge (b. March 8, 1940)

Bank robbery, interstate transportation of stolen property, fraud.

4   Victor Manuel Gerena (b. June 24, 1958)

Bank robbery, interstate flight, armed robbery.

5   Mir Aimal Kansi (b. February 10, 1964)

Unlawful flight to avoid prosecution for a murder resulting from a shooting incident outside CIA headquarters in Langley, Virginia.

Fugitive/crime

6   Juan Garcia-Abrego (b. September 13, 1944)

Conspiracy to possess with intent to distribute cocaine, money laundering, etc.

7   Lamen Khalifa Fhimah (b. April 4, 1956)

Blowing up PanAm flight 103 on December 21, 1988, over Lockerbie, Scotland, UK.

8   Abdel Basset Ali Al-Megrahi (b. April 1, 1952)

Blowing up PanAm flight 103 (see No. 7).

9   O'Neil Vassell (b. September 27, 1976)

Member of drug gangs; unlawful flight to avoid prosecution for murder.

10   Rickey Allen Bright (b. January 13, 1954)

Kidnapping, rape, etc.

64

MURDER MOST FOUL

20TH CENTURY

As well as the multiple murderers appearing in the lists on these pages, there are other American candidates whose infamy is more uncertain. Some authorities have claimed that Donald Henry "Pew Wee" Gaskins, executed in 1991, had killed more than 100, Johann Otto Hoch, executed in 1906, as many as 50, and modern serial killer Randall Brent Woodfield (known as the "I-5 Killer") up to 44. There are also mystery murderers such as the "Green River Killer" who slaughtered 48 in the Seattle-Tacoma area in the period 1982–84, and in California in 1968–74 the "Zodiac Killer" (so-called because he used zodiacal signs at the scenes of his crimes), who may have killed 37 or more.

SERIAL KILLER ANDREI CHIKATILO
Chikatilo successfully led a double life as a married father, schoolteacher, and Communist party member for the 12 years he preyed on the citizens of Rostov-on-Don.

THE 10
WORST GUN MASSACRES* OF ALL TIME

	Perpetrator/location/date	Killed
1	Woo Bum Kong, Sang-Namdo, South Korea, April 28, 1982	57

Off-duty policeman Woo Bum Kong (or Wou Bom-Kon), 27, went on a drunken rampage with rifles and hand grenades, killing 57 and injuring 38 before blowing himself up.

2	Martin Bryant, Port Arthur, Tasmania, Australia, April 28, 1996	35

Bryant used a rifle in an horrific spree that began in a restaurant and ended with a siege in a guesthouse before he was caught by police.

3	Baruch Goldstein, Hebron, Occupied West Bank, Israel, February 25, 1994	29

Goldstein carried out a gun massacre of Palestinians at prayer at the Tomb of the Patriarchs before being beaten to death.

4=	James Oliver Huberty, San Ysidro, California, July 18, 1984	22

Huberty, aged 41, opened fire in a McDonald's restaurant, killing 21 before being shot dead. Another victim died the following day.

4=	George Hennard, Killeen, Texas, October 16, 1991	22

Hennard drove his truck through the window of Luby's Cafeteria and killed 22 with semi-automatic pistols before shooting himself.

6	Thomas Hamilton, Dunblane, Scotland, March 13, 1996	17

Hamilton, 43, shot 16 children and a teacher in Dunblane Primary School before killing himself in the UK's worst shooting incident.

7=	Charles Joseph Whitman, Austin, Texas, July 31 –August 1, 1966	16

Whitman killed his mother and wife on July 31, 1966. The next day he shot 14 and wounded 34 before being shot dead by a police officer.

7=	Michael Ryan, Hungerford, Berkshire, UK, August 19, 1987	16

Ryan, 26, shot 14 dead and wounded 16 others (two of whom died later) before shooting himself.

MASS MURDERER GEORGE HENNARD
Police found over 100 spent cartridges in the carnage that spree-killer Hennard left behind. The killer shot 22 people dead in 11 minutes.

Perpetrator/location/date		Killed
7=	Ronald Gene Simmons, Russellville, Arkansas, December 28, 1987	16

Simmons, a 47-year-old, killed 16, including 14 members of his own family.

10=	Wagner von Degerloch, Muehlhausen, Germany, September 3–4, 1913	14

Wagner von Degerloch, a 39-year-old teacher, murdered his wife and four children before embarking on a random shooting spree.

10=	Patrick Henry Sherrill, Edmond, Oklahoma, August 20, 1986	14

Sherrill, aged 44, shot 14 dead and wounded 6 others at the post office where he worked, before finally killing himself.

10=	Christian Dornier, Luxiol, Doubs, France, July 12, 1989	14

Dornier, a 31-year-old farmer, went on a rampage leaving 14 dead and 9 injured.

10=	Marc Lépine, Université de Montreal, Quebec, Canada, December 6, 1989	14

Lépine went on an armed rampage, killing 14 women before he turned the gun on himself.

* By individuals, excluding terrorist and military actions; totals exclude perpetrator

THE 10

MOST PROLIFIC SERIAL KILLERS OF THE 20TH CENTURY*

Serial killers are mass murderers who kill repeatedly, often over long periods. Because of the secrecy surrounding their horrific crimes, and the time-spans involved, it is almost impossible to calculate the precise number of a serial killer's victims.
The number of murders attributed to these criminals are "best estimates" based on the most reliable evidence available. Such is the magnitude of the crimes of some, however, that the figures may be underestimates.

	Perpetrator	Killed
1	Pedro Alonzo (or Armando) López	over 300

Up to his 1980 capture, López, known as the "Monster of the Andes," led police to 53 graves but probably murdered a total of more than 300 young girls in Colombia, Ecuador, and Peru. He was brought to trial and sentenced to life imprisonment.

	Perpetrator	Killed
2	Henry Lee Lucas	over 200

The subject of the film, Henry, Portrait of a Serial Killer, Lucas (b. 1937) may have committed 200 or more murders, many of them in partnership with Ottis Toole. He admitted in 1983 to 360 and was convicted of 11. Lucas is currently on Death Row in Huntsville, Texas, while Toole's original death sentence was commuted to six life sentences.

	Perpetrator	Killed
3	Delfina and María de Jesús Gonzales	over 91

After abducting girls to work in their Mexican brothel, Rancho El Angel, the Gonzales sisters murdered as many as 80 of them and an unknown number of their customers, burying them in the grounds. In 1964 the two were sentenced to 40 years' imprisonment.

	Perpetrator	Killed
4	Bruno Lüdke	86

Lüdke (b. 1909) was a German who confessed to murdering 86 women between 1928 and January 29, 1943. Declared insane, he was incarcerated in a Vienna hospital where he was subjected to medical experiments, apparently dying on April 8, 1944, after he had been given a lethal injection.

	Perpetrator	Killed
5	Daniel Camargo Barbosa	71

Coincidentally, eight years after the arrest of Pedro Alonzo López in Ecuador, Barbosa was captured following a similar series of horrific murders of children. The probable total number of his victims was 71. Barbosa was sentenced to just 16 years in prison.

	Perpetrator	Killed
6	Kampatimar Shankariya	70

Caught after a two-year spree during which he killed as many as 70 times, Shankariya was hanged in Jaipur, India, on May 16, 1979.

	Perpetrator	Killed
7	Randolph Kraft	67

From 1972 until his arrest on May 14, 1983, Kraft is thought to have murdered 67 men in the US. On November 29, 1989, he was found guilty on 16 counts and was sentenced to death.

	Perpetrator	Killed
8	Dr. Marcel André Henri Felix Petiot	63

Dr. Marcel Petiot (b. 1897) is known to have killed at least 27, but admitted to 63 murders during World War II. He claimed that his victims were collaborators, but it is probable that they were wealthy Jews whom he robbed. Petiot was guillotined on May 26, 1946.

	Perpetrator	Killed
9	Donald Harvey	58

Working as an orderly in hospitals in Kentucky and Ohio, Harvey is believed to have murdered some 58 patients before his arrest in March 1987. He pleaded guilty to 24 murders, for which he received multiple life sentences.

	Perpetrator	Killed
10	Andrei Chikatilo	52

In Rostov-on-Don, in 1992, Russia's worst serial killer was convicted of killing 52 women and children between 1978 and 1990. He was executed on February 14, 1994.

* *Includes only individual murderers and couples; excludes murders by bandits, those carried out by groups, and gangland slayings*

THE 10

MOST PROLIFIC MURDERERS* IN THE US

	Perpetrator	Killed
1	Henry Lee Lucas	over 200

Lucas ranks as America's worst serial killer, with over 200 victims (see No. 2 in The 10 Most Prolific Serial Killers of the 20th Century).

	Perpetrator	Killed
2	Identity to be confirmed	168

The identity of the person or persons responsible for the April 19, 1995 bombing of the Alfred P. Murrah Federal Building in Oklahoma City has not yet been established.

	Perpetrator	Killed
3	Julio Gonzalez	87

On March 25, 1990, following an argument with his girlfriend, Lydia Feliciano, Gonzalez firebombed her place of employment, an illegal disco in New York. He killed 87 – although Lydia Feliciano was one of six survivors.

	Perpetrator	Killed
4	Randolph Kraft	67

See No. 7 in The 10 Most Prolific Serial Killers of the 20th Century.

	Perpetrator	Killed
5	Donald Harvey	58

See No. 9 in The 10 Most Prolific Serial Killers of the 20th Century.

	Perpetrator	Killed
6	John Gilbert Graham	44

In order to claim on six life insurance policies, Graham placed a time bomb in the luggage of his mother, Daisy King, as she boarded an airliner in Denver, Colorado, on November 1, 1955. On the way to San Francisco, it blew up killing all 44 on board. On January 11, 1957, Graham was found guilty and executed.

	Perpetrator	Killed
7	Daniel Burke	43

On a flight from Los Angeles to San Francisco on December 7, 1987, a Pacific Southwest Airlines British Aerospace 146-200 commuter jet crashed near San Luis Obispo, killing 43 on board. Gunshots had been heard over the radio, and the FBI later found a note from a passenger, London-born Jamaican Daniel Burke, an aggrieved former airline employee.

	Perpetrator	Killed
8	Gerald Eugene Stano	40

Convicted of murdering three women, Stano was sentenced in 1981 to a term of imprisonment that would have kept him incarcerated until the age of 103.

	Perpetrator	Killed
9	Ted Bundy	36

After spending nine years on death row, Bundy (b. 1947) was executed on January 24, 1989. Police linked him to 36 murders, and he once admitted that he might have killed 100 people.

	Perpetrator	Killed
10	John Wayne Gacy	34

On March 13, 1980, John Wayne Gacy (b.1942) was sentenced to death for the Chicago murders of 34 men. He was executed on May 10, 1994.

* *Includes only individual murderers; excludes murders by bandits, those carried out by groups, such as terrorist atrocities, and gangland slayings*

CRIMINAL RECORDS

THE 10

MOST COMMON REASONS FOR ARREST IN THE US

	Offense	Estimated arrests (1994)
1	Larceny	1,514,500
2	Driving under the influence	1,384,600
3	Drug-abuse violations	1,351,400
4	Disorderly conduct	746,200
5	Drunkenness	713,200
6	Aggravated assault	547,760
7	Liquor law violations	541,800
8	Fraud	419,800
9	Burglary	396,100
10	Vandalism	323,300
	Total (including others not listed above)	*14,648,700*

Outside this Top 10 are arrests for such offenses as "Weapons (carrying, possessing, etc.)" (259,400 cases) and group categories including "Other assaults" (1,223,600) and "All other offenses" (3,743,200).

THE 10

MOST COMMON OFFENSES IN ENGLAND AND WALES 100 YEARS AGO

	Offense	No. reported
1	Larceny	63,740
2	Burglary and housebreaking	7,495
3	Fraud	2,628
4	Crimes of violence (other than murder)	1,975
5	Attempted suicide	1,861
6	Crimes against morals	1,736
7	Receiving stolen goods	908
8	Robbery and extortion	375
9	Forgery	343
10	Arson	328

These are the annual averages of indictable crimes reported to the police in England and Wales during the period 1893–97. Falling just outside is the now virtually defunct crime of "coining" – the forgery of coins (230 cases) – and murder (143 cases). In the same period, various nonindictable offenses resulted in large numbers of trials – most notably for drunkenness (179,496), assaults (73,048), and vagrancy (25,228).

THE 10

MOST COMMON OFFENSES IN ENGLAND AND WALES IN 1994

	Offense	No. offenders found guilty
1	Driving violations	651,700
2	Minor violations (other than driving)	454,700
3	Theft and handling stolen goods	121,600
4	Other offenses	39,400
5	Burglary	38,000
6	Violence against a person	37,600
7	Drug offenses	27,800
8	Fraud and forgery	18,400
9	Criminal damage	10,000
10	Robbery	4,900
	Total (indictable 314,100/ summary 1,093,500)	*1,407,600*

This list includes both indictable offenses (those normally calling for a trial before a jury) and summary offenses (usually tried before a magistrates' court). In the latter category, driving violations comprise the largest proportion, but other offenses are less precisely itemized and hence appear in official statistics under a general heading. Under the Criminal Justice Act of 1988, a number of offenses were reclassified, and some, such as certain criminal damage offenses, may be either indictable or summary, depending on the value of the property that is damaged. "Other offenses" includes groups of offenses that are grouped as "breach of local and other regulations." It should be noted that direct comparisons cannot be made with offenses under Scottish legal jurisdiction, which employs different categories of offense, some bearing a ring of the age in which they were established, including "theft by opening lockfast places," and "lewd and libidinous practices."

THE 10

LARGEST FEDERAL CORRECTIONAL INSTITUTIONS IN THE US

	Institute	Location	Rated capacity
1	Federal Correctional Institution	Fort Dix, New Jersey	3,621
2	US Penitentiary	Atlanta, Georgia	1,252
3	Federal Detention Center	Miami, Florida	1,214
4	US Penitentiary	Leavenworth, Kansas	1,201
5	Federal Medical Center	Fort Worth, Texas	1,132
6	Federal Medical Center	Lexington, Kentucky	1,116
7	Federal Correctional Institution	Milan, Michigan	1,054
8	Federal Transportation Center	Oklahoma City, Oklahoma	1,053
9	Federal Correctional Institution	Coleman, Florida	1,024
10	Federal Correctional Institution	Allenwood, Pennsylvania	992

Source: Bureau of Federal Prisons

THE 10

EMBASSIES IN THE US WITH THE MOST UNPAID PARKING FINES

	Embassy	Unpaid fines ($)
1	Russia	3,800,000
2	Nigeria	146,030
3	Egypt	77,830
4	Israel	69,340
5	Zimbabwe	65,640
6	Bulgaria	54,630
7	Argentina	45,020
8	Oman	42,280
9	Spain	41,145
10	Guinea-Bissau	40,790

The use of diplomatic immunity by embassy staff to evade both serious criminal offenses and misdemeanours, including parking fines, is an international problem, with some embassies appearing prominently in such lists in different parts of the world: the Soviet Union once consistently headed the comparative list in the UK, for example, although its place has now been taken by the United Arab Emirates. (The United States Embassy in London has not always had an unblemished record, and in 1994 the Embassy failed to pay 22 parking fines.)

THE 10

DIPLOMATIC MISSIONS IN THE UK WITH THE MOST UNPAID PARKING FINES

		No. unpaid fines	
	Mission	1993	1994
1	United Arab Emirates	51	470
2	Angola	30	404
3	Qatar	28	353
4	Nigeria	91	118
5	India	71	79
6	Ghana	35	76
7	Bulgaria	34	66
8	Oman	45	63
9	Pakistan	54	61
10	France	25	58

For many years London diplomatic missions have used their immunity from prosecution to avoid paying parking fines. However, in recent years this practice has been challenged, and thus the total in 1993 was 1,941, a 53.4 percent reduction on the 1992 figure of 4,166. However, 1994 was the first year since 1986 that the figures increased, all but doubling to a total of 3,613. This increase was a result of a change in responsibility for parking offenses from the Metropolitan Police to the London Boroughs.

TOP 10

MOST COMMON REASONS FOR BURGLAR ALARMS BEING ACTIVATED

1	Customer error
2	Rapid changes in temperature
3	Windows left open
4	Pets
5	Small insects (including spiders)
6	Christmas or party decorations and balloons (especially helium-filled)
7	Burglars
8	Electrical storms
9	Telephone faults
10	Faulty equipment

A survey conducted by a leading supplier of centrally monitored systems in domestic premises discloses some suprising results – not least that burglars feature less prominently than insects and other curious causes. These principally relate to the failure of infrared and other sensors to distinguish between disturbances caused by air currents, small creatures, and balloons passing before them, and felonious intruders. However, the inability of human operators to remember to press the right buttons or close their doors remains the No. 1 cause of alarms being activated.

TOP 10

US CITIES WITH THE MOST POLICE OFFICERS

	City	Police officers
1	New York, New York	30,135
2	Chicago, Illinois	12,971
3	Los Angeles, California	7,869
4	Philadelphia, Pennsylvania	6,101
5	Houston, Texas	4,935
6	Washington, DC	4,106
7	Detroit, Michigan	3,855
8	Baltimore, Maryland	3,065
9	Dallas, Texas	2,777
10	Phoenix, Arizona	2,088

TOP 10

US STATES WITH THE LOWEST CRIME RATES

	State	Crimes per 100,000
1	West Virginia	2,528.4
2	North Dakota	2,735.9
3	New Hampshire	2,741.0
4	South Dakota	3,102.2
5	Vermont	3,240.3
6	Kentucky	3,259.7
7	Pennsylvania	3,271.9
8	Maine	3,272.7
9	Iowa	3,654.6
10	Wisconsin	3,944.4

THE 10

US STATES WITH THE HIGHEST CRIME RATES

	State	Crimes per 100,000
1	District of Columbia	11,085.3
2	Florida	8,250.0
3	Arizona	7,924.6
4	Hawaii	6,680.5
5	Nevada	6,677.4
6	Louisiana	6,671.1
7	Oregon	6,296.4
8	New Mexico	6,187.8
9	California	6,173.8
10	Maryland	6,122.6

MURDER FILE

MOST COMMON MURDER WEAPONS AND METHODS IN THE US

	Weapon/method	Victims
1	Handguns	12,769
2	Knives or cutting instruments	2,801
3	"Personal weapons" (hands, feet, fists, etc.)	1,165
4	Firearms (type not stated)	992
5	Shotguns	953
6	Blunt objects (hammers, clubs, etc.)	912
7	Rifles	723
8	Strangulation	287
9	Fire	196
10	Asphyxiation	113

In addition to the weapons listed "other weapons or weapons not stated" were used in 1,079 murders. Relatively less common methods included explosives (10 cases), drowning (25), and poison (10). The total number of murders for the year amounted to 23,305 – equivalent to one person in every 11,290 of the population (an improvement on the previous year's ratio of 1:11,083). The total number of murders committed has escalated dramatically during the 20th century, although the order of the weapons has not changed much in recent years. Perhaps most surprisingly, the proportion of killings involving firearms has scarcely changed at all – and has even gone down compared with the figures for the early years of the century. In 1920, for example, 4,178 out of a total of 5,815 murders were committed with firearms and explosives (formerly a combined statistic), a total of 72 percent, while in 1994, out of a total of 23,305 cases of murder and manslaughter, 15,456, or 66 percent, were committed using firearms.

MOST COMMON MURDER WEAPONS AND METHODS IN ENGLAND AND WALES

	Weapon/method	Victims 1994
1	Sharp instrument	236
2	Hitting and kicking	111
3	Strangulation and asphyxiation	106
4	Shooting	63
5	Blunt instrument	56
6	Burning	42
7	Poison and drugs	23
8	Drowning	14
9	Unknown	10
10	Motor vehicle	8

According to Home Office statistics, there were 677 homicides in 1994 in England and Wales. In addition to those in this list, the apparent method in eight incidents is described as "other." This represents an increase on the previous year, although it should be noted that some offenses first recorded as murders were later reclassified. England and Wales are still relatively safe countries: the odds of being murdered in England and Wales are one in 75,981. You are more than six times as likely to be a murder victim in the US.

COUNTRIES WITH THE HIGHEST MURDER RATES

	Country	Murders p.a. per 100,000 population
1	Swaziland	87.8
2	Lesotho	51.1
3	Colombia	40.5
4	Sudan	30.5
5	Philippines	30.1
6	Guatemala	27.4
7	French Guiana	27.2
8	Nauru	25.0
9	Aruba	24.9
10	Puerto Rico	24.1
	US	9.0

MURDER BY NUMBERS

As the lists on these pages indicate, there are countries with worse murder rates (numbers of victims as a ratio of population) than the US, but nowhere in the world has as many murders each year. This has not always been so: in 1900 there were just 230 murders, a rate of 1.2 per 100,000 inhabitants. The number grew steadily, first exceeding 1,000 in 1906, when there were 1,310 cases, and first topping 10,000 in 1930 (10,331). By 1933 gangland violence pushed the figure up to an all-time peak of 12,124 and a rate of 9.7 per 100,000. This number was not exceeded until 1967, when 13,425 murders were recorded, but a further increase since then means that in 1994 there were 23,305 murders in the US, a rate of 9.0 per 100,000.

RELATIONSHIPS OF MURDER VICTIMS TO PRINCIPAL SUSPECTS IN THE US

	Relationship	Victims
1	Acquaintance	6,125
2	Stranger	2,888
3	Wife	823
4	Friend	733
5	Girlfriend	525
6	Husband	346
7	Son	326
8	Boyfriend	228
9	Daughter	212
10	Neighbor	173

RELATIONSHIPS OF MURDER VICTIMS TO PRINCIPAL SUSPECTS IN THE UK

	Relationship	Victims 1994
1=	Male stranger	113
1=	Male friend or acquaintance	113
3	Wife, ex-wife, or female cohabitant	81
4=	Female friend or acquaintance	41
4=	Daughter	41
6	Female stranger	32
7=	Son	24
7=	Male associate	24
9	Female lover, ex-lover, or lover's spouse	20
10	Husband, ex-husband, or male cohabitant	18

In addition to these offenses, in 1994 15 mothers and seven fathers were killed by their sons or daughters, 19 murder victims were unspecified male or female family members, while 14 men and one woman are described as "other person in course of employment," such as security guards.

WORST STATES FOR MURDER IN THE US

	State	Firearms used	Total murders
1	California	2,790	3,712
2	Texas	1,485	2,027
3	New York	1,356	1,992
4	Florida	647	1,181
5	Illinois*	812	1,177
6	Michigan	646	893
7	Louisiana	682	824
8	North Carolina	483	757
9	Pennsylvania	465	699
10	Georgia	492	678

* Provisional figures

Of the 13,940 murders committed in the 10 states above in 1994, firearms were used in 9,858 cases, or 71 per cent. In that year, there was precisely one more murder in Georgia, ranked 10th in the list, and with an estimated resident population of 5,567,000, than in the whole of England and Wales, which has more than nine times as many inhabitants. These 10 states had murder rates ranging from a low of 7.4 per 100,000 of the population for Pennsylvania to a high of 23.7 per 100,000 in Louisiana.

DYING YOUNG

The odds of your being murdered are increased if you are male, and if you are young. In 1994 in the US 17,309 men were murdered. Murder (along with "legal intervention" – being shot by police or executed) is now, after motor vehicle accidents, the principal cause of death among 15- to 24-year-old men. A quarter (6,790) of the 27,620 deaths recorded in this age group died by this means, followed by suicide (4,770 deaths), cancer (1,070), and heart disease (530). In England and Wales in the same year, 407 men were murdered, 122 of them aged between 16 and 30.

WORST CITIES FOR MURDER IN THE US

	City	Murders (1995)
1	New York, New York	1,182
2	Los Angeles, California	828
3	Chicago, Illinois	823
4	Detroit, Michigan	514
5	Philadelphia, Pennsylvania	404*
6	New Orleans, Louisiana	364
7	Washington, DC	360
8	Baltimore, Maryland	324
9	Houston, Texas	304
10	Dallas, Texas	276

* 1994 figure

The identity of America's 10 murder capitals remains fairly consistent from year to year, with only slight adjustments to the order.

WORST YEARS FOR GUN MURDERS IN THE US

	Year	Victims
1	1993	16,136
2	1994	15,546
3	1992	15,489
4	1991	14,373
5	1980	13,650
6	1990	13,035
7	1981	12,523
8	1974	12,474
9	1975	12,061
10	1989	11,832

MURDER HISTORY

The grisly task of ranking murderers is highly problematic, particularly for murders before the 20th century. Medical diagnoses, policing, and forensic methods were often poor, so poisoning (a particularly popular method) often went undetected. The 19th century was also an age of migrations, especially in the US, when people could simply disappear without a trace with none of the authorities knowing their whereabouts. Earlier still, charges of mass murder were often invented for political motives or as part of broader accusations of witchcraft.

Often the only information we have is that which emerged when people were actually caught and brought to trial, sometimes making dramatic (if not always believable) confessions. Therefore, the victim quota in these lists is based on such reliable evidence as may be available, but with the proviso that some may be underestimates, and that the identities of other similarly active and "successful" murderers (in the sense that they were not discovered and brought to trial) may never be known.

MASS MURDERER GILLES DE RAIS
Gilles de Rais, nicknamed "Bluebeard," was charged with witchcraft, and with the murder of 6 of his 7 wives and perhaps 200 children.

THE 10

MOST PROLIFIC POISONERS IN THE WORLD*

Poisoner	No. of victims
1 Susannah Olah	up to 100

Susi Olah, a Hungarian nurse and midwife, was believed to have prophetic powers after she "predicted" the deaths of up to 100 people, who then died from poisoning. Her victims ranged from the old, handicapped, and newborn, to local husbands – in most cases with the complicity, sometimes even help, of their relatives. She committed suicide when the law caught up with her in 1929.

Poisoner	No. of victims
2 Gesina Margaretha Gottfried	at least 30

Having poisoned her first husband and two children with arsenic in 1815, Gesina Mittenberg, a German, killed her parents and her next husband, Gottfried, whom she married on his deathbed, in the same way. Although she had inherited his fortune, her income dwindled, and she embarked on a series of murders, including those of her brother, a creditor, and most of the family of a Bremen wheelwright called Rumf, for whom she worked as a housekeeper. Rumf became suspicious, and in 1828 Gottfried was arrested. She admitted to over 30 murders and was executed.

Poisoner	No. of victims
3 Hélène Jegado	23

Jegado was a French housemaid believed to have poisoned 23 people with arsenic. She was tried in 1851 and guillotined in 1852.

Poisoner	No. of victims
4 Mary Ann Cotton	up to 20

Cotton (b. 1832), a former nurse, is generally held to be Britain's worst mass murderer. Over a 20-year period, it seems probable that she disposed of 14–20 victims, including her husband, children, and stepchildren, by arsenic poisoning. She was hanged at Durham Prison on March 24, 1873.

Poisoner	No. of victims
5= Dr. William Palmer	14

(See Most Prolific Pre-20th-Century Serial Killers, opposite.)

Poisoner	No. of victims
5= Sadamichi Hirasawa	14

On January 26, 1948, Hirasawa entered the Shiinamachi branch of the Imperial Bank of Tokyo. Posing as a doctor, he gave 16 members of staff what he claimed was a medicine but which was, in fact, cyanide. Fourteen people died, and he was caught and jailed for 40 years.

Poisoner	No. of victims
7= Johann Otto Hoch	at least 12

In 1895 German-born Hoch (1862–1906), who used a variety of aliases, moved to the US. There he preyed on widows, many of whom he married before murdering them, usually with poison. He certainly killed 12, probably 24, and – according to some authorities – as many as 50 before being hanged in Chicago on February 23, 1906.

Poisoner	No. of victims
7= Marie Becker	at least 12

In the 1930s Marie Becker, the 53-year-old wife of a cabinetmaker in Liège, France, carried out a series of poisonings that left at least 12 dead, and possibly as many as 20. In the autumn of 1932 she poisoned her husband Charles with digitalis, followed by her lover Lambert Bayer. In order to finance a somewhat extravagant lifestyle, she then embarked on murdering a series of elderly women whom she nursed. She was sentenced to life imprisonment and died in jail.

Poisoner	No. of victims
9 Lydia Sherman	at least 11

Known as "the Queen Poisoner," American killer Lydia Sherman murdered her husband, a policeman called Edward Struck, and her six children during the 1860s. After this she married and murdered New Haven farmer Dennis Hurlbrut, followed by Nelson Sherman and his two children, all with arsenic, bringing her total to 11 – although it has been suggested that she may have killed at least twice as many (a total of 42 has been claimed by some authorities). She was sentenced to life imprisonment and died in jail on May 16, 1878.

Poisoner	No. of victims
10= Amy Archer-Gilligan	at least 5

While under the care of Amy Archer-Gilligan, a nursing-home owner in Hartford, Connecticut, at least five residents died after being poisoned with arsenic. She was tried in 1917, sentenced to life imprisonment, and died in jail in 1923.

Poisoner	No. of victims
10= Dr. Thomas Neill Cream	5

In 1881 Cream, a Scottish-born doctor, was sentenced to 10 years in prison in the US, for a murder using strychnine. Released in 1891, he moved to London where he soon poisoned four more people and became known as the "Lambeth Poisoner." He was caught and executed on November 15, 1892. It is said that as he died he blurted out, "I am Jack. . .," which some have taken to mean that he was Jack the Ripper. The flaw in this is that the Ripper's crimes were carried out in 1888, when Cream was still firmly behind bars in the US.

Poisoner	No. of victims
10= Herman Billik	5

In the period 1905 to 1906, Herman Billik, a Chicago eccentric who offered his services as a sorcerer, murdered his creditor Martin Vzral and four members of his family using arsenic – although it seems likely that Vzral's widow was an accomplice. At his trial in 1907, Billik was sentenced to death, but this was later commuted to life imprisonment.

* Prior to 1950; excluding poisoners where evidence becomes so confused with legend (such as that surrounding the Borgia family) as to be unreliable.

THE 10

MOST PROLIFIC MURDERESSES

	Murderess	No. of victims
1	Countess Erszébet Báthory	up to 650

(See Most Prolific Pre-20th-Century Serial Killers, below.)

	Murderess	No. of victims
2	Susannah Olah	up to 100

(See Most Prolific Poisoners in the World, opposite.)

	Murderess	No. of victims
3	Delfina and Maria de Jesús Gonzales	80

(See Serial Killers in the 20th Century, p. 65.)

	Murderess	No. of victims
4	Bella Poulsdatter Sorensen Gunness	42

Bella, or Belle, Gunness (1859–1908?), a Norwegian-born immigrant to the US, is believed to have killed her husband Peter Gunness for his life insurance (she claimed that an ax had fallen off a shelf and onto his head). After this she lured between 16 and 28 suitors through "lonely hearts" advertisements, as well as many others – totaling 42 – to her Indiana farm, where she murdered them. Her farm burned down on April 28, 1908, and a headless corpse was found and identified as Gunness. It seemed that she had been murdered – with her three children – by her accomplice Ray Lamphere. However, the truth may be that she faked her own death and disappeared.

	Murderess	No. of victims
5	Gesina Margaretha Gottfried	at least 30

(See Most Prolific Poisoners in the World, opposite.)

	Murderess	No. of victims
6	Jane Toppan	30

Boston-born Nora Kelley, also known as Jane Toppan (1854–1938), was almost certainly insane. She trained as a nurse, and within a few years numerous patients in her care died. Their bodies were exhumed, revealing traces of morphine and atropine poisoning. It seems probable, according to evidence and her own confession, that she killed 30 people. She died on August 17, 1938, in an asylum, aged 84.

	Murderess	No. of victims
7	Hélène Jegado	23

(See Most Prolific Poisoners in the World, opposite.)

	Murderess	No. of victims
8	Genene Jones	21

In 1984 Jones, a nurse, was found guilty of killing a baby, Chelsea McClellan, at the San Antonio Hospital, Texas, by administering the drug succinylcholine. She was sentenced to 99 years. Jones had been dismissed from the previous hospital where she had worked after 20 babies in her care had died of suspicious but uncertain causes. Some authorities link her with as many as 42 deaths.

	Murderess	No. of victims
9	Mary Ann Cotton	20

(See Most Prolific Poisoners in the World, opposite.)

	Murderess	No. of victims
10	Waltraud Wagner	15

Wagner was the ringleader of a group of four nurses found guilty of murder through deliberate drug overdoses and other means at the Lainz Hospital, Vienna, Austria, in the late 1980s. At least 42, and possibly up to several hundred, patients were murdered. Wagner was sentenced to life imprisonment on charges that included 15 counts of murder and 17 of attempted murder.

THE 10

MOST PROLIFIC PRE-20TH-CENTURY SERIAL KILLERS*

	Serial killer	No. of victims
1	Behram	931

Behram (or Buhram) was the leader of the Thugee cult in India, which it was reckoned was responsible for the deaths of up to 2,000 people. At his trial Behram was found guilty of personally committing 931 murders between 1790 and 1830, mostly by ritual strangulation with the cult's traditional cloth known as a ruhmal. From the end of his reign of terror onward, the British in India mounted a campaign against the Thugee, and the cult was eventually suppressed.

	Serial killer	No. of victims
2	Countess Erszébet Báthory	up to 650

In the period up to 1610 in Hungary, Báthory (1560–1614), known as "Countess Dracula" – the title of a 1970 horror film about her life and crimes – was alleged to have murdered between 300 and 650 girls (her personal list of 610 victims was described at her trial) in the belief that drinking their blood would prevent her from aging. She was eventually arrested in 1611. Tried and found guilty, she died on August 21, 1614, walled up in her own castle at Csejthe.

	Serial killer	No. of victims
3	Gilles de Rais	up to 200

A wealthy French aristocrat, Gilles de Laval, Baron de Rais (b. 1404), one-time supporter of Joan of Arc, allegedly dabbled in the occult and committed murders as sacrifices in black magic rituals. He was accused of kidnapping and killing between 60 and 200 children. Found guilty, he was tortured, strangled, and his body burned at Nantes on October 25, 1440.

	Serial killer	No. of victims
4	Herman Webster Mudgett	up to 150

Also known as "H.H. Holmes," Mudgett (b. 1860) was a former doctor. He was believed to have lured over 150 women to his "castle," on 63rd Street, Chicago, which was fully equipped for torturing and murdering them and disposing of the bodies. Arrested in 1894 and found guilty of murder, he confessed to killing 27 but may have killed up to 150.

	Serial killer	No. of victims
5	Gesina Margaretha Gottfried	at least 30

(See Most Prolific Poisoners in the World, opposite.)

	Serial killer	No. of victims
6	Hélène Jegado	23

(See Most Prolific Poisoners in the World, opposite.)

	Serial killer	No. of victims
7	Mary Ann Cotton	up to 20

(See Most Prolific Poisoners in the World, opposite.)

	Serial killer	No. of victims
8	William Burke and William Hare	at least 15

Two Irishmen living in Edinburgh, UK, Burke and Hare murdered at least 15 people in order to sell their bodies to anatomists in the period before human dissection was legal. Burke was hanged on January 28, 1829, while Hare, having turned king's evidence against him, was released and is alleged to have died a blind beggar in London in the 1860s.

	Serial killer	No. of victims
9	Dr. William Palmer	14

Palmer (b. 1824) may have killed at least 13, probably 14, and perhaps as many as 16. His victims included his wife, brother, and children, whom he killed in order to claim insurance, and various men whom he robbed to pay off his gambling debts. He was hanged at Stafford, England, on June 14, 1856. The true number of his victims remains uncertain.

	Serial killer	No. of victims
10	Lydia Sherman	at least 11

(See Most Prolific Poisoners in the World, opposite.)

* Includes only individual murderers; excludes murders by bandits, those carried out by groups, and gangland slayings.

CAPITAL PUNISHMENT

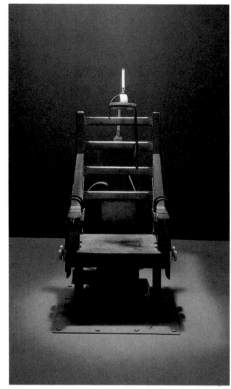

INSTRUMENT OF EXECUTION
*Harold P. Brown and electrical pioneer
Thomas Alva Edison's chief electrician
Dr. A.E. Kennelly jointly take the credit for
inventing the electric chair, first used to
execute murderer William Kemmler in 1890.*

10 US EXECUTION FIRSTS

1 First to be hanged

*John Billington, for the shooting murder
of John Newcomin in Plymouth,
Massachusetts, September 30, 1630.*

2 First to be hanged for witchcraft

*Achsah Young, in Massachusetts on
May 27, 1647. In Salem, Massachusetts, on
September 19, 1692, 80-year-old Giles Cory
became the last man to be pressed to death
(for refusing to plead on charges of
witchcraft); the last executions for witchcraft
(of eight women) also took place at Salem
Village on September 22, 1692.*

3 First to be hanged for treason

*Jacob Leisler, for insurrection against
New York Governor Francis Nicholson, in
City Hall Park, New York, May 16, 1691.*

4 First to be hanged for slave trading

*Captain Nathaniel Gordon (technically
hanged for piracy, which included slave
trading) was executed at the Tombs prison,
New York, February 21, 1862.*

5 First civilian to be hanged for treason

*William Bruce Mumford, for tearing down the
American flag in New Orleans, June 7, 1862.*

6 First man to be electrocuted

*William Kemmler (alias John Hart), for murder,
at Auburn Prison, New York, August 6, 1890.*

7 First woman to be electrocuted

*Martha M. Place, for murder, at Sing Sing
Prison, New York, March 20, 1899.*

8 First to be executed in the gas chamber

*Gee Jon, for murder, in Carson City,
Nevada, February 8, 1924.*

9 First to be electrocuted for treason

*Julius and Ethel Rosenberg, at Sing Sing
Prison, New York, June 19, 1953.*

10 First to be executed by lethal injection

*Charles Brooks, for murder, at the
Department of Corrections, Huntsville,
Texas, December 6, 1982.*

THE 10
FIRST COUNTRIES TO ABOLISH CAPITAL PUNISHMENT

	Country	Abolished
1	Russia	1826
2	Venezuela	1863
3	Portugal	1867
4=	Brazil	1882
4=	Costa Rica	1882
6	Ecuador	1897
7	Panama	1903
8	Norway	1905
9	Uruguay	1907
10	Colombia	1910

A number of countries began by abolishing
capital punishment in peacetime only, or
abolished it for all crimes except treason –
several countries later reinstated it.

THE 10
LAST PEOPLE EXECUTED AT THE TOWER OF LONDON

1 Wilhelm Johannes Roos   Jul 30, 1915

*Roos was a Dutchman who posed as a
cigar salesman and sent coded messages
to a firm in Holland detailing ship
movements in British ports. Roos was the
third spy of World War I to be executed at
the Tower of London. He was shot.*

2 Haike Marinus Petrus Janssen   Jul 30, 1915

*An accomplice of Roos who used the same
methods. The two were tried together and
executed the same day. Janssen was shot
10 minutes after Roos, at 6:10 am.*

3 Ernst Waldemar Melin   Sep 10, 1915

*A German spy who was shot after General
Court Martial during World War I.*

4 Agusto Alfredo Roggen   Sep 17, 1915

*A German who attempted to escape the
death penalty by claiming to be Uruguayan.
He was found guilty of spying on the trials of
a new torpedo at Loch Lomond, then sending
the information in invisible ink.*

5 Fernando Buschman   Oct 19, 1915

*Posing as a Dutch violinist, he spied while
offering entertainment at Royal Navy bases.*

6 Georg T. Breeckow   Oct 26, 1915

*Posing as an American (Reginald Rowland)
with a forged passport, he was caught when
he sent a parcel containing secret messages,
but addressed in German style, with country
and town name preceding that of the street.*

7 Irving Guy Ries   Oct 27, 1915

*A German traveling salesman who was
sentenced to death on spying charges.*

8 Albert Meyer   Dec 2, 1915

*Like Ries, Meyer was a German spy posing
as a traveling salesman.*

9 Y.L. Zender-Hurwitz   Apr 11, 1916

*A spy of Peruvian descent charged with
sending information to Germany about
British troop movements, for which he
received a salary of £30 a month.*

10 Josef Jakobs   Aug 15, 1941

*A German army sergeant who was caught
when he parachuted into England wearing
civilian clothes and carrying an identity card
in the name of James Rymer. Following
General Court Martial, he was shot at
7:15 AM – the only spy executed at the Tower
during the course of World War II.*

THE 10

US STATES WITH THE MOST PRISONERS ON DEATH ROW

	State	No. under death sentence
1	Texas	394
2	California	381
3	Florida	342
4	Pennsylvania	182
5	Illinois	155
6	Ohio	140
7	Alabama	135
8	Oklahoma	129
9	Arizona	121
10	North Carolina	111

As at January 1, 1995, there were 2,890 inmates under sentence of death, and there were 36 states in the Federal Prison System that still operated death penalty laws.

THE 10

US STATES WITH THE MOST WOMEN ON DEATH ROW

	State	Women under death sentence*
1	California	7
2	Texas	6
3=	Florida	5
3=	Illinois	5
3=	Oklahoma	5
6=	Alabama	4
6=	Pennsylvania	4
8=	Missouri	2
8=	North Carolina	2
10=	Arizona	1
10=	Idaho	1
10=	Louisiana	1
10=	Mississippi	1
10=	Nevada	1
10=	Tennessee	1

* As at January 1, 1996

THE 10

US STATES WITH THE MOST EXECUTIONS

	State	Method now in force	Executed 1930–94
1	Georgia	Electrocution	384
2	Texas	Lethal injection	382
3	New York	Lethal injection	329
4	California	Lethal gas	294
5	North Carolina	Lethal gas or injection	269
6	Florida	Electrocution	203
7	Ohio	Electrocution or lethal injection	172
8	South Carolina	Electrocution	166
9	Mississippi	Lethal injection*	158
10	Louisiana	Lethal injection	154

* Lethal gas if sentenced prior to July 1, 1984

THE 10

YEARS WITH THE MOST EXECUTIONS IN THE US*

	Year	Executions
1	1935	199
2	1936	195
3	1938	190
4	1934	168
5=	1933	160
5=	1939	160
7	1930	155
8=	1931	153
8=	1947	153
10	1937	147

* All offenses, 1930 to the present

The total number of executions in the US fell below three figures for the first time this century in 1952, when 82 prisoners were executed, and below double figures in 1965, with seven executions. There were no executions at all between 1968 and 1976, but double figures were recorded again in 1984 and in all subsequent years.

THE 10

LAST MEN HANGED FOR MURDER IN THE UK

	Man	Hanged
1	John Robson Welby	Aug 13, 1964
2	Peter Anthony Allen	Aug 13, 1964
3	Dennis Whitty	Dec 17, 1963
4	Russell Pascoe	Dec 17, 1963
5	Henry Burnett	Aug 15, 1963
6	James Smith	Nov 28, 1962
7	Oswald Grey	Nov 20, 1962
8	James Hanratty	Apr 4, 1962
9	Hendryk Niemasz	Sep 8, 1961
10	Samuel McLaughlin	Jul 25, 1961

THE 10

WORST YEARS OF THE 20TH CENTURY FOR LYNCHINGS IN THE US

	Year	Lynchings
1	1901	130
2	1900	115
3	1903	99
4	1908	97
5	1902	92
6=	1904	83
6=	1919	83
8	1909	82
9	1910	76
10	1915	69

Lynchings are the "rough justice" of a mob who seize a crime suspect and hang him or her without trial. They reached a 19th-century peak in the US in 1892, when 230 victims were recorded. The year 1901 was the last in which more than 100 people met this fate, but the practice declined only slowly. 1932 was the first year with a single-figure tally of eight (although the figure rose again to 28 in the following year). Lynchings continued intermittently up to modern times, with the last three cases recorded in 1964. Mississippi has the worst record, with 577 lynchings in the period 1882–1956.

THE WORLD AT WAR

LARGEST ARMED FORCES OF WORLD WAR I

	Country	Personnel*
1	Russia	12,000,000
2	Germany	11,000,000
3	British Empire#	8,904,467
4	France	8,410,000
5	Austria–Hungary	7,800,000
6	Italy	5,615,000
7	US	4,355,000
8	Turkey	2,850,000
9	Bulgaria	1,200,000
10	Japan	800,000

* *Total at peak strength*
\# *Including Australia, Canada, India, New Zealand, South Africa, and other countries in the Commonwealth*

As well as the 10 principal military powers, several other European nations had forces that were similarly substantial in relation to their populations: Romania had an army of 750,000, Serbia 707,343, Belgium 267,000, Greece 230,000, Portugal 100,000, and Montenegro 50,000 – a total of more than 65,000,000 combatants.

COUNTRIES SUFFERING THE GREATEST MILITARY LOSSES IN WORLD WAR I

	Country	Killed
1	Germany	1,773,700
2	Russia	1,700,000
3	France	1,357,800
4	Austria–Hungary	1,200,000
5	British Empire	908,371
6	Italy	650,000
7	Romania	335,706
8	Turkey	325,000
9	US	116,516
10	Bulgaria	87,500

The number of battle fatalities and deaths from other causes among military personnel varied enormously from country to country: Romania's death rate was highest at 45 percent; Germany's was 16 percent, Austria–Hungary's and Russia's 15 percent, and the British Empire's 10 percent.

BLOODIEST BATTLES OF THE 20TH CENTURY

In the Russo-Japanese War, the 1905 Battle of Mukden left some 163,400 dead, more than 30 percent of the troops. Appalling though this was, it does not begin to compare with the major battles of the two World Wars. In World War I, the first of two major battles of the Somme, fought between June and November 1916, produced the greatest number of casualties of any battle in history: 398,671 British and approximately 650,000 German and 195,000 French troops lost their lives, a total of 1,243,671. In World War II the Battle of Stalingrad, between German and Soviet armies, from August 1942 until February 1943, is reckoned to have cost the lives of 1,109,000.

ALLIES
This World War I badge shows the united flags of France, Britain, and Belgium.

COUNTRIES WITH THE MOST PRISONERS OF WAR, 1914–18

	Country	Prisoners
1	Russia	2,500,000
2	Austria–Hungary	2,200,000
3	Germany	1,152,800
4	Italy	600,000
5	France	537,000
6	Turkey	250,000
7	British Empire	191,652
8	Serbia	152,958
9	Romania	80,000
10	Belgium	34,659

FIRST COUNTRIES TO DECLARE WAR IN WORLD WAR II

	Declaration	Date
1=	UK on Germany	Sep 3, 1939
1=	Australia on Germany	Sep 3, 1939
1=	New Zealand on Germany	Sep 3, 1939
1=	France on Germany	Sep 3, 1939
5	South Africa on Germany	Sep 6, 1939
6	Canada on Germany	Sep 9, 1939
7	Italy on UK and France	Jun 10, 1940
8	France on Italy	Jun 11, 1940
9=	Japan on US, UK, Australia, Canada, New Zealand, and South Africa	Dec 7, 1941
9=	UK on Finland, Hungary, and Romania	Dec 7, 1941

The last of these declarations took place on the day of the Japanese attack on Pearl Harbor, as a result of which the US (as well as the UK and Free France) declared war on Japan the next day. On December 11, 1941, Germany and Italy declared war on the US, which was followed the same day by a counter-declaration by the US. Further declarations followed right up to 1945, some even in the closing months of the war. Italy, for example, declared war on Japan as late as July 14, 1945. The UK did not declare a cessation of war against Germany until July 9, 1951, which was followed by the US on October 19, 1951.

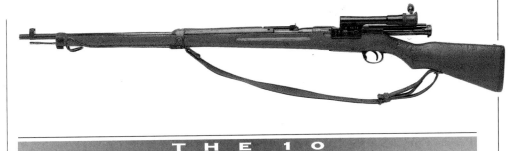

LARGEST ARMED FORCES OF WORLD WAR II

	Country	Personnel*
1	USSR	12,500,000
2	US	12,364,000
3	Germany	10,000,000
4	Japan	6,095,000
5	France	5,700,000
6	UK	4,683,000
7	Italy	4,500,000
8	China	3,800,000
9	India	2,150,000
10	Poland	1,000,000

* Total at peak strength

SMALLEST ARMED FORCES OF WORLD WAR II

	Country	Personnel*
1	Costa Rica	400
2	Liberia	1,000
3=	El Salvador	3,000
3=	Honduras	3,000
3=	Nicaragua	3,000
6	Haiti	3,500
7	Dominican Republic	4,000
8	Guatemala	5,000
9=	Bolivia	8,000
9=	Paraguay	8,000
9=	Uruguay	8,000

* Total at peak strength

Several of the South American countries entered World War II at a very late stage: Argentina, for example, did not declare war on Germany and Japan until March 27, 1945. Denmark, whose maximum strength was 15,000, had the smallest armed force in Europe. Just 13 of the Danish soldiers were killed during the one-day German invasion of April 9, 1940, when Denmark became the second country after Poland to be occupied.

COUNTRIES SUFFERING THE GREATEST MILITARY LOSSES IN WORLD WAR II

	Country	Killed
1	USSR	13,600,000
2	Germany	3,300,000
3	China	1,324,516
4	Japan	1,140,429
5	British Empire* (of which UK	357,116 264,000)
6	Romania	350,000
7	Poland	320,000
8	Yugoslavia	305,000
9	US	292,131
10	Italy	279,800

* Including Australia, Canada, India, South Africa, and other Commonwealth countries

The actual numbers killed in World War II have been the subject of intense argument for nearly 50 years. The immense level of the military casualty rate of the USSR in particular is hard to comprehend. It is included here at its lowest likely level, but most authorities now reckon that of the 30,000,000 Soviets who bore arms, as many as 8,500,000 died in action and up to 2,500,000 of wounds received in battle and disease. Some 5,800,000 were taken prisoner, of which perhaps 3,300,000 may have died in captivity. It should also be borne in mind that these were military losses: to these should be added many untold millions of civilian war deaths. Recent estimates have suggested an additional figure of up to 25,000,000 civilian deaths as a result of Stalinist purges, which began just before the outbreak of war.

TANKS OF WORLD WAR II

	Tank	Introduced	Country	Weight (tons)	No. produced
1	M4A3 Sherman	1942	US	31.0	41,530
2	T34 Model 42	1940	USSR	28.5	35,120
3	T34/85	1944	USSR	32.0	29,430
4	M3 General Stuart	1941	US	12.2	14,000
5	Valentine II	1941	UK	17.5	8,280
6	M3A1 Lee/Grant	1941	US	26.8	7,400
7	Churchill VII	1942	UK	40.0	5,640
8=	Panzer IVD	pre-war	Germany	20.0	5,500
8=	Panzer VG	1943	Germany	44.8	5,500
10	Crusader I	1941	UK	19.0	4,750

The tank named after US Civil War General William Tecumseh Sherman was used in large numbers by both US and British troops. It carried a crew of five and could cruise over a distance of 143 miles/230 km at up to 25 mph/40 km/h. Its weaponry comprised two machine guns and, originally, a 75-mm cannon, but after 1944 about half had this replaced by a cannon capable of firing a powerful 17 lb shell or a 12 lb armor-piercing shell.

ACES HIGH

The term "ace" was first used during World War I for a pilot who had brought down at least five enemy aircraft. The first-ever reference in print to an air "ace" appeared in an article in *The Times* (September 14, 1917), which described Raoul Lufbery as "the 'ace' of the American Lafayette Flying Squadron." The names of French pilots who achieved this feat were recorded in official communiqués, but although American and other pilots followed the same system, the British definition of an "ace" varied from three to 10 aircraft and was never officially approved.

TOP 10
BRITISH AND COMMONWEALTH AIR ACES OF WORLD WAR I

	Pilot	Nationality	Kills claimed
1	Edward Mannock	British	73
2	William Avery Bishop	Canadian	72
3	Raymond Collishaw	Canadian	62
4	James Thomas Byford McCudden	British	57
5=	Anthony Wetherby Beauchamp-Proctor	South African	54
5=	Donald MacLaren	Canadian	54
7=	William George Barker	Canadian	52
7=	Philip Fletcher Fullard	British	52
9	R.S. Dallas	Australian	51
10	George Edward Henry McElroy	Irish	49

AN EARLY GERMAN BOMBER, 1917
The LVG CVI, fitted with guns and able to carry bombs, was one of the most versatile aeroplanes of World War I.

This Top 10 takes account of British Empire pilots belonging to the Royal Flying Corps, the Royal Naval Air Service, and (after April 1, 1918) the Royal Air Force. The total of Edward "Mick" Mannock (1887–1918) may actually be greater than those definitely credited to him. Recent evidence also suggests that Major Raymond Collishaw may have achieved as many as 81 kills, but that interservice rivalries led to many of his kills not being confirmed.

TOP 10
BRITISH AND COMMONWEALTH AIR ACES OF WORLD WAR II

	Pilot	Nationality	Kills claimed*
1	Marmaduke Thomas St. John Pattle	South African	51
2	James Edgar "Johnny" Johnson	British	38
3	Adolf Gysbert "Sailor" Malan	South African	35
4	Brendan "Paddy" Finucane	Irish	32
5	George Frederick Beurling	Canadian	31⅓
6=	John Robert Daniel Braham	British	29
6=	Robert Roland Stanford Tuck	British	29
8	Neville Frederick Duke	British	28⅚
9	Clive Robert Caldwell	Australian	28½
10	Frank Reginald Carey	British	28⅓

* Kills that are expressed as fractions refer to those that were shared with others

TOP 10
US AIR ACES OF WORLD WAR II

	Pilot	Kills claimed
1	Richard I. Bong	40
2	Thomas B. McGuire	38
3	David S. McCampbell	34
4=	Francis S. Gabreski*	28
4=	Gregory "Pappy" Boynington	28
6=	Robert S. Johnson	27
6=	Charles H. MacDonald	27
8=	George E. Preddy	26
8=	Joseph J. Foss	26
10	Robert M. Hanson	25

* Also 6½ kills in Korean War

TOP 10

GERMAN AIR ACES OF WORLD WAR I

	Pilot	Kills claimed
1	Manfred von Richthofen*	80
2	Ernst Udet	62
3	Erich Loewenhardt	53
4	Werner Voss	48
5=	Bruno Loerzer	45
5=	Fritz Rumey	45
7	Rudolph Berthold	44
8	Paul Bäumer	43
9	Josef Jacobs	41
10=	Oswald Boelcke	40
10=	Franz Büchner	40
10=	Lothar Freiherr von Richthofen*	40

* Brothers

Top World War I "ace" Rittmeister Manfred, Baron von Richthofen's claim of 80 kills has been disputed, since only 60 of them have been completely confirmed. Richthofen, known as the "Red Baron" and leader of the so-called "Flying Circus" (because the aircraft of his squadron were painted in distinctive, bright colors), shot down 21 Allied fighters in the single month of April 1917. His own end a year later, on April 21, 1918, has been the subject of controversy ever since, and it remains uncertain whether his Fokker triplane was shot down in aerial combat with British pilot Captain A. Roy Brown (who was credited with the kill) or by shots from Australian machine gunners on the ground.

THE "RED BARON"
The German pilot Rittmeister Manfred, Baron von Richthofen, has passed into legend as the greatest air ace of World War I.

TOP 10

JAPANESE AIR ACES OF WORLD WAR II

	Pilot	Kills claimed
1	Hiroyoshi Nishizawa	87
2	Tetsuzo Iwamoto	80
3	Shoichi Sugita	70
4	Saburo Sakai	64
5	Takeo Okumura	54
6	Toshio Ohta	34
7	Kazuo Sugino	32
8	Shizuo Ishii	29
9	Kaeneyoshi Muto	28
10=	Sadaaki Akamatsu	27
10=	Junichi Sasai	27

Doubts remain concerning the status of some of Japan's air aces: Warrant Officer Hiroyoshi Nishizawa's "score" has been put as high as 102–107, while Shoichi Sugita is sometimes credited with 120 kills. More than half of the pilots appearing in this Top 10 would have higher scores if their victories in China, prior to the outbreak of World War II, were taken into account.

TOP 10

LUFTWAFFE ACES OF WORLD WAR II

	Pilot	Kills claimed
1	Eric Hartmann	352
2	Gerhard Barkhorn	301
3	Günther Rall	275
4	Otto Kittel	267
5	Walther Nowotny	255
6	Wilhelm Batz	237
7	Erich Rudorffer	222
8	Heinrich Baer	220
9	Herman Graf	212
10	Heinrich Ehrler	209

Although these apparently high claims have been dismissed by some military historians as inflated for propaganda purposes, it is worth noting that many of them relate to "kills" on the Eastern Front, where the Luftwaffe was undoubtedly superior to its Soviet opponents, and some of them relate to kills on the ground. All those in the Top 10 were day-fighter aces; the highest "score" by a night-fighter was the 121 kills credited to Heinz-Wolfgang Schnauffer.

TOP 10

US AIR ACES OF THE KOREAN WAR

	Pilot	Kills claimed
1	Joseph McConnell, Jr.	16
2	James Jabara	15
3	Manuel J. Fernandez	14½
4	George A. Davis, Jr.	14
5	Royal N. Baker	13
6=	Frederick C. Blesse	10
6=	Harold H. Fischer	10
6=	Vermont Garrison	10
6=	James K. Johnson	10
6=	Lonnie R. Moore	10
6=	Ralph S. Parr, Jr.	10

The Korean War produced the first air aces among jet fighter pilots. Five of the pilots listed here already had kills to their credit dating from actions in conventional fighters during World War II – in the case of George Davis, a total of seven, making 21 in total, a post-war record that remained unbroken until the more recent Arab–Israeli conflicts.

WAR IN THE AIR

THE 10

AREAS OF EUROPE MOST BOMBED BY ALLIED AIRCRAFT*, 1939–45

	Area	Bombs dropped (tons)
1	Germany	1,350,321
2	France	583,318
3	Italy	366,524
4	Austria, Hungary, and the Balkans	180,828
5	Belgium and Netherlands	88,739
6	Southern Europe and the Mediterranean	76,505
7	Czechoslovakia and Poland	21,419
8	Norway and Denmark	5,297
9	Sea targets	564
10	British Channel Islands	93

* British and US

Between August 1942 and May 1945 alone, Allied air forces (Bomber Command plus 8 and 15 US Air Forces) flew 731,969 night sorties (and Bomber Command a further 67,598 day sorties), dropping a total of 1,850,919 tons of bombs on Europe.

THE 10

EUROPEAN CITIES MOST BOMBED BY THE RAF AND USAF

	City	Estimated civilian deaths
1	Dresden	over 100,000
2	Hamburg	55,000
3	Berlin	49,000
4	Cologne	20,000
5	Magdeburg	15,000
6	Kassel	13,000
7	Darmstadt	12,300
8=	Heilbronn	7,500
8=	Essen	7,500
10=	Dortmund	6,000
10=	Wuppertal	6,000

The high level of casualties in Dresden resulted principally from saturation bombing and the firestorm that ensued after Allied raids on the lightly defended city. The scale of the raids was massive: 775 British bombers took part in the first night's raid on February 13, 1945, followed the next day by 450 US bombers, with a final attack by 200 US bombers on February 15.

THE 10

COUNTRIES SUFFERING THE GREATEST AIRCRAFT LOSSES IN WORLD WAR II

	Country	Aircraft lost
1	Germany	116,584
2	USSR	106,652
3	US	59,296
4	Japan	49,485
5	UK	33,090
6	Australia	7,160
7	Italy	5,272
8	Canada	2,389
9	France	2,100
10	New Zealand	684

Reports of aircraft losses vary considerably from country to country. Some of them include aircraft damaged, lost due to accidents, or scrapped, as well as those destroyed during combat. The Japanese figure for combat-only losses, for example, is often reported as 38,105. The Soviet losses are believed to include aircraft withdrawn from front lines as well as those destroyed.

THE 10

MONTHS OF MOST AIR STRIKES AGAINST JAPAN*

	Month	Bombs (tons) high explosive	incendiary	Total
1	July 1945	9,388	33,163	42,551
2	June 1945	9,954	22,588	32,542
3	May 1945	6,937	17,348	24,285
4	August 1945	8,438	12,591	21,029
5	April 1945	13,209	4,283	17,492
6	March 1945	4,105	11,138	15,243
7	February 1945	2,401	1,619	4,020
8	December 1944	3,051	610	3,661
9	January 1945	2,511	899	3,410
10	November 1944	1,758	447	2,205

* By 20 US Air Force, June 1944 to August 1945

Attacks on Japan by 20 US Air Force began in June 1944, originally flying B-29 bombers from bases in India and later from the captured Marianas Islands.

TOP 10

LUFTWAFFE AIRCRAFT OF WORLD WAR II

	Model	Type	No. produced
1	Messerschmitt Me 109	Fighter	30,480
2	Focke-Wulf Fw 190	Fighter	20,000
3	Junkers Ju 88	Bomber	15,000
4	Messerschmitt Me 110	Fighter-bomber	5,762
5	Heinkel He 111	Bomber	5,656
6	Junkers Ju 87	Dive bomber	4,881
7	Junkers Ju 52	Transport	2,804
8	Fiesler Fi 156	Communications	2,549
9	Dornier Do 217	Bomber	1,730
10	Heinkel He 177	Bomber	1,446

The three-engined version of the Heinkel Ju 52, the Ju 52/3m, was especially ugly and went by such nicknames as "Iron Annie" and "Corrugated Coffin." It was, however, extremely reliable and was used extensively as a troop-carrier and for dropping paratroops. It was also chosen by Hitler as his personal aircraft.

THE DESTRUCTION OF DRESDEN
The massive raids on Dresden caused a firestorm that destroyed the ancient German city, killing perhaps as many as 100,000 – although as their memorial asks, "How many died? Who knows the number?"

THE 10
MOST HEAVILY BLITZED CITIES IN THE UK

	City	Major raids	Tonnage of high explosive
1	London	85	23,949
2	Liverpool/Birkenhead	8	1,957
3	Birmingham	8	1,852
4	Glasgow/Clydeside	5	1,329
5	Plymouth/Devonport	8	1,228
6	Bristol/Avonmouth	6	919
7	Coventry	2	818
8	Portsmouth	3	687
9	Southampton	4	647
10	Hull	3	593

TOP 10
FASTEST FIGHTER AIRCRAFT OF WORLD WAR II

	Aircraft	Country of origin	Maximum speed km/h	mph
1	Messerschmitt *Me 163*	Germany	959	596
2	Messerschmitt *Me 262*	Germany	901	560
3	Heinkel *He 162A*	Germany	890	553
4	*P-51-H Mustang*	US	784	487
5	Lavochkin *La11*	USSR	740	460
6	*Spitfire XIV*	UK	721	448
7	Yakolev *Yak-3*	USSR	719	447
8	*P-51-D Mustang*	US	708	440
9	*Tempest VI*	UK	705	438
10	Focke-Wulf *Fw 190D*	Germany	700	435

Also known as the *Komet*, the Messerschmitt *Me 163* was a short-range, rocket-powered interceptor brought into service in 1944–45, when it scored a number of victories over its slower Allied rivals. The Messerschmitt *Me 262* was the first jet in operational service and the first aircraft to use air-to-air missiles, which were employed with devastating effect against Allied bombers.

TOP 10
ALLIED AIRCRAFT OF WORLD WAR II

	Model/type	No. produced
1	Ilyushin *Il-2m3*, ground-attack	36,200
2	Supermarine *Spitfire*, fighter	20,350
3	Consolidated *Liberator*, bomber	18,500
4	Yakolev *Yak-9D*, fighter	16,800
5	Republic *Thunderbolt*, fighter	15,630
6	North American *Mustang*, fighter	15,470
7	Hawker *Hurricane*, fighter	14,230
8	Curtiss *Kittyhawk*, fighter-bomber	13,740
9	Vought *Corsair*, carrier-fighter	12,750
10	Boeing *Flying Fortress*, bomber	12,700

FAST AND FURIOUS
More than 20,000 of the fast and highly maneuverable Spitfires were built during the course of World War II.

WAR AT SEA

TOP 10

LARGEST NAVIES 100 YEARS AGO

	Country	Guns	No. of personnel	Ships*
1	UK	3,631	94,600	659
2	France	1,735	70,600	457
3	Russia	710	31,000	358
4	Italy	611	23,000	267
5	Germany	608	16,500	217
6	Austria	309	9,000	168
7	Netherlands	256	10,000	140
8	Spain	305	16,700	136
9	Turkey	382	23,000	124
10	US	284	10,000	95

* Including battleships, cruisers, gunboats, and torpedo boats

SINKING SHIPS

The *kami kaze*, or "divine wind" that destroyed an invading Mongol fleet in 1281 was adopted as the name for Japan's World War II suicide pilots. Kamikaze attacks sank a total of 34 and damaged 288 US Navy ships, with the loss of 1,228 pilots. The principal cause of losses of Allied ships during World War II was, however, attack by Axis submarines. Some 2,828 vessels with a combined tonnage of 14,687,231 were sunk by this means, 820 ships (2,889,883 tons) as a result of air assaults, while mines accounted for the loss of 534 ships (1,406,037 tons).

TOP 10

U-BOAT COMMANDERS OF WORLD WAR II

	Commander	U-boats commanded	Ships sunk
1	Otto Kretschmer	U-23, U-99	45
2	Wolfgang Luth	U-9, U-138, U-43, U-181	44
3	Joachim Schepke	U-3, U-19, U-100	39
4	Erich Topp	U-57, U-552	35
5	Victor Schutze	U-25, U-103	34
6	Heinrich Leibe	U-38	30
7	Karl F. Merten	U-68	29*
8	Günther Prien	U-47	29*
9	Johann Mohr	U-124	29*
10	Georg Lassen	U-160	28

* Gross tonnage used to determine ranking

Günther Prien (born January 16, 1908, killed in action March 7, 1941) performed the remarkable feat of penetrating the British naval base at Scapa Flow on October 14, 1939 and sinking the Royal Navy battleship *Royal Oak* at anchor. For this exploit he was awarded the Knight's Cross, the first of 318 to be won by members of the German navy during World War II. Prien was killed when the *U-47* was sunk.

TOP 10

US NAVY SUBMARINE COMMANDERS OF WORLD WAR II

	Commander	Submarines commanded	Ships sunk
1	Richard H. O'Kane	*Tang*	31
2	Eugene B. Fluckley	*Barb*	25
3	Slade D. Cutter	*Seahorse*	21
4	Samuel D. Dealey	*Harder*	20½*
5	William S. Post, Jr.	*Gudgeon* and *Spot*	19
6	Reuben T. Whitaker	*S-44* and *Flasher*	18½*
7	Walter T. Griffith	*Bowfin* and *Bullhead*	17#
8	Dudley W. Morton	*R-5* and *Wahoo*	17#
9	John E. Lee	*S-12*, *Grayling*, and *Croaker*	16
10	William B. Sieglaff	*Tautog* and *Tench*	15

* ½ refers to shared "kills"
# Gross tonnage used to determine ranking order

THE 10

GREATEST MERCHANT SHIPPING LOSSES IN WORLD WAR II

	Country	Vessels sunk Number	Tonnage
1	UK	4,786	21,194,000
2	Japan	2,346	8,618,109
3	Germany	1,595	7,064,600
4	US	578	3,524,983
5	Norway	427	1,728,531
6	Netherlands	286	1,195,204
7	Italy	467	1,155,080
8	Greece	262	883,200
9	Panama	107	542,772
10	Sweden	204	481,864

TOP 10

SUBMARINE FLEETS OF WORLD WAR II

	Country	Submarines
1	Japan	163*
2	US	112*
3	France	77
4	USSR	75
5	Germany	57
6	UK	38
7	Netherlands	21
8	Italy	15*
9	Denmark	12*
10	Greece	6*

Strength in December 1941

This list shows submarine strengths at the outbreak of World War II. During hostilities, the warring nations increased their production prodigiously: from 1939 to 1945 the Axis powers (Germany, Italy, and Japan) commissioned a further 1,337 submarines (1,141 by Germany alone), and the Allies commissioned only 422.

TOP 10

LARGEST BATTLESHIPS OF WORLD WAR II

	Battleship	Country	Status	Length m	ft	Tonnage
1=	*Musashi*	Japan	Sank October 25, 1944	263	862	72,809
1=	*Yamato*	Japan	Sank April 7, 1945	263	862	72,809
3=	*Iowa*	US	Still in service with US Navy	270	887	55,710
3=	*Missouri*	US	Still in service with US Navy	270	887	55,710
3=	*New Jersey*	US	Still in service with US Navy	270	887	55,710
3=	*Wisconsin*	US	Still in service with US Navy	270	887	55,710
7=	*Bismarck*	Germany	Sank May 27, 1941	251	823	50,153
7=	*Tirpitz*	Germany	Sank November 12, 1944	251	823	50,153
9=	*Jean Bart*	France	Survived war, later scrapped	247	812	47,500
9=	*Richelieu*	France	Survived war, later scrapped	247	812	47,500

THE OLD WARHORSE
One of the largest battleships in service during World War II, the 887-ft/270-m USS New Jersey *last saw action as recently as the Gulf War of 1990.*

MODERN MILITARY

AWARDED FOR VALOUR
The Victoria Cross is Britain's highest military award. Established in 1856, its design was chosen by Queen Victoria.

T O P 1 0

LARGEST ARMED FORCES IN THE WORLD

	Country		Estimated active forces		
		Army	Navy	Air Force	Total
1	China	2,200,000	260,000	470,000	2,930,000
2	US	559,900	482,800*	433,800	1,476,500
3	India	1,100,000	55,000	110,000	1,265,000
4	Russia	780,000	295,000	170,000	1,245,000#
5	North Korea	1,000,000	46,000	82,000	1,128,000
6	South Korea	520,000	60,000	53,000	633,000
7	Pakistan	520,000	22,000	45,000	587,000
8	Vietnam	500,000	42,000	15,000	557,000
9	Turkey	393,000	54,000	56,800	503,800
10	Taiwan	289,000	68,000	68,000	425,000

* *Plus 174,000 Marines*
\# *Balance of total comprises Strategic Deterrent Forces, Paramilitary, National Guard, etc.*

In addition to the active forces listed here, many of the world's foremost military powers have considerable reserves on standby. South Korea's are estimated at some 4,500,000; Vietnam's at 3–4,000,000; Russia's, 3,000,000; the US's, 1,784,050; China's, 1,200,000; and Turkey's, 1,107,000. China is also notable for having a massive arsenal of military equipment at its disposal, including some 8,000 tanks and 4,600 fighter aircraft.

T O P 1 0

CAMPAIGNS IN WHICH THE MOST VICTORIA CROSSES HAVE BEEN WON

	Campaign	Year(s)	VCs
1	World War I	1914–18	634
2=	Indian Mutiny	1857–58	182
2=	World War II	1939–45	182
4	Crimean War	1854–56	111
5	Second Boer War	1899–1902	78
6	Zulu War	1879	23
7	Second Afghan War	1878–80	16
8	Waikato–Hauhau Maori War	1863–66	13
9	Third China War	1860	7
10=	Basuto War	1879–82	6
10=	First Boer War	1880–81	6

This Top 10 accounts for all but 92 of the 1,350 VCs ever awarded up to the 1982 Falklands conflict between the UK and Argentina, in which two VCs were posthumously awarded to Lt-Col. "H" Jones and Sgt. Ian McKay, both of the Parachute Regiment.

T H E 1 0

20TH-CENTURY WARS WITH THE MOST MILITARY FATALITIES

	War/years	Approximate no. of fatalities
1	World War II (1939–45)	15,843,000
2	World War I (1914–18)	8,545,800
3	Korean War (1950–53)	1,893,100
4=	Sino-Japanese War (1937–41)	1,000,000
4=	Biafra–Nigeria Civil War (1967–70)	1,000,000
6	Spanish Civil War (1936–39)	611,000
7	Vietnam War (1961–73)	546,000
8=	India–Pakistan War (1947)	200,000
8=	Soviet invasion of Afghanistan (1979–89)	200,000
8=	Iran–Iraq War (1980–88)	200,000

The statistics of warfare have always been an imperfect science. Not only are battle deaths seldom recorded accurately, but figures are often deliberately inflated by both sides in a conflict. For political reasons and to maintain morale, each is anxious to enhance reports of its military success and low casualty figures, so that often quite contradictory reports of the same battle may be issued. These figures thus represent military historians' "best guesses."

TOP 10

RANKS OF THE US NAVY, ARMY, AND AIR FORCE

	Navy	Army	Air Force
1	Admiral	General	General
2	Vice Admiral	Lieutenant General	Lieutenant General
3	Rear Admiral (Upper Half)	Major General	Major General
4	Rear Admiral (Lower Half)	Brigadier General	Brigadier General
5	Captain	Colonel	Colonel
6	Commodore	Lieutenant Colonel	Lieutenant Colonel
7	Lieutenant Commander	Major	Major
8	Lieutenant	Captain	Captain
9	Lieutenant (Junior Grade)	First Lieutenant	First Lieutenant
10	Ensign	Second Lieutenant	Second Lieutenant

STORMIN' NORMAN'S DESERT VICTORY
General Norman Schwarzkopf acknowledges the applause from a special meeting of the US Congress. He declared, "It's a great day to be a soldier and a great day to be an American."

TOP 10

RANKS OF THE ROYAL NAVY, ARMY, AND ROYAL AIR FORCE

	Royal Navy	Army	Royal Air Force
1	Admiral of the Fleet	Field Marshal	Marshal of the Royal Air Force
2	Admiral	General	Air Chief Marshal
3	Vice-Admiral	Lieutenant-General	Air Marshal
4	Rear-Admiral	Major-General	Air Vice-Marshal
5	Commodore	Brigadier	Air Commodore
6	Captain	Colonel	Group Captain
7	Commander	Lieutenant-Colonel	Wing Commander
8	Lieutenant-Commander	Major	Squadron Leader
9	Lieutenant	Captain	Flight Lieutenant
10	Sub-Lieutenant	Lieutenant	Flying Officer

TOP 10

COUNTRIES WITH THE LARGEST UN PEACEKEEPING FORCES*

	Country	Troop totals
1	US	2,449
2	Pakistan	2,298
3	Bangladesh	2,009
4	India	1,986
5	Russia	1,229
6	Nepal	1,141
7	Brazil	1,131
8	Ghana	1,049
9	Finland	1,028
10	Norway	995

* *As of January 31, 1996*

United Nations peacekeeping forces are established by the UN Security Council. Although most UN member states provide troops, they are most frequently drawn from neutral or nonaligned members.

TOP 10

COUNTRIES WITH THE LARGEST DEFENSE BUDGETS

	Country	Budget ($)		Country	Budget ($)
1	US	511,700,000,000	6	UK	34,000,000,000
2	Russia	79,000,000,000	7	Italy	16,100,000,000
3	Germany	47,200,000,000	8	South Korea	14,000,000,000
4	Japan	42,100,000,000	9	Saudi Arabia	13,900,000,000
5	France	35,600,000,000	10	Canada	11,600,000,000

WORLD RELIGIONS

THE WAY OF BUDDHA
Originating in India in the 6th century BC, Buddhism's quest for enlightenment and its espousal of peace and tolerance has contributed to its appeal throughout Asia and beyond.

TOP 10

LARGEST BUDDHIST POPULATIONS IN THE WORLD

	Location	Total Buddhist population
1	China	101,000,000
2	Japan	97,320,000*
3	Thailand	54,340,000
4	Vietnam	48,220,000
5	Myanmar (Burma)	40,760,000
6	South Korea	16,130,000
7	Sri Lanka	12,360,000
8	Taiwan	9,060,000
9	Cambodia	9,050,000
10	India	6,000,000

* Including many who also practice Shintoism

TOP 10

LARGEST CHRISTIAN POPULATIONS IN THE WORLD

	Location	Total Christian population
1	US	222,580,000
2	Brazil	138,300,000
3	Mexico	87,860,000
4	Germany	61,930,000
5	Philippines	61,450,000
6	UK	50,910,000
7	Italy	47,580,000
8	Nigeria	45,800,000
9	France	42,850,000
10	Russia	37,400,000

Surveys indicate that, while almost 90 percent of the US population is Christian, only 63 percent actively practice their religion.

TOP 10

ORGANIZED RELIGIONS IN THE WORLD

	Religion	Members
1	Christianity	1,900,174,000
2	Islam	1,033,453,000
3	Hinduism	764,000,000
4	Buddhism	338,621,000
5	Sikhism	20,204,000
6	Judaism	13,451,000
7	Confucianism	6,334,000
8	Baha'ism	5,835,000
9	Jainism	3,987,000
10	Shintoism	3,387,800

This list excludes the followers of various tribal and folk religions, new religions, and shamanism, who together total more than 400,000,000. Since reforms in the former USSR, many who practiced Christianity in secret while following the Communist anti-religion line in public have now declared their faith openly. This list is based on the work of David B. Barrett, who has been monitoring world religions for many years.

TOP 10

CHRISTIAN AFFILIATIONS IN THE WORLD

	Affiliation	Members
1	Roman Catholicism	872,104,646
2	Slavonic Orthodox	92,523,987
3	United (including Lutheran/Reformed)	65,402,685
4	Pentecostal	58,999,862
5	Anglican	52,499,051
6	Baptist	50,321,923
7	Lutheran (excluding United)	44,899,837
8	Reformed (Presbyterian)	43,445,520
9	Methodist	31,718,508
10	Disciples (Restorationists)	8,783,192

This Top 10 is based on mid-1980s estimates that have not been updated. The difficulty at arriving at figures for religious membership is exemplified by a later report by the Vatican that increased the figure for Roman Catholics to 911,000,000, while independent sources put the number well in excess of 1,000,000,000.

TOP 10

COUNTRIES MOST VISITED BY POPE JOHN PAUL II

	Country	Visits
1	Poland	5
2=	France	4
2=	Spain	4
2=	US*	4
5=	Kenya	3
5=	Mexico	3
5=	Brazil	3
5=	Ivory Coast	3
9=	Argentina, Australia, Austria, Belgium, Benin, Canada, Dominican Republic, Guinea, Papua New Guinea, Peru, Philippines, Portugal, South Korea, Switzerland, Uruguay, West Germany, Zaïre	2

* Includes a 1984 stopover in Alaska

After taking office as Pope in 1978, John Paul II broke with tradition and embarked on a series of travels. Prior to these trips, only one modern Pope had traveled outside Italy (Paul VI went to Israel in 1964).

TOP 10

LARGEST JEWISH POPULATIONS IN THE WORLD

	Location	Total Jewish population		Location	Total Jewish population
1	US	5,900,000	6	UK	300,000
2	Israel	3,755,000	7	Argentina	250,000
3	Russia	1,449,117	8	Brazil	150,000
4	France	600,000	9	South Africa	114,000
5	Canada	350,000	10	Australia	92,000

TOP 10

LARGEST HINDU POPULATIONS IN THE WORLD

	Location	Total Hindu population
1	India	734,000,000
2	Nepal	16,820,000
3	Bangladesh	14,240,000
4	Sri Lanka	2,760,000
5	Pakistan	1,980,000
6	Malaysia	1,370,000
7	US	900,000
8	Mauritius	570,000
9	South Africa	440,000
10	UK	410,000

TOP 10

LARGEST MUSLIM POPULATIONS IN THE WORLD

	Location	Total Muslim population
1	Indonesia	169,840,000
2	Pakistan	127,230,000
3	Bangladesh	101,730,000
4	India	100,000,000
5	Turkey	60,690,000
6	Iran	59,140,000
7	Egypt	52,600,000
8	Nigeria	42,060,000
9	Algeria	27,790,000
10	Morocco	26,240,000

PRACTICING THE JEWISH FAITH
As a result of centuries of persecution, the greatest concentrations of Jewish people are found in the countries to which their ancestors fled as refugees.

TOP 10

RELIGIOUS GROUPS IN THE US

	Religious group	Members
1	Protestant	105,070,000
2	Roman Catholic	54,800,000
3	Eastern Orthodox	5,580,000
4	Jewish	5,560,000
5	Muslim	5,060,000
6	Anglican	2,330,000
7	Hindu	900,000
8	Baha'i	300,000
9	Buddhist	230,000
10	Sikh	190,000

THE BLUE MOSQUE
The superbly decorated Blue Mosque in Istanbul, Turkey, is one of the great centers of the Muslim faith. Islam, the world's fastest-growing religion, has almost 770 million followers in the Top 10 countries alone.

The 1990 Census gave the total US population as 248,709,873, some 86.5 percent of whom claimed to be Christian. Of them 52.7 percent were Protestant and 26.2 percent Roman Catholic. Muslims were reckoned to represent 1.9 percent and Jewish 1.8 percent of the population. It should be noted, however, that nominal affiliation to a particular religious group is generally greater than actual membership, on which this Top 10 is based.

TOWN & COUNTRY

20TH CENTURY

A time traveler from 1900 would be astonished by the changes that have taken place in the human environment during this century. The world's population has more than tripled. The urban landscape itself has been revolutionized by the building of advanced transportation systems, great bridges, tunnels, and other structures, especially skyscrapers: in 1900 the world's tallest building was the Park Row Building, New York, completed in 1899 and standing 386 ft/118 m high. By the year 2001, there will be two buildings, both in China, almost four times as high.

TOP 10

COUNTRIES WHERE MEN MOST OUTNUMBER WOMEN

	Country	Men per 100 women
1	United Arab Emirates	187
2	Qatar	160
3	Bahrain	138
4	Brunei	133
5	Saudi Arabia	124
6	Vanuatu	114
7	Oman	112
8	Hong Kong	110
9	Libya	109
10	Pakistan	108

TOP 10

COUNTRIES WHERE WOMEN MOST OUTNUMBER MEN

	Country	Women per 100 men
1=	Cape Verde	114
1=	Latvia	114
1=	Ukraine	114
4	Antigua	113·
5	Belarus	112
6=	Lithuania	111
6=	Russia	111
8	Georgia	110
9=	Cambodia	109
9=	Moldova	109

The male/female ratio of the world is balanced virtually 50:50, although in many Western countries male births slightly outnumber female by a very small percentage. There are certain countries, however, where one sex dominates more obviously. No one knows why these imbalances occur, or even whether such apparent differentials represent a true picture: in certain Third World countries where births are not accurately recorded and population figures are calculated from census returns, the figures may reflect the numbers of immigrant male workers, or possibly women are regarded as second-class citizens and are simply not counted.

POPULATION EXPLOSION

TOP 10
COUNTRIES WHERE SHEEP MOST OUTNUMBER PEOPLE

	Country	No. of sheep	No. of humans	Sheep per person
1	Falkland Islands	721,000	2,121	339.93
2	New Zealand	51,000,000	3,494,300	14.60
3	Uruguay	25,702,000	3,116,800	8.25
4	Australia	138,102,000	17,938,500	7.70
5	Mongolia	14,657,000	2,156,000	6.80
6	Mauritania	4,800,000	2,143,000	2.24
7	Kazakhstan	33,000,000	16,963,600	1.95
8	Namibia	2,900,000	1,534,000	1.89
9	Iceland	500,000	266,786	1.87
10	Syria	16,000,000	12,958,000	1.23

The estimated total world sheep population is 1,110,782,000 – a global average of 0.2 sheep per person – but, as this Top 10 shows, there are a number of countries where the tables are turned, and sheep considerably outnumber humans.

TOP 10
LEAST POPULATED COUNTRIES IN THE WORLD

	Country	Population
1	Vatican City	738
2	Niue	2,239
3	Tuvalu	9,700
4	Nauru	10,200
5	Wallis and Futuna	13,750
6	Cook Islands	18,300
7	San Marino	24,801
8	Gibraltar	28,800
9	Monaco	29,972
10	Liechtenstein	30,310

These are all independent countries – although some are linked to larger ones (Niue and the Cook Islands are linked to New Zealand, for example). There are numerous dependencies with small populations, among them the Falkland Islands (population 2,121), a British territory, and Midway Islands (450) and Wake Islands (300), both of which are under US military administration. The Pitcairn Islands, settled in 1790 by mutineers from the ship *Bounty*, have a population of 54.

TOP 10
COUNTRIES WITH THE HIGHEST ESTIMATED POPULATION IN THE YEAR 2000

	Country	Population
1	China	1,255,054,000
2	India	1,016,242,000
3	US	275,636,000
4	Indonesia	206,213,000
5	Brazil	172,228,000
6	Russia	149,844,000
7	Pakistan	148,012,000
8	Bangladesh	132,417,000
9	Nigeria	127,806,000
10	Japan	126,840,000

According to World Bank estimates, this Top 10 will represent all the countries in the world with a population of more than 100,000,000 in the year 2000. The closest runner-up will be Mexico, with a population of 98,787,000.

TOP 10
COUNTRIES WITH THE HIGHEST ESTIMATED POPULATION IN THE YEAR 2025

	Country	Population
1	China	1,471,282,000
2	India	1,370,028,000
3	US	322,675,000
4	Indonesia	265,111,000
5	Pakistan	242,811,000
6	Brazil	223,734,000
7	Nigeria	216,900,000
8	Bangladesh	182,313,000
9	Russia	153,498,000
10	Ethiopia	141,345,000

Many countries are predicted to experience substantial population surges between 2000 and 2025, most notably Ethiopia (set to increase by two-and-a-half times its present level) and Pakistan (whose population will almost double). In contrast, it is reckoned that Japan's population will actually decline by 2,546,000. Four other countries – Mexico, Iran, Vietnam, and the Philippines – will all join the 100,000,000-plus club.

IN THE CITY

20TH CENTURY

The progress of the 20th century is especially remarkable in the growth of the populations of the world's great cities. In the opening year of the century, there were only 11 cities in the world with populations in excess of a million: London was the largest with a population of more than 4 million, followed by Paris with 2.5 million, while Tokyo and New York had similar populations of about 1.5 million. At this time, Brooklyn, New York, was marginally larger than Bombay, India. As the following Top 10 lists show, in less than 100 years urban growth has accelerated to such an extent that the million-plus city is now commonplace, and within a decade we face the prospect of urban centers with populations of close to 30 million.

TOP 10

LARGEST CITIES IN THE WORLD IN THE YEAR 2000

	City/country	Estimated population 2000*
1	Tokyo–Yokohama, Japan	29,971,000
2	Mexico City, Mexico	27,872,000
3	São Paulo, Brazil	25,354,000
4	Seoul, South Korea	21,976,000
5	Bombay, India	15,357,000
6	New York, US	14,648,000
7	Osaka–Kobe–Kyoto, Japan	14,287,000
8	Tehran, Iran	14,251,000
9	Rio de Janeiro, Brazil	14,169,000
10	Calcutta, India	14,088,000

* *Based on US Bureau of the Census's unique method of calculating city populations; this gives totals that differ from those calculated by other methods (see Top 10 Most Highly Populated Cities in the World), such as those used by the United Nations*

NON-CAPITALIST CHINESE CITY
China is the most populous country on Earth, with Shanghai, its foremost port and industrial center, the world's largest noncapital city, with a total population of more than 13 million.

TOP 10

LEAST URBANIZED COUNTRIES IN THE WORLD

	Country	Population percentage in towns
1	Rwanda	5.4
2	Burundi	6.3
3	Nepal	9.6
4	Malawi	10.7
5	Oman	11.0
6	Uganda	11.7
7	Ethiopia	12.3
8	Cambodia	12.6
9	Bhutan	13.1
10	Burkina Faso	14.0

TOP 10

MOST URBANIZED COUNTRIES IN THE WORLD

	Country	Population percentage in towns
1=	Bermuda	100.0
1=	Hong Kong	100.0
1=	Monaco	100.0
1=	Singapore	100.0
1=	Vatican City	100.0
6	Macau	99.0
7	Belgium	96.5
8	Kuwait	96.3
9	UK	91.5
10	Iceland	91.4

T O P 1 0

MOST HIGHLY POPULATED CITIES IN THE WORLD

	City/country	Population		City/country	Population
1	Tokyo–Yokohama, Japan	28,447,000	6	Osaka–Kobe–Kyoto, Japan	14,060,000
2	Mexico City, Mexico	23,913,000	7	Bombay, India	13,532,000
3	São Paulo, Brazil	21,539,000	8	Calcutta, India	12,885,000
4	Seoul, South Korea	19,065,000	9	Rio de Janeiro, Brazil	12,788,000
5	New York, US	14,638,000	10	Buenos Aires, Argentina	12,232,000

Calculating the populations of the world's cities is fraught with difficulties, not least that of determining whether the city is defined by its administrative boundaries or by its continuously built-up areas or conurbations. Since different countries adopt different schemes, and some have populations concentrated in city centers while others are spread out in suburbs sprawling over hundreds of square miles, it has been impossible to compare them meaningfully. In order to resolve this problem, the US Bureau of the Census has adopted the method of defining cities as population clusters or "urban agglomerations" with densities of more than 5,000 inhabitants per square mile (equivalent to 1,931 per sq km). It should be stressed that totals based on this system will differ considerably from those based on other methods: by it, for example, the hugely spread-out city of Shanghai is reckoned to have a population of 7,194,000, compared with the total of 12,670,000 estimated for its metropolitan area. On this basis, the city in the Top 10 with the greatest area is New York (1,274 sq miles/3,300 sq km) and the city with the smallest, Bombay (95 sq miles/246 sq km) – which also means that Bombay has the greatest population density, 142,442 inhabitants per sq mile/55,008 per sq km. One recent change to note in the Top 10 is the inexorable rise in the population of Brazil's second-largest city, Rio de Janeiro, the total of which has now overtaken that of Buenos Aires. These two remain the most populous cities in the southern hemisphere, with Jakarta, Indonesia, the runner-up (11,151,000 in 1995, using this method of calculation).

NEW YORK, NEW YORK
During the 20th century, New York City has maintained its place among the 10 most populated cities in the world.

T O P 1 0

MOST DENSELY POPULATED CITIES IN THE WORLD

	City/country	Population per sq mile
1	Hong Kong	247,501
2	Lagos, Nigeria	142,821
3	Jakarta, Indonesia	130,026
4	Bombay, India	127,379
5	Ho Chi Minh City, Vietnam	120,168
6	Ahmadābād, India	115,893
7	Shenyang, China	109,974
8	Tianjin, China	98,990
9	Cairo, Egypt	97,106
10	Bangalore, India	96,041

According to the US Bureau of the Census method of calculating population and population density, the main island of Hong Kong, the capital of which is Victoria, is the most densely populated area in the world – with a cramped 113 sq ft/10.5 sq m per person (London appears positively spacious with 2,673 sq ft/248 sq m per person). If you exclude Hong Kong as having the status of a colony rather than a city, the new No. 10 becomes Chengdu, China, with a population density of 94,870 per sq mile/ 245,712 per sq km.

T O P 1 0

LARGEST NON-CAPITAL CITIES IN THE WORLD*

	City	Country	Population	Capital	Population
1	Shanghai	China	13,400,000	Beijing	10,940,000
2	Bombay	India	12,596,000	Delhi	8,419,000
3	Calcutta#	India	11,022,000	Delhi	8,419,000
4	São Paulo	Brazil	9,394,000	Brasília	1,864,000
5	Tianjin	China	9,090,000	Beijing	10,940,000
6	Karachi#	Pakistan	8,070,000	Islamabad	320,000
7	New York#	US	7,323,000	Washington, DC	598,000
8	Istanbul#	Turkey	6,293,000	Ankara	2,560,000
9	Rio de Janeiro#	Brazil	5,474,000	Brasília	1,864,000
10	St. Petersburg#	Russia	4,456,000	Moscow	8,967,000

* *Based on a comparison of populations within administrative boundaries*
# *Former capital city*

WORLD POPULATION

THE PROGRESSION OF THE GROWTH OF WORLD POPULATION* SINCE AD 1000

Year	Estimated total
1000	254,000,000
1500	460,000,000
1600	579,000,000
1700	679,000,000
1800	954,000,000
1900	1,633,000,000
1950	2,515,312,000
1960	3,019,376,000
1970	3,697,918,000
1980	4,450,210,000
1990	5,266,007,000
1995	5,692,210,000

World population passed the 5,000,000,000 mark in 1987

ESTIMATED PROGRESSIVE GROWTH OF THE WORLD'S POPULATION FROM AD 2000

Year	Low	Medium	High
2000	6,088.506,000	6,251,055,000	6,410,707,000
2005	6,463,211,000	6,728,574,000	6,978,754,000
2010	6,805,064,000	7,190,762,000	7,561,301,000
2015	7,109,736,000	7,639,547,000	8,167,357,000
2020	7,368,995,000	8,062,274,000	8,791,432,000
2025	7,589,731,000	8,466,516,000	9,422,749,000

The United Nations has estimated the future growth of world population within three ranges – "low," "medium," and "high," depending on the extent of birth control measures and other factors during the coming decades. The high scenario assumes that few additional checks are placed on population expansion. It implies a 78 percent global increase by the year 2025. Estimates suggest that as the 21st century ends, more than 60 percent of the world's population will be in Asia. By 2025 the population of China may approach 1,500,000,000 – an increase of over 1,000,000,000 since 1900.

TOP 10

MOST HIGHLY POPULATED COUNTRIES IN THE WORLD

	Country	Population 1985*	Population 1995#
1	China	1,008,175,288	1,193,332,000
2	India	685,184,692	934,228,000
3	US	231,106,727	263,119,000
4	Indonesia	153,030,000	192,543,000
5	Brazil	119,098,922	161,374,000
6	Russia	142,117,000	148,940,000
7	Pakistan	83,780,000	129,704,000
8	Japan	119,430,000	125,213,000
9	Bangladesh	94,700,000	121,110,000
10	Nigeria	82,390,000	111,273,000
	UK	*55,776,422*	*58,288,000*

* Based on closest censuses
# Based on World Bank estimates

The population of China is now more than 20 times that of the UK and represents over 21 percent of the total population of the entire world in 1995 (estimated to be 5,692,210,000), proving the commonly stated statistic that "one person in five is Chinese." Although differential rates of population increase result in changes in the order, the members of this Top 10 account for all the world's countries with populations of more than 100,000,000 – that of closest runner-up, Mexico, was reckoned to be 90,464,000 in 1995.

TOP 10

COUNTRIES OF ORIGIN OF US IMMIGRANTS, 1820–1994

	Country	Population
1	Germany	7,126,132
2	Mexico*	5,969,623
3	Italy	5,421,949
4	Great Britain	5,195,930
5	Ireland	4,771,697
6	Canada/Newfoundland	4,407,840
7	Austria/Hungary#	4,356,208
8	Former USSR✢	3,636,783
9	Caribbean	3,139,648
10	Sweden★	2,154,103

* Unreported 1886–93
# Unreported before 1861; combined 1861–1905; reported separately 1905–, but cumulative total included here; Austria included with Germany 1938–45
✢ Russia before 1917
★ Figures combined with Norway 1820–68

T O P 1 0

FOREIGN BIRTHPLACES OF THE US POPULATION

	Birthplace	Population*
1	Mexico	4,298,014
2	Philippines	912,674
3	Canada	744,830
4	Cuba	736,971
5	Germany	711,929
6	UK	640,145
7	Italy	580,592
8	Korea	568,397
9	Vietnam	543,262
10	China	529,837

* *US Bureau of the Census 1990 figures*

T O P 1 0

MOST DENSELY POPULATED COUNTRIES AND COLONIES IN THE WORLD

	Country/colony	Area sq km	sq miles	Estimated population 1995	Population per sq km
1	Macau	16.06	6.2	415,000	25,841
2	Monaco	1.81	0.7	29,972	16,559
3	Hong Kong	1,037.29	400.5	5,962,000	5,748
4	Singapore	619.01	239.0	2,943,000	4,754
5	Gibraltar	6.47	2.5	28,848	4,459
6	Vatican City	0.44	0.17	738	1,677
7	Malta	313.39	121.0	367,000	1,171
8	Bermuda	53.35	20.6	59,544	1,096
9	Bahrain	675.99	261.0	572,000	846
10	Bangladesh	143,998.15	55,598.0	121,110,000	841
	UK	*244,046.79*	*94,227.0*	*58,288,000*	*239*
	US	*9,372,614.90*	*3,618,787.0*	*263,119,000*	*28*
	World total	*135,597,770.00*	*52,509,600.0*	*5,692,210,000*	*average 42*

T O P 1 0

COUNTRIES OUTSIDE THE US WITH THE MOST RESIDENT US CITIZENS

	Country	Population*
1	Mexico	463,500
2	Canada	422,035
3	UK	215,530
4	Philippines	123,000
5	Italy	121,500
6	Germany	120,188
7	Greece	67,000
8	Australia	66,570
9	Japan	64,311
10	Spain	49,800

* *As at December 31, 1994*

The total number of US citizens living abroad reported to the Bureau of Consular Affairs by individual countries stands at 2,532,863, although this does not include a number of non-reporting countries with large numbers of expatriates, notably Israel.

T O P 1 0

COUNTRIES WITH THE HIGHEST BIRTH RATES

	Country	Birth rate*
1	Oman	61.3
2	Gaza Strip	56.0
3	Malawi	54.5
4	Rwanda	52.1
5	Mali	51.7
6=	Angola	51.3
6=	Niger	51.3
8=	Afghanistan	51.0
8=	Uganda	51.0
10=	Sierra Leone	50.2
10=	Somalia	50.2

* *Live births per annum per 1,000 population*

The 10 countries with the highest birth rates during the 1990s correspond very closely with those countries – mostly in Africa – that have the highest fertility rates (the average number of children born to each woman in that country), which in the case of Rwanda is a modern world record of 8.5.

T O P 1 0

COUNTRIES WITH THE LOWEST BIRTH RATES

	Country	Birth rate*
1	Vatican City	0
2	Japan	9.6
3	Croatia	9.8
4=	Italy	9.9
4=	Spain	9.9
6=	Bulgaria	10.0
6=	Greece	10.0
6=	Slovenia	10.0
9	Estonia	10.2
10	Germany	10.4
	UK	*13.5*
	US	*15.7*

* *Live births per annum per 1,000 population*

As with the highest birth rates, there is a close correlation between the countries with the lowest birth rates and those with the lowest fertility rates, the Top 10 of which is led by Italy, with just 1.4 births per woman. Fertility rates of less than 2.0 would effectively indicate a declining population.

WORLD COUNTRIES

COUNTRIES WITH THE MOST NEIGHBORS

	Country/neighbors	No. of neighbors
1	China	16

Afghanistan, Bhutan, Hong Kong, India, Kazakhstan, Kyrgyzstan, Laos, Macau, Mongolia, Myanmar (Burma), Nepal, North Korea, Pakistan, Russia, Tajikistan, Vietnam

2	Russia	14

Azerbaijan, Belarus, China, Estonia, Finland, Georgia, Kazakhstan, Latvia, Lithuania, Mongolia, North Korea, Norway, Poland, Ukraine

3	Brazil	10

Argentina, Bolivia, Colombia, French Guiana, Guyana, Paraguay, Peru, Surinam, Uruguay, Venezuela

4=	Germany	9

Austria, Belgium, Czech Republic, Denmark, France, Luxembourg, Netherlands, Poland, Switzerland

4=	Sudan	9

Central African Republic, Chad, Egypt, Eritrea, Ethiopia, Kenya, Libya, Uganda, Zaïre

4=	Zaïre	9

Angola, Burundi, Central African Republic, Congo, Rwanda, Sudan, Tanzania, Uganda, Zambia

7=	Austria	8

Czech Republic, Germany, Hungary, Italy, Liechtenstein, Slovakia, Slovenia, Switzerland

7=	France	8

Andorra, Belgium, Germany, Italy, Luxembourg, Monaco, Spain, Switzerland

7=	Saudi Arabia	8

Iraq, Jordan, Kuwait, Oman, People's Democratic Republic of Yemen, Qatar, United Arab Emirates, Yemen Arab Republic

7=	Tanzania	8

Burundi, Kenya, Malawi, Mozambique, Rwanda, Uganda, Zaïre, Zambia

7=	Turkey	8

Armenia, Azerbaijan, Bulgaria, Georgia, Greece, Iran, Iraq, Syria

LONGEST INTERNATIONAL BORDERS IN THE WORLD

	Country	km	miles
1	China	22,143	13,759
2	Russia	20,139	12,514
3	Brazil	14,691	9,129
4	India	14,103	8,763
5	US	12,248	7,611
6	Zaïre	10,271	6,382
7	Argentina	9,665	6,006
8	Canada	8,893	5,526
9	Mongolia	8,114	5,042
10	Sudan	7,697	4,783

The 7,611 miles/12,248 km of US borders include those shared with Canada (3,987 miles/6,416 km of which comprise the longest continuous border in the world), the 1,539-mile/2,477-km boundary between Canada and Alaska, that with Mexico (2,067 miles/3,326 km), and the border between the US naval base at Guantánamo and Cuba (18 miles/29 km). The total length of the world's land boundaries is estimated to be approximately 274,646 miles/442,000 km.

CHINESE PUZZLE
Although China has the third largest land area in the world, it has the most neighbors (16) and the longest borders of any country.

SMALLEST COUNTRIES IN THE WORLD

	Country	Area sq km	Area sq miles
1	Vatican City	0.44	0.17
2	Monaco	1.81	0.7
3	Gibraltar	6.47	2.5
4	Macau	16.06	6.2
5	Nauru	21.23	8.2

	Country	Area sq km	Area sq miles
6	Tuvalu	25.90	10.0
7	Bermuda	53.35	20.6
8	San Marino	59.57	23.0
9	Liechtenstein	157.99	61.0
10	Antigua	279.72	108.0

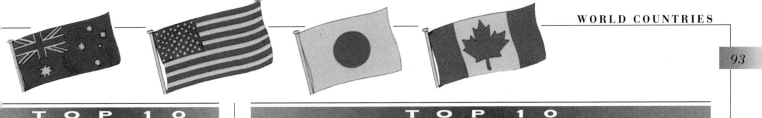

LARGEST LANDLOCKED COUNTRIES IN THE WORLD

	Country	Area sq km	sq miles
1	Kazakhstan	2,717,300	1,049,156
2	Mongolia	1,565,000	604,250
3	Chad	1,284,000	495,755
4	Niger	1,267,080	489,222
5	Mali	1,240,000	478,767
6	Ethiopia	1,128,221	435,609
7	Bolivia	1,098,581	424,165
8	Zambia	752,614	290,586
9	Afghanistan	647,497	250,000
10	Central African Republic	622,984	240,535

There are more than 40 landlocked countries, although the largest, Kazakhstan, and the 12th largest, Turkmenistan, both have coasts on the Caspian Sea – which is itself landlocked. The largest landlocked state in Europe is Hungary (35,919 sq miles/93,030 sq km). Europe also contains the world's smallest landlocked states – Andorra, Liechtenstein, San Marino, and Vatican City – all of which have areas of less than 193 sq miles/500 sq km.

LARGEST COUNTRIES IN THE WORLD

	Country	Area sq km	sq miles
1	Russia	17,070,289	6,590,876
2	Canada	9,970,537	3,849,646
3	China	9,596,961	3,705,408
4	US	9,372,614	3,618,787
5	Brazil	8,511,965	3,286,488
6	Australia	7,686,848	2,967,909
7	India	3,287,590	1,269,346
8	Argentina	2,766,889	1,068,302
9	Kazakhstan	2,717,300	1,049,156
10	Sudan	2,505,813	967,500

LARGEST COUNTRIES IN EUROPE

	Country	Area sq km	sq miles
1	Russia (in Europe)	4,710,227	1,818,629
2	Ukraine	603,700	233,090
3	France	547,026	211,208
4	Spain	504,781	194,897
5	Sweden	449,964	173,732
6	Germany	356,999	137,838
7	Finland	337,007	130,119
8	Norway	324,220	125,182
9	Poland	312,676	120,725
10	Italy	301,226	116,304

MAP OF EUROPE

LARGEST COUNTRIES IN AFRICA

	Country	Area sq km	sq miles		Country	Area sq km	sq miles
1	Sudan	2,505,813	967,500	6	Niger	1,267,080	489,191
2	Algeria	2,381,741	919,595	7	Angola	1,246,700	481,354
3	Zaïre	2,345,409	905,567	8	Mali	1,240,000	478,791
4	Libya	1,759,540	679,362	9	Ethiopia	1,228,121	435,609
5	Chad	1,284,000	495,755	10	South Africa	1,221,031	471,445

LARGEST COUNTRIES IN ASIA

	Country	Area sq km	sq miles
1	China	9,596,961	3,705,408
2	India	3,287,590	1,269,346
3	Kazakhstan	2,717,300	1,049,156
4	Saudi Arabia	2,149,640	830,000
5	Indonesia	1,904,569	735,358
6	Iran	1,648,000	636,296
7	Mongolia	1,565,000	604,250
8	Pakistan	803,950	310,407
9	Turkey (in Asia)	790,200	305,098
10	Myanmar (Burma)	676,552	261,218

COUNTRIES WITH THE LONGEST COASTLINES

	Country	km	miles
1	Canada	243,791	151,485
2	Indonesia	54,716	33,999
3	Greenland	44,087	27,394
4	Russia	37,653	23,396
5	Philippines	36,289	22,559
6	Australia	25,760	16,007
7	Norway	21,925	13,624
8	US	19,924	12,380
9	New Zealand	15,134	9,404
10	China	14,500	9,010

WORLD CITIES

The advantages of city life have appealed to humans for over 4,000 years. Most cities grow through a "snowball" effect. Increases in the population of one area require greater amounts of goods and services. This in turn draws tradespeople to these centers, as well as those generally seeking their fortune, who, like Dick Whittington, believe the city streets to be "paved with gold." The distinction between the city as an administrative area and the city as a highly populated urban zone, perhaps spreading out over a large area and steadily assimilating outlying towns, explains why, according to how it is defined, city populations may appear to vary according to source.

THE 10

FIRST CITIES IN THE WORLD WITH POPULATIONS OF MORE THAN ONE MILLION

	City	Country
1	Rome	Italy
2	Angkor	Cambodia
3	Hangchow (Hangzhou)	China
4	London	UK
5	Paris	France
6	Beijing	China
7	Canton	China
8	Berlin	Germany
9	New York	US
10	Vienna	Austria

Rome's population was reckoned to have exceeded 1,000,000 some time in the 2nd century BC, and Angkor and Hangchow both reached this figure by about AD 900 and 1200 respectively, but all three subsequently declined (Angkor was completely abandoned in the 15th century). No other city attained 1,000,000 until London in the early years of the 19th century. The next cities to pass the million mark did so between about 1850 and the late 1870s. Today, there are at least 300 cities with populations over one million.

TOP 10

LARGEST CITIES IN THE US

	City/state	Population
1	New York, New York	7,311,966
2	Los Angeles, California	3,489,779
3	Chicago, Illinois	2,768,483
4	Houston, Texas	1,690,180
5	Philadelphia, Pennsylvania	1,552,572
6	San Diego, California	1,148,851
7	Dallas, Texas	1,022,497
8	Phoenix, Arizona	1,012,230
9	Detroit, Michigan	1,012,110
10	San Antonio, Texas	966,437

Based on the 1992 US Bureau of the Census update, these are estimates for central city areas only, not for the total metropolitan areas that surround them, which may be several times as large. The populations of both Dallas and Phoenix have recently overtaken that of Detroit, which, along with Chicago and Philadelphia, has declined since the 1980 census was taken. These cities have undergone industrial decline, and there had been a general shift toward the southern and western "sun-belt" states.

NEW YORK CITY

TOP 10

FASTEST-GROWING CITIES IN THE WORLD

	City	Projected annual population-growth rate (%)*
1	Lagos, Nigeria	4.9
2	Taegu, Korea	4.7
3	Kinshasa, Zaïre	4.5
4	Dhaka, Bangladesh	4.1
5=	Poona, India	4.0
5=	Salvador, Brazil	4.0
5=	Tehran, Iran	4.0
8	Karachi, Pakistan	3.8
9	Bangalore, India	3.6
10=	Lima, Peru	3.3
10=	São Paolo, Brazil	3.3

* During the period 1995–2000

TOP 10

MOST HIGHLY POPULATED CITIES IN EUROPE

	City	Country	Population
1	Moscow*	Russia	10,769,000
2	London*	UK	8,897,000
3	Paris*	France	8,764,000
4	Istanbul#	Turkey	7,624,000
5	Essen	Germany	7,364,000
6	Milan	Italy	4,795,000
7	Madrid*	Spain	4,772,000
8	St. Petersburg	Russia	4,694,000
9	Barcelona	Spain	4,492,000
10	Manchester	UK	3,949,000

* Capital city
 # Located in the European part of Turkey

The US Bureau of the Census' method of identifying city populations produces this list – although one based on cities minus their suburbs would present a very different picture. Using this method with other cities shows that Athens, Rome, and Berlin have populations in excess of 3,000,000.

HIGHEST TOWNS AND CITIES IN THE WORLD

	Town	Country	Height m	ft
1	Wenchuan	China	5,099	16,730
2	Potosí	Bolivia	3,976	13,045
3	Oruro	Bolivia	3,702	12,146
4	Lhasa	Tibet	3,684	12,087
5	La Paz	Bolivia	3,632	11,916
6	Cuzco	Peru	3,399	11,152
7	Huancayo	Peru	3,249	10,660
8	Sucre	Bolivia	2,835	9,301
9	Tunja	Colombia	2,820	9,252
10	Quito	Ecuador	2,819	9,249

Lhasa was formerly the highest capital city in the world, a role now occupied by La Paz, the capital of Bolivia. Even the towns and cities at the bottom of this list are more than one-third as high as Everest.

NOT BUILT IN A DAY
The Colosseum, Rome, was built centuries after the city and inaugurated in AD 80. Rome is one of Europe's oldest cities and was the capital of the Roman empire. It was the first city to attain a population of one million.

OLDEST CITIES IN THE US

	City/state	Founded
1	St. Augustine, Florida	1565
2	Santa Fe, New Mexico	1609
3	Hampton, Virginia	1610
4	Newport News, Virginia	1621
5=	Albany, New York	1624
5=	New York City, New York	1624
7	Quincy, Massachusetts	1625
8	Salem, Massachusetts	1626
9=	Jersey City, New Jersey	1629
9=	Lynn, Massachusetts	1629

The oldest permanently inhabited settlements in what is now the US are the subject of much debate. However, the founding years listed here are those from which these cities are generally presumed to date. Some sources give Tallahassee, Florida as having been originally settled in 1539, but this date relates only to the winter camp of the Spanish explorer Hernando de Soto (*c.* 1500–42) and his 600 companions.

OLDEST CITIES IN THE UK

	City	Original charter granted
1	Ripon	886
2	London	1066
3	Edinburgh	1124
4	Chichester	1135
5=	Derby	1154
5=	Lincoln	1154
5=	Oxford	1154
8=	Nottingham	1155
8=	Winchester	1155
10	Exeter	1156

Although most of the 58 British cities were settled in earlier times, some as far back as the 1st century BC, their status as cities is dated from when their charters, issued by the Crown and establishing certain privileges such as the power to enact local laws or collect taxes, were granted.

OLDEST CITIES IN EUROPE

	City/country	First settled
1	Zurich, Switzerland	c. 3000 BC
2=	Lisbon, Portugal	c. 2000 BC
2=	Porto, Portugal	c. 2000 BC
4	Athens, Greece	pre-1200 BC
5	La Coruña, Spain	pre-1100 BC
6=	Málaga, Spain	c. 1100 BC
6=	Cádiz, Spain	c. 1100 BC
8=	Pisa, Italy	c. 1000 BC
8=	Metz, France	c. 1000 BC
8=	Rome, Italy	c. 1000 BC

Although the precise dating of the founding of prehistoric sites is impossible, all these cities have been permanently settled for at least 3,000 years. A world version of such a Top 10 would be dominated by Egypt and other Middle Eastern countries that have many cities dating back to before 2000 BC.

PLACE NAMES

TOP 10

LONGEST PLACE NAMES IN THE US

	Name	Letters
1	Chargoggagoggmanchauggagogg-chaubunagungamaugg (*see* The 10 Longest Place Names in the World, No. 6)	45
2	Nunathloogagamiutbingoi Dunes, Alaska	28
3	Winchester-on-the-Severn, Maryland	21
4	Scraper-Moechereville, Illinois	20
5	Linstead-on-the-Severn, Maryland	19
6=	Kentwood-in-the-Pines, California	18
6=	Lauderdale-by-the-Sea, Florida	18
6=	Vermilion-on-the-Lake, Ohio	18
9=	Chippewa-on-the-Lake, Ohio	17
9=	Fairhaven-on-the-Bay, Maryland	17
9=	Highland-on-the-Lake, New York	17
9=	Kleinfeltersville, Pennsylvania	17
9=	Mooselookmeguntic, Maine	17
9=	Palermo-by-the-Lakes, Ohio	17
9=	Saybrook-on-the-Lake, Ohio	17

*   *Including single-word and hyphenated names (not counting hyphens as characters)*

A number of long American place names are of Native American origin, but some are not as long as they once were: in 1916 the US Board on Geographic Names saw fit to reduce the 26-letter New Hampshire stream known as Quohquinapassakessamanagno to "Beaver Creek," while "Duck" is the new name for the Conamabsqunooncant River.

TOP 10

MOST COMMON PLACE NAMES IN THE US

	Name	No. of occurrences
1	Midway	207
2	Fairview	192
3	Oak Grove	150
4	Five Points	145
5	Pleasant Hill	113
6	Centerville	109
7	Mount Pleasant	108
8	Riverside	106
9	Bethel	105
10	New Hope	98

TOP 10

MOST COMMON PLACE NAMES IN THE UK

	Name	No. of occurrences
1	Newton	150
2	Blackhill/Black Hill	141
3	Mountpleasant/Mount Pleasant	130
4	Castlehill/Castle Hill	127
5	Woodside/Wood Side	116
6	Newtown/New Town	111
7	Greenhill/Green Hill	108
8	Woodend/Wood End	106
9	Burnside	105
10	Beacon Hill	94

TOP 10

COUNTRIES WITH THE LONGEST OFFICIAL NAMES

	Official name*	Common English name	Letters
1	al-Jamāhīrīyah al-ʿArabīya al-Lībīyah ash-Shaʿbīyah al-Ishtirākīyah	Libya	56
2	al-Jumhūrīyah al-Jazāʾirīyah ad-Dīmuqrāṭīyah ash-Shaʿbīyah	Algeria	49
3	United Kingdom of Great Britain and Northern Ireland	United Kingdom	45
4	Sri Lankā Prajathanthrika Samajavadi Janarajaya	Sri Lanka	43
5	Jumhūrīyat al-Qumur al-Ittihādīyah al-Islāmīyah	The Comores	41
6=	al-Jumhūrīyah al-Islāmīyah al-Mūrītānīyah	Mauritania	36
6=	The Federation of St. Christopher and Nevis	St. Kitts and Nevis	36
8	Jamhuuriyadda Dimuqraadiga Soomaaliya	Somalia	35
9	al-Mamlakah al-Urdunnīyah al-Hāshimīyah	Jordan	34
10	Repoblika Demokratika n'i Madagaskar	Madagascar	32

*   *Some official names have been transliterated from languages that do not use the Roman alphabet; their lengths may vary according to the method of transliteration used*

There is clearly no connection between the lengths of names and the longevity of the nation states that bear them. Since this list was first published in 1991, the following three countries have ceased to exist: Socijalisticka Federativna Republika Jugoslavija (Yugoslavia, 45 letters), Soyuz Sovetskikh Sotsialisticheskikh Respublik (USSR, 43), and Ceskoslovenská Socialistická Republika (Czechoslovakia, 36).

T O P 1 0

LONGEST PLACE NAMES IN THE WORLD*

Name	Letters
1 Krung thep mahanakhon bovorn ratanakosin mahintharayutthaya mahadilok pop noparatratchathani burirom udomratchanivetma hasathan amornpiman avatarnsa thit sakkathattiyavisnukarmprasit	167

When the poetic name of Bangkok, capital of Thailand, is used, it is usually abbreviated to "Krung Thep" (City of Angels).

Name	Letters
2 Taumatawhakatangihangakoauau-otamateaturipukakapikimaunga-horonukupokaiwhenuakitanatahu	85

This is the longer version (the other has a mere 83 letters) of the Maori name of a hill in New Zealand. It translates as "The place where Tamatea, the man with the big knees, who slid, climbed, and swallowed mountains, known as land-eater, played on the flute to his loved one."

Name	Letters
3 Gorsafawddacha'idraigodanhed-dogleddollônpenrhynareur-draethceredigion	67

A name contrived by the Fairbourne Steam Railway, Gwynedd, North Wales, UK, for publicity purposes and in order to out-do its rival, No. 4. It means "The Mawddach station and its dragon teeth at the Northern Penrhyn Road on the golden beach of Cardigan Bay."

Name	Letters
4 Llanfairpwllgwyngyllgogerychwyrn-drobwllllantysiliogogogoch	58

This is the place in Gwynedd, UK, famed especially for the length of its railway tickets. It means "St. Mary's Church in the hollow of the white hazel near to the rapid whirlpool of Llantysilio of the Red Cave." Its authenticity is suspect, since its official name comprises only the first 20 letters, and the full name appears to have been invented as a hoax in the 19th century by local inhabitant John Evans.

Name	Letters
5 El Pueblo de Nuestra Señora la Reina de los Angeles de la Porciuncula	57

The site of a Franciscan mission and the full Spanish name of Los Angeles, California, it means "the town of Our Lady the Queen of the Angels of the Little Portion."

Name	Letters
6 Chargoggagoggmanchauggagogg-chaubunagungamaugg	45

The Native American name of a lake near Webster, Massachusetts. Loosely translated, it means "You fish on your side, I'll fish on mine, and no one fishes in the middle." This is an invented extension of its real name (Chagungungamaug Pond, or "boundary fishing place"), devised in the 1920s by Larry Daly, editor of the Webster Times. *The current abbreviation is Chaubunagungamaug.*

Name	Letters
7= Lower North Branch Little Southwest Miramichi	40

Canada's longest place name belongs to a short river in New Brunswick.

Name	Letters
7= Villa Real de la Santa Fe de San Francisco de Asis	40

The full Spanish name of Santa Fe, New Mexico, translates as "Royal city of the holy faith of St. Francis of Assisi."

Name	Letters
9 Te Whakatakanga-o-te-ngarehu-o-te-ahi-a-Tamatea	38

The Maori name of Hammer Springs, New Zealand, like the second name in this list, refers to a legend of Tamatea, explaining how the springs were warmed by "the falling of the cinders of the fire of Tamatea."

Name	Letters
10 Meallan Liath Coire Mhic Dhubhghaill	32

The longest multiple name in Scotland, this is the name of a place near Aultanrynie, Highland, alternatively spelled Meallan Liath Coire Mhic Dhughaill.

* *Including single-word, hyphenated, and multiple names*

T O P 1 0

LONGEST PLACE NAMES IN THE UK

(Single-word and hyphenated names only)

Name	Letters
1 Gorsafawddacha'idraigodanhed-dogleddollônpenrhynareur-draethceredigion (*see* the Top 10 Longest Place Names in the World)	67
2 Llanfairpwllgwyngyllgogerych-wyrndrobwllllantysiliogogogoch (*see* the Top 10 Longest Place Names in the World)	58
3 Sutton-under-Whitestonecliffe, North Yorkshire	27
4 Llanfihangel-yng-Ngwynfa, Powys	22
5= Llanfihangel-y-Creuddyn, Dyfed	21
5= Llanfihangel-y-traethau, Gwynedd	21

Name	Letters
7 Cottonshopeburnfoot, Northumberland	19
8= Blakehopeburnhaugh, Northumberland	18
8= Coignafeuinternich, Inverness-shire	18
10= Claddach-baleshare, North Uist, Outer Hebrides	17
10= Claddach-knockline, North Uist, Outer Hebrides	17

Runners-up include Combeinteignhead, Doddiscombsleigh, Moretonhampstead, Stokeinteignhead, and Woolfardisworthy, all of which are in Devon and have 16 letters. The longest multiple name in England is North Leverton with Habblesthorpe, Nottinghamshire (30 letters), followed by Sulhampstead Bannister Upper End, Berkshire (29). In Wales the longest are Lower Llanfihangel-y-Creuddyn, Dyfed (26), followed by Llansantffraid Cwmdeuddwr, Powys (24); and in Scotland, Meallan Liath Coire Mhic Dhubhghaill, Highland (32), a loch on the island of Lewis called Loch Airidh Mhic Fhionnlaidh Dhuibh (31), and Huntingtower and Ruthvenfield (27). If the British Isles are considered as a whole, including Ireland, Castletownconyersmaceniery (26), Co. Limerick, Muikeenachidirdhashaile (24), and Muckanaghederdauhalia (21) are scooped into the net. The shortest place name in the UK is Ae in Dumfries and Galloway, Scotland.

THE WORLD'S TALLEST BUILDINGS

TOP 10

TALLEST HABITABLE BUILDINGS IN THE WORLD IN THE YEAR 2001

	Building	Location	Year*	Stories	Height m	ft
1	Shanghai World Finance Centre	Shanghai, China	2001	95	460	1,508
2	Chongqing Tower with spire	Chongqing, China	2000	114	457 503	1,500 1,650
3	Petronas Towers	Kuala Lumpur, Malaysia	1996	96	452	1,482
4	Sears Tower with spires	Chicago, Illinois	1974	110	443 520	1,454 1,707
5	Tour Sans Fin	Paris, France	2000	90	419	1,377
6	World Trade Center	New York, New York	1973	110	417	1,368
7	Jin Mao Building with spire	Shanghai, China	1997	93	382 420	1,255 1,378
8	Empire State Building with spire	New York, New York	1931	102	381 449	1,250 1,472
9	T & C Tower	Kao-hsiung, Taiwan	1997	85	348	1,142
10	Amoco Building	Chicago, Illinois	1973	80	346	1,136

* Opened or expected completion year

TOP 10

TALLEST TELECOMMUNICATIONS TOWERS IN THE WORLD

	Building	Location	Year constructed	Height m	ft
1	CN Tower	Toronto, Canada	1975	555	1,821
2	Ostankino Tower	Moscow, Russia	1967	537	1,762
3	Oriental Pearl Broadcasting Tower	Shanghai, China	1995	468	1,535
4	Telecom Tower	Kuala Lumpur, Malaysia	1995	420	1,380
5	Alma-Ata Tower	Alma-Ata, Kazakhstan	1983	370	1,214
6	TV Tower	Berlin, Germany	1969	365	1,198
7	TV Tower	Tashkent, Uzbekistan	1983	357	1,171
8	Tokyo Tower	Tokyo, Japan	1959	333	1,093
9	TV Tower	Frankfurt, Germany	1977	331	1,086
10	National Transcommunications transmitter	Emley Moor, UK	1971	329	1,080

All the towers listed are self-supporting, rather than braced, masts, and all have observation facilities, the highest being that in the CN Tower, Toronto (the world's tallest self-supporting structure of any kind), at 1,467 ft/447 m. The completion of the Telecom Tower, Kuala Lumpur, means that the Eiffel Tower drops out of the Top 10 for the first time.

TOP 10

WORLD CITIES WITH MOST SKYSCRAPERS*

	City	Skyscrapers
1	New York, New York	131
2	Chicago, Illinois	47
3	Houston, Texas	27
4	Los Angeles, California	21
5	Hong Kong	20
6	Dallas, Texas	17
7	Melbourne, Australia	16
8	San Francisco, California	15
9	Boston, Massachusetts	14
10=	Atlanta, Georgia	13
10=	Singapore	13
10=	Sydney, Australia	13

* Habitable buildings of over 500 ft/152 m

TOP 10

CITIES OUTSIDE THE US WITH MOST SKYSCRAPERS*

	City	Skyscrapers
1	Hong Kong	20
2	Melbourne, Australia	16
3=	Singapore	13
3=	Sydney, Australia	13
5	Toronto, Canada	11
6	Tokyo, Japan	10
7	Frankfurt, Germany	4
8=	Caracas, Venezuela	3
8=	Johannesburg, South Africa	3
8=	London, UK	3
8=	Moscow, Russia	3
8=	Paris, France	3
8=	Perth, Australia	3

* Habitable buildings of over 500 ft/152 m

T O P 1 0

TALLEST HABITABLE BUILDINGS IN THE WORLD

	Building	Location	Year completed	Stories	Height m	ft
1	Petronas Towers	Kuala Lumpur, Malaysia	1996	96	452	1,482
2	Sears Tower with spires	Chicago, Illinois	1974	110	443 520	1,454 1,707
3	World Trade Center*	New York, New York	1973	110	417	1,368
4	Empire State Building with spire	New York, New York	1931	102	381 449	1,250 1,472
5	T & C Tower	Kao-hsiung, Taiwan	1997	85	348	1,142
6	Amoco Building	Chicago, Illinois	1973	80	346	1,136
7	John Hancock Center with spire	Chicago, Illinois	1968	100	344 450	1,127 1,476
8	Shun Hing Square with spires	Shenzen, China	1996	80	330 384	1,082 1,263
9	Sky Central Plaza with spires	Guangzhou, China	1996	80	323 391	1,060 1,283
10	Baiyoke II Tower	Bangkok, Thailand	1996	89	319	1,046

* Twin towers; the second tower, completed in 1973, has the same number of stories but is slightly smaller at 415 m/1,362 ft – although its spire takes it up to 521 m/1,710 ft

Heights are of buildings less their television and radio antennae and uninhabited extensions. Although the twin Petronas Towers are now officially accepted as the world's tallest by the Council on Tall Buildings and Urban Habitat, their 1996 completion caused controversy when it became clear that their measurement includes their spires, and that their roof height is "only" 1,328 ft/405 m. The Sears Tower maintains its claim as the tallest building by virtue of having the most floors, the highest occupied floor, and the longest elevator ride.

T O P 1 0

TALLEST BUILDINGS IN THE SOUTHERN HEMISPHERE

	Building	Location	Year Completed	Stories	Height m	ft
1	Rialto Tower	Melbourne, Australia	1985	60	242	794
2	MLC Centre	Sydney, Australia	1977	60	228	748
3	Governor Phillip Tower	Sydney, Australia	1993	54	227	745
4	Central Park Tower	Perth, Australia	1992	52	226	742
5	Bourke Place*	Melbourne, Australia	1991	48	224	735
6=	Carlton Centre	Johannesburg, South Africa	1975	50	220	722
6=	120 Collins Street	Melbourne, Australia	1991	52	220	722
8	Chifley Tower	Sydney, Australia	1992	50	215	705
9	R & I Bank	Perth, Australia	1988	52	214	702
10	Melbourne Central	Melbourne, Australia	1991	55	211	692

* The BHP logo on the top of the building is Australia's highest sign

EMPIRE STATE BUILDING
Located on New York City's Fifth Avenue, this huge skyscraper held the record as the tallest building for more than 40 years. The upper part was built as a mooring mast for airships, although it was never used in this role.

TUNNELS & BRIDGES

LONGEST UNDERWATER TUNNELS IN THE WORLD

	Tunnel	Location	Year completed	Length km	miles
1	Seikan (rail)	Japan	1988	53.90	33.49
2	Channel Tunnel (rail)	France/England	1994	49.94	31.03
3	Dai-Shimizu (rail)	Japan	1982	22.17	13.78
4	Shin-Kanmon (rail)	Japan	1975	18.68	11.61
5	Severn (rail)	UK	1886	7.01	4.36
6	Haneda (rail)	Japan	1971	5.98	3.72
7	Kammon (rail)	Japan	1942	3.60	2.24
8	Kammon (road)	Japan	1958	3.46	2.15
9	Mersey (road)	UK	1934	3.43	2.13
10	Elbe (road)	Germany	1973	3.32	2.06

The need to connect the Japanese islands of Honshu, Kyushu, and Hokkaido has resulted in a wave of underwater-tunnel building in recent years, with the Seikan the most ambitious project of all. Connecting Honshu and Hokkaido, 14.4 miles/23.3 km of the tunnel is 328 ft/100 m below the sea bed, bored through strata that presented such enormous engineering problems that it took 24 years to complete. The long-mooted Channel Tunnel (pilot borings were undertaken more than 100 years ago) was finally opened to the public in 1994. Its overall length is shorter than the Seikan Tunnel, but the undersea portion is longer at 23.6 miles/38.0 km.

HIGHEST-EARNING TOLL LOCATIONS IN THE US

	Location	Income ($)*
1	Manhattan & Staten Island area crossings	483,135,000
2	Thomas E. Dewey Thruway	321,082,000
3	New Jersey Turnpike	317,033,000
4	Pennsylvania Turnpike	280,896,000
5	Florida Turnpike	192,556,000
6	Garden State Parkway	165,935,000
7	Massachusetts Turnpike System	132,927,000
8	Will Rogers Turnpike	98,353,000
9	Ohio Turnpike	95,356,000
10	Chesapeake Bay crossings	90,824,000

* State-administered toll roads and crossing facilities, 1994

LONGEST RAIL TUNNELS IN THE WORLD

	Tunnel/location	Year completed	Length km	miles
1	Seikan, Japan	1988	53.90	33.49
2	Channel Tunnel, France/England	1994	49.94	31.03
3	Moscow Metro (Medvedkovo/Belyaevo section), Russia	1979	30.70	19.07
4	London Underground (East Finchley/Morden Northern Line), UK	1939	27.84	17.30
5	Dai-Shimizu, Japan	1982	22.17	13.78
6	Simplon II, Italy/Switzerland	1922	19.82	12.31
7	Simplon I, Italy/Switzerland	1906	19.80	12.30
8	Shin-Kanmon, Japan	1975	18.68	11.61
9	Apennine, Italy	1934	18.49	11.49
10	Rokko, Japan	1972	16.25	10.10

The first purpose-built passenger rail tunnel was the 2,514-ft/766-m Tyler Hill Tunnel, Kent, UK, opened on May 4, 1830. The longest rail tunnel built in the 19th century is the 9.32-mile/15-km St. Gotthard Tunnel, Switzerland, opened on May 20, 1882.

LONGEST ROAD TUNNELS IN THE WORLD

	Tunnel/location	Year completed	Length km	miles
1	St. Gotthard, Switzerland	1980	16.32	10.14
2	Arlberg, Austria	1978	13.98	8.69
3	Fréjus, France/Italy	1980	12.90	8.02
4	Mt.-Blanc, France/Italy	1965	11.60	7.21
5	Gudvangen, Norway	1992	11.40	7.08
6	Leirfjord, Norway	*	11.11	6.90
7	Kan-Etsu II, Japan	1991	11.01	6.84
8	Kan-Etsu I, Japan	1985	10.93	6.79
9	Gran Sasso, Italy	1984	10.17	6.32
10	Plabutsch, Austria	1987	9.76	6.06

* Under construction

All the tunnels in this Top 10 were built during the past 30 years. Previously, the record for "world's longest" had been held by the 3.13-mile/5.04-km Viella Tunnel, Cataluña, Spain, which was opened in 1941. This tunnel itself overtook the 2.13-mile/3.43-km Mersey Tunnel connecting Liverpool and Birkenhead, UK, which was constructed in 1925–34.

TOP 10

HIGHEST-EARNING TOLL BRIDGES AND TUNNELS IN THE UK

	Crossing	Income (£)
1	Humber Bridge	55,622,000
2	Dartford Bridge	39,197,000
3	Severn Bridge	30,190,000
4	Mersey Tunnel	24,654,000
5	Forth Bridge	8,192,000
6	Tyne Tunnel	5,710,000
7	Eskine Bridge	3,890,000
8	Tamar Bridge	3,187,000
9	Tay Bridge	2,959,000
10	Itchen Bridge	2,015,000

The Humber Bridge is not only the world's longest suspension bridge, but also Britain's highest-earning toll bridge. It took eight years to complete and was officially opened by Queen Elizabeth II on July 17, 1981.

TOP 10

LONGEST SUSPENSION BRIDGES IN THE WORLD

	Bridge/location	Year completed	Length of main span m	ft
1	Humber Bridge, UK	1980	1,410.0	4,626
2	Verrazano Narrows, New York	1964	1,298.5	4,260
3	Golden Gate, San Francisco	1937	1,280.2	4,200
4	Mackinac Straits, Michigan	1957	1,158.2	3,800
5	Minami Bisano-seto, Japan	1988	1,100.0	3,609
6	Bosphorus #2, Istanbul, Turkey	1988	1,090.0	3,576
7	Bosphorus #1, Istanbul, Turkey	1973	1,074.1	3,524
8	George Washington, New York	1931	1,066.8	3,500
9	Ponte 25 Abril (Ponte Salazar), Lisbon, Portugal	1966	1,012.9	3,323
10	Forth Road Bridge, UK	1964	1,005.8	3,300

The Messina Strait Bridge between Sicily and Calabria, Italy, remains a speculative project, but if constructed according to plan it will have by far the longest center span of any bridge at 10,892 ft/3,319.9 m, although at 12,828 ft/3,910 m Japan's Akashi-Kaikyo bridge, scheduled for completion in 1998 and with a main span of 6,529 ft/1,990 m, will be the world's longest overall. The Great Belt East Bridge, Denmark, due for completion in 1997, will have a main span of 5,328 ft/1,624 m.

TOP 10

LONGEST CANTILEVER BRIDGES IN THE WORLD

	Bridge/location	Year completed	Longest span m	ft
1	Pont de Québec, Canada	1917	548.6	1,800
2	Firth of Forth, Scotland	1890	521.2	1,710
3	Minato, Osaka, Japan	1974	509.9	1,673
4	Commodore John Barry, New Jersey/Pennsylvania	1974	494.4	1,622
5	Greater New Orleans, Louisiana	1958	480.1	1,575
6	Howrah, Calcutta, India	1943	457.2	1,500
7	Transbay, San Francisco	1936	426.7	1,400
8	Baton Rouge, Louisiana	1969	376.4	1,235
9	Tappan Zee, Tarrytown, New York	1955	369.4	1,212
10	Longview, Oregon/Washington	1930	365.8	1,200

THE LEGENDARY GOLDEN GATE BRIDGE
Sixty years after its completion, San Francisco's Golden Gate bridge remains the third longest in the world.

OTHER STRUCTURES

LARGEST CEMETERIES IN LONDON

	Cemetery/founded	Area (acres)
1	St. Pancras and Islington, N2 (1854)	182
2	City of London, E12 (1856)	130 *
3	Kensal Green, NW19 (1832)	77
4=	Battersea New, Morden (1891)	70
4=	Streatham Park, SW16 (1909)	70
6	Lee, SE6 (1873)	65
7	Camberwell New, SE23 (1927)	61
8	Great Northern, N11 (1861)	60
9	Merton and Sutton, Morden (1947)	57.5#
10	Tottenham, N17 (1856)	56

* Plus 46 acres in reserve
\# 22 acres in use

LARGEST BELLS IN THE WESTERN WORLD

	Bell/location	Weight (tons)
1	*Tsar Kolokol*, Kremlin, Moscow, Russia	222.56
2	*Voskresenskiy (Resurrection)*, Ivan the Great Bell Tower, Kremlin, Moscow, Russia	72.20
3	*Petersglocke*, Cologne Cathedral, Germany	28.00
4	Lisbon Cathedral, Portugal	26.90
5	St. Stephen's Cathedral, Vienna, Austria	23.58
6	Bourdon, Strasbourg Cathedral, France	22.05
7	*Savoyarde*, Sacre-Coeur Basilica, Paris, France	20.78
8	Bourdon, Riverside Church, New York, USA	20.44
9	Olmütz, Czech Republic	20.05
10	*Campana Gorda*, Toledo Cathedral, Spain	19.04

The largest bell in the world is the 20 ft 2 in/ 6.14 m high, 21 ft 8 in/6.6 m diameter *Tsar Kolokol*, cast in Moscow for the Kremlin. It cracked even before it had been installed and has remained there, unrung, ever since.

LARGEST SPORTS STADIUMS IN THE WORLD

	Stadium/location	Capacity
1	Strahov Stadium, Prague, Czech Republic	240,000
2	Maracaña Municipa Stadium, Rio de Janeiro, Brazil	205,000
3	Rungnado Stadium, Pyongyang, South Korea	150,000
4	Estadio Maghalaes Pinto, Belo Horizonte, Brazil	125,000
5=	Estadio Morumbi, São Paulo, Brazil	120,000
5=	Estadio da Luz, Lisbon, Portugal	120,000
5=	Senayan Main Stadium, Jakarta, Indonesia	120,000
5=	Yuba Bharati Krirangan, nr. Calcutta, India	120,000
9	Estadio Castelão, Fortaleza, Brazil	119,000
10=	Estadio Arrudão, Recife, Brazil	115,000
10=	Estadio Azteca, Mexico City, Mexico	115,000
10=	Nou Camp, Barcelona, Spain	115,000

OLDEST CATHEDRALS IN THE UK

	Cathedral	Founded
1	Canterbury	1071
2	Lincoln	1073
3	Rochester	1077
4=	Hereford	1079
4=	Winchester	1079
6	York	1080
7	Worcester	1084
8	London (now St. Paul's)	1087
9	Durham	1093
10	Exeter	1114

CANTERBURY TALE
The seat of the Anglican Church, Canterbury Cathedral is Britain's oldest, representing superb architectural and decorative work spanning four centuries (AD 1071–1503). This cross-section reveals the nave, transept, and apse details of the interior.

T O P 1 0

LARGEST ARTIFICIAL LAKES IN THE WORLD*

	Dam/lake	Location	Year completed	Volume (m³)
1	Owen Falls	Uganda	1954	204,800,000,000
2	Bratsk	Russia	1964	169,900,000,000
3	High Aswan	Egypt	1970	162,000,000,000
4	Kariba	Zimbabwe	1959	160,368,000,000
5	Akosombo	Ghana	1965	147,960,000,000
6	Daniel Johnson	Canada	1968	141,851,000,000
7	Guri (Raul Leoni)	Venezuela	1986	135,000,000,000
8	Krasnoyarsk	Russia	1967	73,300,000,000
9	W.A.C. Bennett	Canada	1967	70,309,000,000
10	Zeya	Russia	1978	68,400,000,000

* Includes only those formed as a result of dam construction

THE GREAT BARRIER, TARBELA DAM
The complex engineering project of damming the Indus River in Pakistan produced the Tarbela Dam, the world's 4th most massive earth and rockfill structure.

T O P 1 0

OLDEST CHURCHES IN THE US

	Church/location	Built
1	Cervento de Porta Coeli, San German, Puerto Rico*	1609
2	San Estevan del Rey Mission, Valencia County, New Mexico	1629
3	St. Luke's Church, Isle of Wight County, Virginia	1632
4	First Church of Christ and the Ancient Burying Ground, Hartford County, Connecticut	1640
5	St. Ignatius Catholic Church, St. Mary's County, Maryland	1641
6	Merchant's Hope Church, Prince George County, Virginia	1657
7	Flatlands Dutch Reformed Church, King's County, New York	1660
8=	Claflin-Richards House, Essex County, Massachusetts	1661
8=	Church San Blas de Illesces of Coamo, Ponce, Puerto Rico*	1661
8=	St. Mary's Whitechapel, Lancaster County, Virginia	1661

* Not US territory when built, but now a US national historic site

T O P 1 0

LARGEST DAMS IN THE WORLD

(Ranked according to the volume of material used in construction)

	Dam	Location	Completed	Volume (m³)
1	Syncrude Tailings	Alberta, Canada	1992	540,000,000
2	Pati	Paraná, Argentina	1990	230,180,000
3	New Cornelia Tailings	Ten Mile Wash, Arizona	1973	209,500,000
4	Tarbela	Indus, Pakistan	1976	105,922,000
5	Fort Peck	Missouri, Montana	1937	96,050,000
6	Lower Usuma	Usuma, Nigeria	1990	93,000,000
7	Atatürk	Euphrates, Turkey	1990	84,500,000
8	Yacyreta-Apipe	Paraná, Paraguay/Argentina	1991	81,000,000
9	Guri (Raul Leoni)	Caroni, Venezuela	1986	77,971,000
10	Rogun	Vakhsh, Tajikistan	1987	75,500,000

Despite the recent cancelation of several dams on environmental grounds, such as two in the Cantabrian Mountains, Spain, numerous major projects are in development for completion by the end of the century, when this Top 10 will contain some notable new entries. Among several in Argentina is the Chapeton dam under construction on the Paraná and scheduled for completion in 1998; it will have a volume of 296,200,000 m³ and will thus become the 2nd largest dam in the world. The Pati, also on the Paraná, will have a volume of 238,180,000 m³. The Cipasang dam under construction on the Cimanuk, Indonesia, will have a volume of 90,000,000 m³.

CULTURE & LEARNING

20TH CENTURY

"Culture" in all its forms – the transmission of knowledge through education, literature, and art, and the preservation of buildings and sites of historic importance – has become a significant issue during the 20th century. Increasingly, education has been made available to groups to whom it was previously denied, and most countries may now claim literacy levels nearing 100 percent, while many have witnessed a massive escalation in the enrolment figures at their schools and colleges. However, there remain territories, particularly in Africa, where even the most basic reading skills and the provision of educational materials are lacking. Overcoming such imbalances, and managing the costs of maintaining ancient buildings and conserving artistic treasures, are among the greatest cultural challenges facing us in the next century.

TOP 10

LARGEST UNIVERSITIES IN THE UK

(Excluding the Open University)

	University	Full-time students		University	Full-time students
1	London	69,560	6	Sheffield	15,911
2	Manchester Metropolitan	19,706	7	Nottingham Trent	15,730
3	De Montfort (Leicester)	18,392	8	Edinburgh	15,455
4	Leeds	17,197	9	Oxford	15,156
5	Manchester	16,990	10	Birmingham	15,105

THE 10

COUNTRIES WITH THE LOWEST LITERACY RATES IN THE WORLD

	Country	Literacy percentage*
1	Niger	10.8
2	Bhutan	18.0
3	Burkina Faso	18.2
4	Mali	18.8
5	Eritrea	20.0
6	Sierra Leone	20.7
7	Benin	23.4
8	Guinea	24.0
9	Ethiopia	24.3
10	Pakistan	25.6

* *Total of male and female population over the age of 15 that can read*

EDUCATION & HERITAGE

TOP 10

LARGEST UNIVERSITIES IN THE US

	University	Enrolments (1993–94)
1	University of Minnesota (Twin Cities), Minnesota	51,880
2	Ohio State University (Main Campus), Ohio	50,623
3	University of Texas (Austin), Texas	48,555
4	Miami Dade Community College, Florida	48,232
5	Texas A&M University, Texas	42,524
6	Arizona State University, Arizona	41,250
7	University of Wisconsin (Madison), Wisconsin	39,999
8	University of Illinois (Urbana Campus), Illinois	39,912
9	Michigan State University, Michigan	39,743
10	Houston Community College System, Texas	39,321

Source: National Center For Educational Statistics, US Department of Education

DID YOU KNOW

WORLD HERITAGE

Every country has buildings and sites that it considers culturally important, but there are many that are held in such regard that they have world standing. Such are those in the World Heritage List, which was established under terms of the Convention Concerning the Protection of World Culture and Natural Heritage adopted in 1972 at the 17th General Conference of UNESCO. The Convention states that a World Heritage Committee "will establish, keep up-to-date, and publish" a World Heritage List of cultural and natural properties, submitted by the member states and considered to be of universal value. The first 12 sites were all established in 1978.

STUDENT IN UNIVERSITY LIBRARY

THE 10

FIRST UNESCO HERITAGE SITES IN THE US

	Site/location	Year
1=	Mesa Verde National Park, Colorado	1978
1=	Yellowstone National Park, Wyoming/Idaho/Montana	1978
3=	Everglades National Park, Florida	1979
3=	Grand Canyon National Park, Arizona	1979
3=	Independence Hall, Pennsylvania	1979
6	Redwood National Park, California	1980
7=	Mammoth Cave National Park, Kentucky	1981
7=	Olympic National Park, Washington	1981
9	Cahokia Mounds State Historic Site, Illinois	1982
10	Great Smokey Mountains National Park, North Carolina/Tennessee	1983

THE 10

FIRST UNESCO HERITAGE SITES IN THE WORLD

1	L'Anse aux Meadows National Historic Park, Canada
2	Nahanni National Park, Canada
3	Galapagos National Park, Ecuador
4	Old City of Quito, Ecuador
5	Rock-hewn Churches of Lalibela, Ethiopia
6	Simen National Park, Ethiopia
7	Aachen Cathedral, Germany
8	Historic Center of Cracow, Poland
9	Wieliczka Salt Mines, Poland
10=	Island of Goree, Senegal
10=	Mesa Verde National Park, Colorado
10=	Yellowstone National Park, Wyoming/Idaho/Montana

THE 10

FIRST UNESCO HERITAGE SITES IN THE UK

	Site/location	Year
1=	The Giant's Causeway and Causeway Coast, Northern Ireland	1986
1=	Durham Castle and Cathedral, England	1986
1=	Ironbridge Gorge, England	1986
1=	Studley Royal Park, including the ruins of Fountains Abbey, England	1986
1=	Stonehenge, Avebury, and associated sites, England	1986
1=	The Castles and Town Walls of King Edward in Gwynedd, Wales	1986
1=	St. Kilda, Scotland	1986
8=	Blenheim Palace, England	1987
8=	City of Bath, England	1987
8=	Hadrian's Wall, England	1987
8=	Palace of Westminster, Abbey of Westminster, and St. Margaret's Church, England	1987

LIBRARIES OF THE WORLD

LARGEST REFERENCE LIBRARIES IN THE WORLD

	Library	Location	Founded	Books
1	Library of Congress	Washington, DC	1800	29,000,000
2	British Library	London, UK	1753*	18,000,000
3	Harvard University Library	Cambridge, Massachusetts	1638	12,605,537
4	Russian State Library #	Moscow, Russia	1862	11,750,000
5	New York Public Library	New York, New York	1848+	11,300,000★
6	Yale University Library	New Haven, Connecticut	1701	9,937,751
7	Biblioteca Academiei Romane	Bucharest, Romania	1867	9,397,260
8	Bibliothèque Nationale	Paris, France	1480	9,000,000
9	University of Illinois Library	Urbana, Illinois	1867	8,281,455
10	National Library of Russia♦	St. Petersburg, Russia	1795	8,000,000

* *Founded as part of the British Museum 1753; became an independent body 1973*
\# *Founded as Rumyantsev Library; formerly State V.I. Lenin Library*
\+ *Astor Library founded February 1, 1848; consolidated with Lenox Library and Tilden Trust to form New York Public Library in 1895*
★ *Reference holdings only, excluding books in library branches*
♦ *Formerly M.E. Saltykov-Shchedrin State Public Library*

RUSSIAN STATE LIBRARY
Formerly the Lenin Library, this huge building, designed by V.A. Shchuko and V.G. Gel'freytch, was begun in 1928 and completed in the 1950s.

COUNTRIES WITH MOST PUBLIC LIBRARIES

	Country	Public libraries
1	Former USSR	208,146
2	UK	23,678
3	Germany	18,868
4	US	15,870
5	Romania	7,227
6	Canada	6,157
7	Cuba	4,671
8	Spain	3,635
9	France	2,640
10	Mexico	2,269

The very high figure reported by UNESCO for the former Soviet Union's public libraries may owe more to the propaganda value attached to cultural status than to reality. National literary traditions play a major role in determining the ratio of libraries to population. The people of Japan, for example, do not customarily borrow books, and consequently the country has only 1,950 public libraries, whereas Australia, with a strong literary heritage but only one-seventh the population of Japan, has almost as many libraries (1,904), while Finland, which has a population of little over one-twenty-fifth that of Japan, has 1,429 libraries.

FIRST PUBLIC LIBRARIES IN THE UK

	Library	Founded		Library	Founded
1=	Manchester Free Library	1852	6	Nottinghamshire	1868
1=	Liverpool	1852	7	Dundee	1869
3	Sheffield	1856	8	Glasgow (Mitchell Library)	1874
4	Birmingham	1860	9	Aberdeen	1884
5	Cardiff	1862	10	Edinburgh	1890

TOP 10
LARGEST PUBLIC LIBRARIES IN THE US

	Library/no. of branches	Location	Founded	Books
1	New York Public Library (The Branch Libraries) (82)	New York, NY	1895*	10,505,079#
2	Queens Borough Public Library (62)	Jamaica, NY	1896	9,681,898
3	Chicago Public Library (81)	Chicago, IL	1872	6,840,109
4	Boston Public Library (26)	Boston, MA	1852	6,529,998
5	Carnegie Library of Pittsburgh (18)	Pittsburgh, PA	1895	6,409,300
6	Los Angeles Public Library (147)	Los Angeles, CA	1872	6,102,920
7	Free Library of Philadelphia (52)	Philadelphia, PA	1891	5,933,711
8	Brooklyn Public Library (59)	Brooklyn, NY	1896	4,655,894
9	Public Library of Cincinnati and Hamilton County (41)	Cincinnati, OH	1853	4,655,050
10	Houston Public Library (37)	Houston, TX	1901	4,113,095

* *Astor Library founded February 1, 1848; consolidated with Lenox Library and Tilden Trust to form New York Public Library, 1895*
# *Lending library and reference library holdings available for loan*

THE 10
FIRST PUBLIC LIBRARIES IN THE US

	Library/location	Founded
1	Peterboro Public Library, New Hampshire	1833
2	New Orleans Public Library, Louisiana	1843
3	Boston Public Library, Massachusetts	1852
4	Public Library of Cincinnati and Hamilton County, Ohio	1853
5	Springfield City Library, Massachusetts	1857
6	Worcester Public Library, Massachusetts	1859
7	Multnomah County Library, Oregon	1864
8=	Detroit Public Library, Michigan	1865
8=	St. Louis Public Library, Missouri	1865
10	Atlanta-Fulton Public Library, Georgia	1867

TOP 10
LARGEST LIBRARIES IN THE UK*

	Library	Location	Founded	Books
1	British Library	London	1753	18,000,000
2	National Library of Scotland	Edinburgh	1682	6,500,000
3	Bodleian Library	Oxford	1602	5,700,000
4	University of Cambridge Library	Cambridge	c. 1400	4,637,595
5=	National Library of Wales	Aberystwyth	1907	3,500,000
5=	John Rylands University Library of Manchester#	Manchester	1851	3,500,000
7	University of Edinburgh	Edinburgh	1583	2,550,366
8	University of Birmingham	Birmingham	1900	1,917,000
9	University of London	London	1836	1,682,806
10	University of Liverpool	Liverpool	1903	1,282,288

* *Excluding public libraries*
# *In 1972 the John Rylands Library (founded 1900) was amalgamated with Manchester University Library (1851)*

THE BRITISH LIBRARY, LONDON
Until it moves to its new building, the British Library is housed within the British Museum.

WORD POWER

TOP 10

LONGEST WORDS IN THE ENGLISH LANGUAGE

1 Methionylglutaminylarginyltyrosylglut amylserylleucylphenylalanylalanylglutamin ylleucyllysylglutamylarginyllysylglutamylgl ycylalanylphenylalanylvalylprolylphenylala nylvalylthreonylleucylglycylaspartylprolylgl ycylisoleucylglutamylglutaminylserylleucyll ysylisoleucylaspartylthreonylleucylisoleucyl glutamylalanylglycylalanylaspartylalanylleu cylglutamylleucylglycylisoleucylprolylpheny lalanylserylaspartylprolylleucelalanylaspart ylglycylprolylthreonylisoleucylglutaminylas paraginylalanylthreonylleucylarginylalanylp henylalanylalanylalanylglycylvalylthreonylp rolylalanylglutaminylcysteinylphenylalanylg lutamylmethionylleucylalanylleucylisoleucyl arginylglutaminyllysylhistidylprolylthreonyl isoleucylprolylisoleucylglycylleucylleucylme thionyltyrosylalanylasparaginylleucylvalylp henylalanylasparaginyllysylglycylisoleucylas partylglutamylphenylalanyltyrosylalanylglu taminylcysteinylglutamyllysylvalylglycylval ylaspartylserylvalylleucylvalylalanylaspartyl valylprolylvalylglutaminylglutamylserylalan ylprolylphenylalanylarginylglutaminylalany lalanylleucylarginylhistidylasparaginylvalyl alanylprolylisoleucylphenylalanylisoleucylcy steinylprolylprolylaspartylalanylaspartylasp artylaspartylleucylleucylarginylglutaminylis oleucylalanylseryltyrosylglycylarginylglycylt yrosylthreonyltyrosylleucylleucylserylarginy lalanylglycylvalylthreonylglycylalanylgluta mylasparaginylarginylanylalanylleucylproly lleucylaspaaginylhistidylleucylvalylalanyllys ylleucyllysylglutamyltyrosylasparaginylalan ylalanylprolylprolylleucylglutaminylglycylp henylalanylglycylisoleucylserylalanylprolyla spartylglutaminylvalyllysylalanylalanylisole ucylaspartylalanylglycylalanylalanylglycylal anylisoleucylserylglycylserylalanylisoleucylb alyllysylisoleucylisoleucylglutamylglutamin ylhistidylasparaginylisoleucylglutamylprolyl glutamyllysylmethionylleucylalanylalanylle ucyllysylvalylphenylalanylvalylglutaminylpr olylmethionyllysylalanylalanylthreonylargin ylserine (1,909 letters)

The scientific name for tryptophan synthetase A protein, an enzyme made up of 267 amino acids, it has appeared in print several times. The systematic name of deoxyribonucleic acid, or DNA, has an alleged 207,000 letters, but although published in shortened form in Nature *on April 9, 1981, it has never been printed in full. Words for chemical compounds are the most likely to be long since they can be created by linking the scientific names of their components. Words invented with the sole intention of being long words, such as James Joyce's 100-letter examples in* Finnegan's Wake, *have been excluded from this list.*

2 Acetylseryltyrosylserylisoleucylthreony lserylprolylserylglutaminylphenylalanylvalyl phenylalanylleucylserylserylvalyltryptophyla lanylaspartylprolylisoleucylglutamylleucylle ucylasparaginylvalylcysteinylthreonylseryls erylleucylglycllasparaginylglutaminylphenyl alanylglutaminylthreonylglutaminylglutami nylalanylarginylthreonylthreonylglutaminyl valylglutaminylglutaminylphenylalanylseryl glutaminylvalyltryptophyllysylprolylphenyla lanylprolylglutaminylserylthreonylvalylargin ylphenylalanylprolylglycylaspartylvalyltyros yllsyslvalyltyrosylarginyltyrosylasparaginyla lanylvalylleucylaspartylprolylleucylisoleucylt hreonylalanylleucylleucylglycylthreonylphen ylalanylaspartylthreonylarginylasparaginyla rginylisoleucylisoleucylglutamylvalylglutam ylasparaginylglutaminylglutaminylserylprol ylthreonylthreonylalanylglutamylthreonylleu cylaspartylalanylthreonylarginylarginylvalyl aspartylaspartylalanylthreonylvalylalanyliso leucylarginylserylalanylasparaginylisoleucyl asparaginylleucylvallasparaginylglutamylleu cylvalylarginylglycylthreonylglycylleucyltyro sylasparaginylglutaminylasparaginylthreony lphenylalanylglutamylserylmethionylserylgly cylleucylvalyltryptophylthreonylserylalanylp rolylalanylserine (1,185 letters)

The word for the Tobacco Mosaic Virus, Dahlemense Strain, qualifies as the second longest word in English because it has actually been used in print (in the American Chemical Society's Chemical Abstracts).

3 Ornicopytheobibliopsychocrystarroscio aerogenethliometeoroaustrohieroanthropoic hthyopyrosiderochpnomyoalectryoophiobot anopegohydrorhabdocrithoaleuroalphitohal omolybdoclerobeloaxinocoscinodactyliogeoli thopessopsephocatoptrotephraoneirochiroon ychodactyloarithstichooxogeloscogastrogyro cerobletonooenoscapulinaniac (310 letters)

This medieval word means "a deluded human who practices divination or forecasting by means of phenomena, interpretation of acts or other manifestations related to the following animate or inanimate objects and appearances: birds, oracles, Bible, ghosts, crystal gazing, shadows, air appearances, birth stars, meteors, winds, sacrificial appearances, entrails of humans and fishes, fire, red-hot irons, altar smoke, mice, grain picking by rooster, snakes, herbs, fountains, water, wands, dough, meal, barley, salt, lead, dice, arrows, hatchet balance, sieve, ring suspension, random dots, precious stones, pebbles, pebble heaps, mirrors, ash writing, dreams, palmistry, nail rays, finger rings, numbers, book passages, name letterings, laughing manners, ventriloquism, circle walking, wax, susceptibility to hidden springs, wine, and shoulder blades."

4 Lopadotemachoselachogaleokraniol eipsanodrimhypotrimmatosilphioparaomelit okatakechymenokichlepikossyphophattoper isteralektryonoptekephalliokigklopeleiolagoi osiraiobaphetraganopterygon (182 letters)

This is the name of a 17-ingredient dish, transliterated from a 170-letter Greek word in a play by Aristophanes (c. 448–380BC).

5 Aequeosalinocalcalinosetaceoalumino socupreovitriolic (52 letters)

Invented by a medical writer, Dr. Edward Strother (1675–1737), he used this word to describe the spa waters at Bath, UK.

6 Osseocarnisanguineoviscericartilaginon ervomedullary (51 letters)

Coined by Thomas Love Peacock (1785–1866), he used it in his satire Headlong Hall *(1816) to describe the structure of the human body.*

7 Pneumonoultramicroscopicsilicovolcan oconiosis (45 letters)

A lung disease caused by breathing fine dust, it was first printed (ending in "-koniosis") in F. Scully's Bedside Manna *(sic) (1936). It then appeared in* Webster's Dictionary *and is now in the* Oxford English Dictionary.

8 Hepaticocholangiocholecystentero stomies (39 letters)

This is the word for surgical operations to create channels of communication between gall bladders and hepatic ducts or intestines.

9= Pseudoantidisestablishmentarianism (34 letters)

Derived from antidisestablishmentarianism (28), this means "false opposition to the withdrawal of state support from a Church." Another composite (though usually hyphenated) is ultra-antidisestablishmentarianism, which means "extreme opposition to the withdrawal of state support from a Church" (33).

9= Supercalifragilisticexpialidocious (34 letters)

An invented word, it is perhaps now eligible since it has appeared in the Oxford English Dictionary. *It was popularized by the song of this title in the film* Mary Poppins *(1964) where it is used to mean "wonderful," but it was originally written in 1949 in an unpublished song by Parker and Young who spelt it "supercalafajalistickespialadojus" (32 letters). In 1965–66, Parker and Young unsuccessfully sued the makers of* Mary Poppins, *claiming infringement of copyright. In summarizing the case, the US Court decided against repeating this mouthful, stating that "All variants of this tongue-twister will hereinafter be referred to collectively as 'the word'."*

TOP 10

MOST WIDELY SPOKEN LANGUAGES IN THE WORLD

	Language	Approx. no. of speakers
1	Chinese (Mandarin)	931,000,000
2	English	463,000,000
3	Hindustani	400,000,000
4	Spanish	371,000,000
5	Russian	290,000,000
6	Arabic	215,000,000
7	Bengali	193,000,000
8	Portuguese	180,000,000
9	Malay-Indonesian	153,000,000
10	Japanese	126,000,000

According to 1993 estimates by Sidney S. Culbert of the University of Washington, French and German are also spoken by more than 100,000,000 people. A further 12 languages are spoken by between 50,000,000 and 100,000,000 people. They range from Urdu with 99,000,000, to Turkish with 58,000,000. The rest in descending order are: Punjabi, Korean, Telugu, Tamil, Marathi, Cantonese, Wu, Italian, Javanese, and Vietnamese.

TOP 10

COUNTRIES WITH THE MOST ENGLISH-LANGUAGE SPEAKERS

	Country	Approx. no. of speakers
1	US	224,900,000
2	UK	56,830,000
3	Canada	17,700,000
4	Australia	15,188,000
5	South Africa	3,620,000
6	Ireland	3,340,000
7	New Zealand	3,205,000
8	Jamaica	2,350,000
9	Trinidad and Tobago	1,200,000
10	Guyana	900,000

This Top 10 represents the countries with the greatest numbers of inhabitants who are considered English speakers in their daily working lives. Many people who use English in the workplace conduct their home lives in another language – hence the lower number of English speakers given in the list below.

TOP 10

MOST USED LETTERS IN WRITTEN ENGLISH

	i	ii
1	e	e
2	t	t
3	a	a
4	o	i
5	i	n
6	n	o
7	s	s
8	r	h
9	h	r
10	l	d

Column i is the order as indicated by a survey of approximately 1,000,000 words appearing in a wide variety of printed texts, ranging from newspapers to novels. Column ii is the order estimated by Samuel Morse, the inventor in the 1830s of Morse Code, based on his calculations of the respective quantities of type used by a printer. The number of letters in the printer's type trays ranged from 12,000 for "e" to 4,400 for "d," with only 200 for "z."

TOP 10

MOST WIDELY SPOKEN LANGUAGES IN THE EC

	Language	Approx. no. of speakers*
1	German	75,667,000
2	English	59,595,000
3	French	56,943,000
4	Italian	55,370,000
5	Spanish	28,672,000
6	Dutch	20,463,000
7	Portuguese	10,431,000
8	Greek	10,120,000
9	Catalan	6,370,000
10	Danish	5,005,000

* As a "first language," regardless of where they are living in the EC

TOP 10

MOST WIDELY SPOKEN LANGUAGES IN US HOMES

	Language	Approx. no. of speakers
1	English	198,601,000
2	Spanish	17,339,000
3	French	1,702,000
4	German	1,547,000
5	Italian	1,309,000
6	Chinese	1,249,000
7	Tagalog	843,000
8	Polish	723,000
9	Korean	626,000
10	Vietnamese	507,000

TOP 10

MOST COMMON WORDS IN ENGLISH

	Spoken English	Written English*
1	the	the
2	and	of
3	I	to
4	to	in
5	of	and
6	a	a
7	you	for
8	that	was
9	in	is
10	it	that

* Based on a survey of newspaper usages

BOOKS & READERS

MOST TRANSLATED AUTHORS IN THE WORLD

	Author	Translations
1	V.I. Lenin (1870–1924)	3,842
2	Agatha Christie (1890–1976)	1,904
3	Jules Verne (1828–1905)	1,856
4	William Shakespeare (1564–1616)	1,689
5	Enid Blyton (1897–1968)	1,582
6=	Leo Tolstoy (1828–1910)	1,429
6=	Charles Perrault (1628–1703)	1,429
8	Georges Simenon (1903–89)	1,392
9	Karl Marx (1818–83)	1,312
10	Fyodor Dostoevski (1821–81)	1,202

According to a survey conducted by UNESCO of the numbers of translations of books in the postwar period, Lenin leads the field by a long margin, with British crime writer Agatha Christie the world's most ubiquitous novelist. Just outside this Top 10 are such popular children's authors as Hans Christian Andersen and the Brothers Grimm, followed by Mark Twain, Charles Dickens, and Arthur Conan Doyle.

MOST PUBLISHED AUTHORS OF ALL TIME

	Author	Nationality
1	William Shakespeare (1564–1616)	British
2	Charles Dickens (1812–70)	British
3	Sir Walter Scott (1771–1832)	British
4	Johann Goethe (1749–1832)	German
5	Aristotle (384–322 BC)	Greek
6	Alexandre Dumas (*père*) (1802–70)	French
7	Robert Louis Stevenson (1850–94)	British
8	Mark Twain (1835–1910)	American
9	M. Tullius Cicero (106–43 BC)	Roman
10	Honoré de Balzac (1799–1850)	French

FIRST POETS LAUREATE

	Poet	Period of office
1	John Dryden (1631–1700)	1670–88
2	Thomas Shadwell (c. 1642–92)	1689–92
3	Nahum Tate (1652–1715)	1692–1715
4	Nicholas Rowe (1674–1718)	1715–18
5	Rev. Laurence Eusden (1688–1730)	1718–30
6	Colley Cibber (1671–1757)	1730–57
7	William Whitehead (1715–85)	1757–85
8	Rev. Thomas Warton (1728–90)	1785–90
9	Henry James Pye (1745–1813)	1790–1813
10	Robert Southey (1774–1843)	1813–43

The role of "royal versifier" dates back to Geoffrey Chaucer in the 14th century, and perhaps even earlier. Chaucer was followed by other court-appointed poets including Ben Jonson (c. 1572–1637), who served from 1619–37, and Sir William D'Avenant (1606–68), from 1638–68, but none was actually called "Poet Laureate" until Dryden. The principal function of the poet laureate is to write odes to celebrate royal birthdays, marriages, and important state occasions. They are under no obligation to do so, and many of them have done it so badly that they have been ridiculed for their poor, "instant" verses. Poets laureate, who are appointed by the Prime Minister, remain in office until their deaths (although Dryden and Tate were dismissed). The successors of the first 10, some memorable, others completely forgotten, included, in the 19th century, William Wordsworth and Alfred, Lord Tennyson, and in the 20th, John Masefield, Cecil Day Lewis, and Sir John Betjeman, who was followed in 1984 by the present incumbent, Ted Hughes. They receive a salary of £70 ($105) per annum – unchanged since the 17th century.

MOST POPULAR ENGLISH-LANGUAGE POEMS IN THE UK*

1	*If*, Rudyard Kipling (1865–1936)		**6**	*To Autumn*, John Keats (1795–1821)
2	*The Lady of Shallot*, Alfred, Lord Tennyson (1809–92)		**7**	*The Lake Isle of Innisfree*, W.B. Yeats (1864–1939)
3	*The Listener*, Walter De La Mare (1873–1956)		**8**	*Dulce et Decorum*, Wilfred Owen (1893–1918)
4	*Not Waving But Drowning*, Stevie Smith (1902–71)		**9**	*Ode to a Nightingale*, John Keats
5	*Daffodils*, William Wordsworth (1770–1850)		**10**	*He Wishes for the Cloths of Heaven*, W. B. Yeats

* *Based on a survey conducted in the UK on National Poetry Day, 1995*

THE BIRDS OF AMERICA
John James Audubon's sumptuous collection of over 400 large colored engravings was sold for $3,600,000 on June 6, 1989.

THE 10
LAST PULITZER PRIZE WINNERS FOR FICTION

Year	Author	Book
1995	Carol Shields	*The Stone Diaries*
1994	E. Annie Proulx	*The Shipping News*
1993	Robert Olen Butler	*A Good Scent from a Strange Mountain: Stories*
1992	Jane Smiley	*A Thousand Acres*
1991	John Updike	*Rabbit at Rest*
1990	Oscar Hijuelos	*The Mambo Kings Play Songs of Love*
1989	Anne Tyler	*Breathing Lessons*
1988	Toni Morrison	*Beloved*
1987	Peter Taylor	*A Summons to Memphis*
1986	Larry McMurtry	*Lonesome Dove*

THE 10
LAST BOOKER PRIZE WINNERS

Year	Author	Book
1995	Pat Barker	*The Ghost Road*
1994	James Kelman	*How Late It Was, How Late*
1993	Roddy Doyle	*Paddy Clarke Ha Ha Ha*
1992	Michael Ondaatje	*The English Patient*
1992	Barry Unsworth	*Sacred Hunger*
1991	Ben Okri	*The Famished Road*
1990	A. S. Byatt	*Possession: A Romance*
1989	Kazuo Ishiguro	*The Remains of the Day*
1988	Peter Carey	*Oscar and Lucinda*
1987	Penelope Lively	*Moon Tiger*

TOP 10
MOST ANTHOLOGIZED ENGLISH-LANGUAGE POEMS

	Poem/poet	Appearances
1	*The Tyger*, William Blake (1757–1827)	62
2	*Dover Beach*, Matthew Arnold (1822–88)	61
3	*Kubla Khan*, Samuel Taylor Coleridge (1772–1834)	58
4	*La Belle Dame sans Merci*, John Keats (1795–1821)	52
5	*To Autumn*, John Keats	50
6	*Pied Beauty*, Gerard Manley Hopkins (1844–89)	49
7	*Sir Patrick Spens*, Unknown (early Scottish)	48
8	*Stopping by Woods on a Snowy Evening*, Robert Frost (1874–1963)	56
9	*To the Virgins, to Make Much of Time*, Robert Herrick (1591–1674)	55
10	*That Time of Year Thou Mayst in Me Behold*, William Shakespeare (1564–1616)	51

"Appearances" refers to the number of anthologies in which the poem is found, out of a total of more than 400 listed in *Granger's Index to Poetry*, an American guide to poems that can be found in anthologies. *Granger's Index* has been published in numerous editions since 1904. The frequency with which such poems are selected for inclusion in anthologies is a crude indication of their relative popularity – or, at the very least, of their popularity as assumed by the compilers of anthologies.

TOP 10
MOST EXPENSIVE BOOKS AND MANUSCRIPTS EVER SOLD AT AUCTION

	Book/manuscript/sale	Price ($)*
1	*The Codex Hammer*, Christie's, New York, November 11, 1994	30,800,000
2	*The Gospels of Henry the Lion*, c. 1173–75, Sotheby's, London, December 6, 1983	10,841,000
3	*The Gutenberg Bible*, 1455, Christie's, New York, October 22, 1987	5,390,000
4	*The Northumberland Bestiary*, c. 1250–60, Sotheby's, London, November 29, 1990	5,049,000
5	Autographed manuscript of nine symphonies by Wolfgang Amadeus Mozart, c. 1773–74, Sotheby's, London, May 22, 1987	3,854,000
6	John James Audubon's *The Birds of America*, 1827–38, Sotheby's, New York, June 6, 1989	3,600,000
7	The Bible in Hebrew, Sotheby's, London, December 5, 1989	2,932,000
8	*The Monypenny Breviary*, illuminated manuscript, c. 1490–95, Sotheby's, London, June 19, 1989	2,639,000
9	*The Hours and Psalter of Elizabeth de Bohun, Countess of Northampton*, c. 1340–45, Sotheby's, London, June 21, 1988	2,530,000
10	*Biblia Pauperum*, Christie's, New York, October 22, 1987	2,200,000

* *Excluding premiums*

WORLD BESTSELLERS

It is extremely difficult to establish precise sales of contemporary books and virtually impossible to do so with books published long ago. How many copies of the complete works of Shakespeare or Conan Doyle's Sherlock Holmes books have been sold in countless editions? The publication of variant editions, translations, and pirated copies all affect the global picture, and few publishers or authors are willing to expose their royalty statements to public scrutiny. As a result, this Top 10 list offers no more than the "best guess" at the great bestsellers of the past, and it may well be that there are many other books with a valid claim to a place in it.

TOP 10

BESTSELLING BOOKS OF ALL TIME

Title	No. sold
1 The Bible	6,000,000,000

No one really knows how many copies of the Bible have been printed, sold, or distributed. The Bible Society's attempt to calculate the number printed between 1816 and 1975 produced the figure of 2,458,000,000. A more recent survey, for the years up to 1992, put it closer to 6,000,000,000 in more than 2,000 languages and dialects. Whatever the precise figure, the Bible is by far the bestselling book of all time.

2 *Quotations from Chairman Mao Tse-tung (Little Red Book)*	800,000,000 *

Chairman Mao's Little Red Book *could scarcely fail to become a bestseller: between the years 1966 and 1971 it was compulsory for every Chinese adult to own a copy. It was both sold and distributed to the people of China – although what proportion voluntarily bought it must remain open to question. Some 100,000,000 copies of his* Poems *were also disseminated.*

3 *American Spelling Book* by Noah Webster	100,000,000

First published in 1783, this reference book by the American man of letters Noah Webster (1758–1843) remained a bestseller in the US throughout the 19th century.

4 *The Guinness Book of Records*	at least 77,000,000 #

First published in 1955, The Guinness Book of Records *stands out as the greatest contemporary publishing achievement. There have now been 37 editions in the UK alone (it was not published annually until 1964), as well as numerous foreign-language editions.*

5 *The McGuffey Readers* by William Holmes McGuffey	60,000,000

Published in numerous editions from 1853, some authorities have put the total sales of these educational textbooks, originally compiled by American anthologist William Holmes McGuffey (1800–73), as high as 122,000,000. It has also been claimed that 60,000,000 copies of the 1879 edition were printed, but – since this is some 10,000,000 more than the entire population of the US at the time – the publishers must have been extremely optimistic about its success.

6 *A Message to Garcia* by Elbert Hubbard	40–50,000,000

Now forgotten, Hubbard's polemic on the subject of labor relations was published in 1899 and within a few years had achieved these phenomenal sales, largely because many American employers purchased bulk supplies to distribute to their employees. The literary career of Elbert Hubbard (1856–1915) was cut short in 1915 when he went down with the ocean liner Lusitania, *but even in death he was a record breaker: his posthumous* My Philosophy *(1916) was published in one of the largest-ever "limited editions" – a total of 9,983 copies.*

7 *The Common Sense Book of Baby and Child Care* by Dr. Benjamin Spock	at least 39,200,000

Dr. Spock's 1946 manual became the bible of infant care for subsequent generations of parents. Most of the sales have been of the paperback edition of the book.

8 *World Almanac*	at least 38,000,000 #

Having been published annually since 1868 (with a break from 1876 to 1886), this wide-ranging reference book has remained a constant bestseller ever since.

9 *The Valley of the Dolls* by Jacqueline Susann	at least 28,712,000

This tale of sex, violence, and drugs by Jacqueline Susann (1921–74), first published in 1966, is perhaps surprisingly the world's bestselling novel. Margaret Mitchell's Gone With the Wind, *which has achieved sales approaching 28,000,000, is its closest rival.*

10 *In His Steps: "What Would Jesus Do?"* by Rev. Charles Monroe Sheldon	28,500,000

Although virtually unknown today, American clergyman Charles Sheldon (1857–1946) achieved fame and fortune with this 1896 instructive religious treatise on moral dilemmas.

* Number sold and distributed
\# Aggregate sales of annual publication

BESTSELLING CHILDREN'S AUTHORS IN THE WORLD

René Goscinny and Albert Uderzo

René Goscinny (1926–77) and Albert Uderzo (b. 1927) created the comic strip character Astérix the Gaul in 1959. They produced 30 books with total sales of some 250,000,000 copies.

Hergé

Georges Rémi (1907–83), the Belgian author–illustrator who wrote under the pen name Hergé, created the comic strip character Tintin in 1929. Tintin appeared in book form from 1948 onward. He achieved worldwide popularity, and the books have been translated into about 45 languages and dialects. Total sales are believed to be at least 160,000,000.

Enid Blyton

With sales of her Noddy books exceeding 60,000,000 copies, and with more than 700 children's books to her name (UNESCO calculated that there were 974 translations of her works in the 1960s alone), total sales of her works are believed to be over 100,000,000, making her the bestselling English-language author of the 20th century.

Dr. Seuss

His books in the US Top 10 alone total about 30,000,000 copies; to this must be added those titles that have sold fewer than 5,000,000 in the US and all foreign editions of all his books, suggesting total sales of more than 100,000,000.

Beatrix Potter

The Tale of Peter Rabbit (1902) was one of a series of books, the cumulative total sales of which probably exceed 50,000,000.

Lewis Carroll

Total world sales of all editions of Carroll's two classic children's books, Alice's Adventures in Wonderland and Alice Through the Looking Glass, are incalculable. However, just these two books probably place Lewis Carroll among the 20 bestselling children's authors of all time.

It is impossible to make a definitive list of the bestselling children's books in the world. However, based on total sales of their entire output, the authors above have produced titles that have been bestsellers – especially those in numerous translations – over a long period. The sales of Beatrix Potter's *The Tale of Peter Rabbit*, originally published privately in 1901 and by Frederick Warne since 1902, exceed 10,000,000. This makes it possibly the bestselling children's book of all time – although the innumerable editions of other long-established children's classics, such as Robert Louis Stevenson's *Treasure Island* and various works of Hans Christian Andersen, the Brothers Grimm, Mark Twain, Lewis Carroll, and Edward Lear, must collectively have achieved global totals approaching this figure. Among modern children's books are those of the American author Dr. Seuss (Theodor Seuss Giesel), the French duo René Goscinny and Albert Uderzo (Astérix books), and the Belgian author-artist Hergé (Tintin books). The last two have sold totals of more than 220,000,000 and 150,000,000 respectively. The only English-language author to rival them is Enid Blyton: her Noddy books alone have sold more than 60,000,000 copies, and they represent only a fraction of her output of more than 700 titles.

ASTÉRIX THE GAUL
Astérix was created by René Goscinny and Albert Uderzo in 1959. The stories of the intrepid Gauls and their victories over the invading Romans have enthralled readers for almost 40 years.

WORLD'S BESTSELLING FICTION

Author	Title
Richard Bach	*Jonathan Livingstone Seagull*
William Blatty	*The Exorcist*
Peter Benchley	*Jaws*
Erskine Caldwell	*God's Little Acre*
Joseph Heller	*Catch-22*
Harper Lee	*To Kill a Mockingbird*
Colleen McCullough	*The Thorn Birds*
Grace Metalious	*Peyton Place*
Margaret Mitchell	*Gone With the Wind*
George Orwell	*1984*
	Animal Farm
Mario Puzo	*The Godfather*
Harold Robbins	*The Carpetbaggers*
J.D. Salinger	*Catcher in the Rye*

As with the bestselling books of all time, it is virtually impossible to arrive at a definitive list of fiction bestsellers that encompasses all permutations including hardback and paperback editions, book club sales, and translations, and takes account of the innumerable editions of earlier classics such as *Robinson Crusoe* or the works of Jane Austen, Charles Dickens, or popular foreign authors such as Jules Verne. Although only Jacqueline Susann's *The Valley of the Dolls* appears in the all-time list, and publishers' precise sales data remain tantalizingly elusive (it has been said that the most widely published fiction is publishers' own sales figures), there are many other novels that must be close contenders for this list. It seems certain that all the titles in this list have sold in excess of 10,000,000 copies in hardback and paperback worldwide.

ENGLISH-LANGUAGE BESTSELLERS

TOP 10

HARDBACK NON-FICTION BESTSELLERS OF 1995 IN THE US

	Title	Author	Sales
1	Men Are from Mars, Women Are from Venus	John Gray	2,196,935
2	My American Journey	Colin Powell	1,538,469
3	Miss America	Howard Stern	1,398,880
4	The Seven Spiritual Laws of Success	Deepak Chopra	1,085,549
5	The Road Ahead	Bill Gates	775,697
6	Charles Kuralt's America	Charles Kuralt	730,439
7	Mars and Venus in the Bedroom	John Gray	687,726
8	To Renew America	Newt Gingrich	623,435
9	My Point...And I Do Have One	Ellen DeGeneres	600,000
10=	The Moral Compass	William J. Bennett	550,000
10=	The Book of Virtues	William J. Bennett	550,000

Source: Publishers Weekly

STEPHEN KING – KING OF HORROR
Stephen King's novels have been among the bestselling hardback fiction titles on both sides of the Atlantic, while films derived from his books include such smash hits as Carrie, The Shining, The Dead Zone, *and* Creepshow *– in which he makes a cameo appearance.*

TOP 10

HARDBACK FICTION BESTSELLERS OF 1995 IN THE US

	Title/author	Sales
1	The Rainmaker, John Grisham	2,375,000
2	The Lost World, Michael Crichton	1,730,691
3	Five Days in Paris, Danielle Steel	1,550,000
4	The Christmas Box, Richard Paul Evans	1,275,000
5	Lightning, Danielle Steel	1,150,000
6	The Celestine Prophecy, James Redfield	1,048,464
7	Rose Madder, Stephen King	1,020,585
8	Silent Night, Mary Higgins	925,000
9	Politically Correct Holiday Stories, James Finn Garner	906,130
10	The Horse Whisperer, Nicholas Evans	850,000

TOP 10

CHILDREN'S HARDBACKS OF 1995 IN THE US

	Title/author	Sales
1	Pocahontas (Classic), Disney/Mouse Works	1,997,975
2	Pocahontas, Justine Korman	1,368,100
3	The Children's Book of Virtues, William J. Bennett	970,495
4	The Lion King, Justine Korman (adapted)	711,400
5	Guess How Much I Love You, Sam McBratney	622,414
6	Green Eggs and Ham, Dr. Seuss	524,353
7	Cinderella, Ron Dias and Bill Lorencz (illus.)	452,200
8	Pocahontas: Wind's Lullaby, Justine Korman	418,800
9	Daisy-head Mayzie, Dr. Seuss	417,989
10	Winnie the Pooh: The Grand and Wonderful Day, Mary Packard	410,200

TOP 10

CHILDREN'S PAPERBACKS OF 1995 IN THE US

	Title/author	Sales
1	The Horror at Camp Jellyjam, R.L. Stine	1,354,700
2	The Barking Ghost, R.L. Stine	1,303,700
3	Night of the Living Dummy II, R.L. Stine	1,236,000
4	A Shocker on Shock Street, R.L. Stine	1,233,800
5	It Came from Beneath the Sink, R.L. Stine	1,209,100
6	The Cuckoo Clock of Doom, R.L. Stine	1,180,100
7	Monster Blood III, R.L. Stine	1,160,900
8	Revenge of the Snow Gnomes, R.L. Stine	1,143,100
9	Pocahontas, Margot Ludell (adapted)	1,073,800
10	The Indian in the Cupboard, Lynne Reid Banks	1,045,800

TOP 10

TRADE PAPERBACK BESTSELLERS OF 1995 IN THE US

	Title/author	Sales
1	*2nd Helping of Chicken Soup for the Soul*, Jack Canfield & Mark Hansen (eds.)	1,671,446
2	*The Calvin and Hobbes Tenth Anniversary Book*, Bill Watterson	1,325,600
3	*The Far Side Gallery 5*, Gary Larson	804,600
4	*Ten Stupid Things Women Do to Mess Up Their Lives*, Laura Schlessinger	726,686
5	*What to Expect the Toddler Years*, A. Eisenberg	520,837
6	*The Stone Diaries*, Carol Shields	520,000
7	*Microsoft Windows 95 Resource Kit*	500,000
8	*Aladdin Factor*, Jack Canfield & Mark Victor Hansen	491,000
9	*Snow Falling On Cedars*, David Guterson	450,000
10	*Illuminata: A Return to Prayer*, Marianne Williamson	420,000

Source: Publishers Weekly

TOP 10

ALMANACS, ATLASES, AND ANNUALS OF 1995 IN THE US

	Title	Sales
1	*The World Almanac and Book of Facts, 1995*	1,965,000
2	*The World Almanac and Book of Facts, 1996*	1,864,321
3	*The Ernst & Young Tax Guide, 1995*	620,000
4	*The Old Farmer's Almanac 1996*	203,205
5	*What Color is Your Parachute 1996*	183,392
6	*Let's Go: Europe*	134,327
7	*What Color is Your Parachute 1995*	131,839
8	*Birnbaum's Walt Disney World: The Official 1996 Guide*	127,092
9	*Birnbaum's Walt Disney World: The Official 1995 Guide*	121,759
10	*1996 Sports Illustrated Almanac*	114,762

Source: Publishers Weekly

TOP 10

BESTSELLING US AUTHORS OF THE 1990s IN THE UK*

	Author	Titles*	Sales cumulative	Sales average
1	Thomas Harris	1	750,000	750,000
2	John Grisham	6	2,861,440	476,906
3	Barbara Taylor Bradford	4	1,560,734	390,181
4	Danielle Steel	10	3,559,393	355,939
5	Michael Crichton	4	1,322,195	330,549
6	Tom Clancy	6	1,617,977	269,663
7	Stephen King	9	2,262,547	251,394
8	Patricia D. Cornwell	4	983,390	245,848
9	Sidney Sheldon	5	1,205,771	241,154
10	Robert James Waller	2	434,888	217,444

* *Paperback editions published in the UK 1990–95*

Barbara Taylor Bradford is British-born but is married to an American and lives in the US, so she is arguably an American author. If she were disqualified, the 10th entry in this list would be Judith Krantz, whose three novels published in the UK during the 1990s have sold a total of 606,386, an average of 202,129 per title.

TOP 10

LONGEST-RUNNING BESTSELLERS IN THE UK

	Title	Author/ publication*	Appearances#
1	*A Brief History of Time*	Stephen Hawking (H; 1988)	237
2	*The Country Diary of an Edwardian Lady*	Edith Holden (H; 1977)	183
3	*Complete Hip and Thigh Diet*	Rosemary Conley (P; 1989)	169
4	*A Year in Provence*	Peter Mayle (P; 1990)	165 +
5	*Delia Smith's Complete Illustrated Cookery Course*	Delia Smith (H; 1989)	142
6	*Life on Earth*	David Attenborough (H; 1979)	139
7	*Delia Smith's Complete Cookery Course*	Delia Smith (H; 1986)	127
8	*Wild Swans*	Jung Chang (P; 1993)	124
9	*Delia Smith's Summer Collection*	Delia Smith (H; 1993)	121
10	*The Secret Diary of Adrian Mole, Aged 13¾*	Sue Townsend (P; 1983)	119

* H = *hardback*, P = *paperback*
\# *Based on number of appearances in the* Sunday Times *bestseller lists April 14, 1974 to March 24, 1996*
+ *Includes appearances of TV tie-in paperback edition*

THE PRESS

TOP 10

COUNTRIES WITH MOST DAILY NEWSPAPERS

	Country	No. of daily newspapers
1	India	2,300
2	US	1,586
3	Turkey	399
4	Brazil	373
5	Germany	355
6	Russia	339
7	Mexico	292
8	Pakistan	274
9	Argentina	190
10	Spain	148

Certain countries have large numbers of newspapers, each serving relatively small areas and therefore with restricted circulations. The US is the most notable example, with 1,586 daily newspapers, but only four of them with average daily sales of more than 1,000,000. The UK, with fewer individual newspapers, has five with circulations of over 1,000,000. If the table is arranged by total sales of daily newspapers per 1,000 inhabitants, the result – as seen below – is somewhat different:

	Country	Sales per 1,000 inhabitants
1	Hong Kong	819
2	Liechtenstein	700
3	Norway	606
4	Japan	576
5	Iceland	519
6	Finland	515
7	Sweden	511
8	Macau	510
9	South Korea	407
10	Austria	400
	US	*240*

TOP 10

CONSUMERS OF NEWSPRINT

	Country	Consumption per inhabitant kg	lb	oz
1	Sweden	54.32	119	12
2	US	47.633	105	0
3	Austria	46.271	102	0
4	Switzerland	46.235	101	15
5	Norway	42.654	94	1
6	Denmark	42.226	93	1
7	Australia	37.395	82	7
8	Hong Kong	36.500	80	8
9	Singapore	36.367	80	3
10	UK	32.243	71	1

National consumption of newsprint – the cheap wood-pulp paper used for printing newspapers – provides a measure of the extent of the newspaper sales in the Top 10 countries above.

TOP 10

ENGLISH-LANGUAGE DAILY NEWSPAPERS IN THE WORLD

	Newspaper/ founded/country	Average daily circulation (1995)
1	*The Sun,* September 15, 1964, UK	4,075,902
2	*Daily Mirror,* November 2, 1903, UK	2,492,285
3	*Daily Mail,* May 4, 1896, UK	1,894,242
4	*Wall Street Journal,* July 8, 1889, US	1,780,442
5	*USA Today,* September 15, 1982, US	1,570,624
6	*Daily Express,* April 24, 1900, UK	1,252,811
7	*New York Times,* September 18, 1851, US	1,170,869
8	*Los Angeles Times,* December 4, 1881, US	1,058,498
9	*Daily Telegraph,* June 29, 1855, UK	1,052,340
10	*Washington Post,* December 6, 1877, US	840,232

Several long-established English language dailys fail to make the Top 10: in the UK *The Times* has been published since January 1, 1785, while the *New York Post* (formerly the *New York Evening Post*), first published on November 16, 1801, holds the record as America's longest-running daily (the *Hartford Courant* was first issued as a weekly on October 29, 1764 but was not a daily until 1836).

TOP 10

MAGAZINES IN THE US

	Magazine/ no. of issues a year	Circulation*
1	NRTA/AARP Bulletin (10)	21,100,610
2	Modern Maturity (36)	21,064,030
3	Reader's Digest (12)	15,103,830
4	TV Guide (52)	13,175,549
5	National Geographic Magazine (12)	8,988,444
6	Better Homes and Gardens (12)	7,603,207
7	Good Housekeeping (12)	5,372,786
8	Ladies Home Journal (12)	5,045,644
9	Family Circle (17)	5,007,542
10	Woman's Day (17)	4,707,330

* Average for second six months of 1995

National Geographic, the official publication of the National Geographic Society (founded by Gardiner Greene Hubbard, the father-in-law of the great American inventor Alexander Graham Bell), was first published as a monthly magazine in 1896.

TOP 10

MAGAZINES IN THE UK

	Magazine	Average sales per issue
1	Radio Times	1,592,741
2	Reader's Digest	1,521,437
3	What's on TV	1,431,398
4	Bella	1,202,229
5	Take a Break	1,137,283
6	TV Times	1,113,997
7	Viz	875,408
8	Woman's Weekly	826,922
9	Woman	716,837
10	Woman's Own	700,178

In 1916 American bank clerk DeWitt Wallace published a booklet called Getting the Most Out of Farming, which consisted of extracts from various US Government agricultural publications. While recovering from a wound incurred in France during World War I, he contemplated applying the same principle to a general interest magazine and in 1920 produced a sample copy of Reader's Digest.

TOP 10

SPECIAL INTEREST MAGAZINES IN THE US

	Magazine/ no. of issues a year	Circulation*
1	Car & Travel (12)	4,150,352
2	Prevention (12)	3,252,115
3	Sports Illustrated (52)	3,157,303
4	American Legion Magazine (12)	2,852,332
5	Motorland (12)	2,334,938
6	Smithsonian (12)	2,151,172
7	VFW (Veterans of Foreign Wars) Magazine (12)	2,013,258
8	Field and Stream (12)	2,001,875
9	Ebony (12)	1,927,675
10	Money (13)	1,922,737

* Average for second six months of 1995
Source: Magazine Publishers of America

TOP 10

SPECIAL INTEREST MAGAZINES IN THE UK

	Magazine	Average circulation per issue
1	National Trust Magazine	1,163,887
2	Expression! (American Express)	595,513
3	Saga Magazine	540,006
4	Birds (RSPB)	504,611
5	Puzzler Collection	413,432
6	Auto Trader (combined, all editions)	363,927
7	Puzzler	305,500
8	En Route (The Caravan Club)	290,841
9	What Car?	138,274
10	BBC Wildlife	132,217

TOP 10

BESTSELLING BRITISH COMIC BOOKS OF ALL TIME

	Title	Published
1	Beano	1938–present
2	Comic Cuts	1890–1953
3	Dandy	1937–present
4	Eagle	1950–69; 1982–present
5	Film Fun	1920–62
6	Illustrated Chips	1890–1953
7	Mickey Mouse Weekly	1936–57
8	Radio Fun	1938–61
9	Rainbow	1914–56
10	School Friend	1950–65

Information supplied by the Association of Comics Enthusiasts indicates that all 10 comics listed (in alphabetical order) achieved very high circulation figures.

ART AT AUCTION

THE 10
FIRST PAINTINGS AUCTIONED FOR OVER $3M

Work/artist/price	Date
1 *Portrait of Juan de Pareja*, Diego Rodriguez de Silva y Velásquez (Spanish; 1599–1660), Christie's, London, $5,524,000	Nov 27, 1970
2 *The Death of Actaeon*, Titian (Italian; *c.*1488–1576), Christie's, London, $4,036,000	Jun 25, 1971
3 *The Resurrection*, Dirk Bouts (Dutch; 1400–75), Sotheby's, London, $3,740,000	Apr 16, 1980
4 *Saltimbanque Seated with Arms Crossed*, Pablo Picasso (Spanish; 1881–1973), Sotheby's, New York, $3,000,000	May 12, 1980
5 *Paysan en Blouse Bleu*, Paul Cézanne (French; 1839–1906), Christie's, New York, $3,900,000	May 13, 1980
6 *Le Jardin du Poète, Arles*, Vincent van Gogh (Dutch; 1853–80), Christie's, New York, $5,200,000	May 13, 1980
7 *Juliet and Her Nurse*, J.M.W. Turner (British; 1775–1851), Sotheby's, New York, $6,400,000	May 29, 1980
8 *Samson and Delilah*, Sir Peter Paul Rubens (British; 1577–1640), Christie's, London, $5,474,000	Jul 11, 1980
9 *The Holy Family with Saints and Putti*, Nicolas Poussin (French; 1594–1665), Christie's, London, $3,564,000	Apr 10, 1981
10 *Self Portrait: Yo Picasso*, Pablo Picasso, Sotheby's, New York, $5,300,000	May 21, 1981

TOP 10
MOST EXPENSIVE PAINTINGS BY WOMEN ARTISTS

Work/artist/sale	Price ($)
1 *The Conversation*, Mary Cassatt (American; 1845–1926), Christie's, New York, May 11, 1988	4,100,000
2 *Mother, Sara, and the Baby*, Mary Cassatt, Christie's, New York, May 10, 1989	3,500,000
3 *Autoretrato con chango y loro*, Frida Kahlo (Mexican; 1907–54), Sotheby's, New York, May 17, 1995	2,900,000
4 *Augusta Reading to Her Daughter*, Mary Cassatt, Sotheby's, New York, May 9, 1989	2,800,000
5 *Sara Holding Her Dog*, Mary Cassatt, Sotheby's, New York, November 11, 1988	2,500,000
6 *Young Lady in a Loge, Gazing to the Right*, Mary Cassatt, Sotheby's, New York, November 10, 1992	2,300,000
7 *Madame H. de Fleury and Her Child*, Mary Cassatt, Sotheby's, New York, May 25, 1988	1,900,000
8= *Adam et Eve*, Tamara de Lempicka (Polish; 1898–1980), Christie's, New York, March 3, 1994	1,800,000
8= *Black Hollyhocks with Blue Larkspur*, Georgia O'Keeffe (American; 1887–1986), Sotheby's, New York, December 3, 1987	1,800,000
10 *Balskorna – Dancing Shoe*, Helene Schjerfbeck (Finnish; 1862–1946), Sotheby's, London, March 27, 1990	1,630,000

TOP 10
MOST EXPENSIVE PHOTOGRAPHS EVER SOLD AT AUCTION

Photograph/photographer/sale	Price ($)
1 *Egypte et Nubie: Sites et monuments les plus intéressants pour l'étude de l'art et de l'histoire*, Félix Teynard (French; 1817–92) Laurin Guilloux Buffetaud Tailleur, Paris, December 21, 1990	707,000
2 *The North American Indian*, Edward S. Curtis (American; 1868–1952), Sotheby's, New York, October 7, 1993	662,500
3 *The North American Indian*, Edward S. Curtis, Christie's, New York, April 7, 1995	464,500
4 *Georgia O'Keeffe: A Portrait – Hands with Thimble*, Alfred Stieglitz (American; 1864–1946), Christie's, New York, October 8, 1993	398,500
5= *Equivalents (21)*, Alfred Stieglitz, Christie's, New York, October 30, 1989	396,000
5= *The North American Indian*, Edward S. Curtis, Christie's, New York, October 13, 1992	396,000
7 *Noir et blanche*, Man Ray (American; 1890–1976), Christie's, New York, April 21, 1994	354,500
8 *Hier, Demain, Aujourd'hui (triptych)*, Man Ray, Christie's, New York, October 8, 1993	222,500
9 *Noir et blanche*, Man Ray, Christie's, New York, October 5, 1995	206,000
10 *Glass Tears*, Man Ray, Sotheby's, London, May 7, 1993	195,000

CHRISTIE'S

T O P 1 0

MOST EXPENSIVE PAINTINGS EVER SOLD AT AUCTION

Work/artist/sale	Price ($)
1 *Portrait of Dr. Gachet,* Vincent van Gogh (Dutch; 1853–80), Christie's, New York, May 15, 1990	75,000,000

Both this painting and the one in the No. 2 position were bought by Ryoei Saito, head of Japanese Daishowa Paper Manufacturing.

2 *Au Moulin de la Galette,* Pierre-Auguste Renoir (French; 1841–1919), Sotheby's, New York, May 17, 1990	71,000,000
3 *Les Noces de Pierrette,* Pablo Picasso (Spanish; 1881–1973), Binoche et Godeau, Paris, November 30, 1989	51,671,920

The painting was sold by Swedish financier Fredrik Roos to Tomonori Tsurumaki, a property developer, who bid for it by telephone from Tokyo.

4 *Irises,* Vincent van Gogh, Sotheby's, New York, November 11, 1987	49,000,000

After much speculation, the purchaser was confirmed as businessman Alan Bond. However, he was unable to pay for it in full, so its former status as the world's most expensive work of art has been disputed.

5 *Self Portrait: Yo Picasso,* Pablo Picasso, Sotheby's, New York, May 9, 1989	43,500,000

Work/artist/sale	Price ($)
6 *Au Lapin Agile,* Pablo Picasso, Sotheby's, New York, November 15, 1989	37,000,000

The painting depicts Picasso as a harlequin at the bar of the café Lapin.

7 *Sunflowers,* Vincent van Gogh, Christie's, London, March 30, 1987	36,225,000

At the time this was the most expensive picture ever sold.

8 *Acrobate et Jeune Arlequin,* Pablo Picasso, Christie's, London, November 28, 1988	35,530,000

Until the sale of Yo Picasso, this held the world record for a 20th-century painting. It was bought by Mitsukoshi, a Japanese department store. (In Japan, many major stores have important art galleries.)

9 *Portrait of Duke Cosimo I de Medici,* Jacopo da Carucci (Pontormo) (Italy; 1494–1556/7), Christie's, New York, May 31, 1989	32,000,000

This is the record price paid for an Old Master – and the only one in this Top 10. It was bought by the J. Paul Getty Museum, Malibu, California.

10 *Angel Fernandez De Soto,* Pablo Picasso, Sotheby's, New York, May 8, 1995	28,152,500

This painting was sold by one Greek shipowner, George Embiricos, and bought by another, Stavros Niarchos.

T O P 1 0

MOST EXPENSIVE SCULPTURES EVER SOLD AT AUCTION

Work/sculptor/sale	Price ($)
1 *The Dancing Faun,* Adriaen de Vries (Dutch; c. 1550–1626), Sotheby's, London, December 7, 1989	9,796,000
2 *Petite Danseuse de Quatorze Ans,* Edgar Degas (French; 1834–1917), Christie's, New York, November 14, 1988	9,250,000
3 *Petite Danseuse de Quatorze Ans,* Edgar Degas, Sotheby's, New York, May 10, 1988	9,200,000
4 *La Negresse Blonde,* Constantin Brancusi, Sotheby's, New York, May 16, 1990	8,000,000
5 *La Muse Endormie III,* Constantin Brancusi (Romanian; 1876–1957), Christie's, New York, November 14, 1989	7,500,000
6 *L'Homme Qui Marche I,* Alberto Giacometti (Swiss; 1901–66), Christie's, London, November 28, 1988	6,358,000
7 *Grande Femme Debout I,* Alberto Giacometti, Christie's, New York, November 14, 1989	4,500,000
8 *Coming Through the Rye,* Frederic Remington (American; 1861–1909), Christie's, New York, May 25, 1989	4,000,000
9 *Florentine Group of the Rape of a Sabine with Three Nude Figures,* Giambologna (Italian; c. 1529–1608), Christie's, London, December 5, 1989	3,950,000
10 *Cubi V,* David Smith (American; 1906–65), Sotheby's, New York, May 4, 1994	3,700,000

RISING SUN
When it was sold in 1987 for $36,225,000, Vincent van Gogh's Sunflowers *(1888) almost tripled the world record price for a painting. One of several works in a series, its price is equivalent to $2,415,000 per sunflower.*

MODERN ARTISTS

The internationally famed artists of the 20th century represented here share the rare ability to command auction prices in excess of several million dollars. In the case of Pablo Picasso, no fewer than five of his works achieve places among the 10 highest priced paintings of all time.

TOP 10
MOST EXPENSIVE PAINTINGS BY JASPER JOHNS

Work/sale	Price ($)
1 *False Start*, Sotheby's, New York, November 10, 1988	15,500,000
2 *Two Flags*, Sotheby's, New York, November 8, 1989	11,000,000
3 *White Flag*, Christie's, New York, November 9, 1988	6,400,000
4 *Jubilee*, Sotheby's, New York, November 13, 1991	4,500,000
5 *Device Circle*, Christie's, New York, November 9, 1989	4,000,000
6 *Gray Rectangles*, Sotheby's, New York, November 10, 1988	3,900,000
7 *Diver*, Christie's, New York, May 3, 1988	3,800,000
8 *Small False Start*, Christie's, New York, November 12, 1991	3,700,000
9 *Out of the Window*, Sotheby's, New York, November 10, 1986	3,300,000
10 *Colored Alphabet*, Christie's, New York, May 3, 1989	3,200,000

Measured by the prices his works realize at auction, Jasper Johns (b. 1930) is the world's foremost living artist. His work, which is considered as at the vanguard of Pop Art, also includes sculpture and prints.

TOP 10
MOST EXPENSIVE PAINTINGS BY DAVID HOCKNEY

Work/sale	Price ($)
1 *Grand Procession of Dignitaries in the Semi-Egyptian Style*, Sotheby's, New York, May 2, 1989	2,000,000
2 *Deep and Wet Water*, Sotheby's, New York, November 8, 1989	1,300,000
3 *Henry Geldzahler and Christopher Scott*, Sotheby's, New York, November 17, 1992	1,000,000
4 *California Art Collector*, Sotheby's, New York, November 10, 1993	925,000
5 *The Room, Manchester Street*, Christie's, New York, May 3, 1989	800,000
6 *A Neat Lawn*, Sotheby's, London, December 1, 1988	598,400
7 *Different Kinds of Water Pouring into Swimming Pool, Santa Monica*, Sotheby's, New York, May 2, 1989	460,000
8 *The Room, Tarzana*, Christie's, London, December 3, 1987	447,200
9 *The Actor*, Sotheby's, London, June 27, 1991	386,400
10 *Fall Pool with Two Flat Blues*, Christie's, New York, November 12, 1991	380,000

David Hockney (born in Bradford, UK, July 9, 1937) studied at the Royal College of Art and achieved early acclaim in the UK as a representative of Pop Art before settling in California, where the colorful urban landscape ideally suited his evolving style. As well as his paintings, which are avidly collected by the fashionable wealthy, he has produced stage sets and worked with a variety of novel media such as Polaroid, photocollage, and even faxes. Many of his works have become widely known at a more affordable level through poster reproduction.

TOP 10
MOST EXPENSIVE PAINTINGS BY PABLO PICASSO

Work/sale	Price ($)
1 *Les Noces de Pierrette*, Binoche et Godeau, Paris, November 30, 1989	51,671,920
2 *Self Portrait: Yo Picasso*, Sotheby's, New York, May 9, 1989	43,500,000
3 *Au Lapin Agile*, Sotheby's, New York, November 15, 1989	37,000,000
4 *Acrobate et Jeune Arlequin*, Christie's, London, November 28, 1988	35,530,000
5 *Angel Fernandez de Soto*, Sotheby's, New York, May 8, 1995	28,152,500
6 *Le Miroir*, Sotheby's, New York, November 15, 1989	24,000,000
7 *Maternité*, Christie's, New York, June 14, 1988	22,500,000
8 *Les Tuileries*, Christie's, London, June 25, 1990	22,000,000
9 *Le Miroir*, Christie's, New York, November 7, 1995	18,200,000
10 *Mère et Enfant*, Sotheby's, New York, November 15, 1989	17,000,000

By the late 1950s the Spanish painter Pablo Picasso (1881–1973) was already being hailed as the foremost artist of the 20th century. This was progressively reflected in the saleroom: when *Mère et Enfant* (*Mother and Child*) was sold in 1957 for $185,000, it was the highest price ever paid for a painting during an artist's lifetime. The upward spiral continued with *Woman and Child at the Seashore*, sold in 1962 for $304,000. In 1981 Picasso's *Self Portrait: Yo Picasso* (No. 2 in this list) made $5,300,000 – a level considered astonishing at the time. The May 8, 1995, sale of *Angel Fernandez De Soto* achieved the highest price for any painting sold at auction since 1990.

TOP 10

MOST EXPENSIVE PAINTINGS BY JACKSON POLLOCK

	Work/sale	Price ($)
1	*Number 8, 1950*, Sotheby's, New York, May 2, 1989	10,500,000
2	*Frieze*, Christie's, New York, May 23, 1990	5,200,000
3	*Search*, Sotheby's, New York, May 2, 1988	4,400,000
4	*Number 19, 1949*, Sotheby's, New York, May 2, 1989	3,600,000
5	*Number 31, 1949*, Christie's, New York, May 3, 1988	3,200,000
6	*Number 13*, Christie's, New York, November 7, 1990	2,800,000
7=	*Number 26, 1950*, Sotheby's, NewYork, May 4, 1987	2,500,000
7=	*Number 19, 1948*, Christie's, New York, May 4, 1993	2,500,000
9	*Number 20*, Sotheby's, New York, May 8, 1990	2,200,000
10	*Number 24, 1949*, *Number 25, 1949*, *Number 29, 1949 (triptych)*, Christie's, New York, May 2, 1989	2,000,000

The master of "action painting," American artist Jackson Pollock (1912–56) developed a personal style that involved the frenzied dripping and splashing of paint on to large canvases, theorizing that the energy and emotion devoted to the act of painting was of greater importance than the end result.

TOP 10

MOST EXPENSIVE PAINTINGS BY SALVADOR DALI

	Work/sale	Price ($)
1	*Assumpta Corpuscularia Lapislazulina*, Christie's, New York, May 15, 1990	3,700,000
2	*Cygnes Réflétant des Elephants*, Sotheby's, New York, May 9, 1995	3,200,000
3=	*La Bataille de Tetouan*, Sotheby's, New York, November 11, 1987	2,200,000
3=	*L'Ascension de Christ – Pieta*, Christie's, New York, November 2, 1993	2,200,000
5	*La Bataille de Tetouan*, Christie's, New York, May 10, 1994	2,000,000
6	*Portrait de Paul Eluard*, Christie's, New York, November 14, 1989	1,900,000
7	*Bataille Autour d'un Pissenlit*, Guy Loudmer, Paris, March 21, 1988	1,100,000
8	*Le Christ de Gala*, Christie's, New York, May 10, 1994	950,000
9	*Le Someil*, Christie's, London, March 30, 1981	806,000
10	*Portrait de Mon Frère Mort*, Christie's, New York, November 7, 1995	800,000

In the 1920s the Spanish painter Salvador Dali (1904–89) became one of the principal figures in the Surrealist movement. His works feature dreamlike and psychologically disturbing images set in realistic landscapes. The best known are the "melting" watches in his *The Persistence of Memory* (1931).

TOP 10

MOST EXPENSIVE PAINTINGS BY ANDY WARHOL

	Work/sale	Price ($)
1	*Shot Red Marilyn*, Christie's, New York, May 3, 1989	3,700,000
2	*Marilyn Monroe, Twenty Times*, Sotheby's, New York, November 10, 1988	3,600,000
3	*Marilyn x 100*, Sotheby's, New York, November 17, 1992	3,400,000
4	*Shot Red Marilyn*, Christie's, New York, November 2, 1994	3,300,000
5	*Liz*, Christie's, New York, November 7, 1989	2,050,000
6	*Triple Elvis*, Christie's, New York, November 2, 1994	2,000,000
7	*210 Coca-Cola Bottles*, Christie's, New York, May 5, 1992	1,900,000
8	*Ladies and Gentlemen, 1975*, Binoche et Godeau, Paris, November 30, 1989	1,607,000
9=	*The Last Supper*, Sotheby's, New York, November 8, 1989	1,600,000
9=	*Race Riot*, Christie's, New York, November 7, 1989	1,600,000

Born Andrew Warhola, Andy Warhol (1926–87) became one of the most famous American artists of all time through his leadership of the Pop Art movement. He typically featured images derived from popular culture, among them familiar brands, such as Campbell's soup cans and Coca-Cola bottles, and portraits – often multiple images – of well-known celebrities.

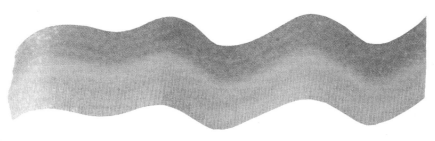

ART ON SHOW

TOP 10

BEST-ATTENDED EXHIBITIONS AT THE NATIONAL GALLERY, WASHINGTON, DC

	Exhibition	Attendance
1	*Rodin Rediscovered,* 1981–82	1,053,223
2	*Treasure Houses of Britain,* 1985–86	990,474
3	*The Treasures of Tutankhamun,* 1976–77	835,924
4	*Archaeological Finds of the People's Republic of China,* 1974–75	684,238
5	*Ansel Adams: Classic Images,* 1985–86	651,652
6	*The Splendor of Dresden,* 1978	620,089
7	*The Art of Paul Gauguin,* 1988	596,058
8	*Circa 1492: Art in the Age of Exploration,* 1991–92	568,192
9	*Post-Impressionism: Cross Currents in European and American Painting,* 1980	557,533
10	*Great French Paintings from The Barnes Foundation,* 1993	520,924

TOP 10

BEST-ATTENDED EXHIBITIONS AT THE METROPOLITAN MUSEUM OF ART, NEW YORK

	Exhibition	Attendance
1	*The Treasures of Tutankhamun,* 1978–79	1,226,467
2	*The Vatican Collection: The Papacy and Art,* 1983	896,743
3	*Origins of Impressionism,* 1994–95	794,108
4	*The Horses of San Marco,* 1980	742,221
5	*Seurat,* 1991–92	642,408
6	*Van Gogh in St. Rémy and Auvers,* 1986–87	630,699
7	*Van Gogh in Arles,* 1984	624,120
8	*Mexico: Splendor of Thirty Centuries,* 1990–91	584,528
9	*Masterpieces of Impressionism and Post-Impressionism: The Annenberg Collection,* 1991	560,734
10	*Velázquez,* 1989–90	556,394

TOP 10

LARGEST PAINTINGS IN THE LOUVRE MUSEUM, PARIS

	Artist/painting	Size (height x width) ft (m)
1	Jean-Pierre Alaux (1783–1856), *Interior of Westminster Abbey*	62 × 131 (19.0 × 40.0)
2	Jean-Pierre Alaux, *Interior of St. Peter's, Rome*	57 × 131 (17.5 × 40.0)
3	Francesco Fontebasso (1709–59), *Palace Ceiling*	26 × 33 (8.0 × 10.0)
4	Paolo Veronese (1525–88), *The Marriage Feast at Cana*	22 × 32 (6.7 × 9.9)
5	Jacques-Louis David (1748–1825), *The Coronation of Napoleon*	20 × 32 (6.2 × 9.9)
6	Charles Lebrun (1619–90), *The Battle of Arbela*	15 × 42 (4.7 × 12.7)
7	Charles Lebrun, *Alexander and Porus*	15 × 41 (4.7 × 12.6)
8	Charles Lebrun, *Crossing the Granicus*	15 × 40 (4.7 × 12.1)
9	Antoine-Jean Gros (1771–1835), *The Battle of Eylau*	17 × 26 (5.2 × 7.8)
10	Antoine-Jean Gros, *Napoleon Visiting the Plague Victims of Jaffa*	17 × 24 (5.2 × 7.2)

Jean-Pierre Alaux's *Interior of Westminster Abbey* measures almost three times the area of a tennis court. As the list shows, a number of paintings celebrating the achievements of Napoleon were also created on a gigantic scale. In terms of paint area, however, even these gargantuan works are dwarfed by panoramas created in France and elsewhere, such as the 45 × 402ft-/ 14 × 123m-painting *Panthéon de la Guerre.*

THE CORONATION OF NAPOLEON
Jacques-Louis David was virtually dictator of the arts in France from the outbreak of the Revolution to the fall of Napoleon. He was Napoleon's painter–advocate and created the Empire style, of which his huge The Coronation of Napoleon *is a superb example.*

TOP 10

BEST-ATTENDED EXHIBITIONS AT THE VICTORIA & ALBERT MUSEUM, LONDON

	Exhibition	Attendance
1	Britain Can Make It, 1946	1,500,000
2	Spanish Art Treasures, 1881	1,022,000
3	Scientific Apparatus, 1876	275,813
4	Wedding Presents (Prince and Princess of Wales), 1863	229,425
5	Six Wives of Henry VIII (BBC drama costumes), 1970	182,825
6	Visions of Japan, 1991	177,669
7	Sovereign, 1992	174,078
8	Meyrick Armour, 1879	172,708
9	Fabergé, 1977	152,645
10	Fabergé: Imperial Jeweler, 1994	151,141

The Victoria & Albert Museum is unusual in having records of exhibitions held dating back as far as 1863.

TOP 10

BEST-ATTENDED EXHIBITIONS AT THE TATE GALLERY, LONDON

	Exhibition	Attendance
1	John Constable, 1976	313,659
2	Picasso: Sculptor/Painter, 1994	296,648
3	Salvador Dali – A Retrospective, 1980	236,615
4	The Pre-Raphaelites, 1984	219,292
5	David Hockney – A Retrospective, 1988–89	173,162
6	Constable, 1991	169,412
7	James McNeil Whistler, 1994	152,226
8	Late Picasso, 1953–72, 1988	139,349
9	The Essential Cubism, 1983	122,246
10	Thomas Gainsborough, 1980–81	112,517

TOP 10

BEST-ATTENDED EXHIBITIONS AT THE BRITISH MUSEUM, LONDON

	Exhibition	Year	Attendance
1	The Treasures of Tutankhamun*	1972–73	1,694,117
2	Turner Watercolours	1975	585,046
3	The Vikings*	1980	465,000
4	Thracian Treasures from Bulgaria	1976	424,465
5	From Manet to Toulouse-Lautrec: French Lithographs 1860-1900	1978	355,354
6	The Ancient Olympic Games	1980	334,354
7	Treasures for the Nation*	1988–89	294,837
8	Excavating in Egypt	1982–83	285,736
9	Heraldry	1978	262,183
10	Drawings by Michelangelo	1975	250,000

* Admission charged, all others free

TREASURE FROM THE TOMB
The centerpiece of the record-breaking The Treasures of Tutankhamun *exhibition was the boy-pharaoh's solid gold mask.*

TOP 10

TALLEST FREE-STANDING STATUES IN THE WORLD

	Statue	Height m	Height ft
1	Chief Crazy Horse, Thunderhead Mountain, South Dakota	172	563

Started in 1948 by Polish–American sculptor Korczak Ziolkowski and continued after his death in 1982 by his widow and eight of his children, this gigantic equestrian statue is even longer than it is high (641 ft/195 m).

2	Buddha, Tokyo, Japan	120	394

This Japanese–Taiwanese project took seven years to complete and weighs 1,000 tons.

3	The Indian Rope Trick, Jönköping, Sweden	103	337

Sculptor Calle Örnemark's 144-ton wooden sculpture depicts a long strand of "rope" held by a fakir, while another figure ascends.

4	Motherland, 1967, Volgograd, Russia	82	270

This concrete statue of a woman with raised sword commemorates the Soviet victory at the Battle of Stalingrad (1942–43).

5	Buddha, Bamian, Afghanistan	53	173

Near this 3rd–4th century AD statue lies the remains of the even taller Sakya Buddha, said to have measured 1,000 ft/305 m.

	Statue	Height m	Height ft
6	Kannon, Otsubo-yama, near Tokyo, Japan	52	170

This immense statue of Kannon, goddess of mercy was unveiled in 1961. It was built in honour of the dead of World War II.

7	Statue of Liberty, New York, New York	46	151

Designed by Auguste Bartholdi and presented to the US by the people of France, the statue was shipped in sections to Liberty (formerly Bedloe's) Island, where it was assembled. It was unveiled on October 28, 1886.

8	Christ, Rio de Janeiro, Brazil	38	125

The work of sculptor Paul Landowski and engineer Heitor da Silva Costa, the figure of Christ weighs 1,282 tons.

9	Tian Tan (Temple of Heaven) Buddha, Po Lin Monastery, Lantau Island, Hong Kong	34	112

Completed after 20 years' work and unveiled on December 29, 1993, the bronze statue weighs 250 tons and cost $9,000,000.

10	Colossi of Memnon, Karnak, Egypt	21	70

The Colossi consist of two seated sandstone figures of Pharaoh Amenhotep III.

124

MUSIC

20TH CENTURY

Since the early years of the century the recorded music business has been dominated by the single. It has usually provided two for the price of one, because the traditional "single" has always been a "double," in that the seven-inch 45-rpm disc contained two recordings, one either side. The "A-side" featured the song with the anticipated selling power, while the "B-side," or "flip," might contain anything from a song of equal worth to a throwaway item designed purely to fill the space on the vinyl.

BRITPOP PHENOMENON
Manchester sibling-led Oasis are the most promising contenders for global singles honors in the second half of the 1990s.

TOP 10

SINGLES OF THE 1960s IN THE US

	Title/artist	Year
1	*I Want to Hold Your Hand*, Beatles	1964
2	*It's Now or Never*, Elvis Presley	1960
3	*Hey Jude*, Beatles	1968
4	*The Ballad of the Green Berets*, Staff Sgt. Barry Sadler	1966
5	*Love Is Blue*, Paul Mauriat	1968
6	*I'm a Believer*, Monkees	1966
7	*Can't Buy Me Love*, Beatles	1964
8	*She Loves You*, Beatles	1964
9	*Sugar Sugar*, Archies	1969
10	*The Twist*, Chubby Checker	1960

TOP 10

SINGLES OF THE 1960s IN THE UK

	Title/artist	Year
1	*She Loves You*, Beatles	1963
2	*I Want to Hold Your Hand*, Beatles	1963
3	*Tears*, Ken Dodd	1965
4	*Can't Buy Me Love*, Beatles	1964
5	*I Feel Fine*, Beatles	1964
6	*We Can Work It Out/ Day Tripper*, Beatles	1965
7	*The Carnival Is Over*, Seekers	1965
8	*Release Me*, Engelbert Humperdinck	1967
9	*It's Now or Never*, Elvis Presley	1960
10	*Green, Green Grass of Home*, Tom Jones	1966

TOP 10

SINGLES OF THE 1970s IN THE US

	Title/artist	Year
1	*You Light Up My Life*, Debby Boone	1977
2	*Le Freak*, Chic	1978
3	*Night Fever*, Bee Gees	1978
4	*Stayin' Alive*, Bee Gees	1978
5	*Shadow Dancing*, Andy Gibb	1978
6	*Disco Lady*, Johnnie Taylor	1976
7	*I'll Be There*, Jackson Five	1970
8	*Star Wars Theme/ Cantina Band*, Meco	1977
9	*Car Wash*, Rose Royce	1976
10	*Joy to the World*, Three Dog Night	1971

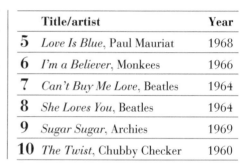

During the last four years of the 1970s, chart-topping records in the US were routinely selling over 2,000,000 copies.

CHART SINGLES

TOP 10

SINGLES OF THE 1970s IN THE UK

	Title/artist	Year
1	*Mull of Kintyre*, Wings	1977
2	*Rivers of Babylon/Brown Girl in the Ring*, Boney M	1978
3	*You're the One That I Want*, John Travolta and Olivia Newton-John	1978
4	*Mary's Boy Child/ Oh My Lord*, Boney M	1978
5	*Summer Nights*, John Travolta and Olivia Newton-John	1978
6	*Y.M.C.A.*, Village People	1979
7	*Bohemian Rhapsody*, Queen	1975
8	*Heart of Glass*, Blondie	1979
9	*Merry Xmas Everybody*, Slade	1973
10	*Don't Give Up On Us*, David Soul	1977

TOP 10

SINGLES OF THE 1980s IN THE US

	Title/artist	Year
1	*We Are the World*, USA for Africa	1985
2	*Physical*, Olivia Newton-John	1981
3	*Endless Love*, Diana Ross and Lionel Richie	1981
4	*Eye of the Tiger*, Survivor	1982
5	*I Love Rock 'n' Roll*, Joan Jett & The Blackhearts	1982
6	*When Doves Cry*, Prince	1984
7	*Celebration*, Kool & The Gang	1981
8	*Another One Bites the Dust*, Queen	1980
9	*Wild Thing*, Tone Loc	1989
10	*Islands in the Stream*, Kenny Rogers and Dolly Parton	1983

TOP 10

SINGLES OF THE 1980s IN THE UK

	Title/artist	Year
1	*Do They Know It's Christmas?*, Band Aid	1984
2	*Relax*, Frankie Goes to Hollywood	1984
3	*I Just Called to Say I Love You*, Stevie Wonder	1984
4	*Two Tribes*, Frankie Goes to Hollywood	1984
5	*Don't You Want Me?*, The Human League	1981
6	*Last Christmas*, Wham!	1984
7	*Karma Chameleon*, Culture Club	1983
8	*Careless Whisper*, George Michael	1984
9	*The Power of Love*, Jennifer Rush	1985
10	*Come on Eileen*, Dexy's Midnight Runners	1982

TOP 10

SINGLES OF THE 1990s IN THE US TO DATE*

	Title/artist	Year
1	*I Will Always Love You*, Whitney Houston	1992
2	*Whoomp! There It Is*, Tag Team	1993
3	*Everything I Do (I Do It for You)*, Bryan Adams	1991
4	*Gangsta's Paradise*, Coolio featuring LV	1995
5	*Baby Got Back*, Sir Mix-A-Lot	1992
6	*Vogue*, Madonna	1990
7	*End of the Road*, Boyz II Men	1992
8	*I'll Make Love to You*, Boyz II Men	1994
9	*I Swear*, All-4-One	1994
10	*Fantasy*, Mariah Carey	1995

* Up to December 31, 1995

BRYAN ADAMS

FEED THE WORLD WITH A SONG FROM THE HEART
The commitment of Bob Geldof to do something for the starving people of Ethiopia brought big names in rock and pop, such as George Michael, Bono, and Freddy Mercury, together.

TOP 10

SINGLES OF THE 1990s IN THE UK TO DATE*

	Title/artist	Year		Title/artist	Year
1	*Unchained Melody*, Robson Green & Jerome Flynn	1995	6	*Think Twice*, Celine Dion	1994
2	*Love is All Around*, Wet Wet Wet	1994	7	*I Would Do Anything for Love (But I Won't Do That)*, Meat Loaf	1993
3	*Everything I Do (I Do It for You)*, Bryan Adams	1991	8	*I Believe/Up on the Roof*, Robson Green & Jerome Flynn	1995
4	*I Will Always Love You*, Whitney Houston	1992	9	*Back For Good*, Take That	1995
5	*Gangsta's Paradise*, Coolio featuring LV	1995	10	*Saturday Night*, Whigfield	1994

* Up to December 31, 1995

SINGLES – WORLD/US/UK

TOP 10

SINGLES OF ALL TIME WORLDWIDE

	Title/artist	Sales exceed
1	*White Christmas*, Bing Crosby	30,000,000
2	*Rock Around the Clock*, Bill Haley & His Comets	17,000,000
3	*I Want to Hold Your Hand*, Beatles	12,000,000
4=	*It's Now or Never*, Elvis Presley	10,000,000
4=	*I Will Always Love You*, Whitney Houston	10,000,000
6=	*Hound Dog/Don't Be Cruel*, Elvis Presley	9,000,000
6=	*Diana*, Paul Anka	9,000,000
8=	*Hey Jude*, Beatles	8,000,000
8=	*I'm a Believer*, Monkees	8,000,000
10=	*Can't Buy Me Love*, Beatles	7,000,000
10=	*Do They Know It's Christmas?*, Band Aid	7,000,000
10=	*We Are the World*, USA for Africa	7,000,000

TOP 10

SONGS REQUESTED AT FUNERALS

	Title/Artist
1	*I Will Always Love You*, Whitney Houston
2	*Nessun Dorma*, Luciano Pavarotti
3	*You'll Never Walk Alone*, Gerry & The Pacemakers
4	*Unforgettable*, Nat "King" Cole
5	*Wind Beneath My Wings*, Bette Midler
6	*Bat Out of Hell*, Meat Loaf
7	*Another One Bites the Dust*, Queen
8	*Who Wants to Live for Ever*, Queen
9	*Memory*, Elaine Paige
10	*(Where Do I Begin) Love Story*, Andy Williams

TOP 10

SINGLES OF ALL TIME IN THE US

	Title/artist	Year
1	*White Christmas*, Bing Crosby	1942
2	*I Want to Hold Your Hand*, Beatles	1964
3	*Hound Dog/Don't Be Cruel*, Elvis Presley	1956
4	*It's Now or Never*, Elvis Presley	1960
5	*I Will Always Love You*, Whitney Houston	1992
6	*Hey Jude*, Beatles	1968
7	*We Are the World*, USA for Africa	1985
8	*Whoomp! There It Is*, Tag Team	1993
9	*Everything I Do (I Do It for You)*, Bryan Adams	1991
10	*The Chipmunk Song*, Chipmunks	1958

White Christmas is still the all-time, most-charted single in the US, having been a major Yuletide seller every Christmas since its original release in 1942. Total US sales are thought to be somewhere in the region of 15,000,000, more than twice the number of the Beatles' biggest seller at No. 2, *I Want to Hold Your Hand*. Whitney Houston's *I Will Always Love You* became the first single to exceed sales of 4,000,000 in the 1990s, joined in 1993 by the quadruple-platinum rap novelty hit *Whoomp! There It Is* by Tag Team.

TOP 10

SINGLES OF ALL TIME IN THE UK

	Title/artist	Year	Approx. sales
1	*Do They Know It's Christmas?*, Band Aid	1984	3,510,000
2	*Bohemian Rhapsody*, Queen	1975/91	2,130,000
3	*Mull of Kintyre*, Wings	1977	2,050,000
4	*Rivers Of Babylon/Brown Girl in the Ring*, Boney M	1978	1,995,000
5	*Relax*, Frankie Goes to Hollywood	1984	1,910,000
6	*She Loves You*, Beatles	1963	1,890,000
7	*You're the One That I Want*, John Travolta and Olivia Newton-John	1978	1,870,000
8	*Unchained Melody*, Robson Green and Jerome Flynn	1995	1,820,000
9	*Mary's Boy Child/Oh My Lord*, Boney M	1978	1,790,000
10	*I Just Called to Say I Love You*, Stevie Wonder	1984	1,775,000

A total of 48 singles have sold over 1,000,000 copies apiece in the UK during the last 40 years, and these are the cream of that crop. The Band Aid single had a host of special circumstances surrounding it, and it is difficult to imagine such sales ever being approached again by a single in this country, even if a similarly special case arose in the future. Two years, 1978 and 1984, were the all-time strongest for million-selling singles, and this chart fittingly has three representatives from each. The pop group Boney M was made up of four singers "assembled" in West Germany to perform a popular disco song.

TOP 10

SINGLES WITH MOST WEEKS AT NO. 1 IN THE US

	Title/artist	Year	Weeks at No. 1
1	*One Sweet Day*, Maria Carey and Boyz II Men	1995	16
2=	*I Will Always Love You*, Whitney Houston	1992	14
2=	*I'll Make Love to You*, Boyz II Men	1994	14
4	*End of the Road*, Boyz II Men	1992	13
5=	*Don't Be Cruel/Hound Dog*, Elvis Presley	1956	11
5=	*I Swear*, All-4-One	1994	11
7=	*Cherry Pink and Apple Blossom White*, Perez Prado	1955	10
7=	*You Light Up My Life*, Debby Boone	1977	10
7=	*Physical*, Olivia Newton-John	1981	10
10=	*Mack the Knife*, Bobby Darin	1959	9
10=	*Hey Jude*, Beatles	1968	9
10=	*Endless Love*, Diana Ross and Lionel Richie	1981	9
10=	*Bette Davis Eyes*, Kim Carnes	1981	9
10=	*Singing the Blues*, Guy Mitchell	1956	9
10=	*Theme from "A Summer Place,"* Percy Faith	1960	9

THE KING REIGNS FOREVER
Elvis Presley's international success is exemplified by his two appearances among the world's 10 bestselling singles of all time.

TOP 10

SINGLES WITH MOST WEEKS AT NO. 1 IN THE UK

	Title/artist	Weeks at No. 1
1	*I Believe*, Frankie Laine	18
2	*Everything I Do (I Do It for You)*, Bryan Adams	16
3	*Love Is All Around*, Wet Wet Wet	15
4	*Bohemian Rhapsody*, Queen	14
5	*Rose Marie*, Slim Whitman	11
6=	*Cara Mia*, David Whitfield	10
6=	*I Will Always Love You*, Whitney Houston	10
8=	*Diana*, Paul Anka	9
8=	*Here in My Heart*, Al Martino	9
8=	*Mull of Kintyre*, Wings	9
8=	*Oh Mein Papa*, Eddie Calvert	9
8=	*Secret Love*, Doris Day	9
8=	*Two Tribes*, Frankie Goes to Hollywood	9
8=	*You're the One That I Want*, John Travolta and Olivia Newton-John	9

TOP 10

YOUNGEST SINGERS TO HAVE A NO. 1 SINGLE IN THE US*

	Artist/title	Age yrs	mths
1	Michael Jackson, *I Want You Back*	11	5
2	Jimmy Boyd, *I Saw Mommy Kissing Santa Claus*	12	11
3	Stevie Wonder, *Fingertips*	13	2
4	Donny Osmond, *Go Away Little Girl*	13	9
5	Laurie London, *He's Got The Whole World In His Hands*	14	3
6	Little Peggy March, *I Will Follow Him*	15	1
7	Brenda Lee, *I'm Sorry*	15	7
8=	Paul Anka, *Diana*	16	1
8=	Tiffany, *I Think We're Alone Now*	16	1
10=	Little Eva, *The Loco-Motion*	17	1
10=	Lesley Gore, *It's My Party*	17	1

* To December 31, 1995

YOUNGEST SINGERS TO HAVE A NO. 1 SINGLE IN THE UK*

	Artist/title	Age yrs	mths
1	Little Jimmy Osmond, *Long Haired Lover from Liverpool*	9	8
2	Donny Osmond, *Puppy Love*	14	6
3	Helen Shapiro, *You Don't Know*	14	10
4	Paul Anka, *Diana*	16	0
5	Tiffany, *I Think We're Alone Now*	16	3
6	Nicole, *A Little Peace*	17	0
7	Glenn Medeiros, *Nothing's Gonna Change My Love*	18	0
8	Mary Hopkin, *Those Were the Days*	18	4
9	Cliff Richard, *Living Doll*	18	8
10	Adam Faith, *What Do You Want?*	19	5

* To December 31, 1995

The totals for *I Believe* and *Bohemian Rhapsody* are the accumulation of more than one run at No. 1. *I Believe* dropped to No. 2 for two weeks in what otherwise would have been a 20-week spell at No. 1. *Bohemian Rhapsody* returned to the top for another long run 16 years after its first, following the tragic death of singer Freddie Mercury. All other totals are for consecutive chart-topping weeks.

THE SUPERGROUPS

ALL-TIME SINGLES BY GROUPS IN THE UK

	Group/single	Year
1	Queen, *Bohemian Rhapsody*	1975
2	Wings, *Mull of Kintyre*	1977
3	Boney M, *Rivers of Babylon/ Brown Girl in the Ring*	1978
4	Frankie Goes to Hollywood, *Relax*	1984
5	Beatles, *She Loves You*	1963
6	Boney M, *Mary's Boy Child/ Oh My Lord*	1978
7	Wet Wet Wet, *Love Is All Around*	1994
8	Beatles, *I Want to Hold Your Hand*	1963
9	Beatles, *Can't Buy Me Love*	1964
10	Frankie Goes to Hollywood, *Two Tribes*	1984

Paul McCartney appears four times, three times with the Beatles and once with Wings. Further high-level consistency sees both Boney M and Frankie Goes To Hollywood represented twice among these 10 titles.

GROUPS OF THE 1960s IN THE US*

1	Beatles	6	Miracles
2	Supremes	7	Temptations
3	Four Seasons	8	Tommy James & the Shondells
4	Beach Boys	9	Dave Clark Five
5	Rolling Stones	10	Herman's Hermits

* *Based on comparative US singles chart performance*

THE INCOMPARABLE SUPREMES

ALL-TIME SINGLES BY GROUPS IN THE US

	Group/single	Year
1	Beatles, *I Want to Hold Your Hand*	1963
2	Beatles, *Hey Jude*	1968
3	Chipmunks, *The Chipmunk Song*	1958
4	Chic, *Le Freak*	1978
5	Monkees, *I'm a Believer*	1966
6	Beatles, *Can't Buy Me Love*	1964
7	Beatles, *She Loves You*	1964
8	Archies, *Sugar Sugar*	1969
9	Bill Haley & the Comets, *Rock Around the Clock*	1955
10	Bee Gees, *Stayin' Alive*	1978

ALL-TIME ALBUMS BY GROUPS IN THE US

	Group/album	Year
1	Eagles, *Their Greatest Hits, 1971–1975*	1976
2	Fleetwood Mac, *Rumours*	1977
3	Led Zeppelin, *Led Zeppelin IV* (untitled)	1971
4	Boston, *Boston*	1976
5	Eagles, *Hotel California*	1976
6=	Pink Floyd, *Dark Side of the Moon*	1973
6=	Guns N' Roses, *Appetite for Destruction*	1987
8	Hootie & The Blowfish, *Cracked Rear View*	1994
9	Boyz II Men, *II*	1994
10	Def Leppard, *Hysteria*	1987

ALL-TIME ALBUMS BY GROUPS IN THE UK

	Group/album	Year
1	Beatles, *Sgt. Pepper's Lonely Hearts Club Band*	1967
2	Dire Straits, *Brothers in Arms*	1985
3	Simply Red, *Stars*	1991
4	Queen, *Greatest Hits*	1981
5	Fleetwood Mac, *Rumours*	1977
6	Pink Floyd, *Dark Side of the Moon*	1973
7	Fleetwood Mac, *Tango in the Night*	1987
8	R.E.M., *Automatic for the People*	1993
9	U2, *The Joshua Tree*	1987
10	Bob Marley and the Wailers, *Legend*	1984

TOP 10

GROUPS OF THE 1960s IN THE UK*

1	Beatles		**6**	Kinks
2	Rolling Stones		**7**	Four Tops
3	Shadows		**8**	Manfred Mann
4	Hollies		**9**	Seekers
5	Beach Boys		**10**	Bachelors

* *Based on comparative UK singles chart performance*

TOP 10

GROUPS OF THE 1970s IN THE US*

1	Bee Gees		**6**	Gladys Knight & the Pips
2	Carpenters		**7**	Dawn
3	Chicago		**8**	Earth, Wind, & Fire
4	Jackson 5/Jacksons		**9**	The Eagles
5	Three Dog Night		**10**	Fleetwood Mac

* *Based on comparative US singles chart performance*

TOP 10

GROUPS OF THE 1970s IN THE UK*

1	Abba		**6**	Showaddywaddy
2	Slade		**7**	Mud
3	T. Rex		**8**	Wings
4	Bay City Rollers		**9**	Electric Light Orchestra
5	Sweet		**10**	Osmonds

* *Based on comparative UK singles chart performance*

TOP 10

GROUPS OF THE 1980s IN THE US*

1	Wham!
2	Kool & the Gang
3	Huey Lewis & the News
4	Journey
5	Duran Duran
6	U2
7	Rolling Stones
8	Alabama
9	Pointer Sisters
10	Jefferson Starship/Starship

* *Based on comparative US singles and album chart performance*

TOP 10

GROUPS OF THE 1980s IN THE UK*

1	Police
2	Wham!
3	Dire Straits
4	U2
5	Queen
6	Simple Minds
7	Pet Shop Boys
8	Duran Duran
9	Adam & the Ants
10	Madness

* *Based on comparative UK singles and album chart performance*

It should be noted that, apart from U2 – who are from the Republic of Ireland – all 10 of these groups are from the UK.

THE ROLLING STONES
One of the leading groups of the 1960s, the Rolling Stones still attract a huge following today. Their most recent "Voodoo Lounge World Tour" consisted of 123 concerts played worldwide on four continents. The tour grossed $320 million and is still the most successful tour by a rock band to date.

LONG PLAYERS

ALBUMS THAT STAYED LONGEST
IN THE US CHARTS*

	Artist/album	First year in chart	Weeks in charts
1	Pink Floyd, *Dark Side of the Moon*	1973	741
2	Johnny Mathis, *Johnny's Greatest Hits*	1958	490
3	Original cast, *My Fair Lady*	1956	480
4	Soundtrack, *Oklahoma!*	1955	305
5	Carole King, *Tapestry*	1971	302
6	Johnny Mathis, *Heavenly*	1959	295
7=	Soundtrack, *The King and I*	1956	277
7=	Tennessee Ernie Ford, *Hymns*	1957	277
9	Original cast, *The Sound of Music*	1959	276
10	Original cast, *Camelot*	1961	265

* To December 31, 1995

With soundtracks or original cast recordings of musicals accounting for half of this Top 10, it is clear that longevity is best earned by a box-office smash or successful Broadway production. It is unlikely, however, that in this century any album will match the extraordinary total reached by Pink Floyd's rock opus, *Dark Side of the Moon*.

ALBUMS THAT STAYED LONGEST
IN THE UK CHARTS*

	Artist/album	First year in chart	Weeks in charts
1	Meat Loaf, *Bat Out of Hell*	1978	471
2	Fleetwood Mac, *Rumours*	1977	443
3	Queen, *Greatest Hits*	1981	426
4	Soundtrack, *The Sound of Music*	1965	382
5	Pink Floyd, *Dark Side of the Moon*	1973	331
6	Simon and Garfunkel, *Bridge over Troubled Water*	1970	304
7	Original cast, *South Pacific*	1958	288
8	Simon and Garfunkel, *Greatest Hits*	1972	283
9	Phil Collins, *Face Value*	1981	274
10	Mike Oldfield, *Tubular Bells*	1973	271

* To December 31, 1995

The 10 longest-staying records virtually took up residence in the album charts (the Top 50, 75, or 100, depending on the years in which the charts were compiled) and in many instances have made comebacks years after their initial release.

ARTISTS WITH THE MOST
CHART ALBUMS IN THE US*

	Artist	Chart albums
1	Elvis Presley	93
2	Frank Sinatra	69
3	Johnny Mathis	63
4=	James Brown	49
4=	Ray Conniff	49
6=	Mantovani	45
6=	Barbra Streisand	45
8=	Beach Boys	41
8=	Temptations	41
8=	Lawrence Welk	41

* To December 31, 1995

Elvis' staggering total will not be matched during this century, and could even pass 100 chart albums by the year 2001 if RCA Records continue to release at least one Elvis album every year.

ARTISTS WITH THE MOST
CHART ALBUMS IN THE UK*

	Artist	Chart albums
1	Elvis Presley	96
2	James Last	60
3	Frank Sinatra	54
4	Cliff Richard	50
5	Rolling Stones	40
6=	Bob Dylan	39
6=	Diana Ross	39#
8	Elton John	35
9	Shirley Bassey	33
10	David Bowie	31+

* To December 31, 1995
 # Excluding albums with the Supremes
+ Excluding two albums with Tin Machine

COVER STORY

Alongside the sales feats represented by these Top 10 lists, the lengthy reign of the 12-inch vinyl album witnessed frequent record-company attempts to hook buyers by means other than just the music. Colored vinyl, gatefold sleeves, and picture discs were regular gimmicks. Far more bizarre were the three-sided album (a double set on which the fourth side was a grooveless blank disc), parallel grooves (as on a Monty Python LP, where the stylus randomly accessed either of two parallel tracks), dual speeds (a Moby Grape LP had one track that required playing at 78 rpm, the rest running at 33 rpm), or insane packaging (an LP by the Fabulous Poodles had a two-foot square sleeve, making it near impossible to handle or house). Sadly, the modern CD offers less scope for the music industry's lateral thinkers.

T O P 1 0

ALBUMS OF ALL TIME WORLDWIDE

	Artist	Album	Estimated sales
1	Michael Jackson	*Thriller*	40,000,000
2	Pink Floyd	*Dark Side of the Moon*	28,000,000
3	Meat Loaf	*Bat Out of Hell*	27,000,000
4	Soundtrack	*The Bodyguard*	26,000,000
5	Soundtrack	*Saturday Night Fever*	25,000,000
6=	Beatles	*Sgt. Pepper's Lonely Hearts Club Band*	24,000,000
6=	Eagles	*Their Greatest Hits 1971–1975*	24,000,000
8	Mariah Carey	*Music Box*	23,000,000
9=	Carole King	*Tapestry*	22,000,000
9=	Simon and Garfunkel	*Bridge over Troubled Water*	22,000,000
9=	Soundtrack	*Grease*	22,000,000
9=	Michael Jackson	*Dangerous*	22,000,000

Total worldwide sales of albums have traditionally been notoriously difficult to gauge, but even with the huge expansion of the album market during the 1980s and multiple million sales of many major releases, this Top 10 is still élite territory.

T O P 1 0

ALBUMS OF ALL TIME IN THE UK

	Artist	Album
1	Beatles	*Sgt. Pepper's Lonely Hearts Club Band*
2	Michael Jackson	*Bad*
3	Dire Straits	*Brothers in Arms*
4	Simply Red	*Stars*
5	Queen	*Greatest Hits*
6	Michael Jackson	*Thriller*
7	Madonna	*The Immaculate Collection*
8	Phil Collins	*. . . But Seriously*
9	Simon and Garfunkel	*Bridge over Troubled Water*
10	Fleetwood Mac	*Rumours*

On the occasion of *Sgt. Pepper's* 25th anniversary in 1992, EMI Records conducted new research into the actual sales of the album and concluded that it had sold over 4,250,000 copies in the UK, substantially more than *Brothers in Arms*, which was previously thought to have bettered it. Michael Jackson's *Bad* has now also overtaken *Brothers*, with UK sales a fraction over 4,000,000 to Dire Straits' 3,700,000 and Simply Red's 3,600,000. The Queen (sales boosted hugely in the 90s by Freddie Mercury's death) and Michael Jackson (*Thriller*) albums have each sold over 3,000,000 copies, while all the others in this list have achieved UK sales in excess of 2,500,000.

T O P 1 0

ALBUMS OF ALL TIME IN THE US

	Artist/album	Estimated sales
1	Michael Jackson, *Thriller*	24,000,000
2	Eagles, *Their Greatest Hits 1971–1975*	22,000,000
3	Fleetwood Mac, *Rumours*	17,000,000
4	Led Zeppelin, *Led Zeppelin IV* (untitled)	16,000,000
5=	Boston, *Boston*	15,000,000
5=	Bruce Springsteen, *Born in the USA*	15,000,000
7=	Soundtrack, *The Bodyguard*	14,000,000
7=	Eagles, *Hotel California*	14,000,000
9=	Pink Floyd, *Dark Side of the Moon*	13,000,000
9=	Guns N' Roses, *Appetite for Destruction*	13,000,000
9=	Garth Brooks, *No Fences*	13,000,000

ON THE RECORD
The long-playing record has undergone notable improvements in the post-war era, from vinyl LPs to modern CDs that represent a significant leap forward in both capacity and quality.

Many of these albums were originally released before the CD age, so have benefited from "second copy" buying as people replace old vinyl copies with CDs.

ALBUMS OF THE DECADES

T O P 1 0

ALBUMS OF THE 1950s IN THE US

	Artist/album	Year
1	Original cast, *South Pacific*	1958
2	Original cast, *My Fair Lady*	1956
3	Soundtrack, *The Music Man*	1958
4	Soundtrack, *Gigi*	1958
5	Soundtrack, *Oklahoma!*	1955
6	Harry Belafonte, *Calypso*	1956
7	Elvis Presley, *Elvis Presley*	1956
8	Nat "King" Cole, *Love Is the Thing*	1957
9	Johnny Mathis, *Johnny's Greatest Hits*	1958
10	Doris Day, *Love Me or Leave Me* (Original soundtrack)	1955

T O P 1 0

ALBUMS OF THE 1960s IN THE US

	Artist/album	Year
1	Soundtrack, *West Side Story*	1961
2	Beatles, *Meet the Beatles*	1964
3	Soundtrack, *The Sound of Music*	1965
4	Beatles, *Sgt. Pepper's Lonely Hearts Club Band*	1967
5	Monkees, *The Monkees*	1966
6	Monkees, *More of the Monkees*	1967
7	Beatles, *Abbey Road*	1969
8	Beatles, *The Beatles* ("White Album")	1968
9	Beatles, *Magical Mystery Tour*	1967
10	Beatles, *Rubber Soul*	1965

Successful film soundtracks often stayed in the charts for years – The Sound of Music managed a run of more than five years.

PINK FLOYD'S WALL OF SOUND
British group Pink Floyd performs The Wall. *The album of the same name, released in 1979, became a multimillion seller and put them in 10th place among US albums of the 1980s.*

T O P 1 0

ALBUMS OF THE 1960s IN THE UK

	Artist/album	Year
1	Beatles, *Sgt. Pepper's Lonely Hearts Club Band*	1967
2	Soundtrack, *The Sound Of Music*	1965
3	Beatles, *With the Beatles*	1963
4	Beatles, *Abbey Road*	1969
5	Original cast, *South Pacific*	1958
6	Beatles, *Beatles for Sale*	1964
7	Beatles, *A Hard Day's Night*	1964
8	Beatles, *Rubber Soul*	1965
9	Beatles, *The Beatles* ("White Album")	1968
10	Soundtrack, *West Side Story*	1962

Not only did the Beatles dominate this Top 10, but three further albums of theirs, *Revolver*, *Please Please Me*, and *Help!*, were in 11th, 12th, and 13th position.

T O P 1 0

ALBUMS OF THE 1970s IN THE US

	Artist/album	Year
1	Fleetwood Mac, *Rumours*	1977
2	Soundtrack, *Saturday Night Fever*	1978
3	Soundtrack, *Grease*	1978
4	Pink Floyd, *Dark Side of the Moon*	1973
5	Carole King, *Tapestry*	1971
6	Boston, *Boston*	1976
7	Led Zeppelin, *Led Zeppelin IV* (untitled)	1971
8	Peter Frampton, *Frampton Comes Alive!*	1976
9	Stevie Wonder, *Songs in the Key of Life*	1976
10	Eagles, *Their Greatest Hits, 1971–1975*	1976

T O P 1 0

ALBUMS OF THE 1970s IN THE UK

	Artist/album	Year
1	Simon and Garfunkel, *Bridge over Troubled Water*	1970
2	Simon and Garfunkel, *Simon and Garfunkel's Greatest Hits*	1972
3	Fleetwood Mac, *Rumours*	1977
4	Pink Floyd, *Dark Side of the Moon*	1973
5	Mike Oldfield, *Tubular Bells*	1973
6	Abba, *Greatest Hits*	1976
7	Meat Loaf, *Bat Out of Hell*	1978
8	Soundtrack, *Saturday Night Fever*	1978
9	Perry Como, *And I Love You So*	1973
10	Carpenters, *The Singles 1969–1973*	1974

TOP 10

ALBUMS OF THE 1980s IN THE US

	Artist/album	Year
1	Michael Jackson, *Thriller*	1982
2	Bruce Springsteen, *Born in the USA*	1984
3	Soundtrack, *Dirty Dancing*	1987
4	Prince & the Revolution, *Purple Rain* (Original soundtrack)	1984
5	Lionel Richie, *Can't Slow Down*	1983
6	Whitney Houston, *Whitney Houston*	1985
7	Def Leppard, *Hysteria*	1987
8	Bon Jovi, *Slippery When Wet*	1986
9	Guns N' Roses, *Appetite for Destruction*	1988
10	Pink Floyd, *The Wall*	1979

On October 30, 1984, *Thriller* became the first album to receive its 20th platinum sales certificate, awarded for sales of 20,000,000 copies in the US.

TOP 10

ALBUMS OF THE 1980s IN THE UK

	Artist/album	Year
1	Dire Straits, *Brothers in Arms*	1985
2	Michael Jackson, *Bad*	1987
3	Michael Jackson, *Thriller*	1982
4	Queen, *Greatest Hits*	1981
5	Kylie Minogue, *Kylie*	1988
6	Whitney Houston, *Whitney*	1987
7	Fleetwood Mac, *Tango in the Night*	1987
8	Phil Collins, *No Jacket Required*	1985
9	Madonna, *True Blue*	1986
10	U2, *The Joshua Tree*	1987

While Michael Jackson's *Thriller* was his bestselling album in most countries around the world, British buyers eventually preferred *Bad*.

TOP 10

ALBUMS OF THE 1990s IN THE US*

	Artist/album	Year
1	Soundtrack, *The Bodyguard*	1992
2	Garth Brooks, *No Fences*	1990
3	Garth Brooks, *Ropin' the Wind*	1991
4	Hootie & The Blowfish, *Cracked Rear View*	1995
5	Boyz II Men, *II*	1994
6	MC Hammer, *Please Hammer Don't Hurt 'Em*	1990
7	Soundtrack, *The Lion King*	1994
8	Kenny G., *Breathless*	1992
9	Pearl Jam, *Ten*	1992
10	Mariah Carey, *Music Box*	1993

* To December 31, 1995

Despite everything rock could come up with, America's real album superstar of the 1990s has been country singer Garth Brooks.

TOP 10

ALBUMS OF THE 1990s IN THE UK*

	Artist/album	Year
1	Simply Red, *Stars*	1991
2	Madonna, *The Immaculate Collection*	1991
3	Elton John, *The Very Best of Elton John*	1990
4	Soundtrack, *The Bodyguard*	1992
5	R.E.M., *Automatic for the People*	1992
6	Robson Green & Jerome Flynn, *Robson & Jerome*	1995
7	Eurythmics, *Greatest Hits*	1991
8	Oasis, *(What's the Story) Morning Glory*	1995
9	Phil Collins, *...But Seriously*	1989
10	Celine Dion, *The Colour of My Love*	1994

* To December 31, 1995

WHITNEY HOUSTON *Making the transition from rock star to actress is not easy. However, Whitney Houston has had two major successes with* The Bodyguard *and* Waiting to Exhale.

ALBUM GREATS

AMERICA'S NO. 1 COUNTRY SINGER
*Seen here in his trademark Stetson,
Garth Brooks has dominated the US
Country charts during the 1990s.*

TOP 10
COUNTRY ALBUMS OF ALL TIME IN THE US

	Title/artist	Year
1	*No Fences*, Garth Brooks	1990
2	*Ropin' the Wind*, Garth Brooks	1991
3	*Some Gave All*, Billy Ray Cyrus	1992
4	*In Pieces*, Garth Brooks	1993
5	*Garth Brooks*, Garth Brooks	1990
6	*The Hits*, Garth Brooks	1995
7	*The Chase*, Garth Brooks	1992
8	*Greatest Hits*, Patsy Cline	1987
9	*Brand New Man*, Brooks & Dunn	1991
10	*Feels So Right*, Alabama	1981

Each of these albums has sold more than
5,000,000 domestic copies, but Garth
Brooks is in a league of his own. Exploding
onto the country scene in 1990, he has sold
55,000,000 albums in the US alone.

TOP 10
COUNTRY ALBUMS OF ALL TIME IN THE UK

	Title/artist	Year
1	*Johnny Cash at San Quentin*, Johnny Cash	1969
2	*20 Golden Greats*, Glen Campbell	1976
3	*The Best of John Denver*, John Denver	1974
4	*40 Golden Greats*, Jim Reeves	1975
5	*Images*, Don Williams	1978
6	*Greatest Hits*, Glen Campbell	1971
7	*The Very Best of Slim Whitman*, Slim Whitman	1976
8	*The Best of Tammy Wynette*, Tammy Wynette	1975
9	*Live in London*, John Denver	1976
10	*Johnny Cash Live at Folsom Prison*, Johnny Cash	1968

TOP 10
JAZZ ALBUMS OF ALL TIME IN THE US

	Title/artist	Year
1	*Time Out*, Dave Brubeck Quartet	1960
2	*Hello Dolly*, Louis Armstrong	1964
3	*Getz & Gilberto*, Stan Getz and Joao Gilberto	1964
4	*Sun Goddess*, Ramsey Lewis	1975
5	*Jazz Samba*, Stan Getz and Charlie Byrd	1962
6	*Bitches Brew*, Miles Davis	1970
7	*The In Crowd*, Ramsey Lewis Trio	1965
8	*Time Further Out*, Dave Brubeck Quartet	1961
9	*Mack the Knife – Ella in Berlin*, Ella Fitzgerald	1960
10	*Exodus to Jazz*, Eddie Harris	1961

Dave Brubeck's *Time Out* album spent
86 weeks in the American Top 40 between
1960 and 1962, an unprecedented
achievement for a jazz album.

TOP 10
JAZZ ALBUMS OF ALL TIME IN THE UK

	Title/artist	Year
1	*We Are in Love*, Harry Connick, Jr.	1990
2	*Blue Light, Red Light*, Harry Connick, Jr.	1991
3	*Jazz on a Summer's Day*, Various Artists	1992
4	*Morning Dance*, Spyro Gyra	1979
5	*In Flight*, George Benson	1977
6	*Duotones*, Kenny G	1987
7	*Best of Ball, Barber, & Bilk*, Kenny Ball, Chris Barber, and Acker Bilk	1962
8	*Sinatra/Basie*, Frank Sinatra and Count Basie	1963
9	*Kenny Ball's Golden Hits*, Kenny Ball	1963
10	*Time Out*, Dave Brubeck Quartet	1960

TOP 10
ORIGINAL CAST RECORDING ALBUMS OF ALL TIME IN THE US

	Title/production	Year
1	*My Fair Lady*, Broadway	1956
2	*The Sound of Music*, Broadway	1959
3	*The Music Man*, Broadway	1958
4	*The Phantom of the Opera*, London	1988
5	*Camelot*, Broadway	1961
6	*West Side Story*, Broadway	1958
7	*Jesus Christ Superstar**	1970
8	*Fiddler on the Roof*, Broadway	1964
9	*Hair*, Broadway	1968
10	*Hello, Dolly!*, Broadway	1964

* *Although an original Broadway cast version
appeared in 1972, the album which
outperformed it here was a studio cast
recording made in 1970 with Deep Purple
vocalist Ian Gillan playing Jesus.*

TOP 10

HEAVY METAL ALBUMS OF ALL TIME IN THE US

	Title/artist	Year
1	*Boston*, Boston	1976
2	*Appetite for Destruction*, Guns N' Roses	1987
3	*Bat Out of Hell*, Meat Loaf	1978
4	*Led Zeppelin IV* (untitled), Led Zeppelin	1971
5	*Slippery When Wet*, Bon Jovi	1986
6	*Hysteria*, Def Leppard	1987
7	*Pyromania*, Def Leppard	1983
8	*Escape*, Journey	1981
9	*Back in Black*, AC/DC	1980
10	*Metallica*, Metallica	1991

All of these albums have sold more than 8,000,000 copies each in the US alone, with *Boston* recently certified for sales over 15,000,000. *Hysteria*'s sales performance is a noteworthy achievement for Def Leppard, the British band whose lineup has suffered a death (that of guitarist Steve Clark in 1991) and a car accident (drummer Rick Allen lost his left arm in 1984).

THE RISE OF LED ZEPPELIN
In 1968 Robert Plant was invited to become the vocalist with the New Yardbirds, soon after renamed Led Zeppelin. Before the band's break-up in 1980, it achieved a steady run of No. 1 albums, two of which are in the UK's all-time heavy metal Top 10.

TOP 10

HEAVY METAL ALBUMS OF ALL TIME IN THE UK

	Title/artist	Year
1	*Bat Out of Hell*, Meat Loaf	1978
2	*Bat Out of Hell II – Back to Hell*, Meat Loaf	1993
3	*Led Zeppelin II*, Led Zeppelin	1969
4	*Hysteria*, Def Leppard	1987
5	*Led Zeppelin IV* (untitled), Led Zeppelin	1971
6	*Cross Road – The Best of Bon Jovi*, Bon Jovi	1994
7	*So Far So Good*, Bryan Adams	1993
8	*Eliminator*, ZZ Top	1983
9	*Appetite for Destruction*, Guns N' Roses	1987
10	*Slippery When Wet*, Bon Jovi	1986

TOP 10

ALBUMS IN THE US, 1995

	Title/artist
1	*Cracked Rear View*, Hootie & The Blowfish
2	*Crazysexycool*, TLC
3	*Jagged Little Pill*, Alanis Morissette
4	*Daydream*, Mariah Carey
5	*The Hits*, Garth Brooks
6	*Live*, Throwing Copper
7	*II*, Boyz II Men
8	*Anthology 1*, Beatles
9	*Hell Freezes Over*, Eagles
10	*The Woman in Me*, Shania Twain

Hootie & The Blowfish have achieved one of the most impressive album debuts in US record history, with over 11,000,000 copies of *Cracked Rear View* sold in 1995.

TOP 10

ALBUMS IN THE UK, 1995

	Title/artist
1	*Robson & Jerome*, Robson Green & Jerome Flynn
2	*(What's the Story) Morning Glory*, Oasis
3	*The Colour of My Life*, Celine Dion
4	*Life*, Simply Red
5	*History – Past Present & Future, Book 1*, Michael Jackson
6	*Stanley Road*, Paul Weller
7	*Made in Heaven*, Queen
8	*Picture This*, Wet Wet Wet
9	*The Great Escape*, Blur
10	*Different Class*, Pulp

TOP 10

INSTRUMENTAL ALBUMS OF ALL TIME IN THE US

	Title/artist	Year
1	*Exodus* (Original Soundtrack), Ernest Gold and the Sinfonia of London Orchestra	1961
2	*Persuasive Percussion*, Enoch Light and the Light Brigade/ Terry and the All-Stars	1960
3	*Breakfast At Tiffany's* (Original Soundtrack), Henry Mancini	1961
4	*Calcutta!*, Lawrence Welk	1961
5	*Around the World in 80 Days* (Original Soundtrack), Victor Young	1957
6	*The Music from Peter Gunn*, Henry Mancini	1959
7	*What Now My Love*, Herb Alpert & The Tijuana Brass	1966
8	*Whipped Cream & Other Delights*, Herb Alpert & The Tijuana Brass	1965
9	*Stereo 35/MM*, Enoch Light and the Light Brigade	1961
10	*Tchaikovsky: Piano Concerto No. 1*, Van Cliburn	1958

MODERN COMPOSERS

TOP 10

US HITS COMPOSED BY GERRY GOFFIN & CAROLE KING

	Title	Charting artist(s)
1	Go Away Little Girl	Happenings, Steve Lawrence, Donny Osmond
2	The Loco-Motion	Grand Funk, Little Eva, Kylie Minogue
3	Will You Love Me Tomorrow?	Roberta Flack, Four Seasons, Dave Mason, Melanie, Shirelles, Dana Valery
4	Up on the Roof	Cryin' Shames, Drifters, Laura Nyro, James Taylor
5	Take Good Care of My Baby	Bobby Vee, Bobby Vinton
6	One Fine Day	Chiffons, Rita Coolidge, Julie, Carole King
7	I'm into Something Good	Earl-Jean, Herman's Hermits
8	Hey Girl	Donny Osmond, Freddie Scott, Bobby Vee
9	Pleasant Valley Sunday	Monkees
10	I Can't Stay Mad at You	Skeeter Davis

TOP 10

UK HITS COMPOSED BY GERRY GOFFIN & CAROLE KING

	Title	Charting artist(s)
1	The Loco-Motion	Little Eva, Kylie Minogue, Dave Stewart and Barbara Gaskin, Vernon Girls
2	I'm into Something Good	Herman's Hermits
3	It Might as Well Rain until September	Carole King
4	Halfway to Paradise	Billy Fury
5	Take Good Care of My Baby	Smokie, Bobby Vee
6	Will You Love Me Tomorrow?	Melanie, Shirelles
7	I Want to Stay Here	Steve & Eydie
8	Don't Bring Me Down	Animals
9	Up on the Roof	Julie Grant, Kenny Lynch
10	Oh No Not My Baby	Manfred Mann, Rod Stewart

A substantially different list from the US ranking of their hits, this list exemplifies the international depth of Goffin and King's extensive catalogue. Although they parted company in 1967, both continued successful solo songwriting careers.

TOP 10

US HITS COMPOSED BY JOHN LENNON & PAUL McCARTNEY

	Title	Charting artist(s)
1	I Want to Hold Your Hand	Beatles, Boston Pops Orchestra
2	Hey Jude	Beatles, Wilson Pickett
3	She Loves You	Beatles
4	Can't Buy Me Love	Beatles
5	Come Together	Aerosmith, Beatles, Ike & Tina Turner
6	Get Back	Beatles with Billy Preston, Billy Preston *
7	I Feel Fine	Beatles
8	Help!	Beatles
9	A Hard Day's Night	Beatles, Ramsey Lewis Trio
10	Let It Be	Joan Baez, Beatles

*   In addition to accompanying the Beatles on the original version, Preston also charted with a solo version in 1978

I Want to Hold Your Hand remains the biggest-selling Lennon and McCartney composition in the US, selling just under 5,000,000 copies in 1964. Successful versions of I Saw Her/Him Standing There, Happiness is a Warm Gun, and Strawberry Fields Forever have all been released in the past decade.

TOP 10

UK HITS COMPOSED BY JOHN LENNON & PAUL McCARTNEY

	Title	Charting artist(s)
1	She Loves You	Beatles
2	I Want to Hold Your Hand	Beatles
3	Can't Buy Me Love	Beatles, Ella Fitzgerald
4	I Feel Fine	Beatles
5	We Can Work It Out	Beatles, Stevie Wonder
6	Help!	Bananarama, Beatles, Tina Turner
7	Day Tripper	Beatles, Otis Redding
8	Hey Jude	Beatles, Wilson Pickett
9	Let It Be	Beatles, Ferry Aid
10	A Hard Day's Night	Beatles, Peter Sellers

The most successful non-Beatles Lennon and McCartney song is A World without Love, a No. 1 hit for Peter & Gordon in 1964, which is their 14th most successful composition behind Get Back, Hello Goodbye, and Ticket To Ride. Yesterday, the most widely-recorded Lennon and McCartney song of all, is missing from this list because virtually all its hundreds of cover versions were album tracks, not hit singles. Indeed, the Beatles' version was exclusive to the Help LP when first released in 1965, and only reached No. 8 as a belated single in 1976.

US HITS COMPOSED
BY BOB DYLAN

	Title/charting artist(s)
1	*Blowin' in The Wind*, Peter, Paul, and Mary, Stevie Wonder
2	*Mr. Tambourine Man*, Byrds
3	*Lay Lady Lay*, Bob Dylan, Ferrante and Teicher, Isley Brothers
4	*Like a Rolling Stone*, Bob Dylan
5	*Rainy Day Women #12 and #35*, Bob Dylan
6	*Don't Think Twice*, Peter, Paul, and Mary, Wonder Who?
7	*It Ain't Me Babe*, Johnny Cash, Turtles
8	*Mighty Quinn (Quinn the Eskimo)*, Manfred Mann
9	*Knockin' on Heaven's Door*, Bob Dylan
10	*All I Really Want to Do*, Byrds, Cher

DYLAN – GURU OF THE 60s
Born Robert Zimmerman, Bob Dylan's adopted stage name is a tribute to his favorite poet, Dylan Thomas.

US HITS COMPOSED BY
BURT BACHARACH & HAL DAVID

	Title	Charting artist(s)
1	*Raindrops Keep Fallin' on My Head*	B.J. Thomas
2	*(They Long to Be) Close to You*	Carpenters, B.T. Express, Jerry Butler & Brenda Lee Eager
3	*This Guy's (Girl's) in Love with You*	Herb Alpert, Dionne Warwick
4	*I Say a Little Prayer*	Dionne Warwick, Aretha Franklin, Glen Campbell & Anne Murray*
5	*Walk on By*	Dionne Warwick, Isaac Hayes, Sybil, Gloria Gaynor, Average White Band
6	*Baby It's You*	Shirelles, Smith
7	*Alfie*	Dionne Warwick, Cher, Eivets Rednow#, Cilla Black
8	*One Less Bell to Answer*	Fifth Dimension
9	*Only Love Can Break a Heart*	Gene Pitney, Margaret Whiting, Bobby Vinton
10	*What the World Needs Now is Love*	Jackie De Shannon, Tom Clay*

UK HITS COMPOSED BY
BURT BACHARACH & HAL DAVID

	Title	Charting artist(s)
1	*Walk on By*	Dionne Warwick, Sybil, Stranglers, D Train, Average White Band
2	*Anyone Who Had a Heart*	Cilla Black, Dionne Warwick, Mary May
3	*Magic Moments*	Perry Como, Ronnie Hilton
4	*Make It Easy on Yourself*	Walker Brothers
5	*I'll Never Fall in Love Again*	Bobbie Gentry, Deacon Blue
6	*The Story of My Life*	Michael Holliday, Dave King, Alma Cogan
7	*Trains and Boats and Planes*	Burt Bacharach, Billy J. Kramer & the Dakotas
8	*(There's) Always Something There to Remind Me*	Sandie Shaw
9	*Raindrops Keep Fallin' on My Head*	Sacha Distel, B.J. Thomas, Bobbie Gentry
10	*This Guy's in Love with You*	Herb Alpert

* Part of a medley # Pseudonym of Stevie Wonder

N FILM

TOP 10

...VIES

		Year
		1978
2	*The Sou...*	1965
3	*Saturday Night Fever*	1977
4	*American Graffiti*	1973
5	*The Best Little Whorehouse in Texas*	1982
6	*Mary Poppins*	1964
7	*Fiddler on the Roof*	1971
8	*Annie*	1982
9	*A Star Is Born*	1976
10	*Flashdance*	1983

Traditional musicals (films in which the cast actually sing) and films in which a musical soundtrack is a major component of the film are included. Several other musical films have also each earned in excess of $30,000,000 in North American rentals, among them *Coal Miner's Daughter* (1980), *The Rocky Horror Picture Show* (1975), *Footloose* (1984), *The Blues Brothers* (1980), and *Purple Rain* (1984), but it would appear that the era of the blockbuster musical film is over. In recent years, animated films with an important musical component appear to have taken on their mantle – and, indeed, both *Aladdin* and *The Lion King* won "Best Original Song" Oscars.

TOP 10

HIGHEST-GROSSING ELVIS PRESLEY MOVIES

	Film	Year	Gross ($)
1	*Viva Las Vegas*	1964	5,500,000
2	*Blue Hawaii*	1961	4,700,000
3	*Love Me Tender*	1956	4,500,000
4	*G.I. Blues*	1960	4,300,000
5	*Jailhouse Rock*	1957	4,000,000
6	*Loving You*	1957	3,700,000
7	*Girls! Girls! Girls!*	1962	3,600,000
8	*Tickle Me*	1965	3,400,000
9	*Roustabout*	1964	3,300,000
10	*Girl Happy*	1965	3,200,000

From his first acting role as Clint Reno in *Love Me Tender* (1956) to that of Dr. John Carpenter in *Change of Habit* (1970), Elvis made 31 films, also appearing as himself in *This is Elvis* (1981) and *Elvis on Tour* (1972). Presley's most successful movie period broadly mirrored his initial spell as the world's biggest-selling pop star, although his biggest-grossing film of all was screened precisely when this initial success was waning, courtesy of the Beatles. The explanation is almost certainly that in *Viva Las Vegas* he had, uniquely, a major-name leading lady – Ann-Margret – with screen dynamism to match Elvis's as well as a huge fan following of her own.

TOP 10

POP MUSIC MOVIES

	Film	Year
1	*The Blues Brothers*	1980
2	*Purple Rain*	1984
3	*La Bamba*	1987
4	*The Doors*	1991
5	*What's Love Got to Do With It*	1993
6	*Xanadu*	1980
7	*The Jazz Singer*	1980
8	*Sergeant Pepper's Lonely Hearts Club Band*	1978
9	*Lady Sings the Blues*	1972
10	*Pink Floyd – The Wall*	1982

Distinct from musicals, these are films that are biographies of pop stars (*La Bamba* told the Ritchie Valens story, *What's Love Got to Do With It* Tina Turner's, and the Diana Ross-starring *Lady Sings the Blues* that of Billie Holiday). Alternatively they are designed as a singing/acting showcase for a pop star (Prince, Neil Diamond, Olivia Newton-John), or – as in the cases of Nos. 8 and 10 – based around an album. Subsequently, the originally fictional Blues Brothers developed into a real performing act.

TOP 10

ELVIS PRESLEY MOVIE SONGS IN THE US*

	Song	Film	Year
1	*Love Me Tender*	*Love Me Tender*	1956
2	*Jailhouse Rock*	*Jailhouse Rock*	1957
3	*Teddy Bear*	*Loving You*	1957
4	*Return to Sender*	*Girls! Girls! Girls!*	1962
5	*Can't Help Falling in Love*	*Blue Hawaii*	1961
6	*Hard Headed Woman*	*King Creole*	1958
7	*Bossa Nova Baby*	*Fun in Acapulco*	1963
8	*One Broken Heart for Sale*	*It Happened at the World's Fair*	1963
9	*Follow That Dream*	*Follow That Dream*	1962
10	*I'm Yours*	*Tickle Me*	1965

* Based on US singles sales

Elvis' film-extracted singles from 1963–69, which actually formed the bulk of his releases during this period, generally sold less well than those from his initial movie forays in the 1950s. *Love Me Tender*, *Jailhouse Rock*, and *Teddy Bear* were all US No. 1 hits, and all multi-million sellers.

THE 10
OSCAR-WINNING SONGS OF THE 1960s

	Song	Film
1960	*Never on Sunday*	*Never on Sunday*
1961	*Moon River*	*Breakfast at Tiffany's*
1962	*Days of Wine and Roses*	*Days of Wine and Roses*
1963	*Call Me Irresponsible*	*Papa's Delicate Condition*
1964	*Chim Chim Cheree*	*Mary Poppins*
1965	*The Shadow of Your Smile*	*The Sandpiper*
1966	*Born Free*	*Born Free*
1967	*Talk to the Animals*	*Dr. Doolittle*
1968	*The Windmills of Your Mind*	*The Thomas Crown Affair*
1969	*Raindrops Keep Falling on My Head*	*Butch Cassidy and the Sundance Kid*

Both Noel Harrison's *The Windmills of Your Mind* and B.J. Thomas' *Raindrops Keep Falling on My Head* hit the US Top 10, while French crooner Sacha Distel's cover version of the 1969 Oscar-winner charted no less than five times in the UK, all in 1970.

THE 10
OSCAR-WINNING SONGS OF THE 1970s

	Song	Film
1970	*For All We Know*	*Lovers and Other Strangers*
1971	*Theme from "Shaft"*	*Shaft*
1972	*The Morning After*	*The Poseidon Adventure*
1973	*The Way We Were*	*The Way We Were*
1974	*We May Never Love Like This Again*	*The Towering Inferno*
1975	*I'm Easy*	*Nashville*
1976	*Evergreen*	*A Star Is Born*
1977	*You Light Up My Life*	*You Light Up My Life*
1978	*Last Dance*	*Thank God It's Friday*
1979	*It Goes Like It Goes*	*Norma Rae*

Barbra Streisand became the first artist since Frank Sinatra to win two Oscar song awards in the same decade. Her two award-winners were *The Way We Were* and *Evergreen*, both of which went on to become huge international hits.

THE 10
OSCAR-WINNING SONGS OF THE 1980s

	Song	Film
1980	*Fame*	*Fame*
1981	*Up Where We Belong*	*An Officer and a Gentleman*
1982	*Arthur's Theme (Best That You Can Do)*	*Arthur*
1983	*Flashdance*	*Flashdance*
1984	*I Just Called to Say I Love You*	*The Woman in Red*
1985	*Say You, Say Me*	*White Nights*
1986	*Take My Breath Away*	*Top Gun*
1987	*(I've Had) The Time of My Life*	*Dirty Dancing*
1988	*Let the River Run*	*Working Girl*
1989	*Under the Sea*	*The Little Mermaid*

Award winners in the 1990s are 1990: *Sooner or Later (I Always Get My Man)* from *Dick Tracy*; 1991: *Beauty and the Beast* from the Disney film of the same name; 1992: *Whole New World* from *Aladdin*; 1993: *Streets of Philadelphia* from *Philadelphia*; 1994: *Can You Feel the Love Tonight* from *The Lion King*; and 1995: *Colors of the Wind* from *Pocahontas*. Of the winning songs during the two decades only those from *The Little Mermaid* and *Dick Tracy* failed to become international hits.

TOP 10
JAMES BOND FILM THEMES IN THE US

	Theme	Year	Artist
1	*A View to a Kill*	1985	Duran Duran
2	*Nobody Does It Better (from The Spy Who Loved Me)*	1977	Carly Simon
3	*Live and Let Die*	1973	Paul McCartney & Wings
4	*For Your Eyes Only*	1981	Sheena Easton
5	*Goldfinger*	1965	Shirley Bassey
6	*Thunderball*	1966	Tom Jones
7	*All Time High (from Octopussy)*	1983	Rita Coolidge
8	*You Only Live Twice*	1967	Nancy Sinatra
9	*Diamonds Are Forever*	1972	Shirley Bassey
10	*Goldfinger*	1965	John Barry

By no means have all the James Bond themes been major US hits, especially those from the later movies which failed to register at all. Every song listed here reached the Top 100, but only the first seven made the Top 40, and only Duran Duran have had a Bond-associated US No. 1 hit. Note the two appearances for *Goldfinger* – a vocal version by Shirley Bassey and an instrumental by John Barry; the film also produced the biggest-selling Bond film soundtrack LP during the same year.

MUSIC IN THE SALEROOM

TOP 10

MOST EXPENSIVE ITEMS OF POP MEMORABILIA EVER SOLD AT AUCTION

(Excluding rock stars' clothing – see opposite)

	Item/sale	Price ($)*
1	John Lennon's 1965 Rolls-Royce Phantom V touring limousine, finished in psychedelic paintwork, Sotheby's, New York, June 29, 1985	2,299,000
2	Jimi Hendrix's Fender Stratocaster electric guitar, Sotheby's, London, April 25, 1990	370,260
3	Acoustic guitar owned by David Bowie, Paul McCartney, and George Michael, Christie's, London, May 18, 1994	341,000
4	Buddy Holly's Gibson acoustic guitar, c. 1945, in a tooled leather case made by Holly, Sotheby's, New York, June 23, 1990	242,000
5	John Lennon's 1970 Mercedes-Benz 600 Pullman four-door limousine, Christie's, London, April 27, 1989	213,125
6	Elvis Presley's 1963 Rolls-Royce Phantom V touring limousine, Sotheby's, London, August 28, 1986	162,800

	Item/sale	Price ($)*
7	Elvis Presley's 1942 Martin D-18 guitar (used to record his first singles, 1954–56), Red Baron Antiques, Atlanta, Georgia, October 3, 1991	180,000
	The same guitar was resold by Christie's, London, May 14, 1993	148,500
8	Charlie Parker's Grafton saxophone, Christie's, London, September 8, 1994	144,925
9	Recording of 16-year-old John Lennon singing at a 1957 church fair in Liverpool, Sotheby's, London, September 15, 1994	121,675
10	Buddy Holly's Fender Stratocaster electric guitar, c.1958, Sotheby's, New York, June 23, 1990	110,000

* *Including 10 percent buyer's premium, where appropriate*

Pioneered by Sotheby's in London, pop memorabilia has become big business – especially if it involves personal association with megastars such as the Beatles and, lately, Buddy Holly (whose eyeglasses were sold by Sotheby's, New York, June 23, 1990, for $45,100). In addition to this Top 10, high prices have been paid for other musical instruments once owned by rock stars, such as a guitar belonging to John Entwistle of the Who, and even the painted bass drumskin featured on the album sleeve of *Sgt. Pepper's Lonely Hearts Club Band* ($80,755 at Sotheby's, London, September 15, 1994) – which would be No. 10, if Charlie Parker's saxophone is eliminated as belonging to the jazz, rather than "pop," genre.

DID YOU KNOW

ELVIS LIVES!

Although he died almost 20 years ago, Elvis Presley continues to reign supreme in the auction room. As well as his cars, guitars, and stage costumes represented in the Top 10s on these pages, recent sales, such as that held by Butterfield & Butterfield in Las Vegas on October 6, 1995, have offered such articles as Elvis's American Express card, a bar of soap used on his private jet, *Lisa Marie*, his revolvers, pajamas, and even a warrant issued for an unpaid parking ticket.

JOHN LENNON'S ROCK 'N' ROLLS ROYCE
The former Beatle's multicolored Phantom V became the most expensive used car ever sold when it was acquired by Jim Pattison, Chairman of the Expo '86 World Fair.

TOP 10

MOST EXPENSIVE ITEMS OF ROCK STARS' CLOTHING EVER SOLD AT AUCTION IN THE UK

Item/sale	Price ($)*
1 Jimi Hendrix's orange floral velvet jacket, Bonham's, London, August 18, 1994	58,900
2 Elvis Presley's one-piece "Shooting Star" stage outfit, *c.* 1972, Phillips, London, August 24, 1988	48,000
3 John Lennon's black leather jacket, *c.* 1960–62, Christie's, London, May 7, 1992	47,916
4 Jimi Hendrix's peacock feather waistcoat, 1967–68, Sotheby's, London, September 13, 1995	37,433
5 Jimi Hendrix's striped wool jacket, Bonham's, London, August 18, 1994	35,650
6 John Lennon's tan suede jacket, 1965, worn for the Beatles' *Rubber Soul* album cover, Christie's, London, May 25, 1995	31,388#

Item/sale	Price ($)*
7 Four "super hero"-style costumes worn by glam rock group Kiss in the film *Kiss Meets the Phantom* (1978), Christie's, London, May 14, 1993	31,350
8 Jimi Hendrix's psychedelic "poppy" jacket, Bonham's, London, August 18, 1994	31,000
9 Jimi Hendrix's green velvet double-breasted jacket, Bonham's, London, August 18, 1994	29,450
10 John Lennon's "Happi" coat, 1966, given to him by Japanese Airlines during the Beatles' trip to Japan, Christie's, London, September 7, 1995	27,900#

* *Including 10 percent buyer's premium unless otherwise noted*
\# *Including 12.5 percent buyer's premium*

TOP 10

MOST EXPENSIVE MUSIC MANUSCRIPTS EVER SOLD AT AUCTION

Manuscript/sale	Price ($)*
1 Nine symphonies by Wolfgang Amadeus Mozart, Sotheby's, London, May 22, 1987	3,854,000
2 Schumann's *Second Symphony*, Sotheby's, London, December 1, 1994	2,085,000
3 Ludwig van Beethoven's *Piano Sonata in E Minor*, Opus 90, Sotheby's, London, December 6, 1991	1,690,000
4 Wolfgang Amadeus Mozart's *Fantasia in C Minor* and *Sonata in C Minor*, Sotheby's, London, November 21, 1990	1,496,000
5 Robert Schumann's *Piano Concerto in A Minor*, Opus 54, Sotheby's, London, November 22, 1989	1,240,000
6 Joseph Haydn's *Four String Quartets*, Opus 50, Sotheby's, London, May 18, 1995	950,000
7 Ludwig van Beethoven's first movement of the *Sonata for Violoncello and Piano in A Major*, Opus 69, Sotheby's, London, May 17, 1990	897,000
8 Johann Sebastian Bach's *Cantata No. 2*, Sotheby's, London, May 15, 1996	679,500
9 Johann Sebastian Bach's cantata *Auf Christi Himmelfahrt allein*, Sotheby's, London, November 22, 1989	604,500
10 Igor Stravinsky's *Rite of Spring*, Sotheby's, London, November 11, 1982	570,000

* *"Hammer price," excluding premiums*

TOP 10

MOST EXPENSIVE MUSICAL INSTRUMENTS EVER SOLD AT AUCTION

Instrument/sale	Price ($)*
1 "Mendelssohn" Stradivarius violin, Christie's, London, November 21, 1990	1,686,740
2 "Cholmondley" Stradivarius violoncello, Sotheby's, London, June 22, 1988	1,145,760
3 Steinway grand piano, decorated by Lawrence Alma-Tadema and Edward Poynter for Henry Marquand, 1884–87, Sotheby Parke Bernet, New York, March 26, 1980	390,000
4 Jimi Hendrix's Fender Stratocaster electric guitar, Sotheby's, London, April 25, 1990	370,260
5 Acoustic guitar owned by David Bowie, Paul McCartney, and George Michael, Christie's, London, May 18, 1994	341,000
6 Verne Powell platinum flute, Christie's, New York, October 18, 1986	187,000
7 Flemish single-manual harpsichord by Johan Daniel Dulken of Antwerp, 1755, Sotheby's, London, March 27, 1990	153,865
8 Charlie Parker's Grafton Saxophone, Christie's, London, September 8, 1994	144,925
9 Two-manual harpsichord by Andreas Ruckers of Antwerp, 1623, Sotheby's, London, November 8, 1995	138,725
10 One-keyed ebony "Quantz" flute made for Frederick the Great of Prussia, *c.* 1750, Sotheby's, Baden-Baden, October 10, 1995	89,280

* *Including 10 percent buyer's premium, where appropriate*

CLASSICAL & OPERA

A PASSION FOR CARMEN
The opera diva Maria Ewing takes the title role in Bizet's popular romantic opera Carmen, *first staged in Paris in 1875. Today it ranks as one of the most performed works on both sides of the Atlantic – at New York's Metropolitan Opera House and London's Royal Opera House.*

TOP 10

OPERAS MOST FREQUENTLY PERFORMED AT THE METROPOLITAN OPERA HOUSE, NEW YORK

	Opera	Composer	Performances
1	*La Bohème*	Giacomo Puccini	728
2	*Aïda*	Giuseppe Verdi	709
3	*La Traviata*	Giuseppe Verdi	579
4	*Tosca*	Giacomo Puccini	559
5	*Carmen*	Georges Bizet	548
6	*Madama Butterfly*	Giacomo Puccini	517
7	*Rigoletto*	Giuseppe Verdi	510
8	*I Pagliacci*	Ruggero Leoncavallo	460
9	*Faust*	Charles Gounod	436
10	*Cavalleria Rusticana*	Pietro Mascagni	428

The Metropolitan Opera House opened on October 22, 1883 with a performance of Charles Gounod's *Faust*. Such is the universality of opera that no fewer than eight of the Met's top operas also appear in the Top 10 performed at London's principal venue, the Royal Opera House, Covent Garden. At Covent Garden, *La Bohème* similarly tops the list of "most performed" operas.

THE 10

LAST WINNERS OF THE "BEST CLASSICAL ALBUM" GRAMMY AWARD

Year	Composer/title/conductor
1996	Claude Debussy, *La Mer*/Pierre Boulez, Cleveland Orchestra
1995	Béla Bartók, *Concerto for Orchestra; Four Orchestral Pieces, Op. 12*/Pierre Boulez, Chicago Symphony Orchestra
1994	Béla Bartók, *The Wooden Prince*/Pierre Boulez, Chicago Symphony Orchestra and Chorus
1993	Gustav Mahler, *Symphony No. 9*/Leonard Bernstein, Berlin Philharmonic Orchestra
1992	Leonard Bernstein, *Candide*/Leonard Bernstein, London Symphony Orchestra
1991	Charles Ives, *Symphony No. 2 (and Three Short Works)*/Leonard Bernstein, New York Philharmonic Orchestra
1990	Béla Bartók, *Six String Quartets*/Emerson String Quartet
1989	Giuseppi Verdi, *Requiem and Operatic Choruses*/Robert Shaw, Atlanta Symphony Orchestra
1988	*Horowitz In Moscow*/Vladimir Horowitz
1987	*Horowitz: The Studio Recordings, New York*/Vladimir Horowitz

THE 10

LAST WINNERS OF THE "BEST OPERA RECORDING" GRAMMY AWARD

Year	Composer/title/principal soloists
1996	Hector Berlioz, *Les Troyens*/Charles Dutoit, Orchestra Symphonie de Montreal
1995	Carlisle Floyd, *Susannah*/Jerry Hadley, Samuel Ramey, Cheryl Studer, Kenn Chester
1994	George Handel, *Semele*/Kathleen Battle, Marilyn Horne, Samuel Ramey, Sylvia McNair, Michael Chance
1993	Richard Strauss, *Die Frau Ohne Schatten*/Placido Domingo, Jose Van Dam, Hildegard Behrens
1992	Richard Wagner, *Götterdämmerung*/Hildegard Behrens, Ekkehard Wlashiha
1991	Richard Wagner, *Das Rheingold*/James Morris, Kurt Moll, Christa Ludwig
1990	Richard Wagner, *Die Walküre*/Gary Lakes, Jessye Norman, Kurt Moll
1989	Richard Wagner, *Lohengrin*/Placido Domingo, Jessye Norman, Eva Randova
1988	Richard Strauss, *Ariadne Auf Naxos*/Anna Tomowa-Sintow, Kathleen Battle, Agnes Baltsa, Gary Lakes
1987	Leonard Bernstein, *Candide*/Ernie Mills, David Eisler, John Lankston

TOP 10

LARGEST OPERA HOUSES IN THE WORLD

	Opera house	Location	seating	Capacity standing	total
1	The Metropolitan Opera	New York	3,800	265	4,065
2	Cincinnati Opera	Cincinnati	3,630	–	3,630
3	Lyric Opera of Chicago	Chicago	3,563	–	3,563
4	San Francisco Opera	San Francisco	3,176	300	3,476
5	The Dallas Opera	Dallas	3,420	–	3,420
6	Canadian Opera Company	Toronto	3,167	–	3,167
7	Los Angeles Music Center Opera	Los Angeles	3,098	–	3,098
8	San Diego Opera	San Diego	2,992	84	3,076
9	Seattle Opera	Seattle	3,017	–	3,017
10	L'Opéra de Montréal	Montreal	2,874	–	2,874

OPERA'S LONDON HOME
Built in 1858 on a site occupied by a succession of theaters since 1732, the Royal Opera House is home to both the Royal Opera and the Royal Ballet companies.

TOP 10

MOST PROLIFIC CLASSICAL COMPOSERS*

	Composer/nationality	Hours
1	Joseph Haydn (1732–1809), Austrian	340
2	George Handel (1685–1759), German/English	303
3	Wolfgang Amadeus Mozart (1656–91), Austrian	202
4	Johann Sebastian Bach (1685–1750), German	175
5	Franz Schubert (1797–1828), German	134
6	Ludwig van Beethoven (1770–1827), German	120
7	Henry Purcell (1659–95), English	116
8	Giuseppe Verdi (1813–1901), Italian	87
9	Antonín Dvořák (1841–1904), Czech	79
10=	Franz Liszt (1811–86), Hungarian	76
10=	Peter Tchaikovsky (1840–93), Russian	76

* *Based on a survey conducted by* Classical Music *magazine, which ranked classical composers by the total number of hours of music each composed.*

TOP 10

CLASSICAL ALBUMS OF ALL TIME IN THE US

	Artist/title	Year
1	Van Cliburn, *Tchaikovsky: Piano Concerto No. 1*	1958
2	Carreras, Domingo, Pavarotti, *The Three Tenors Concert*	1990
3	Soundtrack (Philadelphia Orchestra), *Fantasia (50th Anniversary Edition)*	1990
4	Placido Domingo, *Perhaps Love*	1981
5	Antal Dorati/Minneapolis Symphony Orchestra, *Tchaikovsky: 1812 Overture/ Capriccio Italien*	1959
6	Mantovani, *Strauss Waltzes*	1958
7	Walter Carlos, *Switched-On Bach*	1969
8	Soundtrack (Berlin Philharmonic Orchestra), *2001: A Space Odyssey*	1968
9	Luciano Pavarotti, *O Sole Mio*	1979
10	Van Cliburn, *Rachmaninoff: Piano Concerto No. 3*	1959

Classical recordings held far greater sway in the early years of the US album chart, and most notably during the 1950s, than they have in subsequent decades. This is partly reflected in the vintage nature of much of this Top 10.

TOP 10

OPERAS MOST FREQUENTLY PERFORMED AT THE ROYAL OPERA HOUSE, COVENT GARDEN

	Opera/composer/ first performance	Total*
1	*La Bohème*, Giacomo Puccini, October 2, 1897	510
2	*Carmen*, Georges Bizet, May 27, 1882	495
3	*Aïda*, Giuseppe Verdi, June 22, 1876	467
4	*Faust*, Charles Gounod, July 18, 1863	428
5	*Rigoletto*, Giuseppe Verdi, May 14, 1853	423
6	*Tosca*, Giacomo Puccini, July 12, 1900	375
7	*Don Giovanni*, Wolfgang Amadeus Mozart, April 17, 1834	373
8	*La Traviata*, Giuseppe Verdi, May 25, 1858	355
9	*Norma*, Vincenzo Bellini, July 12, 1833	353
10	*Madama Butterfly*, Giacomo Puccini, July 10, 1905	342

* *Number of performances up to December 31, 1995*

144

STAGE & SCREEN

20TH CENTURY

Almost all the longest-running shows ever staged date from the second half of the 20th century. The century has also witnessed some of the shortest runs, including The Intimate Revue *which opened and closed at the Duchess Theatre, London, on the same night in 1930. On Broadway both* Frankenstein *(1981) and* Little Johnny Jones *(1982) closed after a single performance.*

TOP 10
LONGEST-RUNNING SHOWS ON BROADWAY

	Show	Performances
1	*A Chorus Line* (1975–90)	6,137
2	*Oh! Calcutta!* (1976–89)	5,959
3	*Cats* (1982–)	5,525*
4	*Les Misérables* (1987–)	3,613*
5	*42nd Street* (1980–89)	3,486
6	*Grease* (1972–80)	3,388
7	*Fiddler on the Roof* (1964–72)	3,242
8	*Life with Father* (1939–47)	3,224
9	*Tobacco Road* (1933–41)	3,182
10	*The Phantom of the Opera* (1988–)	3,164*

* Still running; total at December 31, 1995

TOP 10
LONGEST-RUNNING SHOWS IN THE UK

	Show	Performances
1	*The Mousetrap* (1952–)	17,940*
2	*No Sex, Please – We're British* (1971–80; 1982–86; 1986–87)	6,761
3	*Cats* (1981–)	6,108*
4	*Starlight Express* (1984–)	4,905*
5	*Les Misérables* (1985–)	4,182*
6	*Oliver!* (1960–69)	4,125
7	*Oh! Calcutta!* (1970–80)	3,918
8	*The Phantom of the Opera* (1986–)	3,898*
9	*Jesus Christ, Superstar* (1972–80)	3,357
10	*Evita* (1978–86)	2,900

* Still running; total at December 31, 1995

The Mousetrap *opened on November 25, 1952 at the Ambassadors Theatre. After 8,862 performances it transferred to St. Martin's Theatre, where it reopened on March 25, 1974. It is not the only play in the world to have run continuously since the 1950s – Eugène Ionesco's* La Cantatrice Chauve *was first performed in Paris on May 11, 1950 and has run continuously since February 16, 1957.*

LES MISERABLES
The hugely successful musical Les Misérables *was based on the book of the same name by Victor Hugo.*

LONG RUNNERS

THE CLASSIC PHANTOM OF THE OPERA
Andrew Lloyd Webber's The Phantom of the Opera *is a musical version of an old tale. Michael Crawford, who played the original starring role, contributed to the success of the show with songs such as* Music of the Night.

TOP 10
LONGEST-RUNNING MUSICALS ON BROADWAY

	Show	Performances
1	A Chorus Line (1975–90)	6,137
2	Cats (1982–)	5,525*
3	Les Misérables (1987–)	3,613*
4	42nd Street (1980–89)	3,486
5	Grease (1972–80)	3,388
6	Fiddler on the Roof (1964–72)	3,242
7	The Phantom of the Opera (1988–)	3,164*
8	Hello Dolly! (1964–71)	2,844
9	My Fair Lady (1956–62)	2,717
10	Annie (1977–83)	2,377

* Still running; total at December 31, 1995

TOP 10
LONGEST-RUNNING MUSICALS IN THE UK

	Show	Performances
1	Cats (1981–)	6,108*
2	Starlight Express (1984–)	4,905*
3	Les Misérables (1985–)	4,182*
4	Oliver! (1960–69)	4,125
5	The Phantom of the Opera (1986–)	3,898*
6	Jesus Christ, Superstar (1972–80)	3,357
7	Evita (1978–86)	2,900
8	Miss Saigon (1989–)	2,671*
9	The Sound of Music (1961–67)	2,386
10	Salad Days (1954–60)	2,283

* Still running; total at December 31, 1995

TOP 10
LONGEST-RUNNING COMEDIES ON BROADWAY

	Show	Performances
1	Life with Father (1939–47)	3,224
2	Abie's Irish Rose (1922–27)	2,327
3	Gemini (1977–81)	1,788
4	Harvey (1944–49)	1,775
5	Born Yesterday (1946–49)	1,642
6	Mary, Mary (1961–64)	1,572
7	Voice of the Turtle (1943–48)	1,558
8	Barefoot in the Park (1963–67)	1,532
9	Same Time Next Year (1975–78)	1,444
10	Brighton Beach Memoirs (1983–86)	1,299

TOP 10
LONGEST-RUNNING COMEDIES IN THE UK

	Show	Performances
1	No Sex, Please – We're British (1971–80; 1982–86; 1986–87)	6,761*
2	Run for Your Wife (1983–91)	2,638
3	There's a Girl in My Soup (1966–69; 1969–72)	2,547
4	Pyjama Tops (1969–75)	2,498
5	Worm's Eye View (1945–51)	2,245
6	Boeing Boeing (1962–63; 1965–67)	2,035
7	Blithe Spirit (1941–42; 1942; 1942–46)	1,997
8	Dirty Linen (1976–80)	1,667
9	Reluctant Heroes (1950–54)	1,610
10	Seagulls Over Sorrento (1950–54; 1954)	1,551

TOP 10
LONGEST-RUNNING NON-MUSICALS ON BROADWAY

	Show	Performances
1	Oh! Calcutta! (1976–89)	5,959
2	Life with Father (1939–47)	3,224
3	Tobacco Road (1933–41)	3,182
4	Abie's Irish Rose (1922–27)	2,327
5	Deathtrap (1978–82)	1,792
6	Gemini (1977–81)	1,788
7	Harvey (1944–49)	1,775
8	Born Yesterday (1946–49)	1,642
9	Mary, Mary (1961–64)	1,572
10	Voice of the Turtle (1943–48)	1,558

More than half the longest-running non-musical shows on Broadway began their runs before World War II. Off Broadway, these records have all been broken by *The Drunkard*, which was performed at the Mart Theatre, Los Angeles, from July 6, 1933 to September 6, 1953, and then continued as a musical adapation until October 17, 1959.

TOP 10
LONGEST-RUNNING NON-MUSICALS IN THE UK

	Show	Performances
1	The Mousetrap (1952–)	17,940
2	No Sex, Please – We're British (1971–80; 1982–86; 1986–87)	6,761
3	Oh! Calcutta! (1970–80)	3,918
4	Run for Your Wife (1983–91)	2,638
5	There's a Girl in My Soup (1966–69; 1969–72)	2,547
6	Pyjama Tops (1969–75)	2,498
7	Sleuth (1970–75)	2,359
8	Worm's Eye View (1945–51)	2,245
9	Boeing Boeing (1962–63; 1965–67)	2,035
10	Blithe Spirit (1941–42; 1942; 1942–46)	1,997

* Still running; total at December 31,1995

THE WORLD'S A STAGE

THEATER-GOING COUNTRIES IN THE WORLD

	Country	Annual theater attendance per 1,000 population
1	Cuba	2,559
2	Mongolia	1,700
3	Vietnam	1,000
4	UK	720
5	Iceland	658
6	Bulgaria	650
7	Luxembourg	613
8	Albania	590
9	Romania	578
10	Netherlands	575
	US	*170*

AWARDS FOR EXCELLENCE

The Society of West End Theatre Awards was established in 1976 and was renamed in honor of the great British actor, Sir Laurence Olivier, in 1984. The BBC Award for Best Play is presented at this event. The award itself is a bronze bust of Olivier as he appeared at the Old Vic Theatre in 1937 in the title role of *Henry V*. The *Evening Standard* Drama Awards have been presented by the London newspaper since 1955, with awards for best actor, actress, musical, play, and comedy, as well as the Sydney Edwards Award for best director. In the US the most important theater awards include the New York Drama Desk Awards and the Tony Awards. The Pulitzer Drama Awards are the longest established (since 1918).

OLDEST THEATERS IN LONDON

	Theater	Date opened
1	Theatre Royal, Drury Lane	May 7, 1663
2	Sadler's Wells, Rosebery Avenue	Jun 3, 1683
3	The Haymarket (Theatre Royal), Haymarket	Dec 29, 1720
4	Royal Opera House, Covent Garden	Dec 7, 1732
5	The Adelphi (originally Sans Pareil), Strand	Nov 27, 1806
6	The Old Vic (originally Royal Coburg), Waterloo Road	May 11, 1818
7	The Vaudeville, Strand	Apr 16, 1870
8	The Criterion, Piccadilly Circus	Mar 21, 1874
9	The Savoy, Strand	Oct 10, 1881
10	The Comedy, Panton Street	Oct 15, 1881

LAST TONY AWARDS FOR A DIRECTOR

Year	Director	Play
1996	Gerald Gutierrez	*A Delicate Balance*
1995	Gerald Gutierrez	*The Heiress*
1994	Stephen Daldry	*An Inspector Calls*
1993	George C. Wolfe	*Angels in America Part I: Millennium Approaches*
1992	Patrick Mason	*Dancing at Lughnasa*
1991	Jerry Zaks	*Six Degrees of Separation*
1990	Frank Galati	*The Grapes of Wrath*
1989	Jerry Zaks	*Lend Me a Tenor*
1988	John Dexter	*M. Butterfly*
1987	Lloyd Richards	*Fences*

LAST TONY AWARDS FOR AN ACTOR

Year	Actor	Play
1996	George Grizzard	*A Delicate Balance*
1995	Ralph Fiennes	*Hamlet*
1994	Stephen Spinella	*Angels in America Part II: Perestroika*
1993	Ron Leibman	*Angels in America Part I: Millennium Approaches*
1992	Judd Hirsch	*Conversations with My Father*
1991	Nigel Hawthorne	*Shadowlands*
1990	Robert Morse	*Tru*
1989	Philip Bosco	*Lend Me a Tenor*
1988	Ron Silver	*Speed-the-Plow*
1987	James Earl Jones	*Fences*

LAST TONY AWARDS FOR AN ACTRESS

Year	Actress	Play
1996	Zoe Caldwell	*Master Class*
1995	Cherry Jones	*The Heiress*
1994	Diana Rigg	*Medea*
1993	Madeline Kahn	*The Sisters Rosensweig*
1992	Glenn Close	*Death and the Maiden*
1991	Mercedes Ruehl	*Lost in Yonkers*
1990	Maggie Smith	*Lettice and Lovage*
1989	Pauline Collins	*Shirley Valentine*
1988	Joan Allen	*Burn This*
1987	Linda Lavin	*Broadway Bound*

THE 10

LAST NEW YORK DRAMA DESK AWARDS FOR A MUSICAL

Year	Musical
1995	*Showboat*
1994	*Passion*
1993	*Kiss of the Spider Woman*
1992	*Crazy for You*
1991	*The Will Rogers Follies*
1990	*City of Angels*
1989	*Jerome Robbins's Broadway*
1988	*Into the Woods*
1987	*Les Misérables*
1986	*The Mystery of Edwin Drood*

The first New York Drama Critics' Circle Award was presented over 50 years ago for a 1945 production of Richard Rodgers and Oscar Hammerstein II's *Carousel*. Winners over successive years include the popular post-war musicals *Brigadoon*, *South Pacific*, *Guys and Dolls*, and *My Fair Lady*.

THE 10

LAST PULITZER DRAMA AWARDS

Year	Play	Author
1996	*Rent*	Jonathan Larson
1995	*The Young Man from Atlanta*	Horton Foote
1994	*Three Tall Women*	Edward Albee
1993	*Angels in America Part I: Millennium Approaches*	Tony Kushner
1992	*The Kentucky Cycle*	Robert Schenkkan
1991	*Lost in Yonkers*	Neil Simon
1990	*The Piano Lesson*	August Wilson
1989	*The Heidi Chronicles*	Wendy Wasserstein
1988	*Driving Miss Daisy*	Alfred Uhry
1987	*Fences*	August Wilson

THE 10

LAST WINNERS OF THE LAURENCE OLIVIER AWARD FOR BEST COMEDY PERFORMANCE

Year	Performer	Show
1995	Niall Buggy	*Dead Funny*
1994	Griff Rhys Jones	*An Absolute Turkey*
1993	Simon Cadell	*Travels with My Aunt*
1991	Alan Cumming	*Accidental Death of an Anarchist*
1989–90	Michael Gambon	*Man of the Moment*
1988	Alex Jennings	*Too Clever by Half*
1984	Maureen Lipman	*See How They Run*
1983	Griff Rhys Jones	*Charley's Aunt*
1982	Geoffrey Hutchings	*Poppy*
1981	Rowan Atkinson	*Rowan Atkinson in Revue*

THE 10

LAST TONY AWARDS FOR A PLAY

Year	Play	Author
1996	*Master Class*	Terrence McNally
1995	*Love! Valour! Compassion!*	Terrence McNally
1994	*Angels in America Part II: Perestroika*	Tony Kushner
1993	*Angels in America Part I: Millenium Approaches*	Tony Kushner
1992	*Dancing at Lughnasa*	Brian Friel
1991	*Lost in Yonkers*	Neil Simon
1990	*The Grapes of Wrath*	Frank Galati
1989	*The Heidi Chronicles*	Wendy Wasserstein
1988	*M. Butterfly*	David Henry Hwang
1987	*Fences*	August Wilson

THE 10

LAST WINNERS OF THE BBC AWARD FOR BEST PLAY

Year	Play	Author
1995	*Broken Glass*	Arthur Miller
1994	*Arcadia*	Tom Stoppard
1993	*Six Degrees of Separation*	John Guare
1992	*Death and the Maiden*	Ariel Dorfman
1991	*Dancing at Lughansa*	Brian Friel
1989–90	*Racing Demon*	David Hare
1988	*Our Country's Good*	Timberlake Wertenbaker
1987	*Serious Money*	Caryl Churchill
1986	*Les Liaisons Dangereuses*	Christopher Hampton
1985	*Red Noses*	Peter Barnes

THE 10

LAST WINNERS OF THE LAURENCE OLIVIER/ AMERICAN EXPRESS AWARD FOR BEST MUSICAL

Year	Musical
1995	*Once on This Island*
1994	*City of Angels*
1993	*Crazy for You*
1992	*Carmen Jones*
1991	*Sunday in the Park with George*
1989–90	*Return to the Forbidden Planet*
1988	*Candide*
1987	*Follies*
1986	*The Phantom of the Opera*
1985	*Me and My Girl*

THE IMMORTAL BARD

TOP 10

MOST DEMANDING SHAKESPEAREAN ROLES

	Role	Play	Lines
1	Hamlet	*Hamlet*	1,422
2	Falstaff	*Henry IV, Parts I and II*	1,178
3	Richard III	*Richard III*	1,124
4	Iago	*Othello*	1,097
5	Henry V	*Henry V*	1,025
6	Othello	*Othello*	860
7	Vincentio	*Measure for Measure*	820
8	Coriolanus	*Coriolanus*	809
9	Timon	*Timon of Athens*	795
10	Antony	*Antony and Cleopatra*	766

Hamlet speaks over 36 percent of the play – 11,610 words – the most of any character in Shakespeare. Falstaff, however, appearing in *Henry IV, Parts I and II*, and *The Merry Wives of Windsor*, wins with 1,614 lines.

TOP 10

WORDS MOST USED BY SHAKESPEARE

	Word	Frequency
1	the	27,457
2	and	26,285
3	I	21,206
4	to	19,938
5	of	17,079
6	a	14,675
7	you	14,326
8	my	13,075
9	that	11,725
10	in	11,511

In his complete works, William Shakespeare wrote a total of 884,647 words – 118,406 lines comprising 31,959 separate speeches. He used a total vocabulary of 29,066 words, some – such as "America" – appearing only once (*The Comedy of Errors*, III.ii). This Top 10 lists all those words used on over 10,000 occasions.

TO BE OR NOT TO BE, THAT IS THE QUESTION *Mel Gibson, of* Mad Max *and* Lethal Weapon *fame, surprised his fans and critics alike with his masterful portrayal of Hamlet in the 1991 big-screen version of William Shakespeare's longest play. What makes Mel Gibson's success more remarkable is the fact that Hamlet is the most demanding of Shakespearean roles for an actor.*

TOP 10

LONGEST PLAYS BY SHAKESPEARE

	Play	Lines
1	*Hamlet*	3,901
2	*Richard III*	3,886
3	*Coriolanus*	3,820
4	*Cymbeline*	3,813
5	*Othello*	3,672
6	*Antony and Cleopatra*	3,630
7	*Troilus and Cressida*	3,576
8	*Henry VIII*	3,450
9	*Henry V*	3,368
10	*The Winter's Tale*	3,354

THE 10

PRECEPTS FOR LAERTES GIVEN BY POLONIUS

1 *Give thy thoughts no tongue, Nor any unproportioned thought his act.*

2 *Be thou familiar, but by no means vulgar.*

3 *Those friends thou hast, and their adoption tried, Grapple them to thy soul with hoops of steel;*

4 *But do not dull thy palm with entertainment Of each new-hatch'd, unfledged comrade.*

5 *Beware of entrance to a quarrel, but being in, Bear't that the opposed may beware of thee.*

6 *Give every man thy ear, but few thy voice;*

7 *Take each man's censure, but reserve thy judgment.*

8 *Costly thy habit as thy purse can buy, But not express'd in fancy; rich, not gaudy; For the apparel oft proclaims the man, And they in France of the best rank and station Are of a most select and generous chief in that.*

9 *Neither a borrower nor a lender be; For loan oft loses both itself and friend, And borrowing dulls the edge of husbandry.*

10 *This above all: to thine own self be true, And it must follow, as the night the day, Thou canst not then be false to any man.*

In Act I, Scene iii of *Hamlet*, Polonius, the Lord Chamberlain and father of Hamlet's friend Laertes, gives his son these 10 pieces of advice before Laertes sets sail on his voyage to France.

THE 10

FIRST PLAYS BY SHAKESPEARE

	Play	Approx. year written
1	*Titus Andronicus*	1588–90
2	*Love's Labours Lost*	1590
3	*Henry VI, Parts I–III*	1590–91
4=	*The Comedy of Errors*	1591
4=	*Richard III*	1591
4=	*Romeo and Juliet*	1591
7	*The Two Gentlemen of Verona*	1592–93
8	*A Midsummer Night's Dream*	1593–94
9	*Richard II*	1594
10	*King John*	1595

Precise dating of Shakespeare's plays is never easy. Contemporary records of early performances are rare, and only half the plays were published before Shakespeare died in 1616. Even these were much altered from the originals. It was only after 1623, when the "Folios" were published, that the complete works of Shakespeare were published progressively. *Romeo and Juliet* is especially difficult because it may date from as early as 1591 or as late as 1596–97. If the latter is true, then it would be predated by numbers 7–10 and by *The Merchant of Venice* (c. 1596).

TOP 10

MOST PRODUCED PLAYS BY SHAKESPEARE*

	Play	Productions
1	*As You Like It*	65
2	*Twelfth Night*	60
3	*The Merchant of Venice*	59
4	*Hamlet*	58
5	*The Taming of the Shrew*	57
6	*Much Ado About Nothing*	56
7	*A Midsummer Night's Dream*	51
8	*Macbeth*	49
9	*Romeo and Juliet*	48
10	*The Merry Wives of Windsor*	47

* To January 1, 1996

This list, which is based on an analysis of Shakespearean productions from December 31, 1878 to January 1, 1996 given at Stratford-upon-Avon and by the Royal Shakespeare Company in London, provides a reasonable picture of his most popular plays. Records do not, however, indicate the total number of individual performances during each production.

DID YOU KNOW

THE WORLD'S WORST ACTOR

Following a hansom cab accident in London, the death of Robert Coates on February 21, 1848 robbed the world of the man who, it has been claimed, was the worst Shakespearean actor who ever lived. Born in Antigua in 1772, the son of a wealthy merchant and sugar planter, Coates moved to England and took to the stage. Wearing outrageous costumes decked in diamonds, and hats topped with huge ostrich feathers, "Romeo" Coates, as he became known, was celebrated for his total lack of acting ability, frequently forgetting his lines (or writing his own to "improve" Shakespeare's), waving to and chatting with his friends in the audience, and overacting death scenes, such as that of Romeo, which he would often repeat several times as an encore. He frequently argued with the audience, which jeered and pelted him with oranges until theater managers had to drop the curtains to avoid a riot.

MOVIE HITS & MISSES

Movies in these lists are ranked according to the total rental fees paid to the distributors by movie theaters in the US and Canada. The movie industry regards this as a reliable guide to what a movie has earned in these markets. Doubling these receipts is also accepted as a very rough guide to the world total. Rental income is not the same as "box office gross," another way of comparing the success of movies. While valid over a short time, comparing recent releases, for example, it indicates the movie theaters' earnings rather than the film's, and depends on ticket price. Recent movies tend to earn the most money, because as inflation rises so too do ticket prices, box office income, and distributors' fees. If inflation were taken into account, the most successful movie ever would be *Gone with the Wind*.

T O P 1 0
HIGHEST-GROSSING MOVIES OF 1995 IN THE US

	Movie	Distributor	Release date	Box office gross ($)*
1	*Batman Forever*	Warner Bros.	Jun 16	184,031,112
2	*Apollo 13*	Universal	Jun 30	172,071,312
3	*Toy Story*	Buena Vista	Nov 22	146,198,683
4	*Pocahontas*	Buena Vista	Jun 16	141,523,195
5	*Ace Ventura: When Nature Calls*	Warner Bros.	Nov 10	104,194,467
6	*Casper*	Universal	May 26	100,328,194
7	*Die Hard with a Vengeance*	Fox	May 19	100,012,499
8	*Goldeneye*	MGM/UA	Nov 17	92,436,092
9	*Crimson Tide*	Buena Vista	May 12	91,387,195
10	*Waterworld*	Universal	Jul 28	88,246,220

* US and Canada during 1995 only

T O P 1 0
BIGGEST MOVIE FLOPS OF ALL TIME

	Movie	Year	Estimated loss ($)
1	*Cutthroat Island*	1995	100,000,000
2	*The Adventures of Baron Münchhausen*	1988	48,100,000
3	*Ishtar*	1987	47,300,000
4	*Hudson Hawk*	1991	47,000,000
5	*Inchon*	1981	44,100,000
6	*The Cotton Club*	1984	38,100,000
7	*Santa Claus – The Movie*	1985	37,000,000
8	*Heaven's Gate*	1980	34,200,000
9	*Billy Bathgate*	1991	33,000,000
10	*Pirates*	1986	30,300,000

Since the figures here are based upon North American rental earnings balanced against each movie's original production cost, some may recoup a proportion of their losses via overseas earnings, video, and TV revenue. The recent entry of *Cutthroat Island* and other newcomers to the flops league means that *Rambo III* (1988) and *Raise the Titanic* (1980) have finally sunk from this Top 10.

T O P 1 0
HIGHEST-GROSSING MOVIES OF 1995 IN THE WORLD

	Movie	Box office gross ($)
1	*Die Hard with a Vengeance*	354,000,000
2	*Batman Forever*	333,000,000
3	*Apollo 13*	332,000,000
4	*Pocahontas*	318,000,000
5	*Casper*	280,000,000
6	*Waterworld*	255,000,000
7	*Forrest Gump*	207,000,000
8	*Goldeneye*	199,000,000
9	*Outbreak*	188,000,000
10	*Dumb & Dumber*	187,000,000

All 10 of the highest-grossing movies of 1995 were US-made, underlining the fact that today Hollywood productions and world cinema success are synonymous. Internationally, the list broadly reflects the taste of the American movie-going public, except that certain year-end blockbusters, most notably *Toy Story*, were not released overseas until 1996, and hence do not make a showing in the global Top 10.

TOP 10

MOVIES DIRECTED BY WOMEN

	Movie	Director			Movie	Director
1	*Look Who's Talking*	Amy Heckerling		6	*The Prince of Tides*	Barbra Streisand
2	*Sleepless in Seattle*	Nora Ephron		7	*Clueless*	Amy Heckerling
3	*Wayne's World*	Penelope Spheeris		8	*Pet Sematary*	Mary Lambert
4	*Big*	Penny Marshall		9	*National Lampoon's European Vacation*	Amy Heckerling
5	*A League of Their Own*	Penny Marshall		10	*Little Women*	Gillian Armstrong

TOP 10

MOVIE SEQUELS OF ALL TIME

	Movie series	Years
1	*Star Wars/The Empire Strikes Back/Return of the Jedi*	1977–83
2	*Batman/Batman Returns/ Batman Forever*	1989–95
3	*Raiders of the Lost Ark/ Indiana Jones and the Temple of Doom/Indiana Jones and the Last Crusade*	1981–89
4	*Star Trek I–VI/Generations*	1979–94
5	*Rocky I–V*	1976–90
6	*Home Alone 1–2*	1990–92
7	*Back to the Future I–III*	1985–90
8	*Jaws I–IV*	1975–87
9	*Beverly Hills Cop I–III*	1984–94
10	*Ghostbusters I–II*	1984–89

Based on total earnings of the original movie and all its sequels up to the end of 1993, the *Star Wars* trilogy stands head and shoulders above the rest, having made more than $500,000,000 in the North American market alone. All the other movies in this Top 10 have achieved total earnings of around $200,000,000 or more, with recent series that have the potential to catch up – *Lethal Weapon 1–3* and the *Die Hard* movies among them – lagging just outside this Top 10. If the James Bond films were presented as sequels, their total earnings would place them in the 2nd position in this list. A successful movie does not guarantee a successful sequel, however. Although their total earns them a place only just outside this Top 10, each of the four *Superman* films actually earned less than the previous one, with *Superman IV* earning just one-tenth of the original.

DINOSAURS RULE THE EARTH AGAIN
Directed by Steven Spielberg, Jurassic Park *was a major breakthrough in special effects. With the aid of new technology and computers, dinosaurs were brought back to life.*

TOP 10

MOST EXPENSIVE MOVIES EVER MADE

	Movie*	Year	Estimated cost ($)
1	*Waterworld*	1995	160,000,000
2	*True Lies*	1994	115,000,000
3	*Cutthroat Island*	1996	105,000,000
4	*Inchon* (US/Korea)	1981	102,000,000
5	*War and Peace* (USSR)	1967	100,000,000
6	*Terminator 2: Judgment Day*	1991	95,000,000
7	*Total Recall*	1990	85,000,000
8	*The Last Action Hero*	1993	82,500,000
9	*Batman Returns*	1992	80,000,000
10	*Aliens*[3]	1992	75,000,000

* *All US-made unless otherwise stated*

TOP 10

HIGHEST-GROSSING MOVIES OF ALL TIME IN THE UK

	Movie	Year	Box office gross (£)
1	*Jurassic Park*	1993	47,100,000
2	*Four Weddings and a Funeral*	1994	27,800,000
3	*Ghost*	1990	23,300,000
4	*The Lion King*	1994	23,100,000
5	*E.T.: The Extra-Terrestrial*	1983	21,700,000
6	*Crocodile Dundee*	1987	21,500,000
7	*Mrs. Doubtfire*	1994	21,200,000
8	*Robin Hood: Prince of Thieves*	1991	20,500,000
9	*The Flintstones*	1994	20,200,000
10	*Batman Forever*	1995	19,300,000

Inevitably, due to inflation, the top-grossing movies are those of the 1980s and 1990s. However, from the low point of the late 1960s and 1970s, today's movies are more widely viewed than those of 15 to 25 years ago, and they gross much more at the box office.

MOVIES OF THE DECADES

T O P 1 0

MOVIES OF THE 1930s

1	*Gone With the Wind**	1939
2	*Snow White and the Seven Dwarfs*	1937
3	*The Wizard of Oz*	1939
4	*King Kong*	1933
5	*San Francisco*	1936
6=	*Mr. Smith Goes to Washington*	1939
6=	*Lost Horizon*	1937
6=	*Hell's Angels*	1930
9	*Maytime*	1937
10	*City Lights*	1931

* *Winner of "Best Picture" Academy Award*

Both *Gone With the Wind* and *Snow White and the Seven Dwarfs* have generated considerably more income than any other pre-war films, appearing respectively within the Top 40 and the Top 60 films of all time. However, if the income of *Gone With the Wind* is adjusted to allow for inflation in the period since its release, it could, with some justification, be regarded as the most successful film ever. *Gone With the Wind* and *The Wizard of Oz* both celebrated their 50th anniversaries in 1989, the extra publicity generated by these events further enhancing their rental income. The Academy Award-winning *Cavalcade* (1932) is a potential contender for a place in this Top 10, but its earnings have been disputed.

T O P 1 0

MOVIES OF THE 1940s

1	*Bambi*	1942
2	*Fantasia*	1940
3	*Cinderella*	1949
4	*Pinocchio*	1940
5	*Song of the South*	1946
6	*Mom and Dad*	1944
7	*Samson and Delilah*	1949
8=	*The Best Years of Our Lives**	1946
8=	*Duel in the Sun*	1946
10	*This is the Army*	1943

* *Winner of "Best Picture" Academy Award*

With the top four films of the decade classic Disney cartoons (and *Song of the South* part animated/part live action), the 1940s may truly be regarded as the "golden age" of the animated film. The genre was especially appealing in this era as colorful escapism during and after the drabness and grim realities of the war years. The songs from two of these films – *When You Wish Upon a Star* from *Pinocchio* and *Zip-A-Dee-Doo-Dah* from *Song of the South* – won "Best Song" Academy Awards. The cumulative income of a selection of the Disney cartoons has increased as a result of their systematic re-release in theaters and as bestselling videos. *Samson and Delilah* heralded the epic films of the 1950s.

T O P 1 0

MOVIES OF THE 1950s

1	*The Ten Commandments*	1956
2	*Lady and the Tramp*	1955
3	*Peter Pan*	1953
4	*Ben Hur**	1959
5	*Around the World in 80 Days**	1956
6	*Sleeping Beauty*	1959
7=	*South Pacific*	1958
7=	*The Robe*	1953
9	*Bridge on the River Kwai**	1957
10	*This is Cinerama*	1952

* *Winner of "Best Picture" Academy Award*

T O P 1 0

MOVIES OF THE 1960s

1	*The Sound of Music**	1965
2	*101 Dalmatians*	1961
3	*The Jungle Book*	1967
4	*Doctor Zhivago*	1965
5	*Butch Cassidy and the Sundance Kid*	1969
6	*Mary Poppins*	1964
7	*The Graduate*	1968
8	*My Fair Lady**	1964
9	*Thunderball*	1965
10	*Funny Girl*	1968

* *Winner of "Best Picture" Academy Award*

During the 1960s the growth in popularity of soundtrack record albums and featured singles often matched the commercial success of the films from which they were derived. Four of the Top 10 films of the decade were avowed musicals, while all – with the possible exception of *Thunderball* – had a high musical content, generating either an album or, at the very least, a hit single or two. *The Sound of Music*, the highest-earning film of the decade, produced the fastest-selling soundtrack album ever, with over half a million copies sold in two weeks.

WIND-FALL!
Vivien Leigh and Clark Gable are shown in a scene from Gone With the Wind. *In cash terms, the film has earned almost 20 times what it cost to make – but adjusting its earnings for inflation over the 57 years since its release would establish it as Hollywood's all-time money earner.*

T O P   1 0

MOVIES OF THE 1970s

1	*Star Wars*	1977
2	*Jaws*	1975
3	*Grease*	1978
4	*The Exorcist*	1973
5	*The Godfather**	1972
6	*Superman*	1978
7	*Close Encounters of the Third Kind*	1977/80
8	*The Sting**	1973
9	*Saturday Night Fever*	1977
10	*National Lampoon's Animal House*	1978

* *Winner of "Best Picture" Academy Award*

T O P   1 0

MOVIES OF THE 1980s

1	*E.T.: The Extra-Terrestrial*	1982
2	*Return of the Jedi*	1983
3	*Batman*	1989
4	*The Empire Strikes Back*	1980
5	*Ghostbusters*	1984
6	*Raiders of the Lost Ark*	1981
7	*Indiana Jones and the Last Crusade*	1989
8	*Indiana Jones and the Temple of Doom*	1984
9	*Beverly Hills Cop*	1984
10	*Back to the Future*	1985

The 1980s was clearly the decade of the adventure film, with George Lucas and Steven Spielberg continuing to assert their control of Hollywood, dominating the Top 10 between them, with Lucas as producer of 2 and 4 and Spielberg director of 1, 6, 7, 8, and 10. Paradoxically, despite their colossal box office success, they consistently failed to match this with an Academy Award for "Best Picture." *E.T.* and *Raiders of the Lost Ark* were both nominated, but neither won.

In the 1970s the arrival of the two prodigies Steven Spielberg and George Lucas set the scene for the high-adventure blockbusters whose domination in films has continued ever since. Lucas directed his first science-fiction film, *THX 1138*, in 1970 and went on to write and direct *Star Wars* (and wrote its two sequels, *The Empire Strikes Back* and *Return of the Jedi*).

Spielberg directed *Jaws* and wrote and directed *Close Encounters* (which derives its success from the original release as well as the 1980 "Special Edition").

GREASE IS THE WORD
John Travolta's success in Saturday Night Fever *gave him star status, guaranteeing the success of* Grease *the following year.*

T O P   1 0

MOVIES OF THE 1990s TO DATE

1	*Jurassic Park*	1993
2	*The Lion King*	1994
3	*Forrest Gump**	1994
4	*Home Alone*	1990
5	*Terminator 2*	1992
6	*Mrs. Doubtfire*	1993
7	*Batman Forever*	1995
8	*Home Alone 2: Lost in New York*	1992
9	*Batman Returns*	1992
10	*Ghost*	1990

* *Winner of "Best Picture" Academy Award*

Midway through the decade, all 10 of these films have amassed rental income from the North American market alone in excess of $90,000,000, a feat achieved by only 11 films in the whole of the 1980s and just three in the 1970s. Two 1995 releases, *Apollo 13* and *Toy Story*, are hard on their heels. The vagaries of basing such a list on box office gross (rather than rental) would result in a Top 10 with a slightly different order, with new entrants *Aladdin* and *Dances with Wolves* entering the list. However it is presented, *Jurassic Park*'s domestic gross of more than $350,000,000 maintains it as a hard act to follow as the decade progresses.

154 MOVIE GENRES

SCIENCE FICTION AND FANTASY MOVIES

1	E.T.: the Extra-Terrestrial	1982
2	Star Wars	1977
3	Return of the Jedi	1983
4	Batman	1989
5	The Empire Strikes Back	1980
6	Ghostbusters	1984
7	Terminator 2	1991
8	Back to the Future	1985
9	Batman Forever	1995
10	Batman Returns	1992

The first six movies are also in the all-time Top 10, and all 10 are among the 20 most successful movies ever, having earned over $100,000,000 each from North American rentals alone. Similarly high earners just outside this Top 10 include *Close Encounters of the Third Kind*; *Gremlins*; *Honey, I Shrunk the Kids*; *Back to the Future, Part II*; *Teenage Mutant Ninja Turtles*; *Superman II*; *Total Recall*; and *Ghostbusters II*.

WAR MOVIES

1	Platoon	1986
2	Good Morning, Vietnam	1987
3	Apocalypse Now	1979
4	Schindler's List	1993
5	M*A*S*H	1970
6	Patton	1970
7	The Deer Hunter	1978
8	Full Metal Jacket	1987
9	Midway	1976
10	The Dirty Dozen	1967

High-earning war movies have been rare in recent years, suggesting that the days of big-budget movies in this genre may be over. However, this list excludes movies with military, rather than war, themes such as *A Few Good Men* (1992), *The Hunt for Red October* (1990), and *An Officer and a Gentleman* (1982), which would have been in the top five; and *Top Gun* (1986), which would top the list, just beating *Rambo: First Blood 2* (1985), a post-Vietnam War action movie, which is also disqualified.

HORROR MOVIES

1	Jurassic Park	1993
2	Jaws	1975
3	The Exorcist	1973
4	Jaws II	1978
5	Interview with the Vampire	1994
6	Bram Stoker's Dracula	1992
7	Aliens	1986
8	Alien	1979
9	Poltergeist	1982
10	King Kong	1976

This list encompasses supernatural and science fiction horror and monsters (including dinosaurs, gorillas, and oversized sharks), but omits science fiction movies that do not have a major horrific component.

COMEDY MOVIES

1	Forrest Gump	1994
2	Home Alone	1990
3	Mrs. Doubtfire	1993
4	Beverly Hills Cop	1984
5	Ghost	1990
6	Home Alone 2: Lost in New York	1992
7	Tootsie	1982
8	Pretty Woman	1990
9	Three Men and a Baby	1987
10	Beverly Hills Cop II	1987

If the two *Beverly Hills Cop* movies are excluded as "action thrillers" rather than comedies, Nos. 9 and 10 would be *National Lampoon's Animal House* (1978) and *Crocodile Dundee* (1986). High earners also include: *Sister Act* (1992), *City Slickers* (1991), and *Nine to Five* (1980).

BIBLICAL MOVIES

1	The Ten Commandments	1956
2	Ben Hur	1959
3	The Robe	1953
4	Jesus Christ Superstar	1973
5	Quo Vadis	1951
6	Samson and Delilah	1949
7	Jesus	1979
8	The Greatest Story Ever Told	1965
9	King of Kings	1961
10	Solomon and Sheba	1959

Biblical subjects have been standard Hollywood fare since the pioneer days but are now less fashionable – Martin Scorsese's controversial *The Last Temptation of Christ* (1988) actually earned less than the silent versions of the epics *Ben Hur* (1926) and *The Ten Commandments* (1923).

TOP 10

MOVIES IN WHICH THE STAR WEARS DRAG

Movie/year	Star
1	Mrs. Doubtfire (1994)	Robin Williams
2	Tootsie (1983)	Dustin Hoffman
3	The Rocky Horror Picture Show (1974)	Tim Curry
4	Under Siege (1992)	Gary Busey
5	The Crying Game (1993)	Jaye Davidson
6	Dressed to Kill (1980)	Michael Caine
7	Psycho (1960)	Anthony Perkins
8	Some Like It Hot (1959)	Tony Curtis/ Jack Lemmon
9	La Cage aux Folles (1979)	Michel Serrault
10	Jo Jo Dancer, Your Life is Calling (1986)	Richard Pryor

TOP 10

WESTERNS

1	Dances with Wolves	1990
2	Maverick	1994
3	Butch Cassidy and the Sundance Kid	1969
4	Unforgiven	1992
5	Jeremiah Johnson	1972
6	How the West Was Won	1962
7	Pale Rider	1985
8	Young Guns	1988
9	Young Guns II	1990
10	Bronco Billy	1980

Clint Eastwood is in the unusual position of directing and starring in a film that has forced another of his own films out of the Top 10, since the success of *Unforgiven* has ejected *The Outlaw Josey Wales* (1976). Although it has a Western setting, Steven Spielberg's *Back to the Future, Part III* (1990) is essentially a science fiction film; if included, it would be in 2nd position.

TOP 10

DISASTER MOVIES

1	Apollo 13	1995	6	Outbreak	1995
2	The Towering Inferno	1975	7	Airport '75	1974
3	Airport	1970	8	Airport '77	1977
4	The Poseidon Adventure	1972	9	The Hindenburg	1975
5	Earthquake	1974	10	Black Sunday	1977

THE BOND DYNASTY
Pierce Brosnan (right) is the sixth, and current, actor to play James Bond on film. Sean Connery in Dr. No. *was the first, followed by David Niven in* Casino Royale. *George Lazenby played Bond only once, in* On Her Majesty's Secret Service. *He was followed by Roger Moore, who played Bond in seven movies before handing over to Timothy Dalton in 1987.*

TOP 10

JAMES BOND MOVIES

Movie/year	Bond actor
1	Goldeneye (1995)	Pierce Brosnan
2	Octopussy (1983)	Roger Moore
3	Moonraker (1979)	Roger Moore
4	Thunderball (1965)	Sean Connery
5	Never Say Never Again (1983)	Sean Connery
6	The Living Daylights (1987)	Timothy Dalton
7	For Your Eyes Only (1981)	Roger Moore
8	A View to a Kill (1985)	Roger Moore
9	The Spy Who Loved Me (1977)	Roger Moore
10	Goldfinger (1964)	Sean Connery

OSCAR WINNERS – MOVIES

GOLDEN IDOL
Standing 34 cm (13½ in) high, gold-plated "Oscar" was reputedly named for his resemblance to a film librarian's Uncle Oscar.

T O P 1 0

MOVIES NOMINATED FOR THE MOST OSCARS

(Oscar® is a registered trade mark of the Academy of Motion Picture Arts and Sciences)

	Movie	Year	Awards	Nominations
1	All About Eve	1950	6	14
2=	Gone with the Wind	1939	8*	13
2=	From Here to Eternity	1953	8	13
2=	Mary Poppins	1964	5	13
2=	Who's Afraid of Virginia Woolf?	1966	5	13
2=	Forrest Gump	1994	6	13
7=	Mrs. Miniver	1942	6	12
7=	The Song of Bernadette	1943	4	12
7=	Johnny Belinda	1948	1	12
7=	A Streetcar Named Desire	1951	4	12
7=	On the Waterfront	1954	8	12
7=	Ben-Hur	1959	11	12
7=	Becket	1964	1	12
7=	My Fair Lady	1964	8	12
7=	Reds	1981	3	12
7=	Dances with Wolves	1990	7	12
7=	Schindler's List	1993	7	12

* *Plus two special awards*

While *Johnny Belinda* and *Becket* at least had the consolation of winning once out of their 12 nominations, both *The Turning Point* (1977) and *The Color Purple* (1985) suffered the ignominy of receiving 11 nominations without a single win.

T O P 1 0

MOVIES TO WIN MOST OSCARS

	Movie	Year	Awards
1	Ben-Hur	1959	11
2	West Side Story	1961	10
3=	Gigi	1958	9
3=	The Last Emperor	1987	9
5=	Gone with the Wind	1939	8
5=	From Here to Eternity	1953	8
5=	On the Waterfront	1954	8
5=	My Fair Lady	1964	8
5=	Cabaret	1972	8
5=	Gandhi	1982	8
5=	Amadeus	1984	8

DID YOU KNOW

THE STORY OF "OSCAR"

The Academy of Motion Picture Arts and Sciences, founded May 4, 1927, proposed improving the image of the film industry by issuing "awards for merit or distinction." The award took the form of a statuette – a gold-plated, naked male figure clutching a sword and standing on a reel of film with five holes, each representing a branch of the Academy. It was simply called "the statuette" until 1931, when Academy librarian Margaret Herrick commented, "It looks like my Uncle Oscar!". The name stuck as a universally recognized symbol of excellence in movie-making.

T O P 1 0

HIGHEST-EARNING "BEST PICTURE" OSCAR WINNERS

1	Forrest Gump	1994
2	Rain Man	1988
3	The Godfather	1972
4	Dances with Wolves	1990
5	The Sound of Music	1965
6	Gone with the Wind	1939
7	The Sting	1973
8	Platoon	1986
9	Kramer vs. Kramer	1979
10	One Flew Over the Cuckoo's Nest	1975

THE 10

"BEST PICTURE" OSCAR WINNERS OF THE 1930s

1930	All Quiet on the Western Front
1931	Cimarron
1932	Grand Hotel
1933	Cavalcade
1934	It Happened One Night*
1935	Mutiny on the Bounty
1936	The Great Ziegfeld
1937	The Life of Emile Zola
1938	You Can't Take it with You
1939	Gone with the Wind

* Winner of Oscars for "Best Director," "Best Actor," "Best Actress," and "Best Screenplay"

The first Academy Awards, now popularly known as Oscars, were presented at a ceremony at the Hollywood Roosevelt Hotel on May 16, 1929 and were for movies released in the period 1927–28. A second ceremony held at the Ambassador Hotel on October 31 of the same year was for movies released in the period 1928–29.

THE 10

"BEST PICTURE" OSCAR WINNERS OF THE 1940s

1940	Rebecca
1941	How Green Was My Valley
1942	Mrs. Miniver
1943	Casablanca
1944	Going My Way
1945	The Lost Weekend
1946	The Best Years of Our Lives
1947	Gentleman's Agreement
1948	Hamlet
1949	All the King's Men

Several of the "Best Picture" winners are now regarded as movie classics, many critics numbering Casablanca among the greatest movies of all time. Mrs. Miniver (which won a total of six Oscars) and The Best Years of Our Lives (seven Oscars) were both directed by William Wyler and reflected the concerns of wartime and post-war life respectively. How Green Was My Valley and Going My Way each won five Oscars. Rebecca and Hamlet both starred Laurence Olivier, who also directed the latter, winning not only the "Best Picture" award but also that for "Best Actor."

THE 10

"BEST PICTURE" OSCAR WINNERS OF THE 1950s

1950	All About Eve
1951	An American in Paris
1952	The Greatest Show on Earth
1953	From Here to Eternity
1954	On the Waterfront
1955	Marty
1956	Around the World in 80 Days
1957	The Bridge on the River Kwai
1958	Gigi
1959	Ben-Hur

The first movie of the 1950s, All About Eve, received the most nominations (14), while the last, Ben-Hur, won the most (11).

THE 10

"BEST PICTURE" OSCAR WINNERS OF THE 1980s

1980	Ordinary People
1981	Chariots of Fire
1982	Gandhi
1983	Terms of Endearment
1984	Amadeus
1985	Out of Africa
1986	Platoon
1987	The Last Emperor
1988	Rain Man
1989	Driving Miss Daisy

The winners of "Best Picture" Oscars during the 1990s are 1990: Dances with Wolves; 1991: The Silence of the Lambs – which also won Oscars for "Best Director," "Best Actor," "Best Actress," and "Best Screenplay;" 1992: Unforgiven; 1993: Schindler's List – which also won six other awards, for "Best Director," "Best Adapted Screenplay," "Best Film Editing," "Best Art Direction," "Best Cinematography," and "Best Original Score;" 1994: Forrest Gump; and 1995: Braveheart.

THE 10

"BEST PICTURE" OSCAR WINNERS OF THE 1960s

1960	The Apartment
1961	West Side Story
1962	Lawrence of Arabia
1963	Tom Jones
1964	My Fair Lady
1965	The Sound of Music
1966	A Man for All Seasons
1967	In the Heat of the Night
1968	Oliver!
1969	Midnight Cowboy

The Apartment (1960) was the last black-and-white film to receive a "Best Picture" Oscar until Steven Spielberg's Schindler's List in 1993, which won seven Oscars.

THE 10

"BEST PICTURE" OSCAR WINNERS OF THE 1970s

1970	Patton
1971	The French Connection
1972	The Godfather
1973	The Sting
1974	The Godfather, Part II
1975	One Flew Over the Cuckoo's Nest*
1976	Rocky
1977	Annie Hall
1978	The Deer Hunter
1979	Kramer vs. Kramer

* Winner of Oscars for "Best Director," "Best Actor," "Best Actress," and "Best Screenplay"

OSCAR WINNERS – STARS & DIRECTORS

TOP 10

"BEST ACTOR" OSCAR WINNERS OF THE 1980s

Year	Actor	Film
1980	Robert De Niro	*Raging Bull*
1981	Henry Fonda	*On Golden Pond* *
1982	Ben Kingsley	*Gandhi* #
1983	Robert Duvall	*Tender Mercies*
1984	F. Murray Abraham	*Amadeus* #
1985	William Hurt	*Kiss of the Spider Woman*
1986	Paul Newman	*The Color of Money*
1987	Michael Douglas	*Wall Street*
1988	Dustin Hoffman	*Rain Man* #
1989	Daniel Day-Lewis	*My Left Foot*

* Winner of "Best Actress" Oscar   #Winner of "Best Picture" Oscar

The 1990s winners are 1990: Jeremy Irons (*Reversal of Fortune*); 1991: Anthony Hopkins (*The Silence of the Lambs*); 1992: Al Pacino (*Scent of a Woman*); 1993 and 1994: Tom Hanks (*Philadelphia* and *Forrest Gump*); and 1995: Nicholas Cage (*Leaving Las Vegas*).

TOP 10

"BEST ACTRESS" OSCAR WINNERS OF THE 1980s

Year	Actress	Film
1980	Sissy Spacek	*Coal Miner's Daughter*
1981	Katharine Hepburn	*On Golden Pond* *
1982	Meryl Streep	*Sophie's Choice*
1983	Shirley MacLaine	*Terms of Endearment* #
1984	Sally Field	*Places in the Heart*
1985	Geraldine Page	*The Trip to Bountiful*
1986	Marlee Matlin	*Children of a Lesser God*
1987	Cher	*Moonstruck*
1988	Jodie Foster	*The Accused*
1989	Jessica Tandy	*Driving Miss Daisy* #

* Winner of "Best Actor" Oscar   #Winner of "Best Picture" Oscar

The 1990s winners are 1990: Kathy Bates (*Misery*); 1991: Jodie Foster (*The Silence of the Lambs*); 1992: Emma Thompson (*Howard's End*); 1993: Holly Hunter (*The Piano*); 1994: Jessica Lange (*Blue Sky*); and 1995: Susan Sarandon (*Dead Man Walking*).

TOP 10

"BEST ACTOR IN A SUPPORTING ROLE" OSCAR WINNERS OF THE 1980s

Year	Actor	Film
1980	Timothy Hutton	*Ordinary People*
1981	John Gielgud	*Arthur*
1982	Louis Gossett, Jr.	*An Officer and a Gentleman*
1983	Jack Nicholson	*Terms of Endearment*
1984	Haing S. Ngor	*The Killing Fields*
1985	Don Ameche	*Cocoon*
1986	Michael Caine	*Hannah and Her Sisters*
1987	Sean Connery	*The Untouchables*
1988	Kevin Kline	*A Fish Called Wanda*
1989	Denzel Washington	*Glory*

DENZEL WASHINGTON
Denzel Washington's Oscar-winning career spans films from Glory, *to* Cry Freedom *to* Much Ado About Nothing.

TOP 10

"BEST ACTRESS IN A SUPPORTING ROLE" OSCAR WINNERS OF THE 1980s

Year	Actress	Film
1980	Mary Steenburgen	*Melvin and Howard*
1981	Maureen Stapleton	*Reds*
1982	Jessica Lange	*Tootsie*
1983	Linda Hunt	*The Year of Living Dangerously*
1984	Peggy Ashcroft	*A Passage to India*
1985	Anjelica Huston	*Prizzi's Honor*
1986	Diane Wiest	*Hannah and Her Sisters*
1987	Olympia Dukakis	*Moonstruck*
1988	Geena Davis	*The Accidental Tourist*
1989	Brenda Fricker	*My Left Foot*

TOP 10

YOUNGEST OSCAR-WINNING ACTORS

	Actor/actress	Award/film (where specified)	Year	Age
1	Shirley Temple	Special Award – outstanding contribution during 1934	1934	6
2	Margaret O'Brien	Special Award (*Meet Me in St. Louis*)	1944	8
3	Vincent Winter	Special Award (*The Little Kidnappers*)	1954	8
4	Jon Whitely	Special Award (*The Little Kidnappers*)	1954	9
5	Ivan Jandl	Special Award (*The Search*)	1948	9
6	Tatum O'Neal	Best Supporting Actress (*Paper Moon*)	1973	10
7	Anna Paquin	Best Supporting Actress (*The Piano*)	1993	11
8	Claude Jarman, Jr.	Special Award (*The Yearling*)	1946	12
9	Bobby Driscoll	Special Award (*The Window*)	1949	13
10	Hayley Mills	Special Award (*Pollyanna*)	1960	13

CHILD STAR
After winning an Oscar at the age of six, Shirley Temple's film career faded during the 1940s. In 1968 she found a new role as a diplomat, first as a UN and later as a US ambassador.

TOP 10

OLDEST OSCAR-WINNING ACTORS

	Actor/actress	Award/film	Award year	Age*
1	Jessica Tandy	Best Actress (*Driving Miss Daisy*)	1989	80
2	George Burns	Best Supporting Actor (*The Sunshine Boys*)	1975	80
3	Melvyn Douglas	Best Supporting Actor (*Being There*)	1979	79
4	John Gielgud	Best Supporting Actor (*Arthur*)	1981	77
5	Don Ameche	Best Supporting Actor (*Cocoon*)	1985	77
6	Peggy Ashcroft	Best Supporting Actress (*A Passage to India*)	1984	77
7	Henry Fonda	Best Actor (*On Golden Pond*)	1981	76
8	Katharine Hepburn	Best Actress (*On Golden Pond*)	1981	74
9	Edmund Gwenn	Best Supporting Actor (*Miracle on 34th Street*)	1947	72
10	Ruth Gordon	Best Supporting Actress (*Rosemary's Baby*)	1968	72

* At time of award ceremony; those of apparently identical age have been ranked according to their precise age in days at the time of the ceremony

Among those senior citizens who received nominations but did not win Oscars is Ralph Richardson, who was nominated as "Best Supporting Actor" for his role in *Greystoke: The Legend of Tarzan* (1984) at the age of 82. Eva Le Gallienne was the same age when she was nominated as "Best Supporting Actress" for her part in *Resurrection* (1980). Outside the four acting categories, the oldest director to be nominated for a "Best Director" Oscar was John Huston, aged 79 at the time of his nomination for *Prizzi's Honor* (1985), and the oldest winner George Cukor for *My Fair Lady* (1964), when he was 65.

TOP 10

"BEST DIRECTOR" OSCAR WINNERS OF THE 1980s

Year	Director	Film
1980	Robert Redford	*Ordinary People* *
1981	Warren Beatty	*Reds*
1982	Richard Attenborough	*Gandhi* *
1983	James L. Brooks	*Terms of Endearment* *
1984	Milos Forman	*Amadeus* *
1985	Sydney Pollack	*Out of Africa* *
1986	Oliver Stone	*Platoon* *
1987	Bernardo Bertolucci	*The Last Emperor* *
1988	Barry Levinson	*Rain Man* *
1989	Oliver Stone	*Born on the Fourth of July*

* *Winner of "Best Picture" Oscar*

The winners for the 1990s are 1990: Kevin Costner (*Dances With Wolves*); 1991: Jonathan Demme (*The Silence of the Lambs*); 1992: Clint Eastwood (*Unforgiven*); 1993: Steven Spielberg (*Schindler's List*); 1994: Robert Zemeckis (*Forrest Gump*); and 1995: Mel Gibson (*Braveheart*).

AND THE WINNER IS . . .

THE 10

LAST GOLDEN GLOBE AWARDS FOR "BEST MOTION PICTURE – DRAMA"

1996	*Sense and Sensibility*
1995	*Forrest Gump*
1994	*Schindler's List*
1993	*Scent of a Woman*
1992	*Bugsy*
1991	*Dances With Wolves*
1990	*Born on the Fourth of July*
1989	*Rain Man*
1988	*The Last Emperor*
1987	*Platoon*

THE 10

LAST GOLDEN GLOBE AWARDS FOR "BEST MOTION PICTURE – MUSICAL OR COMEDY"

1996	*Babe*
1995	*The Lion King*
1994	*Mrs. Doubtfire*
1993	*The Player*
1992	*Beauty and the Beast*
1991	*Green Card*
1990	*Driving Miss Daisy*
1989	*Working Girl*
1988	*Hope and Glory*
1987	*Hannah and Her Sisters*

THE 10

FIRST GOLDEN GLOBE AWARDS FOR "BEST PICTURE"

1943	*The Song of Bernadette*
1944	*Going My Way**
1945	*The Lost Weekend**
1946	*The Best Years of Our Lives**
1947	*Gentleman's Agreement**
1948	*The Treasure of the Sierra Madre* and *Johnny Belinda*#
1949	*All the King's Men**
1950	*Sunset Boulevard*
1951	*A Place in the Sun*
1952	*The Greatest Show on Earth**

* *Also won "Best Picture" Academy Award*
\# *Joint winners*

The Golden Globe Awards are presented annually by the Hollywood Foreign Press Association, a group of US-based journalists. Although the Golden Globe categories differ in some respects from those of the Academy Awards ("Oscars"), they are often seen as a prediction of Oscars to come: in the "Best Picture" category their awards were identical on six out of 10 occasions in the first 10 years.

DID YOU KNOW

GOING FOR GOLD

Although the Cannes Film Festival was established in 1939, the Second World War delayed its inaugural ceremony until 1946, when the French film *La Bataille du Rail* was one of five winners of a "Best Film" award. The first outright winner of the coveted Palme d'Or (Golden Palm) was the British film *The Third Man* (1949). The US has won on 13 occasions with films that include *M*A*S*H* (1970), *Taxi Driver* (1976), and *Apocalypse Now* (1979).

THE 10

FIRST CANNES FESTIVAL BEST FILM AWARDS

Year	Director	Film	Country of origin
1949	Carol Reed	*The Third Man*	UK
1951	Vittoria De Sica and Alf Sjöberg	*Miracle in Milan* *Miss Julie*	Italy Sweden *
1952	Orson Welles and Renato Castellani	*Othello* *Two Cents Worth of Hope*	Morocco Italy
1953	Henri-Georges Clouzot	*Wages of Fear*	France
1954	Teinosuke Kinugasa	*Gates of Hell*	Japan
1955	Delbart Mann	*Marty*	US
1956	Louis Malle and Jacques-Yves Cousteau	*World of Silence*	France
1957	William Wyler	*Friendly Persuasion*	US
1958	Mikhail Kalatozov	*The Cranes are Flying*	USSR

* *Prize shared*

THE 10

LAST CANNES PALME D'OR FOR BEST FILM

Year	Director	Film	Country of origin
1996	Mike Leigh	*Secrets and Lies*	UK
1995	Emir Kusturica	*Underground*	Yugoslavia
1994	Quentin Tarantino	*Pulp Fiction*	US
1993	Chen Kaige and Jane Campion	*Farewell My Concubine* *The Piano*	China Australia
1992	Bille August	*Best Intentions*	Sweden
1991	Joel Coen	*Barton Fink*	US
1990	David Lynch	*Wild at Heart*	US
1989	Steven Soderbergh	*sex, lies, and videotape*	US
1988	Bille August	*Pelle the Conqueror*	Denmark
1987	Maurice Pialat	*Under Satan's Sun*	France

THE 10

LAST GOLDEN GLOBE AWARDS FOR "BEST PERFORMANCE BY AN ACTOR IN A MOTION PICTURE – DRAMA"

Year	Actor	Film
1996	Nicolas Cage	*Leaving Las Vegas*
1995	Tom Hanks	*Forrest Gump*
1994	Tom Hanks	*Philadelphia*
1993	Al Pacino	*Scent of a Woman*
1992	Nick Nolte	*The Prince of Tides*
1991	Jeremy Irons	*Reversal of Fortune*
1990	Tom Cruise	*Born on the Fourth of July*
1989	Dustin Hoffman	*Rain Man*
1988	Michael Douglas	*Wall Street*
1987	Bob Hoskins	*Mona Lisa*

No fewer than seven of the 10 most recent Golden Globe Awards won by leading actors – those in the 1988–89, 1991, and 1993–96 – were subsequently mirrored by the same actors' Oscar wins.

THE 10

LAST GOLDEN GLOBE AWARDS FOR "BEST PERFORMANCE BY AN ACTRESS IN A MOTION PICTURE – DRAMA"

Year	Actress	Film
1996	Sharon Stone	*Casino*
1995	Jessica Lange	*Blue Sky*
1994	Holly Hunter	*The Piano*
1993	Emma Thompson	*Howard's End*
1992	Jodie Foster	*The Silence of the Lambs*
1991	Kathy Bates	*Misery*
1990	Michele Pfeiffer	*The Fabulous Baker Boys*
1989	Jodie Foster and Shirley MacLaine	*The Accused* * *Madame Sousatzka*
1988	Shirley Kirkland	*Anna*
1987	Marlee Matlin	*Children of a Lesser God*

* Prize shared

THE 10

LAST GOLDEN GLOBE AWARDS FOR "BEST PERFORMANCE BY AN ACTOR IN A MOTION PICTURE – MUSICAL OR COMEDY"

Year	Actor	Film
1996	John Travolta	*Get Shorty*
1995	Hugh Grant	*Four Weddings and a Funeral*
1994	Robin Williams	*Mrs. Doubtfire*
1993	Tim Robbins	*The Player*
1992	Robin Williams	*The Fisher King*
1991	Gerard Depardieu	*Green Card*
1990	Morgan Freeman	*Driving Miss Daisy*
1989	Tom Hanks	*Big*
1988	Robin Williams	*Good Morning, Vietnam*
1987	Paul Hogan	*Crocodile Dundee*

THE 10

LAST GOLDEN GLOBE AWARDS FOR "BEST PERFORMANCE BY AN ACTRESS IN A MOTION PICTURE – MUSICAL OR COMEDY"

Year	Actress	Film
1996	Nicole Kidman	*To Die For*
1995	Jamie Lee Curtis	*True Lies*
1994	Angela Bassett	*What's Love Got To Do With It*
1993	Miranda Richardson	*Enchanted April*
1992	Bette Midler	*For the Boys*
1991	Julia Roberts	*Pretty Woman*
1990	Jessica Tandy	*Driving Miss Daisy*
1989	Melanie Griffith	*Working Girl*
1988	Cher	*Moonstruck*
1987	Sissy Spacek	*Crimes of the Heart*

THE 10

FIRST RECIPIENTS OF THE AMERICAN FILM INSTITUTE LIFETIME ACHIEVEMENT AWARD

1973	John Ford
1974	James Cagney
1975	Orson Welles
1976	William Wyler
1977	Henry Fonda
1978	Bette Davis
1979	Alfred Hitchcock
1980	James Stewart
1981	Fred Astaire
1982	Frank Capra

Initiated in 1973, the award is bestowed on individuals whose "talent has fundamentally advanced the art of American film or television...and whose work has withstood the test of time."

THE 10

LAST RECIPIENTS OF THE AMERICAN FILM INSTITUTE LIFETIME ACHIEVEMENT AWARD

1996	Clint Eastwood
1995	Steven Spielberg
1994	Jack Nicholson
1993	Elizabeth Taylor
1992	Sidney Poitier
1991	Kirk Douglas
1990	David Lean
1989	Gregory Peck
1988	Jack Lemmon
1987	Barbara Stanwyck

The Lifetime Achievement winners in the intervening years between the first and last 10 are 1983 John Huston, 1984 Lillian Gish, 1985 Gene Kelly, and 1986 Billy Wilder.

MOVIE STARS – ACTORS

Like the other Movie Top 10s, the Top 10 films of actors and actresses are ranked according to the total rental fees paid to distributors by cinemas in the US and Canada. This is regarded by the industry as a reliable guide to earnings in those markets. As a rule of thumb, doubling these rental figures roughly corresponds to world totals. However, rental income is not the same as "box-office gross." In addition, these lists should not be taken as the "best" movies by the stars concerned, which is impossible to quantify.

TOP 10

TOM CRUISE MOVIES

1	*Rain Man*	1988
2	*Top Gun*	1986
3	*The Firm*	1993
4	*A Few Good Men*	1992
5	*Interview with the Vampire*	1994
6	*Days of Thunder*	1990
7	*Born on the Fourth of July*	1989
8	*Cocktail*	1988
9	*Risky Business*	1983
10	*Far and Away*	1992

TOP 10

SYLVESTER STALLONE MOVIES

1	*Rambo: First Blood 2*	1985
2	*Rocky IV*	1985
3	*Rocky III*	1982
4	*Rocky*	1976
5	*Cliffhanger*	1993
6	*Rocky II*	1979
7	*Tango and Cash*	1989
8	*Cobra*	1986
9	*Demolition Man*	1993
10	*The Specialist*	1994

TOP 10

HARRISON FORD MOVIES

1	*Star Wars*	1977
2	*Return of the Jedi*	1983
3	*The Empire Strikes Back*	1980
4	*Raiders of the Lost Ark*	1981
5	*Indiana Jones and the Last Crusade*	1989
6	*Indiana Jones and the Temple of Doom*	1984
7	*The Fugitive*	1993
8	*American Graffiti*	1973
9	*Clear and Present Danger*	1994
10	*Presumed Innocent*	1990

TOP 10

TOM HANKS MOVIES

1	*Forrest Gump*	1994
2	*Apollo 13*	1995
3	*Sleepless in Seattle*	1993
4	*A League of Their Own*	1992
5	*Big*	1988
6	*Turner & Hooch*	1989
7	*Splash!*	1984
8	*Philadelphia*	1993
9	*Dragnet*	1987
10	*Bachelor Party*	1984

TOP 10

BRUCE WILLIS MOVIES

1	*Die Hard 2*	1990
2	*Die Hard With a Vengeance*	1995
3	*Die Hard*	1988
4	*Pulp Fiction*	1994
5	*Death Becomes Her*	1992
6	*The Last Boy Scout*	1991
7	*Nobody's Fool*	1994
8	*Blind Date*	1987
9	*Striking Distance*	1993
10	*The Bonfire of the Vanities*	1990

TOP 10

SEAN CONNERY MOVIES

1	*Indiana Jones and the Last Crusade*	1989
2	*The Hunt for Red October*	1990
3	*The Untouchables*	1987
4	*Rising Sun*	1993
5	*Thunderball*	1965
6	*Never Say Never Again*	1983
7	*Goldfinger*	1964
8	*Medicine Man*	1992
9	*Time Bandits*	1981
10	*A Bridge Too Far*	1977

TOP 10

ANTHONY HOPKINS MOVIES

1	*The Silence of the Lambs*	1991
2	*Bram Stoker's Dracula*	1992
3	*Legends of the Fall*	1995
4	*A Bridge Too Far*	1977
5	*Magic*	1978
6	*Howard's End*	1992
7	*The Elephant Man*	1980
8	*Shadowlands*	1993
9	*The Remains of the Day*	1993
10	*The Lion in Winter*	1968

TOP 10

WARREN BEATTY MOVIES

1	*Dick Tracy*	1990
2	*Heaven Can Wait*	1978
3	*Bugsy*	1991
4	*Shampoo*	1975
5	*Bonnie and Clyde*	1967
6	*Reds*	1981
7	*Ishtar*	1987
8	*Splendor in the Grass*	1961
9	*McCabe and Mrs. Miller*	1971
10	*The Fortune*	1975

TOP 10

ARNOLD SCHWARZENEGGER MOVIES

1	Terminator 2: Judgment Day	1991
2	True Lies	1994
3	Total Recall	1990
4	Twins	1988
5	Kindergarten Cop	1990
6	Predator	1987
7	Last Action Hero	1993
8	Conan the Barbarian	1981
9	Junior	1984
10	Commando	1985

TOP 10

JACK NICHOLSON MOVIES

1	Batman	1989
2	A Few Good Men	1992
3	One Flew Over the Cuckoo's Nest	1975
4	Terms of Endearment	1983
5	Wolf	1994
6	The Witches of Eastwick	1987
7	The Shining	1980
8	Broadcast News	1987
9	Reds	1981
10	Easy Rider	1969

TOP 10

MEL GIBSON MOVIES

1	Lethal Weapon 3	1992
2	Lethal Weapon 2	1989
3	Maverick	1994
4	Bird on a Wire	1990
5	Braveheart	1995
6	Lethal Weapon	1987
7	Forever Young	1992
8	Tequila Sunrise	1988
9	Mad Max Beyond Thunderdome	1985
10	Air America	1990

TOP 10

MICHAEL DOUGLAS MOVIES

1	Fatal Attraction	1987
2	Basic Instinct	1992
3	The War of the Roses	1989
4	Disclosure	1994
5	The Jewel of the Nile	1985
6	Romancing the Stone	1984
7	The American President	1995
8	The China Syndrome	1979
9	Black Rain	1989
10	Wall Street	1987

TOP 10

GENE HACKMAN MOVIES

1	Superman	1978
2	The Firm	1993
3	Superman II	1980
4	Unforgiven	1992
5	Crimson Tide	1995
6	The Poseidon Adventure	1972
7	Young Frankenstein	1974
8	Get Shorty	1995
9	The French Connection	1971
10	Bonnie and Clyde	1967

FICTITIOUS ACT OF MURDER
After two huge successes in the late 1970s with Saturday Night Fever *and* Grease, *John Travolta's roles were unmemorable until his Oscar-nominated return as the killer Vincent Vega in Quentin Tarantino's* Pulp Fiction.

TOP 10

CLINT EASTWOOD MOVIES

1	Every Which Way but Loose	1978
2	In the Line of Fire	1993
3	Unforgiven	1992
4	Any Which Way You Can	1980
5	The Bridges of Madison County	1995
6	Sudden Impact	1983
7	Firefox	1982
8	The Enforcer	1976
9	Tightrope	1984
10	Heartbreak Ridge	1986

TOP 10

JOHN TRAVOLTA MOVIES

1	Grease	1978
2	Saturday Night Fever	1977
3	Look Who's Talking	1989
4	Pulp Fiction	1994
5	Staying Alive	1983
6	Get Shorty	1995
7	Urban Cowboy	1980
8	Look Who's Talking Too	1990
9	Carrie	1976
10	Two of a Kind	1983

MOVIE STARS – ACTRESSES

TOP 10

MERYL STREEP MOVIES

1	Kramer vs. Kramer*	1979
2	Out of Africa#	1985
3	The Bridges of Madison County	1995
4	Death Becomes Her	1992
5	The Deer Hunter#	1978
6	Silkwood#	1983
7	Manhattan	1979
8	Postcards From the Edge#	1990
9	Sophie's Choice+	1982
10	Julia	1982

Academy Award for "Best Supporting Actress"
 # Academy Award nomination
+ Academy Award for "Best Actress"

It is perhaps surprising that *Sophie's Choice*, the movie for which Meryl Streep won an Oscar, scores so far down this list, while one of her most celebrated movies, *The French Lieutenant's Woman* (1981), does not make her personal Top 10 at all.

TOP 10

DEMI MOORE MOVIES

1	Ghost	1990
2	A Few Good Men	1992
3	Indecent Proposal	1993
4	Disclosure	1995
5	St. Elmo's Fire	1985
6	About Last Night	1986
7	Young Doctors in Love	1982
8	Blame it on Rio	1984
9	Mortal Thoughts	1991
10	The Seventh Sign	1988

TOP 10

MICHELLE PFEIFFER MOVIES

1	Batman Returns	1992
2	Wolf	1994
3	The Witches of Eastwick	1987
4	Scarface	1983
5	Tequila Sunrise	1988
6	Dangerous Liaisons	1988
7	The Age of Innocence	1993
8	Frankie and Johnny	1991
9	The Russia House	1990
10	The Fabulous Baker Boys	1989

TOP 10

SHARON STONE MOVIES

1	Total Recall	1990	6	Sliver	1993
2	Basic Instinct	1992	7	Police Academy 4: Citizens on Patrol	1987
3	Last Action Hero	1993	8	Intersection	1994
4	The Specialist	1995	9	Action Jackson	1988
5	Casino	1995	10	Above The Law	1988

SUPERSTAR SHARON STONE
Sharon Stone's film career began in 1980 with her nonspeaking and brief appearance as "Pretty Girl on a Train," and was boosted by her notorious scene in Basic Instinct.

Sharon Stone's part in *Last Action Hero* amounted to no more than a brief cameo. If discounted, either of two movies that have been similarly successful would occupy 10th place – *Irreconcilable Differences* (1984) or *King Solomon's Mines* (1985).

TOP 10

MELANIE GRIFFITH MOVIES

1	Working Girl	1988
2	Pacific Heights	1990
3	One-on-One	1977
4	Shining Through	1992
5	Nobody's Fool	1994
6	Paradise	1991
7	The Bonfire of the Vanities	1990
8	The Milagro Beanfield War	1988
9	Body Double	1984
10	Something Wild	1986

TOP 10

MEG RYAN MOVIES

1	Top Gun	1986
2	Sleepless in Seattle	1993
3	When Harry Met Sally	1989
4	When a Man Loves a Woman	1994
5	French Kiss	1995
6	Joe Versus the Volcano	1990
7	The Doors	1991
8	Innerspace	1987
9	I.Q.	1994
10	The Presidio	1988

T O P 1 0

EMMA THOMPSON MOVIES

1	Junior	1994
2	Dead Again	1991
3	Howard's End*	1992
4	In the Name of the Father#	1993
5	The Remains of the Day#	1993
6	Henry V	1989
7	Sense and Sensibility	1995
8	Carrington	1995
9	Much Ado About Nothing	1993
10	The Tall Guy	1989

* Academy Award for "Best Actress"
\# Academy Award nomination

T O P 1 0

JODIE FOSTER MOVIES

1	The Silence of the Lambs*	1990
2	Maverick	1994
3	Sommersby	1993
4	Nell#	1994
5	The Accused*	1988
6	Taxi Driver#	1976
7	Freaky Friday	1976
8	Little Man Tate+	1991
9	Home for the Holidays★	1977
10	Alice Doesn't Live Here Any More	1975

* Academy Award for "Best Actress"
\# Academy Award nomination
+ Acted and directed
★ Directed only

T O P 1 0

SIGOURNEY WEAVER MOVIES

1	Ghostbusters	1984
2	Ghostbusters II	1989
3	Aliens	1986
4	Alien	1979
5	Alien³	1992
6	Dave	1993
7	Working Girl	1988
8	Gorillas in the Mist	1988
9	The Deal of the Century	1983
10	The Year of Living Dangerously	1982

T O P 1 0

JULIA ROBERTS MOVIES

1	Pretty Woman*	1990
2	Hook	1991
3	The Pelican Brief	1993
4	Sleeping with the Enemy	1991
5	Steel Magnolias#	1989
6	Flatliners	1990
7	Something to Talk About	1995
8	Dying Young	1991
9	I Love Trouble	1994
10	Mystic Pizza	1988

* Academy Award for "Best Actress"
\# Academy Award nomination

PRETTY WOMAN
Julia Roberts is best known for her role in Pretty Woman, *which made her one of the most highly paid actresses in Hollywood.*

T O P 1 0

SALLY FIELD MOVIES

1	Forrest Gump	1994
2	Mrs. Doubtfire	1993
3	Smokey and the Bandit	1977
4	Steel Magnolias	1989
5	Smokey and the Bandit II	1980
6	Hooper	1978
7	The End	1978
8	Absence of Malice	1981
9	Places in the Heart*	1984
10	Soapdish	1991

* Academy Award for "Best Actress"

Sally Field provided the voice of Sassy in the animal adventure movie *Homeward Bound: The Incredible Journey* (1993). If taken into account, it would replace *Soapdish* in 10th place. Sally Field's movie career spans three decades and was launched after her success in TV series, including the title role in *Gidget*, which she played at the age of 17, and her role as Sister Bertrille in *The Flying Nun*.

T O P 1 0

HOLLY HUNTER MOVIES

1	The Firm	1993
2	Broadcast News	1987
3	Always	1989
4	The Piano	1993
5	Copycat	1995
6	Raising Arizona	1987
7	Home for the Holidays	1995
8	Once Around	1991
9	Swing Shift	1984
10	Miss Firecracker	1989

COMEDY STARS

TOP 10

WHOOPI GOLDBERG MOVIES

1	Ghost	1990
2	Sister Act	1992
3	The Color Purple	1985
4	Star Trek: Generations	1994
5	Sister Act 2: Back in the Habit	1993
6	Made in America	1993
7	Soapdish	1991
8	National Lampoon's Loaded Weapon 1	1993
9	Jumpin' Jack Flash	1986
10	Corrina, Corrina	1994

Whoopi Goldberg also provided the voice of Shenzi in *The Lion King* (1994). If this film was taken into the reckoning, it would appear in the No. 1 position in her Top 10.

DID YOU KNOW

LAUGH LINES

Many comedy movies continue their humor after the acting is over by including jokes in their credits. The lengthy credits at the end of *Hot Shots!* (1991) include various recipes for desserts before finally advising "If you had left this theater when these credits began, you'd be home now." *Naked Gun 33⅓: The Final Insult* (1994) explains that "No animals were harmed during the filming of this motion picture. However, some species did become extinct." It then lists the species and causes of extinction: "the Northern horned barn owl (approx. 15) – Soundstage fire;" "Striped red heinied tapir (last pair) – Grip truck;" and "Woolly fettered tree squirrel (approx. 100) – Crew lunch."

TOP 10

MEL BROOKS MOVIES

1	Blazing Saddles*#	1974
2	Young Frankenstein#	1975
3	The Muppet Movie*	1979
4	Silent Movie*#	1976
5	High Anxiety*#	1977
6	Spaceballs*#	1987
7	Robin Hood: Men in Tights#	1993
8	History of the World – Part I*#	1981
9	To Be or Not to Be*	1983
10	The Twelve Chairs*#	1970

* Appeared in
\# Directed or codirected

Mel Brooks' voice was heard in *Look Who's Talking Too* (1990). If included, it would take 4th place in this list.

TOP 10

BILL MURRAY MOVIES

1	Ghostbusters	1984
2	Tootsie	1982
3	Ghostbusters II	1989
4	Stripes	1981
5	Groundhog Day	1993
6	Scrooged	1988
7	What About Bob?	1991
8	Meatballs	1979
9	Caddyshack	1980
10	Little Shop of Horrors	1986

TOP 10

JIM CARREY MOVIES

1	Batman Forever	1995
2	Dumb & Dumber	1994
3	The Mask	1994
4	Ace Ventura: When Nature Calls	1995
5	Ace Ventura: Pet Detective	1994
6	The Dead Pool	1988
7	Peggy Sue Got Married	1986
8	Pink Cadillac	1989
9	Once Bitten	1985
10	Earth Girls Are Easy	1989

TOP 10

DAN AYKROYD MOVIES

1	Ghostbusters	1984
2	Indiana Jones and the Temple of Doom	1984
3	Ghostbusters II	1989
4	Driving Miss Daisy	1989
5	Casper	1995
6	Trading Places	1983
7	The Blues Brothers	1980
8	Spies Like Us	1985
9	Dragnet	1987
10	My Girl	1991

If his 20-second cameo appearance as Weber in *Indiana Jones and the Temple of Doom* is excluded, Aykroyd's next most successful film is *Sneakers* (1992). If his unbilled part (as Doctor Raymond Stantz) in *Casper* is eliminated, the Spielberg-directed *1941* joins the list – although it is technically regarded as a "flop" because it cost more to make than it earned at the box office. His directorial debut with *Nothing But Trouble* (1991), in which he also played the starring role, was his least commercially successful film.

TOP 10

EDDIE MURPHY MOVIES

1	Beverly Hills Cop	1984		6	The Golden Child	1986
2	Beverly Hills Cop II	1987		7	Boomerang	1992
3	Coming to America	1988		8	Harlem Nights*	1989
4	Trading Places	1983		9	48 Hours	1982
5	Another 48 Hours	1990		10	The Distinguished Gentleman	1992

* Directed

TOP 10

BETTE MIDLER MOVIES

1	*Get Shorty*	1995
2	*Ruthless People*	1986
3	*Down and Out in Beverly Hills*	1986
4	*Beaches*	1988
5	*Outrageous Fortune*	1987
6	*The Rose*	1979
7	*Big Business*	1988
8	*Hocus Pocus*	1993
9	*Hawaii*	1966
10	*Stella*	1990

Bette Midler's role in *Get Shorty*, her most successful movie, is no more than a cameo, and that in *Hawaii*, her first movie part, is as an extra. If excluded, *For the Boys* (1991), which she also produced, and *Scenes from a Mall* (1991) would join the list.

TOP 10

ROBIN WILLIAMS MOVIES

1	*Mrs. Doubtfire*	1993
2	*Hook*	1991
3	*Good Morning, Vietnam*	1987
4	*Dead Poets Society*	1989
5	*Jumanji*	1995
6	*Nine Months*	1995
7	*Popeye*	1980
8	*Awakenings*	1990
9	*To Wong Foo, Thanks for Everything, Julie Newmar*	1995
10	*The Fisher King*	1991

TOP 10

STEVE MARTIN MOVIES

1	*Parenthood*	1989	6	*Planes, Trains, and Automobiles*	1987
2	*The Jerk*	1979	7	*Three Amigos!*	1986
3	*Father of the Bride*	1991	8	*Little Shop of Horrors*	1986
4	*Housesitter*	1992	9	*Dirty Rotten Scoundrels*	1988
5	*Father of the Bride Part II*	1995	10	*Roxanne*	1987

TOP 10

DANNY DEVITO MOVIES

1	*Batman Returns*	1992
2	*One Flew Over the Cuckoo's Nest*	1975
3	*Twins*	1988
4	*Terms of Endearment*	1983
5	*The War of the Roses*	1989
6	*The Jewel of the Nile*	1985
7	*Romancing the Stone*	1984
8	*Get Shorty*	1995
9	*Ruthless People*	1986
10	*Throw Momma from the Train*	1987

Danny DeVito had a relatively minor role in *One Flew Over the Cuckoo's Nest*. If this is discounted, his 10th movie becomes *Hoffa* (1992), which he also directed.

TOP 10

PETER SELLERS MOVIES

1	*The Revenge of the Pink Panther*	1978
2	*The Return of the Pink Panther*	1974
3	*The Pink Panther Strikes Again*	1976
4	*Murder by Death*	1976
5	*Being There*	1979
6	*Casino Royale*	1967
7	*What's New, Pussycat?*	1965
8	*A Shot in the Dark*	1964
9	*The Pink Panther*	1963
10=	*Dr. Strangelove*	1963
10=	*The Fiendish Plot of Dr. Fu Manchu*	1980

TOP 10

WOODY ALLEN MOVIES

1	*Annie Hall**#+	1977
2	*Hannah and Her Sisters**#+	1986
3	*Manhattan**#+	1979
4	*Casino Royale**	1967
5	*Everything You Always Wanted to Know about Sex (But Were Afraid to Ask)**#+	1972
6	*What's New, Pussycat?**#	1965
7	*Sleeper**#+	1973
8	*Crimes and Misdemeanors**#+	1989
9	*Love and Death**#+	1975
10	*Bullets over Broadway*#+	1994

* *Appeared in*
# *Scriptwriter*
+ *Directed*

This list includes movies that Woody Allen has either written, starred in, or directed. If it were restricted only to movies he has directed, *Casino Royale* and *What's New, Pussycat?* would be dropped from the list, and the new 9th and 10th entries would be *Radio Days* (1987) and *Broadway Danny Rose* (1984), both of which he starred in, wrote, and directed. *Annie Hall* prompted the first occasion since 1941 on which one individual was nominated for "Best Picture," "Best Actor," "Best Director," and "Best Screenplay" (the previous nominee was Orson Welles for *Citizen Kane*; he won only for "Best Screenplay," jointly with Herman J. Manciewicz). For *Annie Hall*, Allen won Oscars for "Best Picture" and "Best Screenplay," and Diane Keaton won the award for "Best Actress."

A WILD AND CRAZY GUY
Before Steve Martin shot to fame on the big screen, he was a successful stand-up comedian, appearing in TV shows such as Saturday Night Live.

THE STUDIOS

20TH CENTURY-FOX
MOVIES OF ALL TIME

1	Star Wars	1977
2	Return of the Jedi	1983
3	The Empire Strikes Back	1980
4	Home Alone	1990
5	Mrs. Doubtfire	1993
6	Home Alone 2: Lost in New York	1992
7	True Lies	1994
8	The Sound of Music	1965
9	Die Hard 2	1990
10	9 to 5	1980

In 1912 William Fox, a nickelodeon owner from New York, founded a film production company in California. Fox was a pioneer in the use of sound, particularly through the medium of Fox Movietone newsreels. In 1935 the Fox company was merged with 20th Century Pictures. Now called 20th Century-Fox, it achieved some of its greatest successes in the 1940s, while under the control of Darryl F. Zanuck and Joseph M. Schenck. This was due mainly to a series of musicals starring Betty Grable. The 1950s and 1960s were less lucrative, however, and despite the box-office success of *The Sound of Music* (1965) the studio suffered a series of setbacks, including the failure of the vastly expensive *Cleopatra* (1963). Its return to prosperity began with *The French Connection* (1971) and was consolidated by the success of *Star Wars* (1977) and its sequels. In 1985 20th Century-Fox was acquired by Rupert Murdoch, thereby permitting Fox television stations to show the company's productions. As the end of the 20th century approaches, the studio is known simply as Fox.

WARNER BROS.
MOVIES OF ALL TIME

1	Batman	1989
2	Batman Forever	1995
3	Batman Returns	1992
4	The Fugitive	1993
5	The Exorcist	1973
6	Robin Hood: Prince of Thieves	1991
7	Superman	1978
8	Lethal Weapon 3	1993
9	Gremlins	1984
10	Lethal Weapon 2	1989

Warner Bros.' *The Jazz Singer* (1927) took its place in cinema history as the first successful film with sound. The 1940s were a prosperous decade for the company, when cartoons such as Bugs Bunny became popular. Concentrating on TV production in the 1960s, film again came to the fore in the 1970s. The company merged with Time, Inc. in 1989 to become Time Warner.

BUENA VISTA/WALT DISNEY
MOVIES OF ALL TIME

1	The Lion King	1994
2	Aladdin	1992
3	Toy Story	1995
4	Pretty Woman	1990
5	Three Men and a Baby	1987
6	Who Framed Roger Rabbit?	1988
7	Snow White and the Seven Dwarfs*	1937
8	The Santa Clause	1994
9	Honey, I Shrunk the Kids	1989
10	Pocahontas	1995

* Originally released by RKO

Walt Disney began his business in 1923, but did not distribute his own films until 1953 when Buena Vista was founded. Touchstone Pictures was established in 1966 to produce films for an adult audience.

MGM MOVIES OF ALL TIME

1	Rain Man	1988
2	Gone with the Wind	1939
3	Rocky IV	1985
4	Rocky III	1982
5	Doctor Zhivago	1965
6	Goldeneye	1995
7	The Goodbye Girl	1977
8	War Games	1983
9	Poltergeist	1982
10	Ben Hur	1959

With "more stars than there are in heaven," Metro Goldwyn Mayer enjoyed huge success in the 1930s and 1940s. However, after Louis B. Mayer left in 1951, it suffered mixed fortunes. Taken over by Kirk Kerkorian in 1969, production virtually ceased until 1981, when it merged with United Artists and was relaunched – James Bond films being the principal money-makers.

ORION MOVIES OF ALL TIME

1	Dances with Wolves	1990
2	Platoon	1986
3	The Silence of the Lambs	1991
4	Arthur	1981
5	Back to School	1986
6	10	1979
7	Throw Momma from the Train	1987
8	Robocop	1987
9	Amadeus	1984
10	First Blood	1982

PARAMOUNT MOVIES OF ALL TIME

1	*Forrest Gump*	1994
2	*Raiders of the Lost Ark*	1981
3	*Indiana Jones and the Last Crusade*	1989
4	*Indiana Jones and the Temple of Doom*	1984
5	*Beverly Hills Cop*	1984
6	*Ghost*	1990
7	*Grease*	1978
8	*The Godfather*	1972
9	*Beverly Hills Cop II*	1987
10	*Top Gun*	1986

Founded in 1912, and with a heyday in the 1930s and 1940s, Paramount's success began to fade in the 1950s. Taken over in 1966, it was not until 1972 and *The Godfather* that the studio's fortunes improved.

TRI-STAR MOVIES OF ALL TIME

1	*Terminator 2*	1991
2	*Rambo: First Blood 2*	1985
3	*Look Who's Talking*	1989
4	*Hook*	1991
5	*Sleepless in Seattle*	1993
6	*Total Recall*	1990
7	*Basic Instinct*	1992
8	*Cliffhanger*	1993
9	*Steel Magnolias*	1989
10	*Philadelphia*	1994

UNIVERSAL MOVIES OF ALL TIME

1	*E.T.: The Extra-Terrestrial*	1982
2	*Jurassic Park*	1993
3	*Jaws*	1975
4	*Back to the Future*	1985
5	*Apollo 13*	1995
6	*The Sting*	1973
7	*Back to the Future, Part II*	1989
8	*National Lampoon's Animal House*	1978
9	*The Flintstones*	1994
10	*On Golden Pond*	1981

Founded in 1912, Universal Pictures changed hands in 1936, 1952, and 1962 – when it was developed as a TV production company. It is now owned by Matsushita, a Japanese multinational.

UNITED ARTISTS MOVIES OF ALL TIME

1	*One Flew Over the Cuckoo's Nest*	1975
2	*Rocky*	1976
3	*Rocky II*	1979
4	*Fiddler on the Roof*	1971
5	*Apocalypse Now*	1979
6	*Moonraker*	1979
7	*Thunderball*	1965
8	*Revenge of the Pink Panther*	1978
9	*The Spy Who Loved Me*	1977
10	*Around the World in 80 Days*	1956

United Artists was formed in 1919 by several actors, including Charlie Chaplin and Douglas Fairbanks, together with director D.W. Griffith, to provide an independent means of producing and distributing their films. United Artists never actually owned a studio, but rented facilities. After many vicissitudes, and a successful run in the 1970s with the consistently successful James Bond films, it merged with MGM in 1981.

COLUMBIA MOVIES OF ALL TIME

1	*Ghostbusters*	1984
2	*Tootsie*	1982
3	*Close Encounters of the Third Kind*	1977/80
4	*A Few Good Men*	1992
5	*City Slickers*	1991
6	*Ghostbusters II*	1989
7	*Kramer vs. Kramer*	1979
8	*Stir Crazy*	1980
9	*The Karate Kid Part II*	1986
10	*A League of Their Own*	1992

Harry Cohn and his brother Jack founded Columbia in 1924, building it up to rival the established giants MGM and Paramount. In 1934 Frank Capra's *It Happened One Night*, starring Clark Gable and Claudette Colbert, won Best Picture, Director, Actor, and Actress Oscars. The studio's success was consolidated by stars such as Rita Hayworth, and films ranging from *Lost Horizon* (1937) and *The Jolson Story* (1946) to serials such as *Batman*. The 1950s saw the founding of a TV production company, Star Gem, and such award-winning films as *The Bridge on the River Kwai* (1957), *On the Waterfront* (1954), and *From Here to Eternity* (1953). Classics of the 1960s include *Lawrence of Arabia* (1962) and *A Man for All Seasons* (1966), plus the Columbia-distributed *Easy Rider*. Taken over by Coca-Cola after an uneasy period in the 1970s, the 1980s produced such hits as *Ghostbusters* (1984). Under the control of English producer David Puttnam for two years, Columbia took over Tri-Star Pictures before it was acquired by the Sony Corporation.

RADIO, TV, & VIDEO

20TH CENTURY

Although there had been earlier low-definition experimental broadcasts, BBC television's high-definition public broadcasting service was inaugurated on a daily basis on November 2, 1936. The US followed in 1939 and soon became the prime mover in many of the major trends in television, from talk shows to the growth of TV as a vehicle for promoting music. The lists here represent some of the milestones in the 60 years since television began, from the pioneer days to the present.

MINI TV
TVs began life with small screens encased in large cabinets. Since the invention of microchips, it is possible to buy a TV with a full-color screen small enough to fit in your pocket.

THE 10
FIRST COUNTRIES TO HAVE TELEVISION*

	Country	Year		Country	Year
1	UK	1936	6	Cuba	1950
2	US	1939	7	Mexico	1950
3	Former USSR	1939	8	Argentina	1951
4	France	1948	9	Denmark	1951
5	Brazil	1950	10	Netherlands	1951

* *High-definition, regular public broadcasting service*

THE 10
FIRST PROGRAMS ON BBC TELEVISION

	Time	Date/program
		Monday November 2, 1936
1	3:02pm	Opening ceremony by Postmaster General G.C. Tryon
2	3:15pm	British Movietone News No. 387 (repeated several times during the next few days)
3	3:23pm	*Variety* – Adele Dixon (singer), Buck and Bubbles (comic dancers), and the Television Orchestra
		(3:31pm close; 3:32pm Television Orchestra continues in sound only with music)
4	9:05pm	Film: *Television Comes to London*
5	9:23pm	*Picture Page* (magazine program featuring interviews with transatlantic flyer Jim Mollison, tennis champion Kay Stammers, King's Bargemaster Bossy Phelps, and others; ghost stories from Algernon Blackwood; and various musical interludes)
6	10:11pm	Speech by Lord Selsdon, followed by close
		Tuesday November 3, 1936
7	3:04pm	Exhibits from the Metropolitan and Essex Canine Society's Show – "Animals described by A. Croxton Smith, OBE"
8	3:28pm	*The Golden Hind* – "A model of Drake's ship, made by L.A. Stock, bus driver"
9	3:46pm	*Starlight* with comedians Bebe Daniels and Ben Lyon (followed by repeat of items 7 and 8)
10	9:48pm	*Starlight* with Manuela Del Rio

TV FIRSTS

FAMILY VIEWING
Although the first proposals to transmit images date back to the 1880s, black-and-white broadcasting did not really progress until after World War II. In the US 1,000,000 receivers were operational by 1949, 10,000,000 by 1951, and more than 100,000,000 by 1975.

THE 10

FIRST GUESTS ON *THE TONIGHT SHOW* – STARRING JOHNNY CARSON

1	Groucho Marx	Comic actor
2	Joan Crawford	Actress
3	Rudy Vallee	Singer/actor
4	Tony Bennett	Singer
5	Mel Brooks	Comic
6	Tom Pedi	Actor
7	The Phoenix Singers	Vocal trio
8	Tallulah Bankhead	Actress
9	Shelley Berman	Comedian
10	Artie Shaw	Band leader

Source: Carson Productions

THE 10

ITEMS IN THE FIRST TOP 10 LIST BROADCAST ON *LATE NIGHT WITH DAVID LETTERMAN*

The Top 10 Words That Almost Rhyme With "Peas"

10	Heats		5	Lens
9	Rice		4	Ice
8	Moss		3	Nurse
7	Ties		2	Leaks
6	Needs		1	Meats

The Top 10 of Everything pays tribute to Mr. Letterman's contribution to Top 10s by publishing this, his first-ever list, from September 18, 1985.

THE 10

FIRST MUSIC VIDEOS BROADCAST BY MTV (USA)

	Video	Artist
1	Video Killed the Radio Star	Buggles
2	You Better Run	Pat Benatar
3	She Won't Dance with Me	Rod Stewart
4	You Better You Bet	Who
5	Little Susie's on the Up	PhD
6	We Don't Talk Anymore	Cliff Richard
7	Brass in Pocket	Pretenders
8	Time Heals	Todd Rundgren
9	Take It on the Run	REO Speedwagon
10	Rockin' the Paradise	Styx

This varied line-up inaugurated the world's first 24-hour music video network on August 1, 1981. What makes this list all the more interesting is that it may be the only occasion on which Cliff Richard has ever been featured on MTV (this song remains his only major hit in the US). Six of the 10 are British acts, there are no R & B videos (a policy with which MTV persevered until the explosion of Michael Jackson's *Thriller* project), and a little-known British duo, PhD, who have never secured a US chart record, make an incongruous appearance at number five.

10 US TV FIRSTS

1 The first President to appear on TV

Franklin D. Roosevelt was seen opening the World's Fair, New York, on April 30, 1939.

2 The first king and queen televised in the US

King George VI and Queen Elizabeth were shown visiting the World's Fair on June 10, 1939.

3 The first televised Major League baseball game

The game between the Cincinnati Reds and the Brooklyn Dodgers at Ebbets Field, Brooklyn, New York, was broadcast on August 26, 1939.

4 The first televised professional football game

The Brooklyn Dodgers vs. Philadelphia Eagles game at Ebbets Field was shown on October 22, 1939.

5 The first TV commercial

A 20-second commercial for a Bulova clock was broadcast by WNBT New York on July 1, 1941.

6 The first soap opera on TV

The first regular daytime serial, DuMont TV network's A Woman to Remember, began its run on February 21, 1947.

7 The first broadcast of a current TV show

NBC's Meet the Press was first broadcast on November 6, 1947.

8 The first televised atomic bomb explosion

An "Operation Ranger" detonation at Frenchman Flats, Nevada, on February 1, 1951, was televised by KTLA, Los Angeles.

9 The first networked coast-to-coast color TV show

The Tournament of Roses parade at Pasadena, California, hosted by Don Ameche, was seen in color in 21 cities nationwide on January 1, 1954.

10 The first presidential news conference televised live

President John F. Kennedy was shown in a live broadcast from the auditorium of the State Department Building, Washington, DC, on January 25, 1961. (A filmed conference with President Eisenhower had been shown on January 19, 1955.)

TOP TELEVISION

TOP 10
NIELSEN'S TV AUDIENCES OF ALL TIME IN THE US

	Program	Date	Households viewing total	percent
1	M*A*S*H Special	February 28, 1983	50,150,000	60.2
2	Dallas	November 21, 1980	41,470,000	53.3
3	Roots Part 8	January 30, 1977	36,380,000	51.1
4	Super Bowl XVI	January 24, 1982	40,020,000	49.1
5	Super Bowl XVII	January 30, 1983	40,500,000	48.6
6	XVII Winter Olympics	February 23, 1994	45,690,000	48.5
7	Super Bowl XX	January 26, 1986	41,490,000	48.3
8	Gone With the Wind Pt.1	November 7, 1976	33,960,000	47.7
9	Gone With the Wind Pt.2	November 8, 1976	33,750,000	47.4
10	Super Bowl XII	January 15, 1978	34,410,000	47.2

© Copyright 1994 Nielsen Media Research

As more and more households acquire television sets (there are currently 94,000,000 "TV households" in the US), the most recently screened programs naturally tend to be watched by larger audiences, which distorts the historical picture. By listing the Top 10 according to percentage of households viewing, we get a clearer picture of who watches what.

WHO SHOT J.R.?
Viewers worldwide tuned in to the episode of Dallas that revealed who shot J. R. Ewing, and discovered it was Kristin Shepard.

TOP 10
TV PROGRAMS IN THE US

	Program	Network	Viewers*
1	Home Improvement	ABC	31,500,000
2	Seinfeld	NBC	30,300,000
3	ER	NBC	28,900,000
4	Grace Under Fire	ABC	27,900,000
5	NFL Monday Night Football	ABC	24,500,000
6	Friends	NBC	24,300,000
7	60 Minutes	CBS	23,200,000
8	NYPD Blue	ABC	22,800,000
9	Roseanne	ABC	22,100,000
10	Murder, She Wrote	CBS	21,800,000

* September 19, 1994 to May 21, 1995
Source: Entertainment Weekly

TOP 10
NIELSEN'S DAYTIME SOAP OPERAS IN THE US, 1993–94

	Program	Households viewing total	percent
1	The Young and the Restless	8,084,000	8.6
2	All My Children	6,204,000	6.6
3	General Hospital	5,828,000	6.2
4	The Bold and the Beautiful	5,730,000	6.1
5	As the World Turns	5,452,000	5.8
6=	Days of Our Lives	5,364,000	5.6
6=	One Life to Live	5,264,000	5.6
8	Guiding Light	5,076,000	5.4
9	Another World	3,290,000	3.5
10	Loving	2,538,000	2.7

© Copyright 1994 Nielsen Media Research

TOP 10
MALE PERFORMERS TO WIN THE MOST EMMYS

	Name	Emmys
1	Ed Asner	7
2	Art Carney	6
3=	Alan Alda	5
3=	Peter Falk	5
3=	Don Knotts	5
3=	Laurence Olivier	5
3=	Dick Van Dyke	5
3=	Hal Holbrook	5
3=	Carroll O'Connor	5
10=	Harvey Korman	4
10=	John Larroquette	4

The Emmy Awards, named after Immy, a nickname given to the tube used in TV image transmission, were first given in 1948 when three awards were handed out. Ed Asner won the 1st of his seven Emmys in 1970–71 for his role in *The Mary Tyler Moore Show*. John Larroquette won all four of his for the same role in *Night Court*.

TOP 10
TV SERIES OF THE 1950s

1	*I Love Lucy*
2	*Texaco Star Theater*
3	*Arthur Godfrey's Talent Scouts*
4	*Dragnet*
5	*Fireside Theater*
6	*Texaco Star Theater*
7	*The Red Skelton Show*
8	*The $64,000 Question*
9	*The Buick Circus Hour*
10=	*Philco TV Playhouse*
10=	*The Colgate Comedy Hour*

TOP 10
FEMALE PERFORMERS TO WIN THE MOST EMMYS

	Name	Emmys
1=	Dinah Shore	8
1=	Mary Tyler Moore	8
3=	Candice Bergen	5
3=	Carol Burnett	5
3=	Cloris Leachman	5
3=	Lily Tomlin	5
3=	Tracey Ullman	5
8=	Valerie Harper	4
8=	Michael Learned	4
8=	Tyne Daly	4
8=	Rhea Perlman	4

The majority of these winners received their Emmys for comedic roles, the exceptions being Michael Learned for *The Waltons* and Tyne Daly for *Cagney and Lacey*. The only non-American included is British comedienne Tracey Ullman, who won most of her five for non-network TV shows. Dinah Shore won her first Emmy in 1956, and Mary Tyler Moore gained her 1st of eight awards in 1963–64 for *The Dick Van Dyke Show*, but won most of them for *The Mary Tyler Moore Show* during the 1970s.

TOP 10
TV SERIES OF THE 1960s

1	*The Beverly Hillbillies*
2	*Gunsmoke*
3	*Bonanza*
4	*Wagon Train*
5	*The Dick Van Dyke Show*
6	*Rowan & Martin's Laugh-In*
7=	*Candid Camera*
7=	*The Red Skelton Show*
9	*Bewitched*
10	*Have Gun Will Travel*

TOP 10
TV SERIES OF THE 1980s

1	*The Cosby Show*
2	*Dallas*
3	*Family Ties*
4	*60 Minutes*
5	*The Dukes of Hazzard*
6	*Cheers*
7	*M*A*S*H*
8	*Murder, She Wrote*
9	*Dynasty*
10	*A Different World*

THE 10
LAST EMMY-WINNING DRAMA SERIES

1995	*N.Y.P.D. Blue*
1994	*Picket Fences*
1993	*Picket Fences*
1992	*Northern Exposure*
1991	*L.A. Law*
1990	*L.A. Law*
1989	*L.A. Law*
1988	*thirtysomething*
1987	*L.A. Law*
1986	*Cagney & Lacey*

TOP 10
TV SERIES OF THE 1970s

1	*All in the Family*
2	*Laverne & Shirley*
3	*Happy Days*
4	*Three's Company*
5=	*Marcus Welby, M.D.*
5=	*Sanford and Son*
7	*Chico and the Man*
8	*Mork and Mindy*
9	*The Flip Wilson Show*
10	*The Waltons*

TOP 10
TV SERIES OF THE 1990s

1	*60 Minutes*
2	*Home Improvement*
3	*Cheers*
4	*Roseanne*
5	*Seinfeld*
6	*ER*
7	*Grace Under Fire*
8	*These Friends of Mine*
9	*Murphy Brown*
10	*NFL Monday Night Football*

THE 10
LAST EMMY-WINNING COMEDY SERIES

1995	*Frasier*
1994	*Frasier*
1993	*Seinfeld*
1992	*Murphy Brown*
1991	*Cheers*
1980	*Murphy Brown*
1989	*Cheers*
1988	*The Wonder Years*
1987	*The Golden Girls*
1986	*The Golden Girls*

VIDEO & CABLE

TOP 10

COUNTRIES WITH MOST VCRs

	Country	Percentage of homes	No. video households
1	US	81.4	78,125,000
2	Japan	78.0	32,224,000
3	Germany	58.5	21,221,000
4	Brazil	42.8	20,458,000
5	UK	77.0	16,771,000
6	France	65.3	14,142,000
7	Italy	44.0	9,879,000
8	Canada	70.3	7,810,000
9	Spain	55.1	6,543,000
10	Russia	13.5	6,515,000

The 1980s has rightly been described as the "Video Decade." According to estimates published by *Screen Digest*, the period from 1980 to 1990 saw an increase in the number of video recorders in use worldwide of more than 27 times, from 7,687,000 to 210,159,000. The estimated 1994 total for the UK alone is more than double the entire world total for 1980. Since 1992 more than one-third of all homes throughout the world with TV have also had video.

TOP 10

VIDEO CONSUMERS IN EUROPE*

	Country	Spending per video household ($)		
		Rental	Purchase	Total
1	Norway	118.49	34.83	153.32
2	Ireland	92.10	33.26	125.36
3	UK	52.93	64.46	117.39
4	Denmark	45.31	58.26	103.57
5	France	25.19	75.42	100.61
6	Italy	28.73	67.03	95.76
7	Switzerland	26.75	49.75	76.50
8	Belgium	25.84	48.74	74.58
9	Luxembourg	25.38	41.13	66.51
10	Netherlands	33.72	31.31	65.03

* *Based on figures prepared by* Screen Digest *for 1993*

On a world basis, total spending per capita, rather than per household with video, produces a different picture. The field is led by Japan on $43.66, the US on $42.64, Canada on $40.63, and Australia on $39.55. Collating these figures on a worldwide basis is not undertaken annually, but when they are next published they may indicate the emergence of new trends and national habits in the ratio of spending on video rentals and purchases.

TOP 10

BESTSELLING EXERCISE VIDEOS OF 1995 IN THE US

1	*Abs of Steel*
2	*Abs of Steel 2*
3	*Abs of Steel 3*
4	*Buns of Steel 3*
5	*Buns of Steel*
6	*Buns and Abs of Steel 2000*
7	*Susan Powter/Burn Fat & Get Fit*
8	*Kathie Lee*
9	*Denise Austin/Non Aerobic Work Out*
10	*Buns of Steel Step 20*

TOP 10

BESTSELLING CHILDREN'S VIDEOS OF 1995 IN THE US

1	*Land Before Time II: The Great Valley Adventure*
2	*Land Before Time III: The Time of the Great Giving*
3	*Sing Along Disney: The Lion King*
4	*Dr. Seuss/ How the Grinch Stole Christmas*
5	*Rudolph the Red-Nosed Reindeer*
6	*Barney: Imagination Island*
7	*Winnie the Pooh: And Christmas Too*
8	*Barney's Alphabet Zoo*
9	*Barney Live! In New York City*
10	*Barney: Families Are Special*

TOP 10

BESTSELLING MUSIC VIDEOS OF ALL TIME IN THE US

1	*Hangin' Tough Live*, New Kids on the Block
2	*Hangin' Tough*, New Kids on the Block
3	*Step by Step*, New Kids on the Block
4	*Moonwalker*, Michael Jackson
5	*This Is Garth Brooks*, Garth Brooks
6	*Garth Brooks*, Garth Brooks
7	*In Concert*, Jose Carreras, Placido Domingo, and Luciano Pavarotti
8	*Billy Ray Cyrus*, Billy Ray Cyrus
9	*A Day at Old MacDonald's Farm*, Kid Songs
10	*Video Anthology 1978–1988*, Bruce Springsteen

In a diverse list ranging from children's music to opera, R&B, rock, and country, the three New Kids on the Block titles are still the only music video releases to sell over 1,000,000 units each in the US.

TOP 10

BASIC CABLE CHANNELS IN THE US

	Channel	Subscribers*
1	ESPN	67,100,000
2	CNN	66,600,000
3	TBS	66,500,000
4=	Arts & Entertainment	66,000,000
4=	The Discovery Channel	66,000,000
6	TNN	65,900,000
7	TNT	65,500,000
8=	C-SPAN	64,500,000
8=	USA Network	64,500,000
10	MTV	64,400,000

* *Covering period August–October 1995*
Source: NCTA

TOP 10

PAY CABLE CHANNELS IN THE US

	Channel	Subscribers*
1	Home Box Office	19,200,000
2	Showtime#	13,300,000
3	The Disney Channel	12,600,000
4	Spice	11,000,000
5	Cinemax	7,800,000
6	Encore	6,000,000
7	Independent channels	3,000,000
8	Adam & Eve	2,700,000
9	Starz	1,000,000
10	Playboy TV	500,000

* *As of August 31, 1995*
# *Includes The Movie Channel and Flix*

TOP 10

VIDEO RENTAL CATEGORIES IN THE US

	Genre	Annual rental earnings ($)*
1	Romantic comedy	10,420,000
2	Comedy	9,180,000
3	Animated	8,730,000
4	Drama	7,960,000
5	Action	6,820,000
6	Thriller	6,350,000
7	Family	6,100,000
8	Science fiction	6,030,000
9	Humor	5,830,000
10	Adventure	5,150,000

* *Sales to stores of videos for rental*

TOP 10

CABLE TV COUNTRIES IN THE WORLD

	Country	Cable TV subscribers
1	US	60,495,090
2	Germany	14,600,000
3	Netherlands	5,700,000
4	Belgium	3,610,000
5	Switzerland	2,235,900
6	Sweden	1,850,000
7	France	1,620,000
8	Austria	1,000,000
9	UK	908,018
10	Finland	830,000

Although the US is the world's most cabled country, its services are fragmented between numerous operators, with TCI the foremost company, followed by Time Warner Cable. Europe has come late to cable, but certain countries are experiencing a phenomenal surge of interest, with annual growth rates of up to 200 percent in certain countries. In Europe a smaller number of large companies dominate the market, with Germany's Deutsche Telekom providing service to more homes than any single US operator.

TOP 10

MOST RENTED VIDEOS OF 1995 IN THE UK

	Film	Approx. rentals
1	*Forrest Gump*	5,175,000
2	*Speed*	4,420,000
3	*Pulp Fiction*	4,390,000
4	*The Mask*	4,315,000
5	*True Lies*	4,100,000
6	*Stargate*	4,095,000
7	*The Specialist*	3,485,000
8	*Dumb and Dumber*	2,980,000
9	*Timecop*	2,650,000
10	*Four Weddings and a Funeral*	2,610,000

The UK public's video rental taste during 1995 divided fairly equally between action thrillers, usually involving a major Hollywood hunk (Sylvester Stallone, Jean Claude Van Damme, Arnold Schwarzenegger, Keanu Reeves), and comedies. *Forrest Gump* was by far the most-watched movie, but more amazing was the longevity of *Four Weddings and a Funeral*, which was also No. 3 in the previous year's list, and is now the most rented film of all time in the UK.

TOP 10

BESTSELLING VIDEOS OF 1995 IN THE UK

1	*The Lion King*
2	*Riverdance*
3	*The Fox and the Hound*
4	*The Aristocats*
5	*Four Weddings and a Funeral*
6	*Pinocchio*
7	*Coronation Street – Feature-length Special*
8	*Batman Forever*
9	*The Mask*
10	*Pulp Fiction*

It is usual on both sides of the Atlantic for Walt Disney, whose titles have well-nigh universal appeal, to dominate the annual bestsellers, and 1995 was certainly no exception, with four Disney titles in this Top 10, and three of those in the Top 4. The No. 2 title *Riverdance*, meanwhile, took less than a year to become the biggest-selling music title ever in the UK, somewhat ironically in view of its non-rock 'n' roll, traditional Irish origins.

ON THE RADIO

MOST LISTENED-TO RADIO STATIONS IN THE US

	Station	City	AQH*
1	WRKS	New York	196,300
2	WQHT	New York	144,100
3	WCBS-FM	New York	123,600
4	WHTZ	New York	118,400
5	WSKQ-FM	New York	117,100
6	WLTW	New York	109,300
7	WABC	New York	108,700
8	WINS	New York	107,700
9	WPLJ	New York	92,900
10	WCBS	New York	92,700

* *Average Quarter Hour statistic based on number of listeners age 12 and over, listening between Monday and Sunday 6:00 am to midnight*

Source: Arbitron, Winter 1995

RADIO STATIONS BY AUDIENCE SHARE IN THE US

	Station	City	Format	Share (%)
1	WIVX-FM	Knoxville, TN	Country	27.0
2	WDRM-FM	Huntsville, AL	Country	24.6
3	WUSY	Chattanooga, TN	Country	22.9
4	WRNS-FM	New Bern/ Morehead City, TN	Country	18.3
5	WWDM	Columbia, SC	R&B	17.5
6=	KRMD-FM	Shreveport, LA	Country	15.7
6=	WSSL-FM	Greenville/ Spartanburg, NC	Country	15.7
8	WIKS	New Bern/ Morehead City, TN	R&B	15.6
9	KSSN	Little Rock, AR	Country	15.3
10	WSIX-FM	Nashville, TN	Country	14.7

LAST GEORGE FOSTER PEABODY AWARDS FOR BROADCASTING WON BY NATIONAL PUBLIC RADIO*

1994	*Tobacco Stories* and *Wade in the Water: African American Sacred Music Traditions* (NPR/Smithsonian Institution)
1993	*Health Reform Coverage 1993*
1992	*Prisoners in Bosnia*
1991	*The Coverage of the Judge Clarence Thomas Confirmation*
1990	*Manicu's Story: The War in Mozambique*
1989	*Scott Simon's Radio Essays on Weekend Edition Saturday*
1988	*Cowboys on Everest*
1983	*The Sunday Show* and *Taylor Made Piano: A Jazz History*
1981	*Jazz Alive*
1979	*Dialogues on a Tightrope: An Italian Mosaic*

* *Includes only programs made or coproduced by NPR.*

In 1938, the National Association of Broadcasters formed a committee to establish a "Pulitzer Prize" for radio. These were inaugurated the following year under the sponsorship of the Henry W. Grady School of Journalism at the University of Georgia, and named in honor of George Foster Peabody, a native Georgian and noted philanthropist. The first awards, for radio programs broadcast in 1940, were presented at a banquet at the Commodore Hotel in New York on March 31, 1941. The ceremony was broadcast live nationwide on CBS and included addresses by CBS founder and chairman William S. Paley, and noted reporter Elmer David, the recipient of the first personal Peabody Award. The Awards are now regarded as the most prestigious in US broadcasting.

RADIO-OWNING COUNTRIES

	Country	Radio sets per 1,000 population
1	US	2,118
2	Guam	1,403
3	Australia	1,273
4	Bermuda	1,260
5	Gibraltar	1,173
6	Netherlands Antilles	1,165
7	UK	1,146
8	Monaco	1,126
9	Denmark	1,033
10	Canada	1,030

The prevalence of radios in island communities is understandable as a method of maintaining contact with the outside world. American Samoa (1,007) and Norfolk Island (1,000) – have ratios equivalent to at least one per inhabitant. South Korea (1,002 radios per 1,000) is the only other country with a ratio greater than one radio per person. Its closest rival is Finland with 997 per 1,000.

TOP 10
LONGEST-RUNNING PROGRAMS ON NATIONAL PUBLIC RADIO

1	*All Things Considered*
2	*National Press Club*
3	*BBC News & Science Magazines*
4	*Weekend All Things Considered*
5	*Marian McPartland's Piano Jazz*
6	*Morning Edition*
7	*Horizons*
8	*NPR Playhouse*
9	*NPR World of Opera*
10	*St. Louis Symphony*

All Things Considered, the longest-running NPR program, was first broadcast on May 3, 1971. Nos. 2 to 7 date from the 1970s, and Nos. 8 to 10 from the early 1980s.

TOP 10
RADIO FORMATS IN THE US

	Format	Share (%)*
1	News/Talk	16.0
2	Adult Contemporary	15.2
3	Country	12.6
4	Top 40	9.1
5=	Urban	8.9
5=	Album Rock	8.9
7	Oldies	7.7
8	Spanish	5.0
9	Classic Rock	3.2
10	Adult Standards	3.0

* *Of all radio listening during an average week, 6 am to midnight, Oct-Dec 1994, for listeners age 12 and over*

News/Talk tops the survey for the first time since spring of 1989.

TOP 10
STATES WITH THE MOST NATIONAL PUBLIC RADIO MEMBER STATIONS

	State	No. of stations
1	New York	33
2	California	23
3	Wisconsin	22
4=	Michigan	20
4=	Ohio	20
6	Minnesota	17
7=	Alaska	15
7=	Illinois	15
7=	Texas	15
10=	Colorado	14
10=	Florida	14
10=	Georgia	14
10=	Oregon	14

Two cities in New York, Buffalo and Watertown, each have three NPR stations. Pennsylvania and New Jersey, two of the most populous states, fail to appear in this Top 10, while Alaska, with a population of fewer than 500,000, is included.

TOP 10
LONGEST-RUNNING PROGRAMS ON BBC RADIO

	Program	First broadcast
1	*The Week's Good Cause*	January 24, 1926
2	*Choral Evensong*	October 7, 1926
3	*Daily Service*	January 2, 1928*
4	*The Week in Westminster*	November 6, 1929
5	*Sunday Half Hour*	July 14, 1940
6	*Desert Island Discs*	January 29, 1942
7	*Saturday Night Theatre*	April 3, 1943
8	*Composer of the Week* (originally *This Week's Composer*)	August 2, 1943
9	*Letter From America* (originally *American Letter*)	March 24, 1946
10	*From Our Own Correspondent*	October 4, 1946

* *Experimental broadcast; national transmission began December 1929*

In November 1922 several radio stations in Britain merged to provide a nationwide service as the BBC (British Broadcasting Corporation). Four of the station's programs that were launched in the 1920s are still running. The oldest is a weekly charity appeal, No. 2 and No. 3 religious broadcasts, and No. 4 a report on the work of Parliament. *Sunday Half Hour* is a program devoted to hymns, while *Desert Island Discs* invites a celebrity to imagine he or she has become a "castaway" on a desert island, and plays the eight records they would most like to take with them. The consistently popular *Letter From America* has been presented since its inception by British-born US broadcaster Alistair Cooke, and takes the form of a commentary on an American topic of the day that Cook considers of interest to his British audience. A further six programs that started in the 1940s are still running: *Woman's Hour* (first broadcast October 7, 1946), *Down Your Way* (December 29, 1946), *Round Britain Quiz* (November 2, 1947), *Any Questions?* (October 12, 1948); *Book at Bedtime* (August 6, 1949), and *Morning Story* (October 17, 1949).

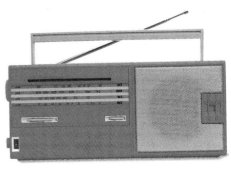

178

THE COMMERCIAL WORLD

20TH CENTURY

*Although the 20th century has seen
some of the worst periods of
unemployment, it has also witnessed
the greatest rise of all time in
numbers among the world's
"economically active populations,"
alongside radical changes in the
structure of the labor force and the
appearance of professions that
barely existed as the century began.
At the same time, manufacturing
industries have been revolutionized,
and intensive agricultural methods,
especially in the Western world, have
led to farms requiring only a fraction
of the labor force of the past.*

TOP 10
MOST COMMON TYPES OF JOB IN THE US

	Job sector	Employees
1	Retail trade	20,437,500
2	Durable goods manufacturing	10,481,300
3	Education (public and private)	10,186,700
4	Health services	10,081,800
5	Government	9,671,300
6	Nondurable goods manufacturing	7,872,500
7	Business services	6,239,100
8	Wholesale trade	6,139,900
9	Construction	5,009,800
10	Transportation	3,774,900

TOP 10
MOST COMMON TYPES OF JOB IN THE UK

	Job sector	Employees
1	Manufacturing	3,942,000
2	Retail trade, incl. auto	3,651,000
3	Real estate and business activities	2,660,000
4	Health and social work	2,503,000
5	Other business activities	1,993,000
6	Education	1,848,000
7	Public administration and defense	1,342,000
8	Transportation and communication	1,294,000
9	Hotels and catering	1,285,000
10	Financial services	944,000

TOP 10
COUNTRIES TAKING THE LONGEST VACATIONS

	Country	Days per annum		Country	Days per annum
1=	Austria	30	8=	Spain	22
1=	Belgium	30	8=	UK	22
3=	Finland	25	10=	Australia	20
3=	France	25	10=	Belgium	20
3=	Norway	25	10=	Netherlands	20
3=	Sweden	25	10=	Switzerland	20
7	Germany	24			

THE WORLD OF WORK

TOP 10

MOST COMMON TYPES OF RETAIL BUSINESS IN THE US

	Type of business	No. of establishments
1	Eating and drinking places	409,836
2	Auto dealers and service stations	178,700
3	Food stores	168,272
4	Apparel and accessory stores	121,283
5	Furniture and home furnishings stores	106,441
6	Building materials and garden supplies stores	66,918
7	Drug stores	41,654
8	General merchandise stores	37,762
9	Jewelry stores	23,503
10	Sporting goods and bicycle stores	22,458
	Total	*1,397,230*

Ranked by total sales, the auto dealers would head this list, with sales in excess of $600 billion, followed by food stores with sales exceeding $400 billion.

TOP 10

MOST COMMON TYPES OF SHOP IN THE UK

	Type of shop	Outlets
1	General (mainly food, drink, and tobacco)	32,169
2	Clothing	29,893
3	Books, newspapers, and stationery	22,870
4	Tobacco products	14,718
5	Alcohol and other drinks	14,085
6	Meat and meat products	13,172
7	Furniture, lighting, and household goods	12,870
8	Electrical goods	10,801
9	Footwear and leather goods	10,517
10	Pharmacies	10,244

TOP 10

COUNTRIES WITH MOST WORKERS

	Country	Economically active population		Country	Economically active population
1	China	584,569,000	6	Japan	65,780,000
2	India	314,904,000	7	Brazil	64,468,000
3	US	128,548,000	8	Bangladesh	50,744,000
4	Indonesia	75,508,000	9	Germany	39,405,000
5	Russia	72,878,000	10	Pakistan	33,829,000

TOP 10

COUNTRIES WITH THE LOWEST PROPORTION OF FARMERS

	Country	Percent in agriculture
1	Singapore	0.8
2	Hong Kong	1.0
3	Bahrain	1.4
4	Belgium/Luxembourg	1.5
5	UK	1.8
6=	United Arab Emirates	2.0
6=	US	2.0
8	Puerto Rico	2.8
9	Netherlands	3.1
10	Sweden	3.3

TOP 10

COUNTRIES WITH THE HIGHEST PROPORTION OF FARMERS

	Country	Percent in agriculture
1	Nepal	91.2
2=	Burundi	90.6
2=	Rwanda	90.6
4	Bhutan	90.0
5	Niger	85.4
6	Burkina Faso	83.4
7	Mozambique	80.4
8	Gambia	79.6
9=	Mali	78.6
9=	Tanzania	78.6

TOP 10

PROFESSIONS THAT WALK THE FARTHEST

	Profession	Average walked per year km	miles
1	Policeman/woman	2,626	1,632
2	Mailman/woman	1,699	1,056
3	TV reporter	1,622	1,008
4	Nurse	1,516	942
5	Doctor	1,352	840
6	Retail clerk	1,294	804
7	Secretary	1,275	792
8	Actor	1,249	776
9	Public relations executive	1,072	666
10	Real estate agent	1,001	622

This Top 10 is based on a survey conducted in the US by healthy-footwear manufacturer Dr. Scholl's and the American Podiatry Association.

PATENTS & INVENTIONS

FIRST WOMEN PATENTEES IN THE US

	Patentee/patent	Date
1	Mary Kies, Straw weaving with silk or thread	May 5, 1809
2	Mary Brush, Corset	Jul 21, 1815
3	Sophia Usher, Carbonated liquid	Sep 11, 1819
4	Julia Planton, Foot stove	Nov 4, 1822
5	Lucy Burnap, Weaving grass hats	Feb 16, 1823
6	Diana H. Tuttle, Accelerating spinning-wheel heads	May 17, 1824
7	Catharine Elliot, Manufacturing moccasins	Jan 26, 1825
8	Phoebe Collier, Sawing wheel-fellies (rims)	May 20, 1826
9	Elizabeth H. Buckley, Sheet-iron shovel	Feb 28, 1828
10	Henrietta Cooper, Whitening leghorn straw	Nov 12, 1828

10 TRADE NAMES THAT HAVE ENTERED THE LANGUAGE

1 Biro

Hungarian sculptor, painter, hypnotist, and journalist, László J. and his brother Georg Biró, a chemist, developed the idea of the ballpoint pen in the 1930s and 1940s from their base in Argentina. The French BiC company (itself derived from its founder, Marcel Bich) presently owns the rights to the trade name "Biro."

2 Escalator

The moving staircases developed in the 1890s and patented in 1900 were made in the US for the Manhattan Elevated Railway by the Otis Elevator Company and originally bore the name "Escalator" (from "escalading elevator"), a word that rapidly entered everyday usage.

3 Zipper

On August 29, 1893 Chicago inventor Whitcomb L. Judson was granted a patent for what was the prototype of the zipper, which was launched as a "Clasp Locker or Unlocker for shoes." A number of improvements followed, especially those of a young Swedish born employee of Judson's called Gideon Sundback, who in 1914 produced his "Hookless No. 2." They were not called zippers until 1923, when the B.F. Goodrich Co. made "Zipper Boots" – rubber galoshes with "Hookless" fasteners. "Zipper" and "Zip" both entered the public domain during the 1920s as clothes with zippers became common on both sides of the Atlantic.

4 Jacuzzi

The "whirlpool bath" is named after Candido Jacuzzi (1903–86), an Italian immigrant to the US and manufacturer of hydraulic pumps. His son was crippled with rheumatoid arthritis, so he hit on the idea of using one of the firm's jet pumps for hydromassage. Developed in the 1950s, the revolutionary bath that became known as the "Jacuzzi" began the cult of the hot tub and was the basis of a multimillion dollar empire.

5 Linoleum

Linoleum was patented in the UK in 1863 by Frederick Walton, and the Linoleum Manufacturing Company was formed the following year. The word soon became so widely used that in 1878 it had to be removed from the Trade Marks Register.

6 Plasticine

The modeling clay invented by William Harbutt (1844–1922) was originally manufactured on a small scale in 1897 for art students, then for children, with commercial manufacturing beginning in 1900 in a converted flour mill in Bathampton, UK.

7 Pullman carriages

In 1864 American inventor George Mortimer Pullman (1831–97) built the first railroad sleeping car. The carriages first came into use in the UK in 1874 and continued to be manufactured by Pullman's British company, but the name became synonymous with any train that had sleeping accommodations.

8 Kleenex

Kleenex tissues were first marketed in the US in 1924 by Kimberly-Clark, a newsprint company established in 1872 by John A. Kimberly and Charles B. Clark. The name, which remains a brand name of the firm, comes from an adapted spelling of "clean" with the suffix "ex", names starting with K and ending with x, from Kodak to Cutex, being considered especially memorable.

9 Velcro

The fastening fabric strip Velcro derives its name from the French words Velours, velvet, and croché, hooked. Invented by Georges de Mestral in Switzerland in 1957, both the product and the word are widely used, but it remains a brand name of the Selectus company.

10 Xerox

The name comes from the Greek xeros, dry, as the Xerox copying process patented by American inventor Chester Carlson (1906–68) does not involve liquid developer. In 1952 it was registered as a trademark by the Rochester, New York, Haloid Company, which later became the Xerox Corporation.

WHEELS OF FORTUNE
The bizarrely named Starley Psycho Safety Bicycle was built in Coventry, UK, in about 1887. The growth in cycling's popularity in the late 1800s mean that "Velocipedes" were among the commonest patent categories of 1900.

DID YOU KNOW

PROLIFIC PATENTEES

Many inventors make their names (and sometimes their fortunes) from a single invention, but there are those whose catalog of patents runs into the hundreds. The most prolific of all time was American inventor Thomas Alva Edison (1847–1931), the pioneer of recorded sound, to whom 1,093 patents were registered. Edwin Herbert Land, best known for his Polaroid camera, patented 533 inventions, while contemporary polymath Jerome H. Lemelson's 500-plus patents range from the Velcro dartboard to the tape drive used in the Sony Walkman. In addition, there are organizations that regularly file large numbers of patents, among them the US Government and IBM, the latter registering a record 1,298 in 1994.

TOP 10

COUNTRIES THAT REGISTER THE MOST TRADEMARKS

	Country	Trademarks
1	Japan	147,191
2	France	78,774
3	US	63,903
4	Spain	63,669
5	China	58,301
6	Argentina	50,287
7	Germany	45,207
8	Mexico	33,717
9	Colombia	29,591
10	UK	28,828

This list includes all trademarks (product names that are thereby legally protected) and service marks (which apply to the names of services rather than products and companies) that were actually registered in 1994. As with patents, more applications are filed than are granted, since many are rejected, for example through being too similar to a trademark or service mark that is already in existence.

THE 10

FIRST PATENTS IN THE UK

	Patentee	Patent	Date
1	Nicholas Hillyard	Engraving and printing the king's head on documents	May 5, 1617
2	John Gason	Locks, mills, and other river and canal improvements	Jul 1, 1617
3	John Miller John Jasper	Oil for suits of armor	Nov 3, 1617
4	Robert Crumpe	Tunnels and pumps	Jan 9, 1618
5	Aaron Rathburne Roger Burges	Making maps of English cities	Mar 11, 1618
6	John Gilbert	River dredger	Jul 16, 1618
7	Clement Dawbeney	Water-powered engine for making nails	Dec 11, 1618
8	Thomas Murray	Sword blades	Jan 11, 1619
9	Thomas Wildgoose David Ramsey	Ploughs, pumps, and ship engines	Jan 17, 1619
10	Abram Baker	Smalt (glass) manufacture	Feb 16, 1619

The world's first patent was granted to the architect Filippo Brunelleschi in Florence in 1421 to make a barge crane to transport marble. John of Utynam was granted the first patent in England in 1449 to make glass for the windows of Eton College. Patents were sometimes granted during the 16th century, such as that issued in 1596 by Queen Elizabeth I to Sir John Harington for a water closet, but the system was not codified until 1617.

THE 10

FIRST TRADEMARKS ISSUED IN THE US*

	Issued to	Invention or discovery
1	Averill Chemical-Paint Company	Liquid paint
2	J.B. Baldy & Co.	Mustard
3	Ellis Branson	Retail coal
4	Tracy Coit	Fish
5	William Lanfair Ellis & Co.	Oyster packing
6	Evans, Clow, Dalzell & Co.	Wrought-iron pipe
7	W.E. Garrett & Sons	Snuff
8	William G. Hamilton	Car wheel
9	John K. Hogg	Soap
10	Abraham P. Olzendam	Woolen hose

* All were registered on the same day, October 25, 1870

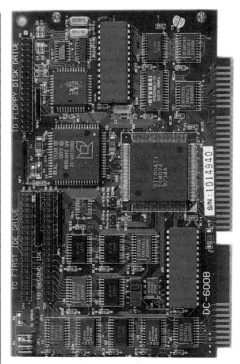

COMPUTER COMPONENTS
Microchips are protected by patent in the competitive computer industry.

TOYS & GAMES

T O P 1 0

MOST EXPENSIVE TOYS EVER SOLD AT AUCTION IN THE UK

	Toy/sale	Price ($)
1	Kämmer and Reinhardt doll, Sotheby's, London, February 8, 1994	292,175
2	*Titania's Palace*, a dollhouse with 2,000 items of furniture, Christie's, London, January 10, 1978	264,600
3	"Teddy Girl," a 1904 Steiff teddy bear, Christie's, London, December 5, 1994	170,500
4	Hornby 00-gauge train set (the largest ever sold at auction), Christie's, London, November 27, 1992	158,752
5	Kämmer and Reinhardt bisque character doll, *c.* 1909, Sotheby's, London, February 16, 1989	139,810
6	William and Mary wooden doll, *c.* 1690, Sotheby's, London, March 24, 1987	109,880
7	Russian carousel (tinplate Ferris wheel), *c.* 1904, Sotheby's, London, February 10, 1993	93,750
8=	Tinplate carousel by Märklin, *c.* 1910, Sotheby's, London, January 23, 1992	93,654
8=	Set of Märklin horse-drawn fire appliances, *c.* 1902, Sotheby's, London, January 23, 1992	93,654
10	Dual-plush Steiff teddy bear, *c.* 1920, Sotheby's, London, September 19, 1989	85,250

T O P 1 0

HAMLEYS' BESTSELLING TOYS AND GAMES IN 1995

1 Barbie (especially Butterfly Princess and Holiday Barbie)

2 Lego (especially Aquazone range)

3 Power Rangers figures

4 Sky Dancers (flying fairies)

5 In-line roller skates

6 Pogs and Pogmakers

7 Sega Lock-on (computer game)

8 Word Spin Scrabble (hand-held word game)

9 Bub-a-loo Bird (marionette)

10 Action Man

FROM PLAYROOM TO SALEROOM
Along with rare toys and teddy bears, fine examples of the doll-maker's craft often attain high prices at auction.

BATTLE OF THE GIANTS
The "Game Boy", produced by Japanese giant Nintendo, became the most popular hand-held games console of the 1990s. Its popularity can perhaps be explained by the variety of games available for this pocket sized machine.

T O P 1 0

MOST EXPENSIVE TOYS SOLD AT AUCTION BY CHRISTIE'S EAST, NEW YORK

	Toy/sale	Price ($)*
1	"The Charles," a fire hose reel made by American manufacturer George Brown & Co, *c.*1875, December 1991	231,000
2	Märklin fire station, December 1991	79,200
3	Horse-drawn, double-decker trolley, December 1991	71,500
4	Mikado mechanical bank, December 1993	63,000
5	Märklin Ferris wheel, June 1994	55,200
6	Girl skipping rope mechanical bank, June 1994	48,300
7	Märklin battleship, June 1994	33,350
8	Märklin battleship, June 1994	32,200
9=	Bing keywind open phaeton tinplate automobile, December 1991	24,200
9=	Märklin fire pumper, December 1991	24,200

* Including 10 percent buyer's premium

TOP 10

HIGHEST-SCORING WORDS IN SCRABBLE

Word/play		Score
1 Quartzy		(i) 164
		(ii) 162

(i) Play across a triple-word-score (red) square with the Z on a double-letter-score (light-blue) square.

(ii) Play across two double-word-score (pink) squares with Q and Y on pink squares.

2= Bezique		(i) 161
4=		(ii) 158

(i) Play across a red square with either the Z or the Q on a light blue square.

(ii) Play across two pink squares with the B and second E on two pink squares.

2= Cazique		(i) 161
4=		(ii) 158

(i) Play across a red square with either the Z or the Q on a light blue square.

(ii) Play across two pink squares with the C and E on two pink squares.

4= Zinkify		158

Play across a red square with the Z on a light-blue square.

5= Quetzal		155

Play across a red square with either the Q or the Z on a light-blue square.

5= Jazzily		155

Using a blank as one of the Zs, play across a red square with the non-blank Z on a light-blue square.

5= Quizzed		155

Using a blank as one of the Zs, play across a red square with the non-blank Z or the Q on a light-blue square.

8= Zephyrs		152

Play across a red square with the Z on a light-blue square.

8= Zincify		152

Play across a red square with the Z on a light-blue square.

8= Zythums		152

Play across a red square with the Z on a light-blue square.

All these Top 10 words contain seven letters and therefore earn the premium of 50 for using all the letters in the rack.

TOP 10

MOST LANDED-ON SQUARES IN MONOPOLY®*

US game		UK game
Illinois Avenue	**1**	Trafalgar Square
Go	**2**	Go
B. & O. Railroad	**3**	Fenchurch Street Station
Free Parking	**4**	Free Parking
Tennessee Avenue	**5**	Marlborough Street
New York Avenue	**6**	Vine Street
Reading Railroad	**7**	King's Cross Station
St. James Place	**8**	Bow Street
Water Works	**9**	Water Works
Pennsylvania Railroad	**10**	Marylebone Station

Monopoly® is a registered trade mark of Parker Brothers division of Tonka Corporation, USA, under licence to Waddington Games Ltd. in the UK

* *Based on a computer analysis of the probability of landing on each square*

TOP 10

MOST POPULAR COSTUME STYLES IN THE UK

Women		Men
Georgian	**1**	Cowboys
1920s	**2**	Cavaliers
Victorian	**3**	Rhett Butler (from *Gone with the Wind*)
Elizabethan	**4**	Georgian
Edwardian	**5**	Medieval
Showgirls	**6**	Roman soldiers
Western	**7**	1940s military/ naval whites
1930s	**8**	Eastern/Indian
Far Eastern	**9**	Futuristic
1940s	**10**	Henley Regatta (striped blazer and boater)

* *Based on loans by The Fancy Dress Emporium, a leading London costume-rental company*

Monopoly was patented in February 1936. It had been devised in Philadelphia during the Depression by Charles Darrow, an unemployed heating engineer. Darrow's streets were derived from those of the New Jersey resort, Atlantic City. There were already several real estate board games around, such as The Landlord's Game, patented in 1904, which, like Monopoly, had a "Go to Jail" square, and Finance, which featured "Chance" and "Community Chest" cards. However, none of the earlier prototypes was commercially successful, and Darrow's version, with its subtle balance of skill and luck, was the first property game that was fun to play. His sales in 1934 rocketed to 20,000, and he entered into a licensing arrangement with Parker Brothers. Darrow rapidly became a millionaire.

TOP 10

BESTSELLING CD-ROM TITLES IN THE US, 1995

	Title	Manufacturer
1	*Microsoft Windows 95*	Microsoft
2	*Myst*	Broderbund
3	*Dark Forces*	LucasArts
4	*Doom II*	ID
5	*Print Shop Deluxe*	Broderbund
6	*Encarta*	Microsoft
7	*Microsoft Plus!*	Microsoft
8	*Quicken Deluxe*	Intuit
9	*Ultimate Doom*	ID
10	*NASCAR Racing*	Sierra

COMMUNICATION

THE 10

FIRST COUNTRIES & CITIES TO ISSUE POSTAGE STAMPS

	Country/city	Stamps issued
1	UK	May 1840
2	New York City	Feb 1842
3	Zurich, Switzerland	Mar 1843
4	Brazil	Aug 1843
5	Geneva, Switzerland	Oct 1843
6	Basle, Switzerland	Jul 1845
7	US	Jul 1847
8	Mauritius	Sep 1847
9	France	Jan 1849
10	Belgium	Jul 1849

The first adhesive postage stamps issued in the US were designed for local delivery and produced by the City Despatch Post, New York City, inaugurated on February 15, 1842 and later that year incorporated into the US Post Office Department. In 1847 the rest of the US followed suit, and the Post Office Department issued its first national stamps: a five-cent Benjamin Franklin stamp and a 10-cent George Washington stamp, both of which first went on sale in New York City on July 1, 1847. By the time they were withdrawn, 3,712,200 and 891,000 Franklin and Washington stamps had been issued, respectively.

TOP 10

COUNTRIES SENDING & RECEIVING THE MOST MAIL

	Country	Items of mail handled per annum
1	US	165,228,428,000
2	Japan	22,723,628,000
3	France	22,344,900,000
4	UK	16,364,000,000
5	Russia	15,075,068,000
6	India	13,314,660,000
7	Canada	9,004,547,000
8	Germany	8,839,012,000
9	Italy	7,711,808,000
10	Netherlands	6,105,000,000

TOP 10

COUNTRIES WITH MOST TELEPHONES

	Country	Telephones
1	US	155,749,790
2	Japan	60,700,000
3	Germany	40,869,190
4	France	31,600,000
5	UK	28,530,000
6	China	27,230,000
7	Italy	24,542,079
8	Russia	24,097,265
9	Republic of Korea	17,646,614
10	Canada	17,000,000

It is estimated that there are some 651,716,000 telephone lines in use in the world, of which 256,118,000 are in Europe, 214,029,000 in North and South America, 58,785,000 in Asia, 11,742,000 in Africa, and 11,042,000 in Oceania. The number of telephones is understandably greater in advanced countries with large populations, and at low levels in small and sparsely populated countries, and those with rural economies. It is remarkable that, given its population, the whole of China has only 27,230,000 telephones – fewer than the UK, which has less than one-twentieth the population. India, similarly, has 9,795,304 telephones, little over half as many as Canada, with barely one-thirtieth as many inhabitants.

TOP 10

COUNTRIES WITH MOST TELEPHONES PER 100 PEOPLE

	Country	Telephones per 100 inhabitants
1	Sweden	68.43
2	Switzerland	60.83
3	Canada	59.24
4	Denmark	58.30
5	US	56.12
6	Luxembourg	55.07
7	Finland	54.57
8	Iceland	54.28
9	Norway	53.00
10	France	51.52

The world average is 10.58 phones per 100 inhabitants. On a continental basis, Oceania (Australia, New Zealand, and their neighbors) has the highest ratio of telephones per 100 people, an average of 37.60, followed by Europe with 29.10. The Americas as a whole have an average of 26.14 because even the high US figure fails to compensate for the much lower numbers in Central and South American countries. Asia's average is 3.97, and Africa's is the lowest at 1.54, with many countries falling well below even this level – Tanzania's, for example, is equivalent to one telephone for every 280 people.

TOP 10

COUNTRIES THAT MAKE THE MOST INTERNATIONAL PHONE CALLS

	Country	Calls per person	Total calls
1	US	9.0	2,342,728,000
2	Germany	17.0	1,384,000,000
3	UK	9.1	528,000,000*
4	Italy	8.7	503,990,000
5	Switzerland	60.0	416,053,000
6	Netherlands	26.5	405,400,000
7	China	0.3	387,350,000
8	Canada	11.9	332,750,000*
9	Spain	7.5	295,450,000
10	Belgium	29.4	291,037,000

* *Estimated*

TOP 10

COUNTRIES WITH THE MOST CELLULAR PHONE USERS

	Country	Cellular phones
1	US	24,134,421
2	Japan	4,331,000
3	UK	3,956,000
4	Germany	2,466,432
5	Australia	2,289,000
6	Italy	2,240,039
7	Canada	1,890,000
8	China	1,566,000
9	Sweden	1,387,000
10	South Korea	960,300

MODERN BUSINESS ON THE LINE
The growth of communications – especially the use of cellular phones – in the 1980s and 1990s has revolutionized business life globally.

TOP 10

COUNTRIES WITH MOST INSTALLED FAX MACHINES

	Country	Fax machines installed (1994)
1	US	2,925,000
2	Japan	2,000,000
3	Germany	850,000
4	UK	454,000
5	France	401,000
6	Italy	260,000
7	Canada	199,000
8	China	187,000
9	India	180,000
10	Australia	135,000

Facsimile transmission from one point to another was suggested in the early 19th century and developed in a primitive form soon after the invention of the telephone. Japanese businesses pioneered the development of the fax as a quick means of sending handwritten documents.

TOP 10

COUNTRIES WITH THE MOST INTERNET USERS

1	US
2	Canada
3	UK
4	Australia
5	Germany
6	Italy
7	Japan
8	Netherlands
9	France
10	Ireland

No one really knows how many people are connected to the Internet. One estimate, published on April 18, 1996, put the global total as 54,829,404 individuals and 233,674 World Wide Web sites – but these figures would have been increased within minutes. The ranking of countries remains more static, with those in this Top 10 list representing the "most wired."

TOP 10

MOST LINKED-TO SITES ON THE WORLD WIDE WEB

	Site	No. of links
1	Download Netscape Software	16,093
2	Yahoo	12,676
3	Welcome to Netscape	12,376
4	WebCrawler	9,700
5	Lycos	5,626
6	Internet Audit Bureau	4,701
7	Infoseek Guide	4,185
8	Starting Point	3,772
9	Microsoft Corporation	3,521
10	The Blue Ribbon Campaign for Online Free Speech	3,113

Source: Global Network Navigator, Inc. April 1996

A survey identified those sites on the Internet that were most frequently signposted, enabling users to "surf" to them from the locations they visit. The analogy of the "Web," by which all sites are interconnected to all others, is very appropriate – although some are better connected than others.

FUEL & POWER

TOP 10

ENERGY CONSUMERS IN THE WORLD

	Country	Energy consumption 1994 (millions of tons of oil equivalent)					
		Oil	Natural gas	Coal	Nuclear power	Hydro-electric	Total
1	US	807.9	533.2	492.5	173.6	21.4	2,028.6
2	China	144.1	14.9	572.0	3.1	14.5	748.7
3	Russia	188.6	360.7	140.8	30.7	15.1	735.9
4	Japan	268.7	54.3	82.0	67.3	6.3	478.6
5	Germany	135.1	61.1	96.3	39.0	1.6	333.2
6	France	90.5	27.7	14.1	92.8	6.9	232.0
7	Canada	79.5	63.5	24.9	27.8	26.8	222.5
8	UK	83.1	60.9	50.2	22.9	0.6	217.8
9	India	67.6	15.7	121.8	1.3	6.0	212.4
10	Italy	92.3	40.9	12.8	–	4.1	150.1
	World	*3,172.4*	*1,824.2*	*2,153.2*	*573.1*	*201.0*	*7,923.9*

TOP 10

NATURAL GAS PRODUCERS IN THE WORLD

	Country	Tons* (1994)
1	Russia	509,600,000
2	US	487,900,000
3	Canada	121,700,000
4	UK	58,900,000
5	Indonesia	55,800,000
6	Algeria	45,300,000
7	Uzbekistan	39,600,000
8	Saudi Arabia	33,900,000
9	Turkmenistan	29,900,000
10	Iran	27,900,000

* Of oil equivalent

TOP 10

COUNTRIES WITH MOST NUCLEAR REACTORS*

	Country	Reactors
1	US	108
2	France	56
3	Japan	50
4	UK	35
5	Russia	29
6	Canada	21
7	Germany	19
8	Ukraine	15
9	Sweden	12
10	South Korea	11

* Civilian nuclear power reactors only, excluding those devoted to military purposes

TOP 10

URANIUM PRODUCERS IN THE WORLD

	Country	Annual production (tons)
1	Canada	9,250
2	Russia	8,200
3	Australia	3,750
4	Niger	3,000
5	France	2,100
6=	South Africa	1,750
6=	US	1,750
8=	Namibia	1,500
8=	Czech Republic	1,500
10	China	1,250

TOP 10

COUNTRIES WITH THE GREATEST NATURAL GAS RESERVES

	Country	Proved reserves (1994)	
		trillion m³	trillion ft³ *
1	Russia	48.1	1,700.0
2	Iran	21.0	741.6
3	Qatar	7.1	250.7
4	Saudi Arabia	5.3	185.9
5	US	4.6	162.4
6	Venezuela	3.7	130.4
7	Algeria	3.6	128.0
8	Nigeria	3.4	120.0
9	Iraq	3.1	109.5
10	Canada	2.2	79.2

* One trillion = 1 million million (10^{12})

The world total reserves of natural gas are put at 4,979.3 trillion ft³/141.0 trillion m³ – the Top 10 countries thus hold 72 percent of the world's supplies. At current rates of production, it is reckoned that natural gas supplies will last until 2060.

NUCLEAR AGE

Because nuclear energy is seen as a modern source, it is easily forgotten that some nuclear power plants are now approaching 40 years of age. Russia's Obinsk research reactor was commissioned in December 1954, and in October 1956 the UK's Calder Hall became the world's first to supply electricity. The US has four and the UK six plants commissioned before 1966, and the dangerous task of decommissioning these reactors now confronts the world's nuclear industries.

TOP 10

OIL PRODUCERS IN THE WORLD

	Producer	Production (barrels per day)
1	Saudi Arabia	8,965,000
2	US	8,355,000
3	Russia	6,385,000
4	Iran	3,600,000
5	Mexico	3,265,000
6	China	2,905,000
7	Abu Dhabi	2,865,000
8	Norway	2,755,000
9=	UK	2,675,000
9=	Venezuela	2,675,000

Despite its huge output, the US produces only just over half the 16,915,000 barrels of oil it consumes every day. Directly through consumption of heating fuel, motor fuel, and so on, or indirectly through consumption of electricity produced by oil-fired power stations, the average US citizen uses one barrel of oil every 23 days.

TOP 10

COUNTRIES WITH THE LARGEST CRUDE OIL RESERVES

	Country	Reserves (barrels*)		Country	Reserves (barrels*)
1	Saudi Arabia	261,200,000,000	6	Venezuela	64,500,000,000
2	Iraq	100,000,000,000	7	Mexico	50,800,000,000
3	Kuwait	96,500,000,000	8	Russia	49,000,000,000
4	Abu Dhabi	92,200,000,000	9	US	30,200,000,000
5	Iran	89,300,000,000	10	China	24,000,000,000

* A barrel of crude oil = 42 US gallons/35 Imperial gallons

Oil accounts for 40 percent of the world's energy market. At the end of 1994, the global "proved reserves" of oil stood at 1,009,300,000,000 barrels, with a Top 10 that controls 857,700,000,000 barrels, or 85 percent of the world's oil.

TOP 10

LARGEST NUCLEAR POWER STATIONS IN THE WORLD

	Station	Country	Reactors in use	Output (megawatts)
1	Bruce	Canada	1–8	6,910
2	Gravelines	France	1–6	5,706
3	Paluel	France	1–4	5,528
4	Washington	US	1–5	5,326
5	Fukushima Daichi	Japan	1–6	4,696
6	Fukushima Daini	Japan	1–4	4,400
7	Pickering	Canada	1–8	4,328
8	Chinon	France	A3; B1–B4	4,051
9=	Kursk	Russia	1–4	4,000
9=	St. Petersburg	Russia	1–4	4,000

TOP 10

ELECTRICITY PRODUCERS IN THE WORLD

	Country	Production kW/hr
1	US	3,074,504,000,000
2	Russia	1,008,450,000,000
3	Japan	895,336,000,000
4	China	753,940,000,000
5	Germany	537,134,000,000
6	Canada	520,857,000,000
7	France	462,263,000,000
8	India	327,913,000,000
9	UK	326,879,000,000
10	Ukraine	252,524,000,000

SAVING THE PLANET

ENVIRONMENTAL CONCERNS IN THE UK

	Environmental problem	Total percent of population worried
1	Air pollution	30
2	Pollution (unspecified)	23
3	Exhaust fumes from cars/trucks	21
4=	Destruction of the ozone layer	18
4=	Pollution of rivers, streams, and water	18
6	Pollution of seas; waste disposal at sea	14
7	Loss of greenbelt/overbuilding	13
8=	Too much traffic	11
8=	Destruction of rainforests	11
10	Greenhouse effect/global warming	9

This survey was carried out in the UK in 1995 by the research organization MORI. Interviewees commented on the issues about which they were "very worried," and this list represents their respective levels of concern. Levels appear to fluctuate according to which issues are currently being debated in the media: a similar survey conducted in 1993 put this entire Top 10 at percentages of 38 or more. Some 60 percent of interviewees formerly considered themselves anxious about radioactive waste and 43 percent with the loss of wildlife species – which, at least temporarily, appear to have faded into matters of little concern.

A RETURN TO BASICS
Today's typical shopping basket includes an increasing proportion of paper, glass, metal, and plastic packaging that can be recycled.

PERSONAL ENVIRONMENTAL IMPROVEMENT ACTIVITIES

	Activity	Percent undertaking
1	Reading/watching TV programs about environmental issues	85
2	Walking in the countryside	81
3	Taking bottles, glass, paper, or cans for recycling	68
4	Giving money to environmental charities	56
5	Using unleaded gasoline	46
6	Selecting environmentally friendly products	41
7	Requesting information from an environmental organization	15
8	Subscribing to an environmental magazine	13
9	Joining an environmental organization	12
10=	Visiting or writing a letter to an elected official about an environmental issue	6
10=	Campaigning about an environmental issue	6

* *Of those taking part in* Business and the Environment, *a 1994 MORI survey of public attitudes and behavior*

WORST TRASH PRODUCERS IN THE WORLD

	Country	Domestic waste per capita per annum kg	lb
1	US	721	1,590
2	Finland	624	1,376
3	Canada	601	1,325
4	Netherlands	497	1,096
5	Denmark	475	1,047
6	Norway	472	1,041
7	Hungary	463	1,021
8	Luxembourg	445	981
9	Switzerland	441	972
10	Japan	411	906

US STATES WITH HIGHEST RECYCLING TARGETS*

	State#/target year	Target percent
1	Rhode Island (not stated)	70
2	New Jersey (1995)	60
3	Massachusetts (2000)	56
4=	California (2000)	50
4=	Hawaii (2000)	50
4=	Indiana (2001)	50
4=	Iowa (2000)	50
4=	Maine (1994)+	50
4=	Nebraska (2002)	50
4=	New Mexico (2000)	50
4=	New York (1997)	50
4=	Oregon (2000)	50
4=	South Dakota (2001)	50
4=	Washington (1995)	50
4=	West Virginia (2010)	50

* *As of December 31, 1994*
# *Ten states have not declared their target for recycling*
+ *Target not yet verified*

WORST DEFORESTING COUNTRIES IN THE WORLD

	Country	Average annual forest loss in 1980s (sq mi)
1	Brazil	14,170
2	Indonesia	4,290
3	Zaïre	2,830
4	Mexico	2,620
5	Bolivia	2,410
6	Venezuela	2,310
7	Thailand	1,990
8	Sudan	1,860
9	Tanzania	1,690
10	Paraguay	1,560

Over the decade of the 1980s the total loss of the Brazilian forest was equivalent to the entire area of Germany.

TOP 10

LEAST POLLUTED CITIES IN THE WORLD*

1	Craiova, Poland
2	Melbourne, Australia
3	Auckland, New Zealand
4	Cali, Colombia
5	Tel Aviv, Israel
6	Bucharest, Romania
7	Vancouver, Canada
8	Toronto, Canada
9	Bangkok, Thailand
10	Chicago, Illinois

* Based on levels of atmospheric sulfur dioxide

Ironically, although the cities in this Top 10 have been identified as the world's "best," some are in countries with notably high national levels of sulfur dioxide, with Canada at the head of the global list.

TOP 10

COMPONENTS OF HOUSEHOLD WASTE IN THE UK

	Waste	percent	Average yearly weight (lb)
1	Putrescibles (kitchen waste)	16.77	234
2	Newspapers	11.40	159
3	Other paper	9.53	132
4	Fines (ash, vacuum cleaner dust)	6.77	95
5	Clear glass	5.37	75
6	Magazines	4.61	64
7	Disposable diapers	4.21	60
8	Plastic wrap	4.18	57
9	Miscellaneous combustibles (shoes, carpets, etc.)	3.90	55
10	Cardboard packaging	3.73	53

THE 10

MOST POLLUTED CITIES IN THE WORLD*

1	Milan, Italy
2	Shengyang, China
3	Tehran, Iran
4	Seoul, South Korea
5	Rio de Janeiro, Brazil
6	São Paulo, Brazil
7	Xian, China
8	Paris, France
9	Peking, China
10	Madrid, Spain

* Based on levels of atmospheric sulfur dioxide

Assessments made by the World Health Authority in the 1980s lacked information from Soviet bloc countries, where pollution levels may be even higher. Many countries have since taken steps to improve matters.

THE 10

US STATES RELEASING THE MOST TOXIC CHEMICALS

	State	kg	Releases lb
1	Louisiana	204,425,459	450,680,961
2	Texas	159,742,417	352,171,723
3	Tennessee	85,369,556	188,207,643
4	Ohio	62,611,427	138,034,559
5	Mississippi	53,532,733	118,019,466
6	Alabama	47,871,421	105,538,411
7	Illinois	45,808,713	100,990,919
8	Indiana	44,381,476	97,844,399
9	Utah	41,662,830	91,850,812
10	North Carolina	41,283,567	91,014,680

A study by the US Environmental Protection Agency determined that in 1993 a total of 2,808,618,413 lb of toxic chemicals were released into the air, water, and land (including underground) of the US, with industries in these states the worst offenders.

THE 10

WORST CARBON DIOXIDE EMITTERS IN THE WORLD

	Country	CO_2 emissions (tons of carbon) per capita p.a.	total
1	US	5.22	1,332,246,000
2	China	0.62	728,161,000
3	Russia	3.85	573,999,000
4	Japan	2.40	298,436,000
5	Germany	2.99	239,666,000
6	India	0.24	210,000,000
7	Ukraine	3.20	166,851,000
8	UK	2.67	154,543,000
9	Canada	4.09	111,862,000
10	Italy	1.92	111,272,000

Dr. Gregg Marland and the Carbon Dioxide Information Analysis Center at Oak Ridge, Tennessee, calculate CO_2 emissions from three principal sources – fossil fuel burning, cement manufacturing, and gas flaring. Their findings show the extent to which increasing industrialization in many countries has resulted in huge increases in pollution caused by carbon emissions.

THE 10

WORST SULFUR DIOXIDE EMITTERS IN THE WORLD

	Country	Annual SO_2 emissions (lb per capita)
1	Canada	261.7
2	US	179.0
3	Germany	155.9
4	UK	136.2
5	Spain	123.7
6	Ireland	116.6
7	Belgium	92.2
8	Finland	84.4
9	Denmark	77.2
10	Italy	75.8

INDUSTRIAL & OTHER DISASTERS

THE 10

OCCUPATIONS FOR FATAL INJURIES AT WORK IN THE US

	Occupation	Fatalities (1994)
1	Truck driver	762
2	Farm worker	261
3	Supervisors, proprietor (sales)	249
4	Construction labourer	247
5	Police, detective (public)	149
6	Aircraft pilot or navigator	131
7	Guard	127
8	Taxi driver	113
9	Lumberjack	112
10	Cashier	110
	Total (including others not listed above)	6,588

THE 10

MOST COMMON CAUSES OF INJURY AT WORK IN THE UK

	Cause	Fatalities	Injuries*
1	Injured while handling, lifting, or carrying	1	47,228
2	Slip, trip, or fall on same level	2	27,813
3	Struck by moving (including flying or falling) object	32	19,527
4	Fall from height	51	10,286
5	Striking something fixed or stationary	1	8,093
6	Contact with moving machinery or material being machined	17	6,374
7	Exposure to, or contact with, harmful substance	5	3,805
8	Struck by moving vehicle	37	3,331
9	Injured by animal	2	760
10	Contact with electricity	10	573
	Total (including causes not listed above)	190	135,940

* Resulting in work absence of more than three days, employees only (excluding self-employed), 1994–95

THE 10

WORST COMMERCIAL AND INDUSTRIAL DISASTERS*

	Location/incident	Date	Killed
1	Bhopal, India (methyl isocyanate gas escape at Union Carbide plant)	December 3, 1984	over 2,500
2	Seoul, Korea (collapse of department store)	June 29, 1995	640
3	Oppau, Germany (explosion at chemical plant)	September 21, 1921	561
4	Mexico City, Mexico (explosion at gas plant)	November 20, 1984	540
5	Brussels, Belgium (fire in L'Innovation department store)	May 22, 1967	322
6	Guadalajara, Mexico (explosions after gas leak into sewers)	April 22, 1992	230
7	São Paulo, Brazil (fire in Joelma bank and office building)	February 1, 1974	227
8	Bangkok, Thailand (fire engulfed a four-story doll factory)	May 10, 1993	187
9	North Sea (Piper Alpha oil rig explosion and fire)	July 6, 1988	173
10	New York City (fire in Triangle Shirtwaist Factory)	March 25, 1911	145

* Including industrial sites, factories, offices, and stores; excluding military, mining, marine, and other transportation disasters

THE 10

WORST MINING DISASTERS IN THE WORLD

	Location	Date	Killed
1	Hinkeiko, China	April 26, 1942	1,549
2	Courrières, France	March 10, 1906	1,060
3	Omuta, Japan	November 9, 1963	447
4	Senghenydd, UK	October 14, 1913	439
5	Coalbrook, South Africa	January 21, 1960	437
6	Wankie, Rhodesia	June 6, 1972	427
7	Dharbad, India	May 28, 1965	375
8	Chasnala, India	December 27, 1975	372
9	Monongah, West Virginia	December 6, 1907	362
10	Barnsley, UK	December 12, 1866	361*

* Including 27 killed the following day while searching for survivors

A mining disaster at the Fushun mines, Manchuria, on February 12, 1931 may have resulted in up to 3,000 deaths, but information was suppressed by the Chinese government. Soviet security was also responsible for obscuring details of an explosion at the East German Johanngeorgendstadt uranium mine on November 29, 1949, where it has been estimated that as many as 3,700 may have died.

WORST EXPLOSIONS IN THE WORLD

(*Excluding mining disasters, and terrorist and military bombs*)

	Location/incident	Date	Killed*
1	Lanchow, China (arsenal)	October 26, 1935	2,000
2	Halifax, Nova Scotia (ammunition ship *Mont Blanc*)	December 6, 1917	1,635
3	Memphis, Tennessee (*Sultana* boiler explosion)	April 27, 1865	1,547
4	Bombay, India (ammunition ship *Fort Stikine*)	April 14, 1944	1,376
5	Cali, Colombia (ammunition trucks)	August 7, 1956	1,200
6	Salang Tunnel, Afghanistan (gasoline tanker collision)	November 2, 1982	over 1,100
7	Chelyabinsk, USSR (liquid gas beside railroad)	June 3, 1989	up to 800
8	Texas City, Texas (ammonium nitrate on *Grandcamp* freighter)	April 16, 1947	752
9	Oppau, Germany (chemical plant)	September 21, 1921	561
10	Mexico City, Mexico (PEMEX gas plant)	November 20, 1984	540

* All these "best estimate" figures should be treated with caution, since, as with fires and shipwrecks, body counts are notoriously unreliable

MEXICO CITY GAS EXPLOSION
The PEMEX gas plant explosion of November 20, 1984, that left 540 dead, is not only one of the worst industrial disasters, but one of the worst explosions of all time.

MOST COMMON TYPES OF ACCIDENT AT HOME IN THE UK

	Accident	No. per year
1	Falls	1,004,000
2	Cutting/piercing	333,000
3	Striking a static object	186,000
4	Struck by a moving object	179,000
5	Foreign body	138,000
6	Burning	96,000
7	Jamming/pinching	85,000
8	Animal/insect bite	76,000
9	Poisoning	54,000
10	Overexertion	25,000

Falls includes everything from tripping over (233,800 cases), through to falling on or down stairs (197,800), to falling off ladders (23,200) or buildings (8,400). Official statistics also list 176,500 accidents of unknown cause and 79,100 as "other." Figures cover only nonfatal accidents within homes and yards, and do not include self-inflicted injury, suspected suicide attempts, or attack by other people.

MOST COMMON TYPES OF FATAL ACCIDENT AT HOME IN THE UK

	Accident	No. per year
1	Unspecified falls	1,391
2	Poisoning/inhalation	558
3	Fall from stairs	515
4	Uncontrolled fire	432
5	Foreign body	245
6	Fall between two levels	117
7	Fall on same level	98
8	Suffocating/choking	81
9	Drowning	68
10	Fall from building	61

THE WORLD'S RICHEST

T O P   1 0

RICHEST PEOPLE IN THE WORLD*

	Name	Country	Business	Assets ($)
1	Bill Gates	US	Computer software	14,800,000,000
2	Warren Buffett	US	Textiles, etc.	9,200,000,000
3=	Hans Rausing	Sweden	Packaging	9,000,000,000
3=	Yoshiaki Tsutsumi	Japan	Property	9,000,000,000
5	Paul Sacher	Switzerland	Roche drug company	8,600,000,000
6	Tsai Wan-lin	Taiwan	Insurance	8,500,000,000
7=	Lee Shau Kee	Hong Kong	Property	6,500,000,000
7=	Kenneth T. Thomson	Canada	Publishing	6,500,000,000
9	Chung Ju-yung	Korea	Hyundai (cars)	6,200,000,000
10	Li Ka-shing	Hong Kong	Property, etc.	5,900,000,000

* *Excluding royalty*

Based on data published by Forbes Magazine

T O P   1 0

COUNTRIES WITH THE MOST DOLLAR BILLIONAIRES*

	Country	Billionaires
1	US	129
2	Germany	48
3	Japan	34
4=	Hong Kong	12
4=	Thailand	12
6	France	11
7=	Indonesia	10
7=	Mexico	10
9=	Brazil	8
9=	Switzerland	8

* *With a net worth of $1,000,000,000 or more*

Based on data published in Forbes Magazine

T O P   1 0

HIGHEST-EARNING ENTERTAINERS IN THE WORLD*

	Entertainer	Profession	1994–95 income ($)
1	Steven Spielberg	Film producer/director	285,000,000
2	Oprah Winfrey	TV host/producer	146,000,000
3	David Copperfield	Illusionist	81,000,000
4	Andrew Lloyd Webber	Theatre producer/composer	48,000,000
5	Stephen King	Novelist/screenwriter	43,000,000
6=	Sheryl Leach (Barney)	Singer/dancer/children's educator	40,000,000
6=	Siegfried & Roy	Illusionists	40,000,000
8	Michael Crichton	Novelist	39,000,000
9	Robert Zemeckis	Film director	37,000,000
10	Charles M. Schulz	*Peanuts* cartoonist	36,000,000

* *Other than actors and pop stars*

Used by permission of Forbes Magazine

Receiving eight percent of gross receipts from his blockbuster film *Forrest Gump* rocketed Robert Zemeckis into this list for the first time. Meanwhile, the global success of *Jurassic Park* accounts for two prominent placings in this Top 10: Steven Spielberg has been a long-standing resident of this élite group of high-earning entertainers, but the 1990s have been exceptional years even for him (his $250,000,000 take from the film represents the greatest amount any individual has ever earned from a single movie), while Michael Crichton, the highest-earning novelist in the list, was the author of *Jurassic Park*. Runners-up in this distinguished list are TV host David Letterman ($29,000,000) and novelists John Grisham ($29,000,000) and Tom Clancy ($28,000,000), authors of bestselling books that have been successfully adapted as films, including Grisham's *The Firm* and Clancy's *Patriot Games*.

T H E   1 0

HIGHEST-EARNING DECEASED PEOPLE

	Name	Year died
1	Elvis Presley	1977
2	John Lennon	1980
3	James Dean	1955
4	Jimi Hendrix	1970
5	Albert Einstein	1955
6	Marilyn Monroe	1962
7	Jim Morrison	1971
8	Humphrey Bogart	1957
9	Orson Welles	1985
10	Babe Ruth	1948

Under copyright law, the estates of numerous authors, movie stars, singers, and songwriters continue to receive posthumous royalty income. Added to this, the commercial exploitation of iconic images in advertisements and other media has become a major business, with Einstein, for example, used to promote everything from whisky to computer software. The estates of innumerable other deceased celebrities similarly accrue substantial income, but like the rights themselves, the actual amounts are jealously protected by lawyers.

TOP 10

RICHEST PEOPLE IN THE US

In 1995 *Forbes Magazine*, which annually surveys the 400 wealthiest people in the US, ranked more than 70 American individuals and families as dollar billionaires – that is, with assets in excess of $1,000,000,000. The *Forbes 400* includes both the inheritors of great family fortunes and self-made individuals. A placing in the list is extremely volatile, however – particularly during recent times, when many who made vast fortunes in a short period lost them with even greater rapidity. Events such as stock market falls and the decline in property values have led to a fall in the assets of many members of this élite club, while deaths such as that in 1996 of David Packard have removed former entrants from the list.

Name	Assets ($)
1 Bill Gates	14,800,000,000

In 1975, at the age of 19, Gates left Harvard University to co-found (with Paul G. Allen, who rates No. 4 in this list) the Microsoft Corporation of Seattle, now one of the world's leading computer software companies, and one that has experienced phenomenal growth: a $2,000 investment in 1986 was worth nearly $70,000 in 1993. Gates, a self-described "hard-core technoid," first ascended to number one position in 1992. Formerly a bachelor devoted only to his business and fast cars, he married Microsoft executive Melinda French in 1994; the launch of Windows 95 the following year further enhanced his fortune.

Name	Assets ($)
2 Warren Buffett	9,200,000,000

Buffett was born and still lives in Omaha, Nebraska. He started his professional career as a pinball service engineer, after which he published a horse-race tip sheet. His diverse business interests include the New England textile company, Berkshire Hathaway, which has in turn acquired major stakes in the Washington Post and Coca-Cola. In 1992 Buffett was ranked 4th in the Forbes 400, in 1993 he was elevated to 1st place, but in 1994 he dropped back behind Bill Gates.

Name	Assets ($)
3 John Werner Kluge	6,700,000,000

Kluge was the founder of the Metromedia Company of Charlottesville, Virginia. The family of German-born Kluge settled in Detroit in 1922, where he worked on the Ford assembly line. He won a scholarship to Columbia University and earned a degree in economics. He started a radio station and in 1959, with partners, acquired the Metropolitan Broadcasting Company, developing it into Metromedia, a corporation that owns TV and radio stations, cellular telephone franchises, and other varied

properties. He also owned an 80,000-acre estate and castle in Scotland. Kluge, who was placed as America's richest man in 1989, has diversified his interests and is developing Orion Pictures as part of a media group.

Name	Assets ($)
4 Paul G. Allen	6,100,000,000

Co-founder with Bill Gates of Microsoft, Allen has maintained his connections with the computer and multimedia industry and pursues such interests as his ownership of the Portland Trailblazers basketball team.

Name	Assets ($)
5 Sumner Murray Redstone	4,800,000,000

Formerly in 6th place, Redstone, who comes from a theater-owning family, built up his own cinema company, National Amusements, Inc., coining the word "multiplex" for his multi-screen cinema complexes. The company now has more than 750 screens across the US and has acquired the cinema company Viacom.

Name	Assets ($)
6= Richard Marvin De Vos and Jay Van Andel ($8,600,000,000 shared)	4,300,000,000

Relative newcomers to this Top 10, De Vos and Van Andel are partners in the Amway Corporation, the success of which is founded on its hugely successful soap distribution operation. The corporation is also involved in real estate, jewelry, and hotels. De Vos owns the Orlando Magic basketball team.

Name	Assets ($)
6= Samuel Irving Newhouse, Jr. and Donald Edward Newhouse ($8,600,000,000 shared)	4,300,000,000

The New York City-based Newhouse brothers are the owners of America's largest privately owned chain of newspapers. They also have interests that include book publishing and cable television. Samuel ("Si") Newhouse runs book publisher Random House and magazine publisher Condé Nast, the publishers of Vogue. This famous magazine was bought by their father in 1959 as an anniversary gift for his wife ("She asked for a fashion magazine, and I went out and got her Vogue."). Donald controls their newspaper group.

Name	Assets ($)
6= Helen Walton, S. Robson Walton, John T. Walton, Jim C. Walton, and Alice L. Walton ($21,500,000,000 shared)	4,300,000,000

Samuel Moore Walton, the founder of Wal-Mart Stores, headed the list of America's richest people for several years. One of the largest retail chains in the US, its more than 2,000 stores achieved sales of

$55,500,000,000 in 1992, the year in which Sam Walton died. His widow Helen and four children share the fortune he created.

Name	Assets ($)
9= Ronald Owen Perelman	4,200,000,000

Perelman is a wide-ranging entrepreneur who acquired Revlon, Max Factor, and other cosmetics businesses. He is the former owner of Technicolor and has professional interests that encompass firms from Marvel Comics and cigars to a camping goods company, with TV assets under the control of the newly formed New World Communications.

Name	Assets ($)
9= Lawrence J. Ellison	4,200,000,000

Based in Atherton, California, Ellison worked with IBM before establishing his own computer software company, Oracle Corporation.

Close runners-up in the more-than-three-billion dollars league include Walter Annenberg ($3,900,000,000), Rupert Murdoch ($3,300,000,000), and the Mars family (of Mars candy fame) – four members sharing $12,000,000,000.

GOLDEN GATES OF FORTUNE
Seattle-born Bill Gates's fortune has grown along with the global success of his Microsoft Corporation, making him the world's richest nonroyal with a fortune nudging $15 billion.

THE WEALTH OF NATIONS

TOP 10

COUNTRIES WITH THE HIGHEST INFLATION

	Country	Annual inflation rate (percent)
1	Zaïre	542.0
2	Suriname	238.5
3	Russia	197.4
4	Brazil	184.4
5	Turkey	93.6
6	Venezuela	59.9
7	Madagascar	49.1
8	Uruguay	42.2
9	Lithuania	39.7
10	Mexico	35.0

These figures are for 1995 and indicate the rise in consumer prices over the previous year, as calculated by the International Monetary Fund. A 100 percent inflation rate would mean that consumer prices had doubled since the previous year.

TOP 10

COUNTRIES IN WHICH IT IS EASIEST TO BE A MILLIONAIRE

	Country	Currency unit	Value of 1,000,000 units £	$
1	Ukraine	Karbovanets	3.95	6.13
2	Turkey	Lira	13.35	20.73
3	Guinea-Bissau	Peso	38.46	59.71
4	Belarus	Rouble	56.01	86.96
5	Vietnam	Dông	58.46	90.76
6	Mozambique	Metical	67.07	104.13
7	Zaïre	Zaïre	118.77	184.39
8	Madagascar	Franc	144.75	224.72
9	Afghanistan	Afghani	145.01	225.13
10	Azerbaijan	Manat	146.56	227.53

Runaway inflation in many countries has reduced the value of their currencies to such an extent as to make them virtually worthless. Thus with an exchange rate running at an average of 392,872 Ukrainian Karbovanets to the dollar, total assets of just $6.13 will qualify one as an Ukrainian millionaire. Occasionally currencies are realigned (effectively devalued). In 1993, for example, there were 5,789,293 Zaïres to the dollar, so that anyone with 17 cents could have claimed to be a Zaïre millionaire; in 1995 the exchange rate was Zaïre 5,423.28/$1.00. Now a Zaïre millionaire would require assets of $184.39.

TOP 10

RICHEST COUNTRIES IN THE WORLD

	Country	GDP per capita ($)
1	Switzerland	36,399
2	Luxembourg	35,583
3	Japan	31,451
4	Bermuda	28,293
5	Denmark	26,514
6	Norway	26,340
7	Sweden	24,833
8	US	24,753
9	Iceland	23,985
10	Germany	23,561

Gross Domestic Product (GDP) is the total value of all the goods and services produced annually within the country (Gross National Product – GNP – also includes income from overseas). Dividing the GDP by the country's population produces the GDP per capita.

THE 10

POOREST COUNTRIES IN THE WORLD

	Country	GDP per capita ($)
1	Sudan	63
2	Somalia	78
3	Mozambique	81
4	Tanzania	94
5	Ethiopia	102
6	Afghanistan	111
7	Sierra Leone	145
8	Nepal	156
9	Bhutan	165
10	Vietnam	169

About 30 industrialized nations have per capita GDPs in excess of $10,000, while a similar number of Third World countries, particularly in Africa, have per capita GDPs of less than $300, with those in this Top 10 at the bottom of the world income league.

TOP 10

RICHEST STATES IN THE US

	State	Average income per capita ($)
1	District of Columbia	31,136
2	Connecticut	29,402
3	New Jersey	28,038
4	New York	25,999
5	Massachusetts	25,616
6	Maryland	24,933
7	Hawaii	24,057
8	Nevada	24,023
9	Alaska	23,788
10	Illinois	23,784

The US Bureau of Economic Analysis produces data to show the average income, and the District of Columbia is commonly used as a state for comparisons such as this. In the 20th century the average income received by each US resident has risen from $418 in 1900 to $21,809 in 1994.

TOP 10

COUNTRIES WITH THE HIGHEST PER CAPITA EXPENDITURE

	Country	Expenditure per capita ($)
1	Switzerland	20,720
2	Japan	16,830
3	Iceland	15,550
4	US	15,530
5	Luxembourg	13,880
6	France	13,800
7	Sweden	13,760
8	Belgium	13,720
9	Norway	13,700
10	Italy	13,480
	UK	*9,970*

Average per capita expenditure varies greatly from country to country, from the levels in this Top 10 to those in the low hundreds of dollars or less. In Western industrial economies the proportion of expenditure devoted to food is often about 20 percent. The more disposable expenditure that is not allocated to such essential items, the more may be spent on consumer goods, education, and leisure activities.

THE 10

POOREST STATES IN THE US

	State	Average income per capita ($)
1	Mississippi	15,838
2	Arkansas	16,898
3	Utah	17,043
4	New Mexico	17,106
5	West Virginia	17,208
6	Louisiana	17,651
7	South Carolina	17,695
8	Oklahoma	17,744
9	Kentucky	17,807
10	Alabama	17,865

THE 10

COUNTRIES WITH THE LOWEST PER CAPITA EXPENDITURE

	Country	Expenditure per capita ($)
1	Somalia	17
2	Mozambique	70
3	Tanzania	77
4	Ethiopia	80
5	Nepal	110
6	Sierra Leone	115
7	Malawi	130
8	Laos	140
9=	India	160
9=	Rwanda	160

It is hard for people in Western consumer cultures to comprehend the poverty of the countries appearing in this list, where the total average annual expenditure of an individual would barely cover the cost of a few meals in the West. These poorer economies inevitably rely on a greater degree of self-sufficiency in food production. In such countries, spending on transportation, recreation, and other staple household items is virtually zero in comparison to that of other countries.

TOP 10

COINS AND BILLS IN CIRCULATION IN THE US*

	Unit	Value in circulation ($)
1	$100 bill	236,398,620,700
2	$20 bill	79,881,915,120
3	$50 bill	45,754,743,300
4	$10 bill	13,351,167,780
5	$5 bill	7,146,421,670
6	$1 bill	6,033,686,002
7	Quarter	5,768,500,000
8	Dime	2,724,700,000
9	$2 bill	1,045,269,832
10	Nickel	900,950,000

As of January 1, 1996

TOP 10

COUNTRIES WITH MOST CURRENCY IN CIRCULATION 100 YEARS AGO

	Country	Total currency in circulation ($)
1	US	2,142,000,000
2	France	2,104,000,000
3	India	960,000,000
4	Germany	900,000,000
5	UK	845,000,000
6	Russia	720,000,000
7	China	700,000,000
8	Italy	510,000,000
9	Austria	460,000,000
10	Spain	390,000,000

TOP 10

COINS AND BILLS IN CIRCULATION IN THE UK*

	Unit	Value in circulation (£)
1	£20 bill	7,723,000,000
2	£10 bill	5,348,000,000
3	£50 bill	2,852,000,000
4	£5 bill	1,072,000,000
5	£1 coin	1,033,000,000
6	20p coin	296,800,000
7	50p coin	240,000,000
8	10p coin	136,400,000
9	5p coin	140,000,000
10	2p coin	82,700,000

As of January 1, 1996

Bills in circulation in April 1996 (which included a total of £1,004,000,000 "other notes," such as the high-value bills used internally by the Bank of England) totaled £19,888,927,680 – the equivalent of a pile of £5 notes 316 km/196 miles high. There are also 6,799,000,000 1p coins worth £67,990,000, and 57,000,000 £1.00 notes – which are legal tender only in Scotland.

FOOD & DRINK

20TH CENTURY

The brand naming of products begin in earnest in the last century, but in the present has acquired huge commercial importance. In a competitive international market, major companies have sought to establish and enhance their share of it by ensuring that their names, those of their products, their slogans, and even the shape of their packaging and the style and color of its lettering, are instantly recognizable and respected by potential buyers the world over. This is nowhere truer than in the field of food and drink, and here we present a range of lists that give just a flavor of this global business: Heinz, Mars, Cadbury Schweppes, Coca-Cola, and Kellogg's, all of which have become 20th-century household names.

"57 VARIETIES"
The Heinz company was already established in the US and UK when its founder devised its familiar slogan.

TOP 10

HEINZ PRODUCTS IN THE WORLD

1	Ketchup, sauces, and other condiments		**6**	Weight loss products and services
2	Pet food		**7**	Soups
3	Baby food		**8**	Beans
4	Seafood		**9**	Pasta
5	Frozen potatoes		**10**	Coated vegetables, cheese, and fish

Henry John Heinz, the founder of the huge food processing and canning empire that bears his name, was born in Pittsburgh, Pennsylvania in 1844, of German immigrant parents. In 1869 he formed a partnership with a family friend, L.C. Noble, selling horseradish in clear glass jars (previously green glass disguised the dishonest practice of packing out the horseradish with turnip), beginning the Heinz reputation for quality and integrity. Their products were also sold on their lack of artificial flavoring and coloring long before these factors were thought desirable. In 1876, with his brother John and cousin Frederick, he formed the firm of F. & J. Heinz. One of their first products was ketchup – a staple product in every American household, but one previously home-made, a task that involved the whole family stirring a huge cauldron over an open fire for an entire day. The business was sufficiently well established by 1886 for the Heinz family to visit Europe, and H.J. sold the first Heinz products in Britain to Fortnum & Mason, the fashionable Piccadilly emporium. H.J. also devised the famous "57 Varieties" slogan in 1896; while travelling on the New York Third Avenue railway, he was inspired by a sign advertising "21 Styles" of shoe.

FOOD BRANDS

THE 10
FIRST MARS PRODUCTS

	Product	Introduced
1=	Milky Way bar	1923
1=	Snickers bar (non-chocolate)	1923
3	Snickers bar (chocolate)	1930
4	3 Musketeers bar	1932
5	Maltesers	1937
6	Kitekat (catfood; now Whiskas)	1939
7	Mars almond bar	1940
8	M&M's plain chocolate candies	1941
9	Uncle Ben's Converted brand rice	1942
10=	M&M's peanut chocolate candies	1954
10=	Pal (dogfood)	1954

American candy manufacturer Franklin C. Mars established his first business in Tacoma, Washington, USA, in 1911 and formed the Mar-O-Bar company in Minneapolis (later moving it to Chicago) in 1922 with the first of its internationally known products, the Milky Way bar. The founder's son Forrest E. Mars set up in the UK in 1932, merging the firm with its American counterpart in 1964.

THE SWEET TASTE OF SUCCESS
The name of its first product, the Milky Way bar, and successors such as Galaxy, recall the name of the Mars company's founder.

A Mars a day...

THE 10
FIRST COCA-COLA PRODUCTS

	Product	Introduced
1	Coca-Cola	May 1886
2	Fanta	June 1960
3	Sprite	February 1961
4	TAB	May 1963
5	Fresca	February 1966
6	Mr. PiBB*	June 1972
7	Hi-C Soft Drinks	August 1977
8	Mello Yello	March 1979
9	Ramblin' Root Beer	June 1979
10	Diet Coke	July 1982

* *Mr. PiBB without Sugar launched Sep 1974; changed name to Sugar free Mr. PiBB, 1975*

TOP 10
CADBURY SCHWEPPES WORLD BRANDS

1	Dr. Pepper
2	7-Up
3	Schweppes "Mixers"
4	Canada Dry Ginger Ale
5	Crush Orange
6	A&W (US – root beer and cream soda)
7	Sunkist
8	Penafiel (Mexico – mineral waters)
9	Squirt (US – fruit carbonates)
10	Cottee's (Australia)

Schweppe & Co. (later Schweppes Ltd.) was founded by German-born Jean Jacob Schweppe (1740–1821), an amateur scientist interested in the manufacture of artificial mineral waters. He moved to London in 1792 and in his Drury Lane factory began producing his own brand of soda water. By the 1870s Schweppe & Co. was also making ginger ale and "Indian Tonic Water" by adding quinine to sweetened soda water, after the style of the British in India who drank it as an antidote to malaria. Schweppes merged with Cadbury Brothers Ltd. in 1969.

TOP 10
CONSUMERS OF KELLOGG'S CORN FLAKES*

1	Ireland	6	Norway
2	UK	7	Canada
3	Australia	8	US
4	Denmark	9	Mexico
5	Sweden	10	Venezuela

* *Based on per capita consumption*

In 1894 the brothers Dr. John Harvey and Will Keith Kellogg were running their "Sanatorium," a health resort in Battle Creek, Michigan. Attempting to devise healthy foods for their patients, they experimented with wheat dough that they boiled and passed through rollers. By accident, they discovered that if the dough was left overnight it came out as flakes, and that when these were baked they turned into a tasty cereal. The Kellogg brothers first made their new product on a small scale, providing cereal by mail order to former patients. In 1898 they replaced wheat with corn, thereby creating the Corn Flakes we know today. The Kellogg Company now achieves annual worldwide sales worth more than $6,000,000,000. The value of the Kellogg brand is rated second in the world (after Coca-Cola).

CEREAL STORY
Born a century ago, Kellogg's Corn Flakes started their globally successful life as a health-food product at the Kellogg brothers' Battle Creek Sanatorium.

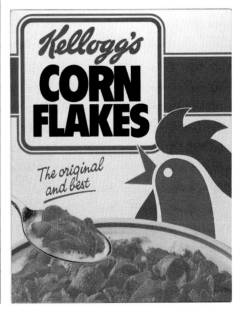

Kellogg's **CORN FLAKES** *The original and best*

CANDY IS DANDY

TOP 10

CANDY-CONSUMING NATIONS IN THE WORLD

	Country	Annual consumption (lbs per head) chocolate	other sweets	total
1	Netherlands	18.10	12.52	30.62
2	Denmark	15.23	14.09	29.32
3	Switzerland	22.11	6.39	28.51
4	UK	16.36	11.40	27.76
5	Belgium/Luxembourg	16.82	10.71	27.54
6	Ireland	14.66	12.74	27.40
7	Norway	17.39	9.63	27.03
8	Germany	14.48	12.52	27.01
9	Sweden	12.24	11.57	23.81
10	Austria	16.14	6.28	22.42
	US	*10.27*	*7.58*	*17.86*

TOP 10

COCOA-CONSUMING COUNTRIES IN THE WORLD

	Country	Total cocoa consumption (tons)
1	US	545,700
2	Germany	244,100
3	UK	181,600
4	France	157,300
5	Russian Federation	148,000
6	Japan	115,500
7	Brazil	88,100
8	Italy	81,400
9	Spain	65,400
10	Belgium/Luxembourg	60,000

Cocoa is the principal ingredient of chocolate, and its consumption is therefore closely linked to the production of chocolate in each consuming country. Like coffee, the consumption of chocolate tends to occur mainly in the Western world and in more affluent countries. Since some of the Top 10 consuming nations also have large populations, the list for cocoa consumption per capita is somewhat different in composition, being dominated by those countries with a long-established tradition of manufacturing chocolate products:

	Country	Consumption per capita lb	oz
1	Belgium/ Luxembourg	12	10
2	Switzerland	10	0
3	Austria	7	3
4	Iceland	6	15
5	UK	6	14
6	Germany	6	10
7	Norway	6	8
8	Denmark	6	1
9	France	6	0
10	Netherlands	5	12

TOP 10

CANDY AND SNACK PRODUCTS IN THE US

	Type	Sales percent*
1	Chocolate bars	45.5
2	Potato chips and pretzels	22.0
3	Cookies	9.4
4	Non-chocolate bars	8.7
5	Gums	3.4
6	Filled crackers	2.8
7	Nuts	2.5
8	Mints	2.3
9	Granola bars	1.5
10	Crackers	1.4

* Based on percentages of total purchases by stores, by value
Source: Manufacturing Confectioner

TOP 10

OLDEST-ESTABLISHED BRITISH CHOCOLATE PRODUCTS

	Product	Year introduced
1	Fry's Chocolate Cream	1866
2	Cadbury's Dairy Milk	1905
3	Cadbury's Bournville	1908
4	Fry's Turkish Delight	1914
5	Cadbury's Milk Tray	1915
6	Cadbury's Creme Egg	1920
7=	Cadbury's Fruit & Nut	1921
7=	Terry's 1767 Bitter Bar	1921
9	Terry's Neapolitan	1922
10	Terry's Spartan	1923

DID YOU KNOW

CHOCOLATE LOVERS

Cocoa had been drunk by the Aztecs and was taken from South America to Spain in the 16th century. Sugar was added to make the bitter cocoa more palatable, and then milk to create chocolate, the diarist Samuel Pepys recording his first drink of "jocolatte" on November 24, 1664. In Britain the industry came under the control of three Quaker families, Fry, Rowntree, and Cadbury, who encouraged drinking cocoa or chocolate as an alternative to alcohol.

TOP 10

ICE CREAM BRANDS IN THE US

	Brand	Sales ($)*
1	Private labels	727,700,000
2	Good Humor-Breyers	328,000,000
3	Dreyer's/Edy's Grand	229,700,000
4	Häagen-Dazs	118,700,000
5=	Ben & Jerry's	99,500,000
5=	Blue Bell	99,500,000
7	Sealtest	50,200,000
8	Turkey Hill	49,500,000
9	Blue Bell Supreme	49,300,000
10	Dreyer's/Edy's Light	42,600,000

Year to September 10, 1995
Source: International Dairy Foods Association

The memorably titled Häagen-Dazs ice cream was the brainchild of Reuben Mattus, who in 1961 created a range of high-quality ice creams, choosing a meaningless but Danish-sounding name to emphasize the rich, creamy nature of his product.

TOP 10

ICE CREAM-CONSUMING COUNTRIES IN THE WORLD

	Country	Production per capita pints
1	USA	47.04
2	New Zealand	37.70
3	Denmark	36.01
4	Australia	32.65
5	Belgium/Luxembourg	31.51
6	Sweden	30.09
7	Canada	27.03
8	Norway	25.66
9	Ireland	19.32
10	Switzerland	15.79

Global statistics for ice cream consumption are hard to come by, but this list presents recent and reliable International Ice Cream Association estimates for per capita production of ice cream and related products (frozen yogurt, sherbert, water ices, etc.) – and since only small amounts of such products are exported, consumption figures can be presumed to be similar. In 1992 US production of all ice cream products was put at a remarkable 1,492,510,149 gallons.

TOP 10

GUM BRANDS IN THE US

	Brand	Sales 1993 ($)*
1	Wrigley's Extra	108,288,122
2	Trident	76,374,560
3	Carefree	73,746,912
4	Wrigley's Doublemint	39,397,616
5	Freedent	36,320,686
6	Wrigley's Big Red	25,086,000
7	Wrigley's Gum	22,593,408
8	Wrigley's Juicy Fruit	21,305,330
9	Dentyne Cinn-A-Burst	19,077,312
10	Bubblicious	15,117,924

Through grocery stores only – total sales of some brands through drug stores, mass merchandisers, and other outlets including vending machines, gas stations, etc. may more than double these figures

Source: Information Resources, Inc.

TOP 10

BEN & JERRY'S ICE CREAM/FROZEN YOGURT FLAVORS

1	Chocolate Chip Cookie Dough
2	Cherry Garcia
3	Chocolate Fudge Brownie
4	New York Super Fudge Chunk
5	Cherry Garcia Frozen Yogurt
6	Chunky Monkey
7	Chocolate Fudge Brownie Frozen Yogurt
8	English Toffee Crunch
9	Peanut Butter Cup
10	Chubby Hubby

The late Grateful Dead founder Jerry Garcia is probably the only rock musician to have two bestselling ice cream or frozen yogurt varieties named in his honor.

FOOD FOR THOUGHT

T O P 1 0

CALORIE-CONSUMING COUNTRIES IN THE WORLD

	Country	Average daily consumption per capita
1	Ireland	3,847
2	Greece	3,815
3	Cyprus	3,779
4	US	3,732
5	Spain	3,708
6	Belgium/Luxembourg	3,681
7	New Zealand	3,669
8	Denmark	3,664
9	Portugal	3,634
10	France	3,633
	World average	*2,718*

The calorie requirement of the average man is 2,700 and of the average woman, 2,500. Inactive people need fewer Calories, and those engaged in heavy labor might need to increase, perhaps even to double these figures. Calories that are not consumed as energy are stored as fat – which is why Calorie-counting is one of the key aspects of most diets. The high Calorie intake of certain countries reflects the high proportion of starchy foods in the national diet. In many Western countries the high figures simply reflect overeating – especially since these figures are averages that include men, women, and children, suggesting that large numbers in each country are greatly exceeding them.

T O P 1 0

FOOD AND DRINK ITEMS CONSUMED IN THE US

	Item	Average annual consumption per capita	
		lb	oz
1	Fresh and processed vegetables	231	02
2	Milk and cream	225	11
3	Flour and cereal products (bread, breakfast cereals, etc.)	198	11
4	Meat, poultry, and fish	193	08
5	Sugar and sweeteners	147	10
6	Fruit (fresh, frozen, dried, and canned)	145	10
7	Potatoes (fresh, frozen, and sweet)	81	13
8	Oils and fats	69	13
9	Eggs	30	10
10	Frozen dairy products (ice cream, frozen yogurt, etc.)	30	00

The American passion for ice cream means that it comprises more than half the total of frozen dairy products. Falling just outside this Top 10 are cheese (26 lb 13 oz) and fish (15 lb 2 oz).

DID YOU KNOW

BIRTH OF THE BURGER

"Hamburger" first appeared in print on January 5, 1889, in the *Walla Walla Union*, a Washington State newspaper, concealed in a phrase that was itself a mouthful: "You are asked if you will have porkchopbeefsteakhamandegghamburgersteakorliverandbacon." The hamburger derives its name not from any ham content but from the German city of Hamburg, and was originally called a "Hamburg steak." A century ago a type of hamburger known as a "Salisbury steak" appeared. This was revived during World War I as part of an anti-German campaign in the UK.

T O P 1 0

FOOD AND DRINK ITEMS CONSUMED IN THE UK*

	Item	Average annual consumption per capita (1994)	
		lb	oz
1	Milk and cream	246	15
2	Vegetables (other than potatoes)	130	12
3	Meat	108	0
4	Potatoes	93	0
5	Bread	86	14
6	Fruit and nuts	83	5
7	Biscuits, cakes, cereals, etc.	46	8
8	Fruit juices	27	9
9=	Butter, oils, and fats	26	0
9=	Sugar and honey	26	0

* Excluding beer and other alcoholic drinks

The National Food Survey, on which this list is partly based, revealed that a number of changes in British eating habits had taken place during the 1980s. Most notable were a move from whole milk to other types, such as semiskimmed, and a more than 50 percent reduction in the amount of butter and sugar consumed.

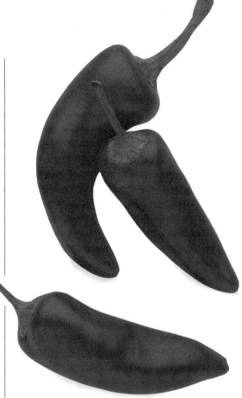

TOP 10

SUGAR-CONSUMING COUNTRIES IN THE WORLD

	Country	Annual consumption per capita	
		kg	lb
1	Swaziland	169.5	373.7
2	Singapore	79.8	175.9
3	Belize	62.6	138.0
4	Australia	61.2	134.9
5	Cuba	60.5	133.4
6	Iceland	60.2	132.7
7	Israel	57.7	127.2
8	Denmark	57.6	127.0
9	Barbados	57.5	126.8
10	Costa Rica	57.4	126.5

THE 10

DEGREES OF HOTNESS OF CHILIES

1	Delicate	6	Hot
2	Mild	7	Burning
3	Medium	8	Fiery
4	Warm	9	Incendiary
5	Piquant	10	Volcanic

It is said that Christopher Columbus "discovered" chili peppers on the island of Hispaniola in 1492, from where they were introduced to the rest of the world. Various scales have been devised for measuring the "hotness" of chilies, of which this is one.

TOP 10

PASTA PRODUCTS

	Pasta	Market share (%)
1	Spaghetti	26.0
2	Twists	18.0
3	Assorted shapes	13.5
4	Lasagne	9.2
5	Shells	9.0
6	Tagliatelle	8.0
7	Noodles	7.1
8	Macaroni	6.3
9	Tortellini	2.5
10	Cannelloni	0.4

TOP 10

LARGEST CHEESES EVER MADE

1 40,060 lb/18,171 kg

Making gigantic cheeses is not a modern eccentricity: in his Natural History, *the Roman historian Pliny the Elder describes a 1,000-lb/ 454-kg cheese that was made in the Tuscan town of Luni. The current world record holder is this monster Cheddar manufactured on March 13–14, 1988 by Simon's Specialty Cheese of Little Chute, Wisconsin.*

2 34,591 lb/15,690 kg

Made on January 20–22, 1964 for the World's Fair, New York, by the Wisconsin Cheese Foundation, it was 14½ ft /4.35 m long, 6½ ft/1.95 m wide, and 6 ft/1.8 m high. It took 183 tons of milk – equivalent to a day's output by a herd of 16,000 cows. It was toured and displayed until 1968, when it was cut up to be sold. As late as 1978 the last two chunks were sold at a charity auction for $200 each.

3 13,440 lb/6,096 kg

Using the milk from 6,000 cows, production started on July 12, 1937 and the cheese was exhibited at the New York State Fair.

4 11,815 lb/5,359 kg

This Cheddar was made in January 1957 in Flint, Michigan, from the milk pooled by a group of 367 farmers from their 6,600 cows.

5 8,000 lb/3,629 kg

This large Canadian Cheddar was made especially for the 1883 Toronto Fair.

6 1,474 lb/ 669 kg

A cheese 13 ft/3.90 m in circumference was made by James Elgar of Peterborough, UK, in 1849.

7 1,400 lb/653 kg

This Cheddar was given to President Jackson. After maturing for two years in the White House, it was given to the people of Washington, DC, on George Washington's birthday.

8= 1,200 lb/544 kg

A huge Cheshire presented to President Thomas Jefferson by a preacher, John Leland, in 1801, it was appropriately made by the town of Cheshire, Massachusetts.

8= 1,200 lb/544 kg

Made on March 3, 1989 in the village of West Pennard, Somerset, UK, by John Green to recreate the "Great Pennard Cheese" (see No. 10) and as an exhibit at the May 1989 Festival of British Food and Farming. It took 1,200 gallons/5,455 l of milk and measured 3 ft/75 cm in diameter.

10 1,100 lb/499 kg

This 9-ft/2.7-m circumference Cheddar, named the "Great Pennard Cheese" after the Somerset, UK, village in which it was made, was presented to Queen Victoria as a wedding gift in 1840. It was taken to London and exhibited, but on its return it was found to have suffered so much in the heat of the exhibition that the Queen refused to accept it.

ALCOHOLIC BEVERAGES

MOST EXPENSIVE BOTTLES OF WINE EVER SOLD AT AUCTION

	Wine/sale	Price ($)
1	Château Lafite 1787, Christie's, London, December 5, 1985	140,700

The highest price ever paid for a bottle of red wine resulted from the bottle having been initialled by Thomas Jefferson. Purchased by Christopher Forbes, it is now on display in the Forbes Magazine Galleries, New York.

	Wine/sale	Price ($)
2	Château d'Yquem 1784, Christie's, London, December 4, 1986	58,608

The highest price ever paid for a bottle of white wine.

	Wine/sale	Price ($)
3	Château Mouton-Rothschild 1945 (jeroboam – equivalent to four bottles), Christie's, Geneva, May 14, 1995	56,229

The highest price ever paid for a post-war wine.

	Wine/sale	Price ($)
4	Château Lafite Rothschild 1832 (double magnum), International Wine Auctions, London, April 9, 1988	40,320
5	Château Pétrus 1945 (jeroboam), Sotheby's, New York, September 16, 1995	37,375
6	Château Mouton Rothschild 1986 (Nebuchadnezzar – equivalent to 20 bottles), Sotheby's, New York, April 22, 1995	36,800
7	Château Lafite 1806, Sotheby's, Geneva, November 13, 1988	36,456

	Wine/sale	Price ($)
8	Château Lafite 1811 (tappit-hen – equivalent to three bottles), Christie's, London, June 23, 1988	33,600
9	Cheval-blanc 1947 (Imperial – equivalent to eight bottles), Christie's, London, December 1, 1994	33,248
10	Château Mouton Rothschild 1945 (jeroboam), Sotheby's, New York, February 4, 1995	31,050

As well as these high prices paid at auction, rare bottles of wine have also been sold privately for sums in excess of $38,750.

BEER-DRINKING COUNTRIES IN THE WORLD

	Country	Annual consumption per capita	
		liters	US pints
1	Czech Republic	160.6	338.1
2	Germany	139.6	295.0
3	Ireland	135.2	285.7
4	Luxembourg	122.9	259.7
5	Denmark	121.5	256.8
6	Austria	117.0	247.3
7	Slovakia	103.9	219.6
8	Hungary	103.0	217.7
9	UK	102.3	216.2
10	New Zealand	102.1	215.8

Perhaps surprisingly, despite its position as the world's leading producer of beer, the US is ranked outside this Top 10 in terms of consumption (180 pints per head/85.2 liters), beaten by such countries as Australia, Belgium, and the Netherlands.

ALCOHOL-DRINKING COUNTRIES IN THE WORLD

	Country	Annual consumption per capita (pure alcohol)	
		liters	quarts
1	Luxembourg	12.5	13.2
2	France	11.4	12.0
3	Portugal	10.7	11.3
4=	Germany	10.3	10.9
4=	Hungary	10.3	10.9
6	Czech Republic	10.1	10.7
7=	Austria	9.9	10.5
7=	Denmark	9.9	10.5
9=	Spain	9.7	10.3
9=	Switzerland	9.7	10.3
	US	*6.6*	*7.0*

After heading this list for many years – with a figure that peaked at 17.4 liters/18.4 quarts per head – France has been overtaken by Luxembourg, which is now acknowledged as the world's leading alcohol consumer.

NOT A GOOD YEAR

After surviving for over 200 years, the first entry in the "Most Expensive Bottles of Wine Ever Sold at Auction" list suffered a disastrous fate in New York. The world's most expensive single bottle was exhibited in a cabinet where the heat from the display light dried out the cork, allowing the contents to evaporate. Another bottle, a 1784 Château Margaux that had been bought by Jefferson when he was ambassador to France and that had his initials scratched into the glass, was sold at auction in 1987. Its Presidential association had increased its post-auction price tag to $500,000, and an offer of nearly $300,000 had been refused. On April 25, 1989 it was on show at a tasting in the Four Seasons restaurant, New York, when it was inadvertently smashed by a waiter's tray. A small quantity of the wine was salvaged, but, as the wine merchant who drank it reported, "It tasted like it still had wine taste, but not very good." Fortunately, it was insured.

TOP 10

LARGEST BREWERIES IN THE WORLD

	Brewery	Location	Annual sales liters	US gallons
1	Anheuser-Busch, Inc.	US	10,430,000,000	2,755,314,640
2	Heineken NV	Netherlands	5,350,000,000	1,413,320,550
3	Miller Brewing Co.	US	5,260,000,000	1,389,545,060
4	Kirin Brewery Co. Ltd.	Japan	3,240,000,000	885,917,490
5	Foster's Brewing Group	Australia	3,050,000,000	805,724,800
6	Companhia Cervejaria Brahma	Brazil	2,530,000,000	668,355,330
7	Groupe BSN	France	2,500,000,000	660,430,160
8	Coors Brewing Co.	US	2,370,000,000	626,087,795
9	South Africa Breweries Ltd.	South Africa	2,270,000,000	599,670,600
10	Companhia Antartica Paulista	Brazil	2,000,000,000	528,344,130

TOP 10

DISTILLED SPIRIT-DRINKING NATIONS IN THE WORLD

	Country	Annual consumption per capita liters	quarts		Country	Annual consumption per capita liters	quarts
1	Russia	4.40	4.65	6	Bulgaria	2.84	3.00
2	China	4.02	4.02	7	Greece	2.80	2.96
3	Poland	3.50	3.70	8	Spain	2.50	2.64
4	Cyprus	3.30	3.49	9	France	2.49	2.63
5	Hungary	3.06	3.23	10	Germany	2.40	2.54

TOP 10

WINE PRODUCERS IN THE US

	Producer	Storage capacity (US gallons)
1	E. & J. Gallo Winery	330,000,000
2	Canandaigua Wine Co.	186,300,000
3	Grand Metropolitan/ Heublein	112,000,000
4	Vie-Del Company	59,200,000
5	The Wine Group	56,000,000
6	Bronco	43,800,000
7	Delicato Vineyards	40,000,000
8	Golden State Vintners	35,660,000
9	Korbel & Bros/ Heck Cellars	34,000,000
10	Robert Mondavi Winery	18,760,000

TOP 10

WINE-DRINKING COUNTRIES IN THE WORLD

	Country	Liters per capita per annum	Equiv. 75 cl bottles
1	France	62.5	83.3
2	Luxembourg	60.5	80.7
3	Italy	58.5	78.0
4	Portugal	50.7	67.6
5	Switzerland	44.3	59.1
6	Argentina	43.2	57.6
7	Greece	33.8	45.1
8	Hungary	33.1	44.1
9	Austria	32.8	43.7
10	Spain	32.2	42.9

TOP 10

IMPORTERS OF SCOTCH* IN THE WORLD

	Country	Annual imports liters	quarts
1	US	101,100,000	106,831,183
2	France	58,990,000	62,334,041
3	Spain	51,350,000	54,260,942
4	Japan	40,570,000	42,869,843
5	Venezuela	23,060,000	24,367,548
6	Germany	22,690,000	23,976,257
7	Greece	22,460,000	23,733,218
8	Australia	18,640,000	19,696,669
9	South Africa	16,240,000	17,160,617
10	Italy	16,070,000	16,980,980

Including Northern Irish whiskey

More than 100 years ago, the expensive processes of distilling malt whisky and maturing it for several years were joined by the scientific blending of different grain and malt Scotch whiskies to achieve a consistent and less costly result. The unique brands that were produced by this method became recognized worldwide, establishing a major export business that continues to flourish today.

TOP 10

COUNTRIES THAT HAVE INCREASED THEIR WINE CONSUMPTION

	Country	Change in consumption 1970–94 (%)
1	Denmark	343.5
2	UK	333.7
3	Ireland	264.5
4	Japan	243.8
5	Netherlands	204.7
6	New Zealand	186.5
7	Iceland	174.3
8	Finland	166.6
9	Norway	156.4
10	Algeria	114.3

SOFT DRINKS

T O P   1 0

BOTTLED WATER BRANDS IN THE US

	Brand	1994 sales ($)
1	Arrowhead	235,400,000
2	Poland Spring	167,000,000
3	Evian	154,500,000
4	Sparklets	152,000,000
5	Hinckley-Schmitt	108,000,000
6	Ozarka	79,300,000
7	Zephyrhills	75,100,000
8	Alpine Springs	67,500,000
9	Mountain Valley	59,800,000
10	Perrier	56,600,000

Source: Beverage Marketing Corporation

T O P   1 0

MILK-DRINKING COUNTRIES IN THE WORLD

	Country*	Annual consumption per capita	
		liters	quarts
1	Iceland	174.2	184.0
2	Finland	165.1	179.5
3	Norway	142.9	151.0
4	Sweden	122.5	129.4
5	Spain	111.6	117.9
6	UK	111.5	117.8
7	Denmark	111.3	117.6
8	Switzerland	98.3	103.9
9	New Zealand	97.9	103.4
10	Australia	95.6	101.0

* Those reporting to the International Dairy Federation only

T O P   1 0

TEA-DRINKING COUNTRIES IN THE WORLD

	Country	Annual consumption per capita			
		kg	lb	oz	cups*
1	Irish Republic	3.21	7	01	1,412
2	UK	2.60	5	12	1,144
3	Kuwait	2.14	4	12	942
4	Turkey	2.08	4	09	915
5	Qatar	1.94	4	04	854
6	Syria	1.67	3	11	735
7	Hong Kong	1.62	3	09	713
8=	Iran	1.46	3	03	642
8=	Tunisia	1.46	3	03	642
10	Bahrain	1.30	2	14	572
	US	0.35	0	12	154

* Based on 440 cups per kg/2 lb 3 oz

Notwithstanding the UK's traditional passion for tea, during recent years its consumption has consistently lagged behind that of Ireland. In the same period, Qatar's tea consumption has dropped from its former world record of 8 lb 12 oz/3.97 kg (1,747 cups) per head. Within Europe, consumption varies enormously from the current world-leading Irish figure down to just 3 oz/0.09 kg (40 cups) in Italy, while in the rest of the world, Thailand's 0.4 oz/0.01 kg (4 cups) is one of the lowest.

T O P   1 0

COFFEE-DRINKING COUNTRIES IN THE WORLD

	Country	Annual consumption per capita			
		kg	lb	oz	cups*
1	Finland	12.38	27	05	1,857
2	Sweden	11.44	25	03	1,716
3	Norway	11.32	24	15	1,698
4	Denmark	10.48	23	02	1,572
5	Netherlands	8.28	18	04	1,242
6	Austria	8.16	18	00	1,224
7	Switzerland	8.10	17	15	1,215
8	Germany	7.42	16	05	1,113
9	France	5.32	11	11	798
10	Italy	5.00	11	00	750
	US	4.07	8	00	610

* Based on 150 cups per kg/2 lb 3 oz

The coffee consumption of many countries declined during the 1980s – that of Belgium and Luxembourg went down by almost 70 percent, from 15 lb 13 oz/7.17 kg (1,076 cups) in 1986 to 5 lb 0 oz/2.27 kg (341 cups) in 1990, but has recently risen again. That of both Finland and Sweden has remained high, however. Ireland's consumption is the EC's lowest, at 4lb 9oz/2.08 kg (312 cups) – but as the comparative table shows, the country more than compensates with its preeminence in tea-drinking.

TOP 10

CONSUMERS OF PERRIER WATER IN THE WORLD

1	France
2	US
3	UK
4	Belgium
5	Canada
6	Germany
7	Middle East
8	Hong Kong
9	Switzerland
10	Greece

In 1903 St. John Harmsworth, a wealthy Englishman on a tour of France, visited Vergèze, a spa town near Nîmes. Its spring, Les Bouillens (which was believed to have been discovered by the Carthaginian soldier Hannibal *c.* 218 BC), was notable for the occurrence of carbon dioxide, which is released from the surrounding rock, permeating through the water and making it "naturally sparkling." Harmsworth recognized the potential for selling the spa water and proceeded to buy the spring, naming it after its former owner, Dr. Louis Perrier, a local doctor, and bottling it in distinctive green bottles said to have been modeled on the Indian clubs with which he exercised. The company was sold back to the French in 1948 (and in 1992 the firm was bought by the Swiss company Nestlé). Perrier water has maintained a reputation as a popular drink in sophisticated circles. In 1960, in the book *For Your Eyes Only*, Ian Fleming even has James Bond drink it – "He always stipulated Perrier. . . ." In the late 1970s a combination of increased health consciousness and advertising and marketing enabled Perrier to broaden its appeal and to achieve its world dominance of the burgeoning mineral water business. Perrier is now drunk in 145 countries around the world, and its name has become synonymous with mineral water. The strength of US sales of Perrier, and the cachet and brand profile attaching to it, are all the more remarkable when the economics of shipping water across the Atlantic Ocean are considered, while through its ownership of other companies, the Perrier Group's share of the US bottled water market is a dominant 23.2 percent, considerably ahead of all its competitors.

TOP 10

SOFT-DRINK CONSUMERS IN THE WORLD

	Country	Annual consumption per capita liters	quarts
1	Switzerland	105.0	111.0
2	Barbados	81.4	86.0
3	Bahamas	75.0	79.3
4	USA	74.7	78.4
5	Australia	73.9	78.1
6	Germany	72.0	76.1
7	Canada	69.3	73.2
8=	Belgium	65.0	68.7
8=	Japan	65.0	68.7
10	Singapore	61.4	64.9

As one might expect, affluent Western countries feature prominently in this list. Despite the spread of the so-called "Coca-Cola culture," former Eastern Bloc and Third World countries rank very low – some African nations recording consumption of less than one liter/1.06 quarts per annum.

TOP 10

SOFT DRINKS IN THE US

	Brand	1994 sales (gallons)*
1	Coca-Cola Classic	2,621,000,000
2	Pepsi	2,066,000,000
3	Diet Coke	1,268,000,000
4	Dr. Pepper	768,000,000
5	Diet Pepsi	760,000,000
6	Mountain Dew	683,000,000
7	Sprite	581,000,000
8	7-Up	381,000,000
9	Caffeine Free Diet Coke	265,000,000
10	Caffeine Free Diet Pepsi	153,000,000

* *Wholesale sales*
Source: Beverage Marketing Corporation

A total of 13,275,000,000 gallons of soft drinks was sold in the US in 1994. Such is the international nature of the soft drinks market that a comparative British list would show Coca-Cola, Pepsi, and 7-Up in identical positions. Alongside them in a UK list, however, would be long-established domestic brands that include Lucozade, which dates from the 1930s, and Schweppes products that have been sold for more than 200 years.

TOP 10

CONSUMERS OF COCA-COLA

	Country	Servings consumed per person (1995)
1	USA	343
2	Mexico	322
3	Germany	201
4=	Argentina	179
4=	Spain	179
6	South Africa	147
7	Japan	136
8	Brazil	122
9	UK	114
10	Philippines	105

The first Coca-Cola was served in Jacob's Pharmacy, a drug store in Atlanta, Georgia, on May 8, 1886, the creation of pharmacist Dr. John Styth Pemberton (1831–88). Three weeks after its launch, the first advertisement appeared in the *Atlanta Journal*, describing Coca-Cola as "Delicious! Refreshing! Exhilarating! Invigorating!" The new drink proved an immediate success – especially after a local Prohibition Act of July 1886 banned alcohol. "Coke," as it became know, was first served in bottles in 1894.

TRANSPORTATION & TOURISM

20TH CENTURY

When the 20th century started, the car was just five years old and still something of a rarity: in 1900, just 4,192 cars were sold in the entire US, while today annual sales of cars and commercial vehicles in the US top 12 million. Cars have gone from being luxuries to being commonplace in most countries, with more than 600 million vehicles on the world's roads. Their impact is such that road-traffic safety and environmental issues have become important international concerns.

TOP 10

VEHICLE-OWNING COUNTRIES IN THE WORLD

	Country	Cars	Commercial vehicles	Total registered vehicles
1	US	146,314,296	47,722,186	194,036,482
2	Japan	40,772,325	22,590,209	63,362,534
3	Germany	39,202,066	2,687,225	41,889,291
4	Italy	29,600,000	2,745,500	32,345,500
5	France	24,385,000	5,065,000	29,450,000
6	UK	23,402,347	3,603,518	27,005,865
7	Commonwealth of Independent States (CIS)	13,549,000	9,856,000	23,405,000
8	Canada	13,477,896	3,712,486	17,190,382
9	Spain	13,440,694	2,859,438	16,300,132
10	Brazil	11,613,000	3,246,800	14,859,800
	World total	*469,460,221*	*147,626,840*	*617,087,061*

Three-quarters of the world's vehicles are registered in the Top 10 countries. Of this number, some 227,079,966 are in Europe, 226,653,590 are in North America, 107,544,327 are in Asia, 27,754,370 are in South America, 14,873,241 are in Africa, and 13,181,567 are in Oceania. Outside this Top 10, only two countries (Mexico and Australia) have more than 10,000,000 vehicles. In the years from 1960 to 1994 world motor vehicle ownership increased almost fivefold, from a total of 126,954,817. As vehicles have proliferated, the ratio of people to vehicles has fallen from 23 in 1960 to nine people per vehicle today. In car-conscious and affluent countries the ratio is much higher: 1.3 per vehicle in the US and 2.2 in the UK. A few small countries, such as San Marino, claim the equivalent of more than one vehicle per person. The biggest disparities naturally occur in the least developed economies, with 177 people per vehicle in India, 195 in China, 998 in Ethiopia, and 1,814 in Bangladesh. In the car ownership stakes, Bangladesh also scores worst, with 3,792 people per car, contrasting with the UK's 2.5 and the US's 1.8. Only rarely do numbers of commercial vehicles outnumber those of cars, but this is true in China, which has two-and-a-half times as many trucks as cars. Despite having the greatest population of any country, it has just one car for every 676 people.

ON THE ROAD

VOLKSWAGEN BEETLE

TOP 10

BESTSELLING CARS OF ALL TIME

	Model/year first produced	Estimated no. made
1	Volkswagen Beetle, 1937*	21,220,000
2	Toyota Corolla, 1963	20,000,000
3	Ford Model T, 1908	15,007,033
4	Volkswagen Rabbit, 1974	14,800,000
5	Lada Riva, 1970	13,500,000
6	Ford Escort/Orion, 1967	12,000,000
7	Nissan Pulsar/Sunny, 1966	10,200,000
8	Mazda 323, 1977	9,500,000
9	Renault 4, 1961	8,100,000
10	Honda Civic, 1972	8,000,000

* Still produced in Mexico and Brazil

THE 10

FIRST COUNTRIES TO MAKE SEAT BELTS COMPULSORY

	Country	Introduced
1	Czechoslovakia	Jan 1969
2	Ivory Coast	Jan 1970
3	Japan	Dec 1971
4	Australia	Jan 1972
5=	Brazil	Jun 1972
5=	New Zealand	Jun 1972
7	Puerto Rico	Jan 1974
8	Spain	Oct 1974
9	Sweden	Jan 1975
10=	Netherlands	Jun 1975
10=	Belgium	Jun 1975
10=	Luxembourg	Jun 1975

Seat belts, long in use in aircraft, were not designed for use in private cars until the 1950s. Ford was the first manufacturer in Europe to fit anchorage-points, and belts were first fitted as standard equipment in Swedish Volvos from 1959. They were optional extras in most cars until the 1970s.

TOP 10

FASTEST PRODUCTION CARS IN THE WORLD

	Model	Maximum speed km/h	mph
1	Jaguar XJ220	349	217
2	Lamborghini Diablo	325	202
3	Ferrari Testarossa	290	180
4=	Ferrari 348ts	277	172
4=	Ferrari 348tb	277	172
6	Porsche 928 GT	274	170
7	Porsche 911 Turbo	270	168
8	Porsche 928S Series 4	266	165
9	Porsche 911 Carrera 2	259	161
10=	Lotus Esprit Turbo SE	257	160
10=	TVR 450SEAC	257	160

This list excludes production models that are no longer available, such as the 197 mph/317 km/h Porsche 959 and the 186 mph/299 km/h Aston Martin Zagato; "souped up" versions of production cars; and "limited edition" cars such as the Ferrari F40, which is said to be capable of 201 mph/323 km/h.

TOP 10

COUNTRIES WITH THE LONGEST ROAD NETWORKS

	Country	km	miles
1	US	6,243,103	3,879,284
2	India	1,970,000	1,224,101
3	Brazil	1,670,148	1,037,782
4	France	1,511,200	939,016
5	Japan	1,111,974	690,949
6	China	1,029,000	639,391
7	Russia	934,000	580,361
8	Canada	849,404	527,795
9	Australia	837,872	520,629
10	Germany	636,282	395,367

TOP 10

COMMERCIAL VEHICLE-OWNING COUNTRIES

	Country	Commercial vehicles		Country	Commercial vehicles
1	US	47,722,186	6	Mexico	3,797,000
2	CIS	23,405,000	7	Canada	3,712,486
3	Japan	22,590,209	8	UK	3,603,518
4	France	5,065,000	9	Brazil	3,246,800
5	China	4,349,218	10	Spain	2,859,438

UAE 576

IN THE AIR

20TH CENTURY

No century in history has witnessed change at the rate it has occurred in the 20th century, and this is no more evident than in the rise of public air transportation. At the turn of the century ships and trains were the only means by which one could travel long distances in comfort and safety, so usually only the wealthy undertook long journeys. Since the arrival of the world's airlines in the 1930s, however, this pattern has changed dramatically. Today the US leads the world among airline users, each year carrying 515 million passengers a total of 511 billion passenger miles on scheduled flights – a distance equivalent to more than one million return trips to the moon.

TOP 10

BUSIEST AIRPORTS IN THE WORLD

	Airport	Location	Terminal passengers per annum*
1	Chicago O'Hare	Chicago	65,091,000
2	Dallas/Ft. Worth International	Dallas/Ft. Worth	49,655,000
3	LA International	Los Angeles	47,845,000
4	Hartsfield Atlanta International	Atlanta	47,775,000
5	London Heathrow	London	47,602,000
6	Tokyo-Haneda International	Tokyo, Japan	41,507,000
7	San Francisco International	San Francisco	32,769,000
8	Stapleton International	Denver	32,627,000
9	Frankfurt	Frankfurt, Germany	31,945,000
10	Miami International	Miami	28,660,000

* *International and domestic flights*

CHICAGO O'HARE AIRPORT
Like the other six US airports in the world's 10 busiest, O'Hare handles mainly domestic passengers. Only JFK sees enough international flights to put it in the international Top 10.

TOP 10

BUSIEST AIRPORTS IN EUROPE

	Airport	Location	Passengers per annum
1	London Heathrow	London, UK	47,602,000
2	Frankfurt	Frankfurt, Germany	31,945,000
3	Charles de Gaulle	Paris, France	25,695,000
4	Orly	Paris, France	25,251,000
5	Schiphol	Amsterdam, Netherlands	20,770,000
6	London Gatwick	London, UK	20,065,000
7	Fiumicino	Rome, Italy	19,370,000
8	Madrid	Madrid, Spain	17,339,000
9	Zurich	Zurich, Switzerland	13,130,000
10	Düsseldorf	Düsseldorf, Germany	12,922,000

TOP 10

AIRLINES IN THE WORLD

	Airline/location	Aircraft in service	Passenger miles flown per annum*
1	United Airlines (US)	564	107,989,400,000
2	American Airlines (US)	665	98,711,000,000
3	Delta Airlines (US)	566	86,276,700,000
4	Northwest Airlines (US)	366	57,837,000,000
5	British Airways (UK)	214	52,181,750,000
6	Aeroflot (Russia)	n/a	39,911,500,000
7	JAL (Japan)	121	39,105,500,000
8	USAir (US)	509	37,930,800,000
9	Continental Airlines (US)	307	37,500,600,000
10	Lufthansa (Germany)	218	35,128,250,000

* *Total distance traveled by aircraft multiplied by number carried*

TOP 10

BUSIEST AIRPORTS IN THE US

	Airport	Total passengers* (1994)
1	Chicago O'Hare	31,285,725
2	Dallas/Ft. Worth (Regional)	26,229,812
3	Hartsfield Atlanta International	26,126,457
4	Los Angeles International	25,081,546
5	San Francisco International	16,544,351
6	Denver (Stapleton International)	15,772,858
7	Miami	14,742,476
8	Newark	13,944,647
9	JFK International	13,916,470
10	Detroit	12,996,818

Source: Federal Aviation Administration

* Departures only

TOP 10

BUSIEST INTERNATIONAL AIRPORTS IN THE WORLD

	Airport/location	International passengers* per annum
1	London Heathrow, UK	40,848,000
2	Frankfurt, Germany	25,119,000
3	Hong Kong International	24,421,000
4	Charles de Gaulle, France	22,336,000
5	Schiphol, Amsterdam, Netherlands	20,658,000
6	Tokyo/Narita, Japan	18,947,000
7	Singapore International	18,796,000
8	London Gatwick, UK	18,656,000
9	JFK International, New York	14,821,000
10	Bangkok, Thailand	12,789,000

* Departures and arrivals

TOP 10

INTERNATIONAL FLIGHT ROUTES WITH MOST AIR TRAFFIC

	City A	City B	Passengers per route A to B	B to A	Total passengers
1	London	Paris	1,637,000	1,728,000	3,365,000
2	Hong Kong	Taipei	1,227,000	1,161,000	2,388,000
3	London	New York	1,204,000	1,182,000	2,386,000
4	Kuala Lumpur	Singapore	1,161,000	1,109,000	2,270,000
5	Seoul	Tokyo	980,000	964,000	1,944,000
6	Honolulu	Tokyo	949,000	946,000	1,895,000
7	Hong Kong	Tokyo	908,000	891,000	1,799,000
8	Bangkok	Hong Kong	899,000	880,000	1,779,000
9	Amsterdam	London	877,000	877,000	1,754,000
10	Dublin	London	773,000	787,000	1,560,000

TOP 10

COUNTRIES WITH THE MOST AIRPORTS

	Country	Airports
1	US	15,032
2	Brazil	3,467
3	Russia	2,517
4	Mexico	1,841
5	Argentina	1,602
6	Canada	1,386
7	Bolivia	1,382
8	Colombia	1,307
9	Paraguay	929
10	South Africa	853

Airports, as defined by the Central Intelligence Agency (which monitors them for strategic reasons), range in size and quality from those with paved runways over 10,000 ft/3,048 m in length to those with only short landing strips. Among European countries, those with the most airports are Germany (660) and the UK (505).

HIGH-FLYING FLEET
American Airlines has more aircraft than any other airline, but United Airlines achieve the highest number of passenger miles flown.

ON THE RIGHT TRACK

FIRST COUNTRIES WITH RAILROADS

	Country	First railroad established
1	UK	September 27, 1825
2	France	November 7, 1829
3	US	May 24, 1830
4	Ireland	December 17, 1834
5	Belgium	May 5, 1835
6	Germany	December 7, 1835
7	Canada	July 21, 1836
8	Russia	October 30, 1837
9	Austria	January 6, 1838
10	Netherlands	September 24, 1839

Although there were earlier horse-drawn railroads, the Stockton and Darlington Railway in the north of England inaugurated the world's first steam service. In their early years some of these listed here offered only limited services over short distances, but their opening dates mark the generally accepted beginning of each country's steam railroad system. By 1850, railroads had also begun operating in several other countries, including Italy, Hungary, Denmark, and Spain.

SURVIVING STEAM LOCOMOTIVES IN THE US

	Class	No. surviving
1	2-8-0	206
2	0-4-0	202
3	0-6-0	143
4	2-8-2	131
5	4-6-0	108
6	2-6-0	83
7	2-6-2	78
8	4-6-2	76
9	Shay	74
10	4-4-0	58

The number of surviving steam locomotives bears a close relation to the numbers of each class built – in the case of the 2-8-0s, some 21,000. Of these survivors, only a relatively small number are operational – again led by the 2-8-0s with 35 functioning examples, down to just 12 in the case of the 4-4-0s. There are instances of classes built in thousands, such as 2,200 2-10-2s, where fewer than 10 have survived and none are operational. The Shay was a geared, rather than wheeled, locomotive, introduced in 1880 and designed for steep gradients.

FIRST BRITISH TRAINS TO EXCEED 100MPH

	Train/railway	Date
1	*City of Truro*, GW	May 9, 1904
2	*Flying Scotsman*, LNER	Nov 30, 1934
3	*Papyrus*, LNER	Mar 5, 1935
4	*Silver Link*, LNER	Sep 27, 1935
5	*Silver Fox*, LNER	Aug 27, 1936
6	*Coronation Scot*, LMS	Jun 29, 1937
7	*Dominion of Canada*, LNER	Jun 30, 1937
8	*Commonwealth of Australia*, LNER	Aug 1937
9	*Mallard*, LNER	Jul 3, 1938
10	*Builth Castle*, GWR	Jul 31, 1939

The first train in the world to exceed 100 mph/160.9 km/h was the *Empire State Express* on the run from Syracuse to Buffalo, NY, on May 9, 1893, when a maximum of 102.8 mph/165.4 km/h was recorded. There is some controversy over the *City of Truro*'s early claim of 102.3 mph/164.6 km/h (said to have been attained descending Wellington's Bank on the Plymouth to Bristol line), although 100 mph/160.9 km/h seems probable and hence qualifies it as the first British train to exceed the magic 100 mph. The *Flying Scotsman*'s claim is similarly questioned by some authorities. *Mallard*'s remarkable 126 mph/202.8 km/h remains the world speed record for a steam locomotive and was not surpassed in the UK until June 12, 1973, when the British prototype *High Speed Train* achieved 143.0 mph/230.1 km/h. The current world record is held by the French TGV, which clocked 320.0 mph/515.0 km/h on May 18, 1990.

COUNTRIES WITH THE FASTEST RAIL JOURNEYS*

	Country/journey/train	Distance km	miles	Speed km/h	mph
1	France, Paris–Lille (TGV 587)	204.2	126.9	250.0	155.3
2	Japan, Hiroshima-Kokuru (31 *Nozomi*)	192.0	119.3	230.4	143.2
3	Spain, Madrid-Ciudad Real (AVE 9744)	170.7	106.1	217.9	135.4
4	Germany, Fulda–Kassel (ICE *Frankfurter Römer*)	90.0	55.9	200.0	124.3
5	UK, Stevenage–Doncaster (InterCity 225)	206.6	128.4	177.1	110.0
6	Sweden, Hallsberg–Skövde (X2000 429)	113.8	70.7	175.1	108.8
7	Italy, Rome-Florence (*Cristoforo Colombo*)	261.9	162.7	162.0	100.7
8	US, Baltimore-Wilmington (*Metroliner*)	110.1	68.4	153.6	95.4
9	Canada, Toronto-Dorval (*Metropolis*)	519.5	322.8	144.3	89.7
10	Russia, St. Petersburg-Moscow (ER 200)	649.9	403.8	130.4	81.0

* *Fastest journey for each country; all those in this Top 10 have other services that are sometimes just as fast*

TOP 10

LONGEST UNDERGROUND RAIL NETWORKS IN THE WORLD

	Location	Opened	Stations	Total track length km	miles
1	London, UK	1863	270	401	251
2	New York, US	1904	469	398	249
3	Paris, France*	1900	432	323	202
4	Tokyo, Japan#	1927	250	289	181
5	Moscow, Russia	1935	150	244	153
6	Mexico City, Mexico	1969	154	178	112
7	Chicago, US	1943	138	173	108
8	Copenhagen, Denmark✛	1934	79	170	106
9	Berlin, Germany	1902	135	167	104
10	Seoul, Korea	1974	130	165	103

* *Metro + RER* \# *Through-running extensions raise total to 391 miles/683 km, with 502 stations*
✛ *Only partly undergound*

NEW YORK'S SUBTERRANEAN LABYRINTH
The New York subway runs a close second among the world's longest underground railroad networks and has the most stations.

TOP 10

OLDEST UNDERGROUND RAILROAD SYSTEMS IN THE WORLD

	Location	Opened
1	London, UK	1863
2	Budapest, Hungary	1896
3	Glasgow, UK	1896
4	Boston, US	1897
5	Paris, France	1900
6	Wuppertal, Germany	1901
7	Berlin, Germany	1902
8	New York, US	1904
9	Philadelphia, US	1907
10	Hamburg, Germany	1912

TOP 10

LONGEST RAIL NETWORKS IN THE WORLD

	Location	Total rail length km	miles
1	US	240,000	149,129
2	Russia	154,000	95,691
3	Canada	78,148	48,559
4	China	65,780	40,874
5	India	62,211	38,656
6	Germany	45,457	28,246
7	Australia	40,478	25,152
8	France	34,572	21,482
9	Argentina	34,074	21,173
10	Brazil	30,612	19,021

US rail mileage has declined considerably since its 1916 peak of 254,000 miles/408,773 km. The total of all world networks is today reckoned to be 746,476 miles/1,201,337 km.

TRAIN A GRANDE VITESSE
The current world rail speed record is held by the French TGV, which on May 18, 1990 reached 320 mph/515 km/h.

TOP 10

LONGEST RAIL PLATFORMS IN THE WORLD

	Station	Platform length m	ft
1	Washington–Monroe– Jackson platform, Chicago	1,067	3,500
2	Kharagpur, India	833	2,733
3	Perth, Australia	762	2,500
4	Sonepur, India	736	2,415
5	Bournemouth, UK	720	2,362
6	Bulawayo, Zimbabwe	702	2,302
7	New Lucknow, India	686	2,250
8	Bezwada, India	640	2,100
9	Gloucester, UK	624	2,047
10	Jhansi, India	617	2,025

The presence of India in five out of the 10 entries in this list emphasizes the importance of the railroads in the daily life of the country. India's first railroad opened on April 18, 1853, since when the network has grown to become the fifth longest in the world, today providing more than three-and-a-half billion passenger journeys a year.

LAND TRANSPORTATION DISASTERS

THE 10

WORST MOTOR VEHICLE AND ROAD DISASTERS IN THE WORLD

	Location/date/incident	No. killed
1	Afghanistan, November 3, 1982	2,000+

Following a collision with a Soviet army truck, a gasoline tanker exploded in the 1.7-mile/2.7-km long Salang Tunnel. Some authorities estimate that the death toll could be as high as 3,000.

2	Colombia, August 7, 1956	1,200

Seven army ammunition trucks exploded at night in the center of the city of Cali, destroying eight city blocks.

3	Thailand, February 15, 1990	150+

A dynamite truck exploded.

4	Nepal, November 23 1974	148

Hindu pilgrims were killed when a suspension bridge over the River Mahahali collapsed.

5	Egypt, August 9, 1973	127

A bus drove into an irrigation canal.

6	Togo, December 6, 1965	125+

Two trucks collided with a group of dancers during a festival at Sotouboua.

7	Spain, July 11, 1978	120+

A liquid gas tanker exploded in a camping site at San Carlos de la Rapita.

	Location/date/incident	No. killed
8	Gambia, November 12, 1992	c. 100

A bus full of passengers plunged into a river when its brakes failed.

9	Kenya, early December 1992	nearly 100

A bus carrying 112 passengers skidded, hit a bridge, and plunged into a river.

10=	Lesotho, December 16, 1976	90

A bus fell into the Tsoaing River.

10=	India, March 16, 1988	90

In the state of Madhya Pradesh, the driver of a bus carrying a wedding party lost control of the vehicle and crashed while trying to change a tape cassette.

The worst-ever accident involving a single car occurred on December 17, 1956, when eight adults and four children were killed when their car was hit by a train in Phoenix, Arizona. Although hurled into a tree, a 20-month-old baby survived.

THE 10

US STATES WITH THE HIGHEST NUMBER OF ROAD DEATHS

	State	Total deaths (1995)
1	California	4,175
2	Texas	3,130
3	Florida	2,855
4	New York	1,680
5	Illinois	1,565
6	Michigan	1,520
7	Pennsylvania	1,480
8	Georgia	1,475
9	North Carolina	1,430
10	Ohio	1,360

While they have the greatest number of motor vehicle deaths, most of the states appearing are also among the nation's foremost vehicle users, and if this is taken into account they have fatality rates below the national average. The highest rates actually occur in states with relatively few vehicles, including Alaska, Arkansas, Mississippi, Nevada, and New Mexico. Connecticut and Massachusetts have the lowest rates of all. Total road deaths in the US in 1994 amounted to 41,700.

THE 10

COUNTRIES WITH THE HIGHEST NUMBER OF ROAD DEATHS

	Country	Total deaths*
1	US	41,700
2	Japan	14,886
3	Germany	10,631
4	France	9,900
5	Italy	8,029
6	Poland	7,901
7	Spain	7,818
8	Turkey	6,189
9	UK	3,650
10	Canada	3,485

* In latest year for which figures are available

WORST RAIL DISASTERS IN THE WORLD

Location/date/incident	No. killed
1 Bagmati River, India, June 6, 1981	c. 800

The cars of a train plunged off a bridge when the engineer braked, apparently to avoid a sacred cow. Rescuers recovered 268 bodies, but it has been claimed that the train was so full that in reality over 800 died, making it probably the worst rail disaster of all time.

| **2** Chelyabinsk, Russia, June 3, 1989 | up to 800 |

Two Trans-Siberian passenger trains, going to and from the Black Sea, were destroyed when liquid gas from a nearby pipeline exploded.

| **3** Guadalajara, Mexico, January 18, 1915 | 600+ |

A train derailed on a steep incline, but details of the disaster were suppressed.

| **4** Modane, France, December 12, 1917 | 573 |

A troop-carrying train ran out of control and was derailed. It was probably overloaded, and as many as 1,000 people may have died.

| **5** Balvano, Italy, March 2, 1944 | 521 |

Passengers were asphyxiated when a train stalled in the Armi Tunnel. Wartime secrecy prevented true figures from being declared.

| **6** Torre, Spain, January 3, 1944 | 500+ |

A double collision and fire in a tunnel caused many deaths. Wartime secrecy prevented full details from being published.

| **7** Awash, Ethiopia, January 13, 1985 | 428 |

A derailment hurled a train laden with some 1,000 passengers into a ravine.

| **8** Cireau, Romania, January 7, 1917 | 374 |

An overcrowded passenger train crashed into a military train and was derailed. In addition to the high death toll, 756 were injured.

| **9** Quipungo, Angola, May 31, 1993 | 355 |

A train was derailed by UNITA guerrilla action.

| **10** Sangi, Pakistan, January 4, 1990 | 306 |

A train was diverted onto the wrong line, resulting in a fatal collision.

Casualty figures for rail accidents are often very imprecise, especially during wartime. Uncertain cases have been omitted.

WORST RAIL DISASTERS IN THE US

Location/date/incident	No. killed
1 Nashville, Tennessee, July 9, 1918	101

On the Nashville, Chattanooga, and St. Louis Railroad, a head-on collision resulted in a death toll that remains the worst in US history, with 171 injured.

| **2** Brooklyn, New York, November 2, 1918 | 97 |

A subway train was derailed in the Malbone Street tunnel.

| **3=** Eden, Colorado, August 7, 1904 | 96 |

A bridge washed away during a flood smashed Steele's Hollow Bridge as the "World's Fair Express" was crossing.

| **3=** Wellington, Washington, March 1, 1910 | 96 |

An avalanche swept two trains into a canyon.

| **5** Bolivar, Texas, September 8, 1900 | 85 |

A train traveling from Beaumont encountered the hurricane that destroyed Galveston, killing 6,000. Attempts to load the train on to a ferry were abandoned, and it turned back but was destroyed by the storm.

| **6** Woodbridge, New Jersey, February 6, 1951 | 84 |

A Pennsylvania Railroad train crashed while speeding through a sharply curving detour.

| **7** Chatsworth, Illinois, August 10, 1887 | 82 |

A trestle bridge caught fire and collapsed as the Toledo, Peoria, & Western train was passing over. As many as 372 were injured.

| **8** Ashtabula, Ohio, December 29, 1876 | 80 |

A bridge collapsed in a snow storm, and the Lake Shore train fell into the Ashtabula river. The death toll may have been as high as 92.

| **9=** Frankford Junction, Pennsylvania, September 6, 1943 | 79 |

Pennsylvania's worst railroad accident (since that at Camp Hill on July 17, 1856 when two trains crashed, resulting in the deaths of 66 school children on a church picnic outing).

| **9=** Queens, New York, November 22, 1950 | 79 |

A Long Island Railroad commuter train rammed into the rear of another, leaving 79 dead and 363 injured.

THE FIRST RAILROAD PASSENGER DEATH

On September 15, 1830, British MP William Huskisson attended the opening of the Liverpool and Manchester Railway. The visitors boarded the *Northumbrian*, which stopped to take on water. Against their instructions, the passengers disembarked and wandered about. Huskisson headed across the adjacent line to speak to the Duke of Wellington just as Stephenson's *Rocket* came steaming down it. Huskisson tripped and fell beneath the wheels of the oncoming train, thereby becoming the world's first railroad passenger fatality.

WORST YEARS FOR ROAD DEATHS IN THE US

	Year	Deaths per 100,000,000 VMT*	Total deaths#
1	1972	4.3	54,589
2	1973	4.1	54,052
3	1969	5.0	53,543
4	1968	5.2	52,725
5	1970	4.7	52,627
6	1971	4.5	52,542
7	1979	3.3	51,093
8	1980	3.3	51,091
9	1966	5.5	50,894
10	1967	5.3	50,724

* *Vehicle Miles of Travel*
\# *Deaths occurring within 30 days of accident*

Although 1972 was the worst year on record for total fatalities, it is important to take into account the progressive increases in population and numbers of vehicles on the road, so the ratio of fatalities to vehicle miles of travel is more significant. This has steadily declined since 1921, the first year it was recorded, when there were 24.1 deaths per 100,000,000 VMT. By 1993 this figure had plunged to 1.7 per 100,000,000 VMT.

WATER TRANSPORTATION

TOP 10

SHIPPING COUNTRIES IN THE WORLD

	Country	Ships*
1	Panama	3,323
2	Liberia	1,515
3	Russia	1,443
4	Cyprus	1,373
5	China	1,311
6	Greece	970
7	Japan	881
8	Bahamas	863
9	Malta	852
10	Norway	665
	World total, including those not in this Top 10	*23,767*

* *The list includes only ships of more than 1,000 GRT – Gross Registered Tonnage*

The Top 10 countries account for more than 55 percent of the world's merchant ships of more than 1,000 gross tons (gross tonnage is not the weight of a ship but its displacement). The US and UK have fallen out of this Top 10 because their merchant fleets have gradually declined in recent years.

TOP 10

BUSIEST PORTS IN THE WORLD

	Port	Location	Goods handled p.a. (tons)
1	Rotterdam	Netherlands	287,700,000
2	New Orleans	US	189,300,000
3	Singapore	Singapore	187,800,000
4	Kobe	Japan	171,500,000
5	Shanghai	China	133,000,000
6	Houston	US	131,200,000
7	Nagoya	Japan	128,900,000
8	New York	US	126,200,000
9	Yokohama	Japan	123,900,000
10	Antwerp	Belgium	102,000,000

THE IMPORTANCE OF THE ORIENTAL PORT
With the rise of the economies of the Far East, ports such as Singapore have steadily eclipsed many of those in the US and Europe, and now occupy half the world's Top 10 busiest ports.

TOP 10

COUNTRIES WITH THE LONGEST INLAND WATERWAY NETWORKS*

	Country	km	miles
1	China	138,600	86,122
2	Russia	100,000	62,137
3	Brazil	50,000	31,069
4	US#	41,009	25,482
5	Indonesia	21,579	13,409
6	Vietnam	17,702	11,000
7	India	16,180	10,054
8	Zaïre	15,000	9,321
9	France	14,932	9,278
10	Colombia	14,300	8,886

* *Canals and navigable rivers*
\# *Excluding Great Lakes*

The longest ship canal in the world is the St. Lawrence Seaway (Canada/US). It opened in 1959 and is 189 miles/304 km in length. The Main-Danube Canal, Germany, completed in 1992, is the second longest at 106 miles/171 km. The Suez Canal, Egypt, opened in 1869, measures 101 miles/162 km – almost double the length of the Panama Canal (1914; 52 miles/82 km).

TOP 10

CATEGORIES OF BOAT NAMES IN THE US

	Category	No. in survey
1	Picturesque	144
2	Seagoing	75
3=	Children	67
3=	Geographical	67
5	Birds	63
6	Man and wife	62
7	Foreign	61
8	Whimsical	50
9	Alcoholic	45
10=	Fictitious/mythological	40
10=	Zoological	40

In a survey off the east coast of Florida, John McNamara noted the names of 1,000 vessels of all kinds and produced this analysis, which was published as "Reflections on Nautical Onomastics" in the journal *Names*. Among these and other categories, such as numbers, surnames, and "unexplained," he personally considered that the dullest name borne by a boat was *Investment Broker*.

T O P 1 0

LARGEST PASSENGER LINERS IN THE WORLD

	Ship	Year built	Country built in	Passenger capacity	Gross tonnage
1	*France/Norway* (renamed)	1961	France	2,565	76,049
2=	*Majesty of the Seas*	1992	France	2,766	73,937
2=	*Monarch of the Seas*	1991	France	2,764	73,937
4	*Sovereign of the Seas*	1987	France	2,600	73,192
5=	*Sensation*	1993	Finland	2,634	70,367
5=	*Ecstasy*	1991	Finland	2,634	70,367
5=	*Fantasy*	1990	Finland	2,634	70,367
8=	*Crown Princess*	1990	Italy	1,590	69,845
8=	*Regal Princess*	1991	Italy	1,900	69,845
10	*Oriana*	1995	Germany	1,975	69,153

T O P 1 0

LARGEST OIL TANKERS IN THE WORLD

	Ship	Year built	Country built in	Deadweight tonnage*
1	*Jahre Viking*	1979	Japan	564,650
2	*Kapetan Giannis*	1977	Japan	516,895
3	*Kapetan Michalis*	1977	Japan	516,423
4	*Nissei Maru*	1975	Japan	484,276
5	*Stena King*	1978	Taiwan	457,927
6	*Stena Queen*	1977	Taiwan	457,841
7	*Kapetan Panagiotis*	1977	Japan	457,062
8	*Kapetan Giorgis*	1976	Japan	456,368
9	*Sea Empress*	1976	Japan	423,677
10	*Mira Star*	1975	Japan	423,642

* The total weight of the vessel, including its cargo, crew, passengers, and supplies

T O P 1 0

LONGEST PASSENGER LINERS IN THE WORLD

	Ship/year built/ country	Length m	ft	in
1	*France/Norway,** 1961, France	315.53	1,035	2
2	*QE2,* 1969, UK	293.53	963	0
3=	*Majesty of the Seas,* 1992, France	268.32	880	4
3=	*Monarch of the Seas,* 1991, France	268.32	880	4
3=	*Sovereign of the Seas,* 1987, France	268.32	880	4
6=	*Sensation,* 1993, Finland	262.00	859	7
6=	*Ecstasy,* 1991, Finland	262.00	859	7
8	*Fantasy,* 1990, Finland	260.60	855	0
9	*Oriana,* 1995, Germany	260.00	853	0
10	*Canberra,* 1961, UK	249.49	818	6

* Renamed

THE MAJESTIC OCEAN LINER *QE2*
The QE2 was built as a replacement for the liner Queen Elizabeth. *It offers luxury accommodation for up to 1,700 passengers and made its maiden voyage in 1969.*

D I D   Y O U   K N O W

"THE BIGGEST SHIP IN THE WORLD"

The 692-ft/211-m steamship *Great Eastern*, designed by Isambard Kingdom Brunel, was five times bigger than any vessel ever built until then, a record held for nearly 50 years. Built in Millwall, London, and almost as long as the Thames was wide, it was decided to launch it sideways. Thousands turned out for the event, but the ship would not budge. She was finally launched in 1858 and in 1866 laid the first commercially successful transatlantic telegraph cable. However, dogged by misfortune, she was broken up for scrap 30 years after her launch.

MARINE DISASTERS

THE SINKING OF THE UNSINKABLE
The collision of the supposedly unsinkable British liner Titanic *with an iceberg was one of the worst marine disasters in peacetime.*

DID YOU KNOW

RIVERBOAT DISASTERS

On April 27, 1865, the boilers of the *Sultana*, a 1,700-ton Mississippi paddle wheeler exploded. Although designed to carry fewer than 400, in the chaos at the end of the Civil War the loading regulations were overlooked and 2,500 had boarded, of whom an estimated 1,547 were killed in America's worst marine disaster. The assassination of Abraham Lincoln had occurred just over a week earlier and eclipsed the reporting of the *Sultana* incident. The number of casualties from this tragedy was far worse than that resulting from the sinking of the more famous *Titanic* less than 50 years later. The worst riverboat disaster in the UK occurred on September 3, 1878 when the 250-ton paddle wheeler *Princess Alice* was struck by the *Bywell Castle*, a steamship more than five times her size. There was no official passenger list, but some authorities put the total at 786, with 640 bodies recovered. Amid the folklore surrounding the incident there is the claim that a Swedish woman called Elizabeth Stride was widowed and lost both her children in the tragedy. Her resultant poverty led her on to the streets, where 10 years later she became the third victim of Jack the Ripper.

THE 10

WORST PASSENGER FERRY DISASTERS OF THE 20TH CENTURY

	Ferry	Location	Date	Approx. no. killed
1	*Dona Paz*	Philippines	December 20, 1987	3,000
2	*Neptune*	Haiti	February 17, 1992	1,800
3	*Toya Maru*	Japan	September 26, 1954	1,172
4	*Don Juan*	Philippines	April 22, 1980	over 1,000
5	*Estonia*	Baltic Sea	September 28, 1994	853
6	*Samia*	Bangladesh	May 25, 1986	600
7	*Salem Express*	Egypt	December 14, 1991	480
8	*Tampomas II*	Indonesia	January 27, 1981	431
9	*Nam Yung Ho*	South Korea	December 15, 1970	323
10	*Atlas Star*	Bangladesh	April 20, 1986	up to 300

The *Dona Paz* sank in the Tabias Strait, Philippines, after the ferry was struck by the oil tanker *MV Victor*. The loss of life may have been much higher than the official figure (up to 4,386 has been suggested by some authorities) due to excessive overcrowding, but – as with many similar disasters – there was no accurate record of the numbers who actually boarded.

THE 10

WORST OIL TANKER SPILLS OF ALL TIME

	Tanker	Location	Date	Approx. spillage (tons)
1	*Atlantic Empress* and *Aegean Captain*	Trinidad	July 19, 1979	300,000
2	*Castillio de Bellver*	Cape Town, South Africa	August 6, 1983	255,000
3	*Olympic Bravery*	Ushant, France	January 24, 1976	250,000
4	*Showa-Maru*	Malacca, Malaya	June 7, 1975	237,000
5	*Amoco Cadiz*	Finistère, France	March 16, 1978	223,000
6	*Odyssey*	Atlantic, off Canada	November 10, 1988	140,000
7	*Torrey Canyon*	Scilly Isles, UK	March 18, 1967	120,000
8	*Sea Star*	Gulf of Oman	December 19, 1972	115,000
9	*Irenes Serenada*	Pilos, Greece	February 23, 1980	102,000
10	*Urquiola*	Corunna, Spain	May 12, 1976	101,000

In addition to major slicks, it is estimated that an average of 2,000,000 tons of oil is spilled into the world's seas every year. The grounding of the *Exxon Valdez* in Prince William Sound, Alaska, on March 24, 1989 ranks outside the 10 worst spills at about 35,000 tons, but resulted in major ecological damage. All the accidents in this Top 10 were caused by collision, grounding, fire, or explosion, but worse tanker oil spills have been caused by military action. Between January and June 1942, for example, German U-boats torpedoed a number of tankers off the east coast of the US with a loss of some 600,000 tons of oil, and in June 1991, during the Gulf War, various tankers were sunk in the Persian Gulf, spilling a total of more than 1,000,000 tons of oil.

THE 10
WORST MARINE DISASTERS
OF THE 20TH CENTURY

	Incident	Date	Approx. no. killed
1	*Wilhelm Gustloff*	January 30, 1945	up to 7,700

This German liner, laden with refugees, was torpedoed off Danzig by a Soviet submarine, S-13. The precise death toll remains uncertain, but is in the range 5,348–7,700.

	Incident	Date	Approx. no. killed
2	Unknown vessel	November 1947	over 6,000

An unidentified Chinese troopship carrying Nationalist soldiers from Manchuria sank off Yingkow. The exact date is unknown.

	Incident	Date	Approx. no. killed
3	*Cap Arcona*	May 3, 1945	4,650

A German ship carrying concentration camp survivors was bombed and sunk by British aircraft in Lübeck harbor.

	Incident	Date	Approx. no. killed
4	*Lancastria*	June 17, 1940	over 4,000

A British troop ship sank off St. Nazaire.

	Incident	Date	Approx. no. killed
5	*Yamato*	April 7, 1945	3,033

A Japanese battleship sank off Kyushu Island.

	Incident	Date	Approx. no. killed
6	*Dona Paz*	December 20, 1987	3,000

The ferry Dona Paz *was struck by oil tanker* MV Victor *in the Tabias Strait, Philippines.*

	Incident	Date	Approx. no. killed
7	*Kiangya*	December 3, 1948	over 2,750

An overloaded steamship carrying refugees struck a Japanese mine off Woosung, China.

	Incident	Date	Approx. no. killed
8	*Thielbeck*	May 1945	2,750

A refugee ship sank during the British bombardment of Lübeck harbor in the closing weeks of World War II.

	Incident	Date	Approx. no. killed
9	*Arisan Maru*	October 24, 1944	over 1,790

A Japanese vessel carrying American prisoners of war was torpedoed by a US submarine in the South China Sea.

	Incident	Date	Approx. no. killed
10	*Mont Blanc*	December 6, 1917	1,600

A French ammunition ship collided with Belgian steamer Imo *and exploded, Halifax, Nova Scotia.*

Due to a reassessment of the death tolls in some World War II marine disasters, the most famous of all, the sinking of the *Titanic* (the British liner that struck an iceberg in the North Atlantic on April 15, 1912, and went down with the loss of 1,517 lives), no longer ranks in this list. However, the *Titanic* tragedy remains one of the worst-ever peacetime disasters, along with such notable incidents as that involving the *General Slocum*, an excursion liner that caught fire in the port of New York on June 15, 1904, with the loss of 1,021. Among other disasters occurring during wartime are that of the sinking of the British cruiser *HMS Hood* by the German battleship *Bismarck* in the Denmark Strait on May 24, 1941, with 1,418 killed, the torpedoing by German submarine *U-20* of the *Lusitania*, a British passenger liner, off the Irish coast on May 7, 1915, with the loss of 1,198 civilians, and the accidental sinking by a US submarine of *Rakuyo Maru*, a Japanese troopship carrying Allied prisoners of war, on September 12, 1944, killing some 1,141.

THE 10
WORST SUBMARINE DISASTERS OF ALL TIME
(Excluding those as a result of military action)

	Incident	Date	Approx. no. killed
1	*Le Surcouf*	February 18, 1942	159

A French submarine accidentally rammed by a US merchant ship.

	Incident	Date	Approx. no. killed
2	*Thresher*	April 10, 1963	129

A three-year-old US nuclear submarine, worth $45,000,000, sank in the North Atlantic, 220 miles/350 km east of Boston.

	Incident	Date	Approx. no. killed
3	*I-12*	January 1945	114

A Japanese submarine sank in the Pacific in unknown circumstances.

	Incident	Date	Approx. no. killed
4	*I-174*	April 3, 1944	107

A Japanese submarine sank in the Pacific in unknown circumstances.

	Incident	Date	Approx. no. killed
5	*I-26*	October 1944	105

A Japanese submarine sank east of Leyte, cause and date unknown.

	Incident	Date	Approx. no. killed
6	*I-169*	April 4, 1944	103

A Japanese submarine flooded and sank while in harbor at Truk.

	Incident	Date	Approx. no. killed
7	*I-22*	October, 1942	100

A Japanese submarine sank off the Solomon Islands, exact date unknown.

	Incident	Date	Approx. no. killed
8=	*Seawolf*	October 3, 1944	99

A US submarine sunk in error by USS Rowell *off Morotai.*

	Incident	Date	Approx. no. killed
8=	*Thetis*	March 13, 1943	99

A British submarine sank on June 1, 1939 during trials in Liverpool Bay, with civilians on board. Her captain and three crew members escaped. Thetis was later salvaged and renamed Thunderbolt. *She was sunk by an Italian ship with the loss of 63 lives.*

	Incident	Date	Approx. no. killed
8=	*Scorpion*	May 21, 1968	99

A US nuclear submarine was lost in the North Atlantic, southwest of the Azores. The wreck was located on October 31 of that year.

The loss of the *Thresher* is the worst accident ever involving a nuclear submarine. It sank while undertaking tests off the US coast and was located by the bathyscaphe *Trieste*. The remains of the submarine were scattered over the ocean floor at a depth of 8,400 ft/2,560 m. The cause of the disaster remains a military secret.

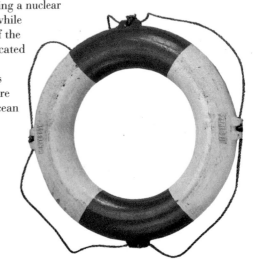

THE FIRST TO FLY

T H E   1 0

FIRST MANNED BALLOON FLIGHTS*

1 November 21, 1783

François Laurent, Marquis d'Arlandes, and Jean-François Pilâtre de Rozier took off from the Bois de Boulogne, Paris, France, in a hot-air balloon designed by Joseph and Etienne Montgolfier. This first-ever manned flight covered a distance of about 5½ miles/9 km in 23 minutes, landing safely near Gentilly. (Unfortunately, on June 15, 1785, de Rozier and his passenger were killed near Boulogne when their hydrogen balloon burst into flames during an attempted Channel crossing, thereby making them the first air fatalities.)

2 December 1, 1783

A crowd of 400,000 watched as Jacques Alexandre César Charles and Nicholas-Louis Robert made the first-ever flight in a hydrogen balloon. They took off from the Tuileries, Paris, and traveled about 27 miles/43 km north to Nesle in about two hours. Charles then took off again alone, thus becoming the first solo flier.

3 January 19, 1784

La Flesselle was a 131-ft/40-m high Montgolfier hot-air balloon named after its sponsor. It was piloted by Pilâtre de Rozier with Joseph Montgolfier, Prince Charles de Ligne, and the Comtes de La Porte d'Anglefort, de Dampierre, and de Laurencin. There was one other, the first aerial stowaway, a man called Fontaine, who leaped in as it was taking off.

4 February 25, 1784

Chevalier Paolo Andreani and the brothers Augustino and Carlo Giuseppi Gerli (the builders of the balloon) made the first-ever flight outside France. They took off from Moncuco near Milan, Italy.

5 March 2, 1784

Jean-Pierre François Blanchard made his first flight in a hydrogen balloon from the Champ de Mars, Paris. He had made experimental hops during the preceding months.

6 April 14, 1784

A Mr. Rousseau and an unnamed 10-year-old drummer boy flew from Navan to Ratoath in Ireland, the first ascent in the British Isles.

7 April 25, 1784

Guyton de Morveau, a French chemist, and L'Abbé Bertrand flew at Dijon.

8 May 8, 1784

Bremond and Maret flew at Marseilles.

9 May 12, 1784

Brun ascended at Chambéry.

10 May 15, 1784

Adorne and an unnamed passenger took off, but crash-landed near Strasbourg.

* *The first 10 flights of the ballooning pioneers all took place within a year. Several of the balloonists listed also made subsequent flights, but in each instance only their first flights are included*

After the first 10 flights, the pace of ballooning accelerated rapidly. On June 4, 1784, Monsieur Fleurant took Mme. Elisabeth Thiblé, an opera singer, on his flight at Lyons. This makes her the first woman to fly (the Marchioness de Montalembert and other aristocratic ladies had ascended on May 20, 1784, but in a tethered balloon). On August 27, James Tytler (known as "Balloon Tytler"), a doctor and newspaper editor, took off from Comely Gardens, Edinburgh, achieving an altitude of 350 ft/107 m in a ½-mile/0.8 km hop in a homemade balloon – the first hot-air balloon flight in Great Britain. On September 15, watched by a crowd of 200,000, Vincenzo Lunardi ascended from the Artillery Company Ground, Moorfields, London, flying to Standon in Hertfordshire, the first balloon flight in England.

T H E   1 0

FIRST FLIGHTS OF MORE THAN ONE HOUR

	Pilot	Location	Duration			Date
			hr	min	sec	
1	Orville Wright	Fort Meyer, VA	1	2	15.0	Sep 9, 1908
2	Orville Wright	Fort Meyer, VA	1	5	52.0	Sep 10, 1908
3	Orville Wright	Fort Meyer, VA	1	10	0.0	Sep 11, 1908
4	Orville Wright	Fort Meyer, VA	1	15	20.0	Sep 12, 1908
5	Wilbur Wright	Auvours, France	1	31	25.8	Sep 21, 1908
6	Wilbur Wright	Auvours, France	1	7	24.8	Sep 28, 1908
7	Wilbur Wright*	Auvours, France	1	4	26.0	Oct 6, 1908
8	Wilbur Wright	Auvours, France	1	9	45.4	Oct 10, 1908
9	Wilbur Wright	Auvours, France	1	54	53.4	Dec 18, 1908
10	Wilbur Wright	Auvours, France	2	20	23.2	Dec 31, 1908

* *First-ever flight of more than one hour with a passenger (M.A. Fordyce)*

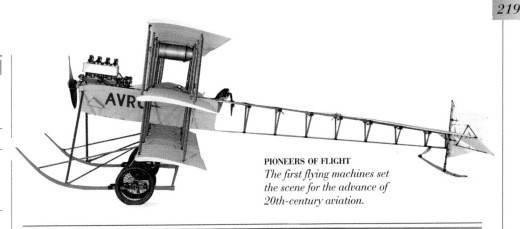

PIONEERS OF FLIGHT
The first flying machines set the scene for the advance of 20th-century aviation.

THE 10

FIRST PEOPLE TO FLY IN HEAVIER-THAN-AIR AIRCRAFT

1 Orville Wright (1871–1948), US

On December 17, 1903 at Kitty Hawk, North Carolina, Wright made the first-ever manned flight in his Wright Flyer I. It lasted 12 seconds and covered a distance of 120 ft/37 m.

2 Wilbur Wright (1867–1912), US

On the same day, Orville's brother made his first flight in the Wright Flyer I (59 seconds).

3 Alberto Santos-Dumont (1873–1932), Brazil

At Bagatelle, Bois de Boulogne, Paris, Santos-Dumont made a 193-ft /60-m hop on October 23, 1906 in his clumsy No. 14-bis.

4 Charles Voisin (1882–1912), France

Voisin made a short, 6-second hop of 197 ft/ 60m at Bagatelle on March 30, 1907. The aircraft was built by Voisin and his brother Gabriel to the commission of Léon Delagrange.

5 Henri Farman (1874–1958), UK (later a French citizen)

Farman first flew on October 7, 1907 and by 26 October had achieved 2,530 ft/771 m.

6 Léon Delagrange (1873–1910), France

On November 5, 1907 at Issy-les-Moulineaux, Delagrange flew his Voisin-Delagrange I for 40 seconds.

7 Robert Esnault-Pelterie (1881–1957), France

On November 16, 1907 at Buc, he first flew his REP 1 (55 sec; 1,969 ft/600 m).

8 Charles W. Furnas (1880–1941), US

On May 14, 1908 at Kitty Hawk, Wilbur Wright took Furnas, his mechanic, for a spin in the Wright Flyer III (29 sec; 1,968 ft/600 m). Furnas was thus the first passenger in the US.

9 Louis Blériot (1872–1936), France

After some earlier short hops, on June 29, 1908 at Issy, Blériot flew his Blériot VIII. On July 25, 1909 he became the first to fly across the English Channel.

10 Glenn Hammond Curtiss (1878–1930), US

On July 4, 1908 at Hammondsport, New York, Curtiss flew an AEA June Bug (1 min 42.5 sec; 5,090 ft/1,551 m), the first "official" flight in the US that was watched by a large crowd.

THE 10

FIRST TRANSATLANTIC FLIGHTS

1 May 16–27, 1919*, Trepassy Harbor, Newfoundland to Lisbon, Portugal, US Navy/Curtiss flying boat NC-4

Lt.-Cdr. Albert Cushing Read and a crew of five (Elmer Fowler Stone, Walter Hinton, James Lawrence Breese, Herbert Charles Rodd, and Eugene Saylor Rhoads) crossed the Atlantic in a series of hops, refueling at sea.

2 June 14–15, 1919, St. John's, Newfoundland to Galway, Ireland, Twin Rolls-Royce-engined converted Vickers Vimy bomber

British pilot Capt. John Alcock and Navigator Lt. Arthur Whitten Brown achieved the first non-stop flight. They ditched in Derrygimla bog after their epic 16 hr 28 min journey.

3 July 2–6, 1919, East Fortune, Scotland to Roosevelt Field, New York, British R-34 airship

Major George Herbert Scott and a crew of 30 (including the first-ever transatlantic air stowaway, William Ballantyne) made the first east–west crossing. It was the first airship to do so and, when it returned to Pulham, England, on July 13, it became the first to complete a double crossing.

4 March 30–June 5, 1922, Lisbon, Portugal to Recife, Brazil, Fairey IIID seaplane *Santa Cruz*

Portuguese pilots Admiral Gago Coutinho and Commander Sacadura Cabral were the first to fly the South Atlantic in stages, although they replaced one damaged aircraft with another.

5 August 2–31, 1924, Orkneys, Scotland to Labrador, Canada, Two Douglas seaplanes, *Chicago* and *New Orleans*

Lt. Lowell H. Smith and Leslie P. Arnold in one biplane and Erik Nelson and John Harding in another crossed the North Atlantic together. The crossing was achieved by a series of hops via Iceland and Greenland.

6 October 12–15, 1924, Friedrichshafen, Germany to Lakehurst, New Jersey, *Los Angeles*, a renamed German-built ZR 3 airship

Piloted by its inventor, Dr. Hugo Eckener.

7 January 22–February 10, 1926, Huelva, Spain to Recife, Brazil, *Plus Ultra*, a Dornier Wal twin-engined flying boat

The Spanish crew – General Franco's brother Ramón with Julio Ruiz De Alda, Ensign Beran, and mechanic Pablo Rada – crossed in stages.

8 February 8–24, 1927, Cagliari, Sardinia to Recife, Brazil, *Santa Maria*, a Savoia-Marchetti S.55 flying boat

Francesco Marquis de Pinedo, Capt. Carlo del Prete, and Lt. Vitale Zacchetti crossed in stages as part of a goodwill trip to South America from fascist Italy.

9 March 16–17, 1927, Lisbon, Portugal to Natal, Brazil, Dornier Wal flying boat

Portuguese flyers Sarmento de Beires and Jorge de Castilho flew via Casablanca.

10 April 28–May 14, 1927, Genoa, Italy to Natal, Brazil, Savoia-Marchetti flying boat

A Brazilian crew of João De Barros, João Negrão, Newton Braga, and Vasco Cinquini set out on October 17, 1926, flying in stages via the Canaries and Cape Verde Islands.

* All dates refer to the actual Atlantic legs of the journeys; some started earlier and ended beyond their first transatlantic landfalls

AIR DISASTERS

THE 10
WORST AIR DISASTERS IN THE WORLD

Incident	Killed
1 March 27, 1977, Tenerife, Canary Islands	583

Two Boeing 747s (Pan Am and KLM, carrying 364 passengers with 16 crew, and 230 passengers with 11 crew, respectively) collided and caught fire on the runway of Los Rodeos airport after the pilots received incorrect control tower instructions.

2 August 12, 1985, Mt. Ogura, Japan	520

A JAL Boeing 747 on a domestic flight from Tokyo to Osaka crashed, killing all but four on board in the worst-ever disaster involving a single aircraft.

3 January 8, 1996, Kinshasa, Zaïre	350

A Zaïrean Antonov-32 cargo plane crashed shortly after take-off, killing shoppers in a city-center market in Kinshasa. The final death toll has not yet been officially announced.

4 March 3, 1974, Paris, France	346

A Turkish Airlines DC-10 crashed at Ermenonville, north of Paris, immediately after take-off for London, with many English rugby supporters among the dead.

5 June 23, 1985, off the Irish coast	329

An Air India Boeing 747, on a flight from Vancouver to Delhi, exploded in mid-air, perhaps as a result of a terrorist bomb.

6 August 19, 1980, Riyadh, Saudi Arabia	301

A Saudia (Saudi Arabian) Airlines Lockheed TriStar caught fire during an emergency landing.

7 July 3, 1988, off the Iranian coast	290

An Iran Air A300 Airbus was shot down in error by a missile fired by the USS Vincennes.

8 May 25, 1979, Chicago, Illinois	275

The worst air disaster in the US occurred when an engine fell off a DC-10 as it took off from Chicago O'Hare airport. The aircraft plunged out of control, killing all 273 on board and two on the ground.

9 December 21, 1988, Lockerbie, Scotland, UK	270

Pan Am Flight 103 from London Heathrow to New York exploded in mid-air as a result of a terrorist bomb, killing 243 passengers, 16 crew, and 11 on the ground in the UK's worst-ever air disaster.

10 September 1, 1983, Sakhalin Island, off the Siberian coast	269

A Korean Air Lines Boeing 747 that had strayed into Soviet airspace was shot down by a Soviet fighter.

Four other air disasters have resulted in the deaths of more than 250 people: on April 26, 1994, at Nagoya airport, Japan, a China Airlines Airbus A300-600 crashed while landing, killing 262; on July 11, 1991, a DC-8 carrying Muslim pilgrims from Mecca crashed on takeoff, killing 261; on November 28, 1979, an Air New Zealand DC-10 crashed near Mt. Erebus, Antarctica, killing 257; and on December 12, 1985, an Arrow Air DC-8 crashed on takeoff at Gander, Newfoundland, killing all 256 on board, including 248 members of the 101st US Airborne Division.

THE 10
WORST AIR DISASTERS IN THE US

Incident	Killed
1 May 25, 1979, Chicago, Illinois	275

(See The 10 Worst Air Disasters in the World, No. 8.)

2 August 16, 1987, Romulus, Michigan	156

A Northwest Airlines McDonnell Douglas MD-80 crashed onto a road following an engine fire after takeoff from Detroit. Out of 157 people a four-year-old girl was the only person to survive.

3 July 9, 1982, Kenner, Louisiana	154

A Pan Am Boeing 727 crashed after takeoff from New Orleans, killing all 138 passengers, the crew, and eight people on the ground.

4 September 25, 1978, San Diego, California	144

A Pacific Southwest Boeing 727 collided with a Cessna 172 light aircraft, killing 135 in the airliner, two in the Cessna, and seven on the ground.

5 December 16, 1960, New York, New York	135

A United Air Lines DC-8 with 77 passengers and a crew of seven collided in a snow storm with a TWA Super Constellation carrying 39 passengers and a crew of four. The DC-8 crashed in Brooklyn, killing eight on the ground; the TWA airplane crashed in the harbour off Staten Island.

6 August 2, 1985, Dallas–Ft. Worth Airport, Texas	133

A Delta Airlines TriStar crashed when a severe wind shear sent it out of control just before it was about to touch down.

7 September 8, 1994, Pittsburgh, Pennsylvania	132

A USAir Boeing 737-400, en route from Chicago to West Palm Beach, Florida, crashed seven miles from Pittsburgh airport, killing all the passengers as well as the crew members.

8 June 30, 1956, Grand Canyon, Arizona	128

A United Airlines DC-7 and a TWA Super Constellation collided in mid-air, killing every person on board each aircraft.

9 June 24, 1975, JFK Airport, New York	113

An Eastern Air Lines Boeing 727 on a flight from New Orleans crashed while attempting to land in a storm.

10 May 11, 1996, Everglades, Florida	110

A ValuJet DC-9 on a flight from Miami International to Atlanta attempted to return to Miami but plunged into the swamp, killing all on board.

The 1988 Lockerbie crash (see The 10 Worst Air Disasters in the World, No. 9) is the worst US air disaster not occurring within US territory. A domestic incident that could potentially have resulted in a huge number of casualties, but in fact killed only 14 with another 25 injured, was the July 28, 1945, crash, of a US Army B-25 bomber into the 78th and 79th floors of the Empire State Building. Blazing wreckage was hurled throughout the building, and the crew of three, plus 11 office workers, were killed. The worst pre-war American air disaster was the April 4, 1933, crash into the ocean off the New Jersey coast of the *Akron* dirigible airship, with the loss of 73 lives.

T H E 1 0
WORST AIRSHIP DISASTERS IN THE WORLD

Incident	Killed
1 April 4, 1933, off the Atlantic coast of US	73

US Navy airship Akron *crashed into the sea in a storm, leaving only three survivors in the world's worst airship tragedy.*

2 December 21, 1923, over the Mediterranean	52

French airship Dixmude *is assumed to have been struck by lightning, broken up, and crashed into the sea. Wreckage, believed to be from the airship, was found off Sicily 10 years later.*

3 October 5, 1930, near Beauvais, France	50

British airship R101 *crashed into a hillside leaving 48 dead, with two dying later, and six saved.*

4 August 24, 1921, off the coast near Hull, UK	44

Airship R38, *sold by the British Government to the US and renamed USN ZR-2, broke in two on a training and test flight.*

5 May 6, 1937, Lakehurst, New Jersey	36

German Zeppelin Hindenburg *caught fire when mooring.*

6 February 21, 1922, Hampton Roads, Virginia	34

Roma, *an Italian airship bought by the US Army, crashed killing all but 11 men on board.*

7 October 17, 1913, Berlin, Germany	28

German airship LZ18 *crashed after engine failure during a test flight at Berlin-Johannisthal.*

8 March 30, 1917, Baltic Sea	23

German airship SL9 *was struck by lightning on a flight from Seerappen to Seddin, and crashed into the sea.*

9 September 3, 1915, mouth of the River Elbe, Germany	19

German airship L10 *was struck by lightning and plunged into the sea.*

10= September 9, 1913, off Heligoland	14

German Navy airship L1 *crashed into the sea, leaving six survivors out of the 20 on board.*

10= September 3, 1925, Caldwell, Ohio	14

US dirigible Shenandoah, *the first airship built in the US and the first to use safe helium instead of flammable hydrogen, broke up in a storm, scattering sections over many miles of the Ohio countryside.*

From its earliest years, the history of the airship has been a mixture of triumphs and disasters. Following a series of accidents in the 1920s, the world's largest airship, the 777-ft/237-m British-built *R101* crashed in France, broke in two and burst into flames. Britain's interest in airships promptly ended, as did that of the US after the loss of the *Akron* less than three years later. Germany's enthusiasm lasted until 1937, when the 803.8-ft/245-m *Hindenburg* arrived at Lakehurst, New Jersey, after a three-day trip from Frankfurt. As she moored, she caught fire and turned into an inferno, the last moments of which remain among the most haunting sights ever captured on newsreel, with commentator Herb Morrison describing the horrific scene through floods of tears.

T H E 1 0
WORST AVIATION DISASTERS WITH GROUND FATALITIES

Disaster/cause	Ground deaths
1 January 8, 1996, Kinshasa, Zaïre	350

(See The 10 Worst Air Disasters in the World, No. 3.)

2 March 16, 1969, Maracaibo, Venezuela	76

A DC-9 crashed into the city.

3 October 4, 1992, Amsterdam, Netherlands	70

An El Al cargo aircraft crashed into a suburban apartment house.

4 August 28, 1988, US air base, Ramstein, Germany	67

Three fighter aircraft in an Italian aerobatic team collided, one of them crashing into the crowd, leaving 70 dead and 150 spectators injured.

5 July 24, 1938, Campo de Marte, Bogota, Colombia	53

A low-flying stunt aircraft crashed into a stand, broke up, and hurled blazing wreckage into the crowd.

6 August 23, 1944, Freckelton, Lancashire, UK	51

A B-24 bomber crashed into a school.

7= September 6, 1952, Farnborough Air Show, UK	27

A de Havilland 110 broke up and scattered wreckage into the crowd, killing 27 spectators and injuring 60 others.

7= May 6, 1988, Hanover, Germany	27

Helicopters crashed during an airshow.

9= December 21, 1988, Lockerbie, Scotland, UK	11

Wreckage fell on the town after the explosion of a terrorist bomb (see The 10 Worst Air Disasters in the World, No. 9).

9= July 28, 1945, New York, New York	11

A B-25 bomber crashed into the Empire State Building.

DOWN IN FLAMES
Overweight and unstable, British airship R101 crashed en route for India and was engulfed in a fireball when its 141,585 cu m/ 5,000,000 cu ft of hydrogen exploded, killing all but six on board.

WORLD TOUR

TOP 10

TOURIST COUNTRIES IN THE WORLD

	Country	World total %	Total visitors (1995)
1	France	10.7	60,584,000
2	Spain	8.0	45,125,000
3	US	7.9	44,730,000
4	Italy	5.1	29,184,000
5	China	4.1	23,368,000
6	UK	4.0	22,700,000
7	Hungary	3.9	22,087,000
8	Mexico	3.5	19,870,000
9	Poland	3.4	19,225,000
10	Austria	3.0	17,173,000

Source: World Tourism Organization

TOP 10

AMUSEMENT AND THEME PARKS IN EUROPE

	Park/location	Estimated visitors (1995)
1	EuroDisney, Marne-la-Vallée, France	10,700,000
2	Blackpool Pleasure Beach, Blackpool, UK	7,200,000
3	Alton Towers, Staffordshire, UK	3,000,000
4	Port Aventura, Salou, Spain	2,700,000
5	De Efteling, Kaatsheuvel, Netherlands	2,680,000
6	Europa Park, Rust, Germany	2,550,000
7	Bakken, Klampenborg, Denmark	2,438,000
8=	Tivoli Gardens, Copenhagen, Denmark	2,400,000
8=	Gardaland, Casteinuovo Del Garda, Italy	2,400,000
10	Liseberg, Gothenburg, Sweden	2,200,000

Despite appearing at the top of this list, EuroDisney continues to lose money at an alarming rate (although in the first half of 1995 this was reduced from F.Fr 1,055,000,000/$210,000,000 to F.Fr 241,000,000/ $48,000,000). Meanwhile, competition is mounting both from existing theme parks and from newly-opened complexes, such as Spain's Port Aventura, with Warner Brothers' new operation in Germany scheduled for opening in 1996.

TOP 10

MOST COMMON TYPES OF LOST PROPERTY ON LONDON TRANSPORT

	Type	Number of items found								
		1986–87	1987–88	1988–89	1989–90	1990–91	1991–92	1992–93	1993–94	1994–95
1	Books, check books, and credit cards	19,013	19,329	19,148	20,006	20,270	20,436	20,187	18,818	20,038
2	"Value items" (handbags, purses, wallets, etc.)	21,940	19,868	18,628	18,397	18,634	17,342	18,270	17,364	17,708
3	Clothing	16,497	15,211	14,954	15,088	14,624	13,704	14,328	14,626	15,045
4	Umbrellas	21,080	23,250	17,129	13,889	10,828	10,917	13,634	13,357	13,212
5	Cases and bags	9,222	9,317	9,155	9,272	9,034	8,513	8,056	8,432	9,029
6	Keys	9,923	9,265	8,793	8,595	8,348	7,559	7,694	6,960	7,023
7	Cameras, electronic articles, and jewelry	5,550	5,304	5,493	5,352	5,732	5,298	5,394	5,426	6,129
8	Eyeglasses	5,975	5,754	5,756	5,985	5,944	5,362	5,683	5,486	5,912
9	Gloves (pairs)	5,625	4,402	3,770	3,428	3,446	3,268	3,188	3,380	2,886
10	Gloves (odd)	844	701	576	577	606	520	540	653	571
	Total items in Top 10:	*115,669*	*112,401*	*103,402*	*100,589*	*97,466*	*92,919*	*96,974*	*94,502*	*97,553*

As we have noted in previous editions of *The Top 10 of Everything*, there is an inexplicable consistency in the numbers of most categories of articles handed in to London Transport's Lost Property Office from year to year. Why, we may speculate, do an average of rather more than 100 individuals leave their spectacles on London's buses and subway trains every week? Why did the number losing their umbrellas halve and then begin to increase again? Alongside the mysterious pattern that emerges, a clear decline in the total can also be discerned, raising the question of whether the traveling public are becoming more careful with their property or less scrupulous about handing in finds. Books remain in the No. 1 position (check books and credit cards are now included with them), but changes in fashion have meant that hats, once one of the most common lost items, no longer even warrant a separate category.

TOP 10

AMUSEMENT AND THEME PARKS IN THE WORLD

	Park/location	Estimated visitors (1995)
1	Tokyo Disneyland, Tokyo, Japan	15,509,000
2	Disneyland, California	14,100,000
3	Magic Kingdom at Walt Disney World, Florida	12,900,000
4=	EuroDisney, Marne-la-Vallée, France	10,700,000
4=	EPCOT at Walt Disney World, Florida	10,700,000
6	Disney-MGM Studios Theme Park at Walt Disney World, Florida	9,500,000
7	Universal Studios Florida, Florida	8,000,000
8	Yong-In Farmland, Kyonggi-Do, South Korea	7,300,000
9	Blackpool Pleasure Beach, Blackpool, UK	7,200,000
10	Yokohama Hakkeijima Sea Paradise, Japan	6,000,000

Source: Amusement Business

TOP 10

LONDON TOURIST ATTRACTIONS

	Attraction	Visitors (1995)
1	British Museum	5,745,866
2	National Gallery	4,469,019
3	Madame Tussaud's	2,703,283
4	Tower of London	2,536,680
5	Funland and Laserbowl, Trocadero	2,500,000
6	Westminster Abbey	2,245,000
7	St. Paul's Cathedral	2,220,000
8	Tate Gallery	1,769,662
9	Science Museum	1,556,368
10	Victoria & Albert Museum	1,224,030

PARIS TOURIST ATTRACTION
When the Eiffel Tower was erected for the Universal Exhibition of 1889, it was meant to be a temporary addition to the Paris skyline. In fact, it outraged many Parisians, who felt it was an eyesore. The world's tallest structure until New York's Empire State Building was completed in 1931, the Eiffel Tower has become the symbol of Paris.

TOP 10

COUNTRIES EARNING MOST FROM TOURISM

	Country	World total %	Total ($) receipts (1995)
1	US	15.7	58,370,000,000
2	France	7.3	27,322,000,000
3	Italy	7.3	27,072,000,000
4	Spain	6.7	25,065,000,000
5	UK	4.7	17,468,000,000
6	Austria	3.4	12,500,000,000
7	Germany	3.2	11,922,000,000
8	Hong Kong	2.4	9,075,000,000
9	China	2.3	8,733,000,000
10	Thailand	2.0	7,556,000,000

Source: World Tourism Organization

In 1995 tourism earned a total of $372,585,000,000 worldwide, of which the Top 10 countries earned $205,083,000,000 and the Top 40, $329,869,000,000.

TOP 10

TOURIST SPENDING COUNTRIES IN THE WORLD

	Tourist country of origin	World total %	Total expenditure ($) (1995)
1	Germany	14.7	47,304,000,000
2	US	13.9	44,825,000,000
3	Japan	11.4	36,737,000,000
4	UK	7.6	24,625,000,000
5	France	5.0	16,038,000,000
6	Italy	3.8	12,366,000,000
7	Netherlands	3.4	11,050,000,000
8	Austria	2.9	9,500,000,000
9	Canada	2.9	9,484,000,000
10	Taiwan	2.7	8,595,000,000

Source: World Tourism Organization

SPORTS

20TH CENTURY

The 1996 Olympic Games in Atlanta, GA, mark the 100th anniversary of the modern Olympics. The first Games were staged at Athens, Greece, in 1896 and attracted 311 competitors representing just 13 countries. In contrast, the 1992 Games in Barcelona were attended by 9,369 sportsmen and women from 169 countries. Due to the two World Wars, there were no Games in 1916, 1940, or 1944.

SUPER FIT
Daly Thompson brought home gold for the UK by winning the 1984 decathlon.

THE 10

LAST COUNTRIES TO WIN THEIR FIRST OLYMPIC GOLD MEDAL

	Country	Year
1=	Algeria	1992
1=	Indonesia	1992
1=	Lithuania	1992
4	Suriname	1988
5=	China	1984
5=	Morocco	1984
5=	Portugal	1984
8	Zimbabwe	1980
9=	South Korea	1976
9=	Trinidad	1976

RUNNING LIKE THE WIND TO VICTORY
Joan Benoit won the gold medal in the 1st Olympic women's marathon in 1984 in Los Angeles. In 1985 she received the Sullivan Award, which is presented every year to the best US amateur athlete.

TOP 10

MEDAL-WINNING COUNTRIES

	Country	Gold	Silver	Bronze	Total
			Medals		
1	US	789	603	518	1,910
2	Russia/USSR/CIS	442	361	333	1,136
3	Germany/West Germany	186	227	236	649
4	UK	177	224	218	619
5	France	161	175	191	527
6	Sweden	133	149	171	453
7	East Germany	154	131	126	411
8	Italy	153	126	131	410
9	Hungary	136	124	144	404
10	Finland	98	77	112	287

THE OLYMPIC GAMES

T O P 1 0

INDIVIDUAL GOLD-MEDAL WINNERS OF ALL TIME AT THE SUMMER OLYMPICS

	Medallist/nationality	Sport	Years	Gold medals
1	Ray Ewry (US)	Track & Field	1900–08	10
2=	Paavo Nurmi (Fin)	Track & Field	1920–28	9
2=	Larissa Latynina (USSR)	Gymnastics	1956–64	9
2=	Mark Spitz (US)	Swimming	1968–72	9
5=	Sawao Kato (Jap)	Gymnastics	1968–76	8
5=	Carl Lewis (US)	Track & Field	1984–92	8
5=	Matt Biondi (US)	Swimming	1984–92	8
8=	Aladár Gerevich (Hun)	Fencing	1932–60	7
8=	Viktor Chukarin (USSR)	Gymnastics	1952–56	7
8=	Boris Shakhlin (USSR)	Gymnastics	1956–64	7
8=	Vera Čáslavská (Cze)	Gymnastics	1964–68	7
8=	Nikolay Andrianov (USSR)	Gymnastics	1972–80	7

T O P 1 0

LONGEST-STANDING CURRENT OLYMPIC TRACK & FIELD RECORDS

	Event/competitor/nationality	Winning distance/time/score	Date
1	Men's long jump, Bob Beamon (US)	8.90 m	Oct 18, 1968
2	Men's javelin, Miklos Nemeth (Hungary)	94.58 m	Jul 25, 1976
3	Women's shot, Ilona Slupianek (GDR)	22.41 m	Jul 24, 1980
4	Women's 800 meters, Nadezhda Olizarenko (USSR)	1 min 53.43 sec	Jul 27, 1980
5	Women's 4 × 100 meters, Romy Müller, Bärbel Wöckel, Ingrid Amerswald, Marlies Göhr (GDR)	41.60 sec	Aug 1, 1980
6	Men's 1,500 meters, Sebastian Coe (UK)	3 min 32.53 sec	Aug 1, 1980
7	Women's marathon, Joan Benoit (US)	2 hr 24 min 52 sec	Aug 5, 1984
8	Men's 800 meters, Joaquim Cruz (Brazil)	1 min 43.00 sec	Aug 6, 1984
9	Decathlon, Daley Thompson (UK)	8,847 points	Aug 9, 1984
10	Men's 5,000 meters, Said Aouita (Morocco)	13 min 05.59 sec	Aug 11, 1984

T O P 1 0

SUMMER OLYMPICS WITH THE MOST COMPETITORS

	Country	Year	Competing countries	Competitors
1	Barcelona	1992	172	9,369
2	Seoul	1988	159	9,101
3	Munich	1972	122	7,156
4	Los Angeles	1984	141	7,058
5	Montreal	1976	92	6,085
6	Mexico City	1968	112	5,530
7	Rome	1960	83	5,346
8	Moscow	1980	81	5,326
9	Tokyo	1964	93	5,140
10	Helsinki	1952	69	4,925

T O P 1 0

GOLD-MEDAL-WINNING HOST COUNTRIES

	Country	Venue	Year	Gold medals
1	US	Los Angeles	1984	83
2=	US	St. Louis	1904	80
2=	USSR	Moscow	1980	80
4	UK	London	1908	56
5	US	Los Angeles	1932	41
6	Germany	Berlin	1936	33
7	France	Paris	1900	29
8	Sweden	Stockholm	1912	24
9	Japan	Tokyo	1964	16
10	Belgium	Antwerp	1920	14

GOLDEN OPPORTUNITY IN SPAIN
The opening ceremony of the 1992 Olympics took place at Barcelona. Three countries won their first gold medals at these Games.

BASEBALL – THE CHAMPIONS

PLAYERS WHO PLAYED THE MOST GAMES IN A CAREER

	Player	Games
1	Pete Rose	3,562
2	Carl Yastrzemski	3,308
3	Hank Aaron	3,298
4	Ty Cobb	3,034
5	Stan Musial	3,026
6	Willie Mays	2,992
7	Dave Winfield	2,973
8	Rusty Staub	2,951
9	Brooks Robinson	2,896
10	Robin Yount	2,856

"CHARLIE HUSTLE" PROVES CRIME DOES NOT PAY
So-called for his aggressive play, Pete Rose holds the record for the most hits (4,256) in a Major League baseball career. He was banned from baseball for life in 1989 for betting on games, and convicted of tax offenses in 1990.

PLAYERS WHO ACHIEVED THE MOST RUNS IN A CAREER*

	Player	Runs
1	Ty Cobb	2,245
2=	Babe Ruth	2,174
2=	Hank Aaron	2,174
4	Pete Rose	2,165
5	Willie Mays	2,062
6	Stan Musial	1,949
7	Lou Gehrig	1,888
8	Tris Speaker	1,881
9	Mel Ott	1,859
10	Frank Robinson	1,829

* Regular season only, excluding World Series

FIRST PLAYERS TO HIT FOUR HOME RUNS IN ONE GAME

	Player	Club	Date
1	Bobby Lowe	Boston Red Sox	May 30, 1884
2	Ed Delahanty	Philadephia Phillies	June 3, 1932
3	Lou Gehrig	New York Yankees	June 3, 1932
4	Chuck Klein	Philadelphia Phillies	July 10, 1936
5	Pat Seerey	Chicago White Sox	July 18, 1948
6	Gil Hodges	Brooklyn Dodgers	August 31, 1950
7	Joe Adcock	Milwaukee Brewers	July 31, 1954
8	Rocky Colavito	Cleveland Indians	June 10, 1959
9	Willie Mays	San Francisco Giants	April 30, 1961
10	Mike Schmidt	Philadelphia Phillies	April 17, 1976

The only other players to score four homers in one game are Bob Horner, who did so for Atlanta on July 6, 1986, and Mark Whitten, for St. Louis, on September 7, 1993.

A WAY OF SAVING FACE
With a hard, leather-covered ball traveling at speed toward them, it is imperative for players to wear face guards to avoid accidents.

PLAYERS WITH THE HIGHEST CAREER BATTING AVERAGES

	Player	At bat	Hits	Average*
1	Ty Cobb	11,429	4,191	.367
2	Rogers Hornsby	8,137	2,930	.360
3	Joe Jackson	4,981	1,774	.356
4	Ed Delahanty	7,502	2,591	.345
5=	Billy Hamilton	6,284	2,163	.344
5=	Tris Speaker	10,208	3,515	.344
5=	Ted Williams	7,706	2,654	.344
8	Willie Keeler	8,585	2,947	.343
9=	Dan Brouthers	6,711	2,296	.342
9=	Harry Heilmann	7,787	2,660	.342
9=	Babe Ruth	8,399	2,873	.342

* Calculated by dividing the number of hits by the number of times a batter was "at bat"

The players appearing in this list represent a bygone era, several of them achieving their remarkable averages in the last century, and it is unlikely that any modern-day player will join them. Wade Boggs flirted with an average of more than .340, but he is more likely to see his average decrease than increase the longer he plays. Ted Williams was the last hitter to bat .400 in a season, although Tony Gwynn came close in the strike-shortened 1994 season with an average of .394. Curiously, of the 11 batters on this list, eight of them were left-handed.

TOP 10

OLDEST STADIUMS IN MAJOR LEAGUE BASEBALL

	Stadium	Home club	Year built
1=	Tiger Stadium	Detroit Tigers	1912
1=	Fenway Park	Boston Red Sox	1912
3	Wrigley Field	Chicago Cubs	1914
4	Yankee Stadium	New York Yankees	1923
5	Mile High Stadium	Colorado Rockies	1948*
6	County Stadium	Milwaukee Brewers	1953
7	Candlestick Park	San Francisco Giants	1960
8	Dodger Stadium	Los Angeles Dodgers	1962
9	Shea Stadium	New York Mets	1964
10	Astrodome	Houston Astros	1965

* *First used for baseball in 1993*

Each stadium has a unique history, but the Yankee Stadium is particularly notable for its association with Babe Ruth, the best-known name in baseball. The stadium was built during the early 1920s to hold the huge crowds that he attracted and was known as "The House Babe Built" because the revenue he brought in financed the construction of the stadium.

TOP 10

TEAMS WITH THE MOST WORLD SERIES WINS

	Team*	Wins
1	New York Yankees	22
2=	Philadelphia/Kansas City/Oakland Athletics	9
2=	St. Louis Cardinals	9
4	Brooklyn/Los Angeles Dodgers	6
5=	Boston Red Sox	5
5=	Cincinnati Reds	5
5=	New York/San Francisco Giants	5
5=	Pittsburgh Pirates	5
9	Detroit Tigers	4
10=	St. Louis/Baltimore Orioles	3
10=	Washington Senators/Minnesota Twins	3

* *Teams separated by / indicate changes of franchise and are regarded as the same team for Major League record purposes*

TOP 10

SALARIES IN MAJOR LEAGUE BASEBALL IN 1995

	Player	Team	Salary ($)*
1	Cecil Fielder	Detroit Tigers	9,237,000
2	Barry Bonds	San Francisco Giants	8,000,183
3	David Cone	Toronto Blue Jays	8,000,000
4=	Joe Carter	Toronto Blue Jays	7,500,000
4=	Ken Griffey, Jr.	Seattle Mariners	7,500,000
6	Frank Thomas	Chicago White Sox	7,150,000
7	Mark McGwire	Oakland Athletics	6,900,000
8	Jeff Bagwell	Houston Astros	6,875,000
9	Carl Ripken, Jr.	Baltimore Orioles	6,871,671
10=	Lenny Dykstra	Philadelphia Phillies	6,200,000
10=	Kirby Puckett	Minnesota Twins	6,200,000
10=	Ruben Sierra	Oakland Athletics	6,200,000

* *Figures include base salary and prorated signing bonuses as of opening day but do not reflect the 11.1 percent reduction in base salary due to the players' strike*

TOP 10

LARGEST MAJOR LEAGUE BALLPARKS*

	Stadium/home team	Capacity
1	Anaheim Stadium, California Angels	64,593
2	Candlestick Park, San Francisco Giants	63,000
3	Veterans Stadium, Philadelphia Phillies	62,136
4	The Kingdome, Seattle Mariners	59,166
5	Yankee Stadium, New York Yankees	57,545
6	Busch Stadium, St. Louis Cardinals	57,078
7	Hubert H. Humphrey, Metrodome, Minnesota Twins	56,783
8	Dodger Stadium, Los Angeles Dodgers	56,000
9	Shea Stadium, New York Mets	55,601
10	The Astrodome, Houston Astros	54,350

* *By capacity*

BASKETBALL

TEAMS WITH
THE MOST NBA TITLES

	Team*	Titles
1	Boston Celtics	16
2	Minnesota/Los Angeles Lakers	11
3=	Chicago Bulls	3
3=	Philadelphia/Golden State Warriors	3
3=	Syracuse Nationals/ Philadelphia 76ers	3
6=	Detroit Pistons	2
6=	Houston Rockets	2
6=	New York Knicks	2
9=	Baltimore Bullets	1
9=	Houston Rockets	1
9=	Milwaukee Bucks	1
9=	Rochester Royals#	1
9=	St Louis Hawks+	1
9=	Seattle Supersonics	1
9=	Portland Trail Blazers	1
9=	Washington Bullets	1

* Teams separated by / indicate change of franchise: they have won the championship under both names
\# Now the Sacramento Kings
\+ Now the Atlanta Hawks

Basketball is one of the few sports that can trace its exact origins. It was invented by Dr. James Naismith in Springfield, Massachusetts, in 1891. Professional basketball in the US dates to 1898, but the National Basketball Association (NBA) was not formed until 1949 when the National Basketball League and Basketball Association of America merged. The NBA consists of 27 teams split into Eastern and Western Conferences. At the end of an 82-game regular season, the top eight teams in each Conference play off and the two Conference champions meet in a best-of-seven final for the NBA Championship.

BIGGEST ARENAS IN THE NBA

	Arena	Location	Home team	Capacity
1	Charlotte Coliseum	Charlotte, North Carolina	Charlotte Hornets	24,042
2	SkyDome	Toronto, Canada	Toronto Raptors	22,911
3	United Center	Chicago, Illinois	Chicago Bulls	21,711
4	The Palace of Auburn Hills	Auburn Hills, Michigan	Detroit Pistons	21,454
5	The Rose Garden	Portland, Washington	Portland Trail Blazers	21,300
6	The Alamodome	San Antonio, Texas	San Antonio Spurs	20,662
7	Gund Arena	Cleveland, Ohio	Cleveland Cavaliers	20,562
8	Meadowlands Arena	East Rutherford, New Jersey	New Jersey Nets	20,039
9	General Motors Place	Vancouver, Canada	Vancouver Grizzlies	20,004
10	Delta Center Arena	Salt Lake City, Utah	Utah Jazz	19,911

The smallest arena is the 15,025 capacity Oakland Coliseum Arena, home of the Golden State Warriors (although the Washington Bullets play some games in the Baltimore Arena, which has a capacity of 12,756).

PLAYERS TO HAVE PLAYED
MOST GAMES IN THE NBA
AND ABA

	Player	Games played
1	Kareem Abdul-Jabbar	1,560
2	Robert Parish*	1,494
3	Moses Malone*	1,455
4	Artis Gilmore	1,329
5	Elvin Hayes	1,303
6	Caldwell Jones	1,299
7	John Havlicek	1,270
8	Paul Silas	1,254
9	Julius Erving	1,243
10	Dan Issel	1,218

* Still active at end of 1994–95 season

The ABA (American Basketball Association) was established as a rival to the NBA in 1968 and survived until 1976. Because many of the sport's top players "defected," their figures are still included in this list. During the 1995–96 season, Robert Parish moved to the top of this list by playing his 1,561st game on April 6, 1996.

PLAYERS WITH THE MOST
CAREER ASSISTS

	Player	Assists
1	John Stockton*	10,394
2	Magic Johnson*	9,921
3	Oscar Robertson	9,887
4	Isiah Thomas	9,061
5	Maurice Cheeks	7,392
6	Lenny Wilkens	7,211
7	Bob Cousy	6,995
8	Guy Rodgers	6,917
9	Nate Archibald	6,476
10	John Lucas	6,454

* Still active at end of 1995–96 season

Magic Johnson's figure needs to have his comeback stats from this season. John Stockton's now stands at 11,310. With John Stockton surpassing the 11,000 figure at the end of his 12th season in the NBA, and with his tally increasing by close to 1,000 assists per season, it is unlikely that his record will ever be broken.

TOP 10

POINTS AVERAGE (PPG) IN AN NBA SEASON

	Player	Club	Season	Average
1	Wilt Chamberlain	Philadelphia	1961–62	50.4
2	Wilt Chamberlain	San Francisco	1962–63	44.8
3	Wilt Chamberlain	Philadelphia	1960–61	38.4
4	Elgin Baylor	Los Angeles	1961–62	38.3
5	Wilt Chamberlain	Philadelphia	1959–60	37.6
6	Michael Jordan	Chicago	1986–87	37.1
7	Wilt Chamberlain	San Francisco	1963–64	36.9
8	Rick Barry	San Francisco	1966–67	35.6
9	Michael Jordan	Chicago	1987–88	35.0
10=	Elgin Baylor	Los Angeles	1960–61	34.8
10=	Kareem Abdul-Jabbar	Milwaukee	1971–72	34.8

TOP 10

HIGHEST-EARNING PLAYERS IN THE NBA, 1995–96

	Player	Team	Earnings ($)
1	Patrick Ewing	New York Knicks	18,700,000
2	Clyde Drexler	Houston Rockets	9,800,000
3	David Robinson	San Antonio Spurs	7,700,000
4	Shaquille O'Neal	Orlando Magic	5,700,000
5=	Hakeen Olajuwon	Houston Rockets	5,300,000
5=	Sean Elliott	San Antonio Spurs	5,300,000
7	Anfernee Hardaway	Orlando Magic	5,230,000
8	Charles Barkley	Phoenix Suns	4,760,000
9	Alonzo Mourning	Miami Heat	4,050,000
10	Grant Hill	Detroit Pistons	4,000,000

TOP 10

MOST SUCCESSFUL NBA COACHES

	Coach	Games won*		Coach	Games won*
1	Lenny Wilkens#	1,000	6	Don Nelson#	817
2	Red Auerbach	938	7	Cotton Fitzsimmons#+	805
3	Dick Motta#	892	8	Gene Shue	784
4	Jack Ramsay	864	9	Pat Riley#	756
5	Bill Fitch#	862	10	John MacLeod	707

* Regular season games only
# Still active 1995-96 season
+ Reappointed as coach of the Phoenix Suns during the 1995–96 season

TOP 10

POINT-SCORERS IN AN NBA CAREER*

	Player	Total points
1	Kareem Abdul-Jabbar	38,387
2	Wilt Chamberlain	31,419
3	Moses Malone#	27,409
4	Elvin Hayes	27,313
5	Oscar Roberston	26,710
6	John Havlicek	26,395
7	Alex English	25,613
8	Dominique Wilkins#	25,389
9	Jerry West	25,192
10	Adrian Dantley	23,177

* Regular season games only
# Still active at end of 1995 season

If points from the ABA were also considered, then Abdul-Jabbar would still be number one, with the same total. He was born as Lew Alcindor but adopted a new name when he converted to the Islamic faith in 1969. The following year he turned professional, playing for Milwaukee. Despite scoring an NBA record 38,387 points he could not emulate the great Wilt Chamberlain by scoring 100 points in a game, which Chamberlain achieved for Philadelphia against New York at Hershey, Pennsylvania, on March 2, 1962.

DID YOU KNOW

"WILT THE STILT"

The 7-ft 1-in player Wilt Chamberlain, affectionately known as "Wilt the Stilt," stands second only to Kareem Abdul-Jabbar in career points and is the all-time rebounder, as well as holding more season records than any other player. Wilton Norman Chamberlain was born August 21, 1936, in Philadelphia, Pennsylvania – one of the two cities, with Los Angeles, with which he spent most of his career. After a year with the Harlem Globetrotters, Chamberlain joined the NBA in 1959, playing for 14 years and winning four MVPs and two world championships. In the Top 10 of points scored in a game, Chamberlain's name appears six times. His unrivaled catalog of individual game records encompasses such categories as most points, rebounds, field goals attempted, field goals made, field goals percentage, free throws attempted, and free throws made. He was inducted into the Basketball Hall of Fame in 1978. He became best known in his retirement for his alleged lifetime sexual conquests, the reputed number of which may well have been confused with one of his basketball statistics.

AMERICAN FOOTBALL

BIGGEST WINNING MARGINS IN THE SUPER BOWL

	Winners	Runners-up	Year	Score	Margin
1	San Francisco 49ers	Denver Broncos	1990	55–10	45
2	Chicago Bears	New England Patriots	1986	46–10	36
3	Dallas Cowboys	Buffalo Bills	1993	52–17	35
4	Washington Redskins	Denver Broncos	1988	42–10	32
5	LA Raiders	Washington Redskins	1984	38–9	29
6	Green Bay Packers	Kansas City Chiefs	1967	35–10	25
7	San Francisco 49ers	San Diego Chargers	1995	49–26	23
8	San Francisco 49ers	Miami Dolphins	1985	38–16	22
9	Dallas Cowboys	Miami Dolphins	1972	24–3	21
10=	Green Bay Packers	Oakland	1968	33–14	19
10=	New York Giants	Denver Broncos	1987	39–20	19

COLLEGES WITH THE MOST BOWL WINS

	College	Wins
1	Alabama	27
2	University of Southern California (USC)	24
3=	Oklahoma	20
3=	Penn State	20
3=	Tennessee	20
6=	Georgia Tech	17
6=	Texas	17
8=	Georgia	15
8=	Nebraska	15
8=	Florida State	15

PLAYERS WITH THE MOST TOUCHDOWNS IN AN NFL CAREER*

	Player	Touchdowns		Player	Touchdowns
1	Jerry Rice	156	6	Lenny Moore	113
2	Jim Brown	126	7	Don Hutson	105
3=	Walter Payton	125	8	Steve Largent	101
3=	Marcus Allen	125	9	Franco Harris	100
5	John Riggins	116	10	Eric Dickerson	96

* To end of 1995–96 season

BROWN RUNS FOR THE BROWNS
Star running-back for the Cleveland Browns from 1957 to 1966, Brown rushed 12,312 yards and scored 126 touchdowns.

MOST SUCCESSFUL RUSHERS IN AN NFL CAREER

	Player	Total yards gained rushing
1	Walter Payton	16,726
2	Eric Dickerson	13,259
3	Tony Dorsett	12,739
4	Jim Brown	12,312
5	Franco Harris	12,120
6	John Riggins	11,352
7	O.J. Simpson	11,236
8	Marcus Allen*	11,002
9	Ottis Anderson	10,273
10	Barry Sanders*	10,172

* Still active at end of 1995–96 season

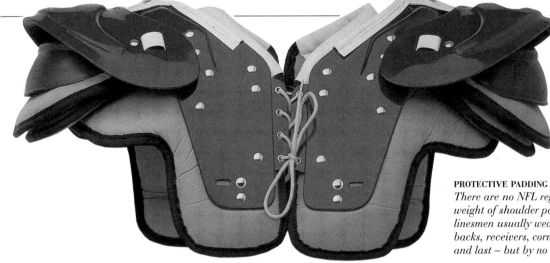

PROTECTIVE PADDING
There are no NFL regulations concerning the size and weight of shoulder pads, but offensive and defensive linesmen usually wear the biggest, followed by the backs, receivers, corners and safeties, quarterbacks, and last – but by no means least – kickers.

T O P 1 0
LARGEST NFL STADIUMS*

	Stadium	Home team	Capacity
1	Clemson Memorial Stadium	Carolina Panthers	81,000
2	Pontiac Silverdrome	Detroit Lions	80,500
3	Rich Stadium	Buffalo Bills	80,290
4	Cleveland Stadium	Cleveland Browns	80,098
5	Arrowhead Stadium	Kansas City Chiefs	78,067
6	Giants Stadium	New York Giants/Jets	76,891
7	Mile High Stadium	Denver Broncos	76,283
8	Joe Robbie Stadium	Miami Dolphins	75,000
9	Tampa Stadium	Tampa Bay Buccaneers	74,321
10	Sun Devil Stadium	Phoenix Cardinals	73,500

* As at end of 1995–96 season
Source: National Football League

T O P 1 0
MOST SUCCESSFUL TEAMS*

	Team	Wins	Runners-up	Points
1	Dallas Cowboys	4	3	11
2	San Francisco 49ers	5	0	10
3	Pittsburgh Steelers	4	1	9
4	Washington Redskins	3	2	8
5=	Oakland/Los Angeles Raiders	3	1	7
5=	Miami Dolphins	2	3	7
7=	Green Bay Packers	2	0	4
7=	New York Giants	2	0	4
9=	Buffalo Bills	0	4	4
9=	Denver Broncos	0	4	4
9=	Minnesota Vikings	0	4	4

* Based on two points for a Super Bowl win, and one for runner-up

T O P 1 0
POINT-SCORERS IN AN NFL SEASON

	Player	Team	Year	Points
1	Paul Hornung	Green Bay Packers	1960	176
2	Mark Moseley	Washington Redskins	1983	161
3	Gino Cappelletti	Boston Patriots	1964	155*
4	Emitt Smith	Dallas Cowboys	1995	150
5	Chip Lohmiller	Washington Redskins	1991	149
6	Gino Cappelletti	Boston Patriots	1961	147
7	Paul Hornung	Green Bay Packers	1961	146
8	Jim Turner	New York Jets	1968	145
9=	John Riggins	Washington Redskins	1983	144
9=	Kevin Butler#	Chicago Bears	1985	144

* Including a two-point conversion
 # The only rookie in this Top 10

T O P 1 0
MOST SUCCESSFUL COACHES IN AN NFL CAREER

	Coach	Games won
1	Don Shula	347
2	George Halas	324
3	Tom Landry	270
4	Curly Lambeau	229
5	Chuck Noll	209
6	Chuck Knox	193
7	Paul Brown	170
8	Bud Grant	168
9	Steve Owen	154
10	Dan Reeves*	143

* Still active at end of 1995–96 season

GOLF – THE MAJORS

PLAYERS TO WIN THE MOST MAJORS IN A CAREER

	Player	Country	British Open	US Open	Masters	PGA	Total
1	Jack Nicklaus	US	3	4	6	5	18
2	Walter Hagen	US	4	2	0	5	11
3=	Ben Hogan	US	1	4	2	2	9
3=	Gary Player	South Africa	3	1	3	2	9
5	Tom Watson	US	5	1	2	0	8
6=	Harry Vardon	UK	6	1	0	0	7
6=	Gene Sarazen	US	1	2	1	3	7
6=	Bobby Jones	US	3	4	0	0	7
6=	Sam Snead	US	1	0	3	3	7
6=	Arnold Palmer	US	2	1	4	0	7

The four Majors are the British Open, the US Open, the US Masters, and the US PGA (Professional Golfers Association). The oldest is the British Open, first played at Prestwick in 1860 and won by Willie Park. The first US Open was held at the Newport Club, Rhode Island, in 1895 and was won by Horace Rawlins. The US PGA Championship, probably the least prestigious of the four Majors, was first held at the Siwanoy Club, New York. Jim Barnes beat Jock Hutchison by one hole in the match-play final. It did not become a stroke-play event until 1958. The youngest of the four Majors is the Masters, played over the Augusta National Course in Georgia. Entry is by invitation only, and the first winner was Horton Smith.

LOWEST FOUR-ROUND SCORES IN THE BRITISH OPEN

	Player	Country	Year	Venue	Score
1	Greg Norman	Australia	1993	Sandwich	267
2=	Tom Watson	US	1977	Turnberry	268
2=	Nick Price	South Africa	1994	Turnberry	268
4=	Jack Nicklaus	US	1977	Turnberry	269
4=	Nick Faldo	UK	1993	Sandwich	269
4=	Jesper Parnevik	Sweden	1994	Turnberry	269
7=	Nick Faldo	UK	1990	St. Andrews	270
7=	Bernhard Langer	Germany	1993	Sandwich	270
9=	Tom Watson	US	1980	Muirfield	271
9=	Fuzzy Zoeller	US	1994	Turnberry	271

The first time the Open Championship was played over four rounds of 18 holes was at Muirfield in 1892, when the amateur Harold H. Hilton won with scores of 78, 81, 72, and 74 for a total of 305. Since then the record has kept falling, and at Turnberry in 1977 Tom Watson and Jack Nicklaus decimated British Open records, with Watson winning by one stroke with a championship record 268. It remained unbeaten for 16 years until Australia's Greg Norman became the first champion to shoot four rounds under 70 when he won with a 267 at Sandwich in 1993. The lowest individual round is 63, which has been achieved by seven golfers: Mark Hayes (US), Turnberry 1977; Isao Aoki (Japan), Muirfield 1980; Greg Norman (Australia), Turnberry 1986; Paul Broadhurst (UK), St. Andrews 1990; Jodie Mudd (US), Royal Birkdale 1991; Nick Faldo (UK), Sandwich 1993; and Payne Stewart (US), Sandwich 1993. Hubert Green (1980), Tom Watson (1980), Craig Stadler (1983), Christy O'Connor, Jr. (1985), Seve Ballesteros (1986), Rodger Davis (1987), Ian Baker-Finch (1990 and 1991), Fred Couples (1991), Nick Faldo (1992 and 1994), Raymond Floyd (1992), Steve Pate (1992), Wayne Grady (1993), Greg Norman (1993), Fuzzy Zoeller (1994), Anders Forsbrand (1994), Larry Mize (1994), and Mark Brooks (1994) have all recorded rounds of 64. Thirty more men have registered rounds of 65.

MOST USED COURSES FOR THE BRITISH OPEN

	Course	First used	Last used	Times used
1	St. Andrews	1873	1995	25
2	Prestwick	1860	1925	24
3	Muirfield	1892	1992	14
4	Royal St. George's, Sandwich	1894	1993	12
5	Hoylake	1897	1967	10
6	Royal Lytham	1926	1988	8
7	Royal Birkdale	1954	1991	7
8=	Musselburgh	1874	1889	6
8=	Royal Troon	1923	1989	6
10	Carnoustie	1931	1975	5

The first Open in 1860 was organized by the Prestwick Club, which was also solely responsible for the first 11 championships. After Tom Morris, Jr. won the title for a 3rd consecutive year in 1870, he was allowed to keep the winner's prize, a red morocco leather belt. With no trophy to play for, there was no championship in 1871. It was revived, however, the following year by the Prestwick Club, the Honourable Company of Edinburgh Golfers, and the Royal and Ancient. That same year the now famous claret jug was first presented to the winner, Tom Morris, Jr., again.

THE 10

LOWEST WINNING SCORES IN THE US OPEN

	Player	Country	Year	Venue	Score
1=	Jack Nicklaus	US	1980	Baltusrol	272
1=	Lee Janzen	US	1993	Baltusrol	272
3	David Graham	Australia	1981	Merion	273
4=	Jack Nicklaus	US	1967	Baltusrol	275
4=	Lee Trevino	US	1968	Oak Hill	275
6=	Ben Hogan	US	1948	Riviera	276
6=	Fuzzy Zoeller	US	1984	Winged Foot	276
8=	Jerry Pate	US	1976	Atlanta	277
8=	Scott Simpson	US	1987	Olympic Club	277
10=	Ken Venturi	US	1964	Congressional	278
10=	Billy Casper	US	1966	Olympic Club	278
10=	Hubert Green	US	1977	Southern Hills	278
10=	Curtis Strange	US	1988	Brookline	278
10=	Curtis Strange	US	1989	Oak Hill	278

In winning the 1980 US Open at Baltusrol, 18 years after his first success in the tournament, Jack Nicklaus did so in record-breaking style. Not only was his four-round aggregate a new championship record, but on day one he shot a record-equaling 63. His second round 71 also lowered the aggregate record for 36 holes, and after three rounds his total of 204 established yet another new record.

THE 10

LOWEST WINNING SCORES IN THE US MASTERS

	Player*	Year	Score
1=	Jack Nicklaus	1965	271
1=	Raymond Floyd	1976	271
3=	Ben Hogan	1953	274
3=	Ben Crenshaw	1995	274
5=	Severiano Ballesteros (Spain)	1980	275
5=	Fred Couples	1992	275
7=	Arnold Palmer	1964	276
7=	Jack Nicklaus	1975	276
7=	Tom Watson	1977	276
7=	Nick Faldo (UK)	1996	276

All US players unless otherwise stated

The US Masters, the brainchild of American amateur golfer Robert Tyre "Bobby" Jones, is the only Major played on the same course each year, at Augusta, Georgia. The course was built on the site of an old nursery, and the abundance of flowers, shrubs, and plants is a reminder of its former days, with each of the holes named after the plants growing adjacent to it.

TOP 10

MOST SUCCESSFUL BRITONS IN MAJORS

	Player	Titles
1	Harry Vardon	7
2=	James Braid	5
2=	Nick Faldo	5
2=	John Henry Taylor	5
5=	Tom Morris, Sr.	4
5=	Tom Morris, Jr.	4
5=	Willie Park, Sr.	4
8=	Willie Anderson	3
8=	Robert Ferguson	3
8=	Henry Cotton	3

All, except Vardon (US Open, 1900) and Faldo (US Masters, 1989 and 1990), won their Majors on British soil.

TOP 10

HIGHEST-EARNING GOLFERS ON THE PGA TOUR

	Player	Country	Winnings ($)
1	Greg Norman	Australia	9,592,829
2	Tom Kite	US	9,337,998
3	Payne Stewart	US	7,389,479
4	Nick Price	South Africa	7,338,119
5	Fred Couples	US	7,188,408
6	Corey Pavin	US	7,175,523
7	Tom Watson	US	7,072,113
8	Paul Azinger	US	6,957,324
9	Ben Crenshaw	US	6,845,235
10	Curtis Strange	US	6,791,618

Source: PGA Tour

GOLFER'S GOLDEN OPPORTUNITY
Jack Nicklaus, known as "The Golden Bear," is the winner of 18 professional majors since 1962. His record seems unlikely to be challenged in the foreseeable future.

HORSE RACING

US JOCKEYS WITH HIGHEST WINNINGS IN 1995

	Jockey	1st places	Winnings ($)
1	Jerry Bailey	287	16,311,876
2	Corey Nakatani	302	15,156,276
3	Gary Stevens	221	14,526,108
4	Pat Day	239	11,750,800
5	Mike Earl Smith	263	11,704,157
6	Chris McCarron	166	11,306,603
7	Kent Desormeaux	235	10,767,379
8	Ed Delahoussaye	170	9,180,455
9	Alexis Solis	210	8,702,970
10	Jorge Chavez	248	8,528,229

US JOCKEYS WITH MOST WINS IN A CAREER

	Jockey	Years riding	Wins
1	Willie Shoemaker	42	8,833
2	Laffit Pincay, Jr.	29	8,417
3	Angel Cordero, Jr.	31	7,057
4	Jorge Velasquez	32	6,877
5	David Gall	38	6,611
6	Pat Day	23	6,545
7	Larry Snyder	35	6,388
8	Carl Gambardella	39	6,349
9	Chris McCarron	19	6,241
10	Sandy Hawley	27	6,204

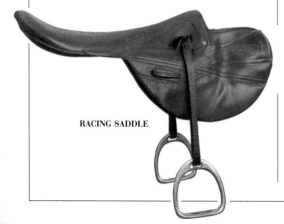

RACING SADDLE

JOCKEYS IN ENGLISH CLASSICS

	Jockey	Years	1,000 Guineas	2,000 Guineas	Derby	Oaks	St. Leger	Total
1	Lester Piggott	1954–92	2	5	9	6	8	30
2	Frank Buckle	1792–1827	6	5	5	9	2	27
3	Jem Robinson	1817–48	5	9	6	2	2	24
4	Fred Archer	1874–86	2	4	5	4	6	21
5=	Bill Scott	1821–46	0	3	4	3	9	19
5=	Jack Watts	1883–97	4	2	4	4	5	19
7	Willie Carson	1972–94	1	5	4	4	3	17
8=	John Day	1826–41	5	4	0	5	2	16
8=	George Fordham	1859–83	7	3	1	5	0	16
10	Joe Childs	1912–33	2	2	3	4	4	15

TRAINERS OF ENGLISH CLASSIC WINNERS

	Trainer	Years	1,000 Guineas	2,000 Guineas	Derby	Oaks	St. Leger	Total
1	John Scott	1827–63	4	7	5	8	16	40
2	Robert Robson	1793–1827	9	6	7	12	0	34
3	Mat Dawson	1853–95	6	5	6	5	6	28
4	John Porter	1868–1900	2	5	7	3	6	23
5	Alec Taylor	1905–27	1	4	3	8	5	21
6=	Fred Darling	1916–47	2	5	7	2	3	19
6=	Noel Murless	1948–73	6	2	3	5	3	19
8	Dixon Boyce	1805–29	3	5	5	4	0	17
10=	Vincent O'Brien	1957–84	1	4	6	2	3	16
10=	Dick Hern	1962–89	1	2	3	3	6	16

FASTEST WINNING TIMES OF THE KENTUCKY DERBY

	Horse	Year	Time min	Time sec		Horse	Year	Time min	Time sec
1	Secretariat	1973	1	59.4	6=	Affirmed	1978	2	01.2
2	Northern Dancer	1964	2	00.0	6=	Thunder Gulch	1995	2	01.2
3	Spend a Buck	1985	2	00.2	9	Whirlaway	1941	2	01.4
4	Decidedly	1962	2	00.4	10=	Middleground	1950	2	01.6
5	Proud Clarion	1967	2	00.6	10=	Hill Gail	1952	2	01.6
6=	Lucky Debonair	1965	2	01.2	10=	Bold Forbes	1976	2	01.6

TOP 10
EPSOM DERBY-WINNING JOCKEYS

	Jockey	Years	Wins
1	Lester Piggott	1954–83	9
2=	Jem Robinson	1817–36	6
2=	Steve Donoghue	1915–25	6
4=	John Arnull	1784–99	5
4=	Bill Clift	1793–1819	5
4=	Frank Buckle	1792–1823	5
4=	Fred Archer	1877–86	5
8=	Sam Arnull	1780–98	4
8=	Tom Goodison	1809–22	4
8=	Bill Scott	1832–43	4
8=	Jack Watts	1887–96	4
8=	Charlie Smirke	1934–58	4
8=	Willie Carson	1979–94	4

Lester Piggott has been so dominant in the postwar era that his total of nine Derby winners is five more than Willie Carson's and six more than the next highest postwar winning jockeys, Rae Johnstone, Pat Eddery, and Walter Swinburn.

TOP 10
TRAINERS OF EPSOM DERBY WINNERS

	Trainer	Years	Wins		Trainer	Years	Wins
1=	Robert Robson	1793–1823	7	**4=**	Vincent O'Brien	1962–82	6
1=	John Porter	1868–99	7	**7=**	Richard Prince	1795–1819	5
1=	Fred Darling	1922–41	7	**7=**	Dixon Boyce	1805–28	5
4=	Frank Neale	1782–1804	6	**7=**	James Edwards	1811–36	5
4=	Mat Dawson	1860–95	6	**7=**	John Scott	1835–53	5

John Porter's fourth Derby winner was Ormonde in 1896, ridden by Fred Archer. Ormonde was one of the great racehorses of the late 19th century and won all 16 races he entered, including the 1886 British Triple Crown. He won the 1886 Champion Stakes at odds of 100–1 on.

TOP 10
JOCKEYS IN US TRIPLE CROWN RACES

	Jockey	Kentucky Derby	Preakness Stakes	Belmont Stakes	Total
1	Eddie Arcaro	5	6	6	17
2	Willie Shoemaker	4	2	5	11
3=	Bill Hartack	5	3	1	9
3=	Earle Sande	3	1	5	9
5	Jimmy McLaughlin	1	1	6	8
6	Pat Day	1	4	2	7
7=	Angel Cordero, Jr.	3	2	1	6
7=	Chas Kurtsinger	2	2	2	6
7=	Ron Turcotte	2	2	2	6
10=	Eddie Delahoussaye	2	1	2	5
10=	Lloyd Hughes	0	3	2	5
10=	Johnny Loftus	2	2	1	5
10=	Chris McCarron	2	2	1	5
10=	Willie Simms	2	1	2	5

TOP 10
JOCKEYS IN THE BREEDERS CUP

	Jockey	Years	Wins
1	Pat Day	1984–94	8
2=	Eddie Delahoussaye	1984–93	7
2=	Laffit Pincay, Jr.	1985–93	7
4=	Pat Valenzuela	1986–92	6
4=	Chris McCarron	1985–95	6
4=	Mike Smith	1992–95	6
7=	José Santos	1986–90	5
7=	Jerry Bailey	1991–95	5
9	Angel Cordero, Jr.	1985–89	4
10=	Craig Perret	1984–90	3
10=	Randy Romero	1987–89	3
10=	Gary Stevens	1990–94	3

Held at a different venue each year, the Breeders Cup is an end-of-season gathering with seven races run during the day, and with the season's best thoroughbreds competing in each category.

CAR RACING – FORMULA ONE

YOUNGEST WORLD CHAMPIONS OF ALL TIME

	Driver/country	Year	Age* yrs	Age* mths
1	Emerson Fittipaldi (Brazil)	1972	25	9
2	Michael Schumacher (Germany)	1994	25	10
3	Niki Lauda (Austria)	1975	26	7
4	Jim Clark (UK)	1963	27	7
5	Jochen Rindt (Austria)	1970	28	6
6	Ayrton Senna (Brazil)	1988	28	7
7=	James Hunt (UK)	1976	29	2
7=	Nelson Piquet (Brazil)	1981	29	2
9	Mike Hawthorn (UK)	1958	29	6
10	Jody Scheckter (South Africa)	1979	29	8

* If a driver is eligible to appear on the list twice, only his youngest age is considered

Some branches of the media reported that Michael Schumacher had become the youngest world champion in 1994. This was not the case. At the time of his capturing the title in Adelaide on November 13, 1994, he was 25 years and 314 days (born January 3, 1969), but Emerson Fittipaldi (born December 12, 1946) secured his first world title at the Monza Grand Prix on September 10, 1972, when he was merely 25 years and 273 days old.

OLDEST WORLD CHAMPIONS OF ALL TIME

	Driver/country	Year	Age* yrs	Age* mths
1	Juan Manuel Fangio (Argentina)	1957	46	2
2	Giuseppe Farina (Italy)	1950	43	11
3	Jack Brabham (Australia)	1966	40	6
4	Graham Hill (UK)	1968	39	9
5	Mario Andretti (US)	1978	38	8
6	Alain Prost (France)	1993	38	7
7	Nigel Mansell (UK)	1992	37	11
8	Niki Lauda (Austria)	1984	35	8
9	Nelson Piquet (Brazil)	1987	35	3
10	Alberto Ascari (Italy)	1953	35	1

* If a driver is eligible to appear on the list twice, only his oldest age is considered

The oldest man to compete in a World Championship Grand Prix was Louis Chiron (Monaco), who was 55 years 8 months old when he joined the competition in the 1955 Monaco Grand Prix. The oldest man to win a race was Luigi Fagioli (Italy), who was 53 years 1 month when he won the 1951 French Grand Prix.

FANGIO FIRST AND FOREMOST
Argentina's Juan Manuel Fangio was the foremost driver in the early days of world championship Grand Prix racing. His record of 24 wins out of 51 starts seemed invincible until it was surpassed by the equally formidable Jim Clark.

DRIVERS WITH THE MOST WORLD TITLES

	Driver/country	Titles
1	Juan Manuel Fangio (Argentina)	5
2	Alain Prost (France)	4
3=	Jack Brabham (Australia)	3
3=	Niki Lauda (Austria)	3
3=	Nelson Piquet (Brazil)	3
3=	Ayrton Senna (Brazil)	3
3=	Jackie Stewart (UK)	3
8=	Alberto Ascari (Italy)	2
8=	Jim Clark (UK)	2
8=	Graham Hill (UK)	2
8=	Emerson Fittipaldi (Brazil)	2
8=	Michael Schumacher (Germany)	2

DRIVERS WITH THE MOST GRAND PRIX WINS

	Driver/country	Years	Wins
1	Alain Prost (France)	1981–93	51
2	Ayrton Senna (Brazil)	1985–93	41
3	Nigel Mansell (UK)	1985–94	31
4	Jackie Stewart (UK)	1965–73	27
5=	Jim Clark (UK)	1962–68	25
5=	Niki Lauda (Austria)	1974–85	25
7	Juan Manuel Fangio (Argentina)	1950–57	24
8	Nelson Piquet (Brazil)	1980–91	23
9	Michael Schumacher (Germany)	1992–95	18
10	Stirling Moss (UK)	1955–61	16

T O P 1 0

BRITISH DRIVERS WITH THE MOST GRAND PRIX WINS

	Driver	Years	Wins
1	Nigel Mansell	1985–94	31
2	Jackie Stewart	1965–73	27
3	Jim Clark	1962–68	25
4	Stirling Moss	1955–61	16
5	Graham Hill	1962–69	14
6	James Hunt	1975–77	10
7	Damon Hill	1993–94	9
8=	Tony Brooks	1957–59	6
8=	John Surtees	1963–67	6
10	John Watson	1976–83	5

Of all the drivers in this list, all but Stirling Moss, Damon Hill, Tony Brooks, and John Watson were world champions – a situation that many believe will be altered when Damon Hill, son of Graham Hill (at No. 5), finally achieves his goal.

DRIVERS WITH THE MOST GRAND PRIX POINTS

	Driver/country	Years	Points
1	Alain Prost (France)	1980–93	798.5
2	Ayrton Senna (Brazil)	1985–94	614
3	Nelson Piquet (Brazil)	1978–91	485.5
4	Nigel Mansell (UK)	1980–94	482
5	Niki Lauda (Austria)	1971–85	420.5
6	Jackie Stewart (UK)	1965–73	360
7	Gerhard Berger (Austria)	1984–95	338
8	Carlos Reutemann (Argentina)	1972–82	310
9	Michael Schumacher (Germany)	1991–95	303
10	Graham Hill (UK)	1958–75	289

The World Drivers' Championship often takes into consideration only those points earned over a certain number of successful drives. This Top 10, however, is a list of all points obtained, whether they counted toward the Championship or not.

T O P 1 0

DRIVERS WITH THE MOST WINS IN A SEASON

	Driver/country	Season	Wins
1	Nigel Mansell (UK)	1992	9
2=	Ayrton Senna (Brazil)	1988	8
2=	Michael Schumacher (Germany)	1994	8
2=	Michael Schumacher (Germany)	1995	8
5=	Jim Clark (UK)	1963	7
5=	Alain Prost (France)	1984	7*
5=	Alain Prost (France)	1988	7*
5=	Alain Prost (France)	1993	7
5=	Ayrton Senna (Brazil)	1991	7
10=	Alberto Ascari (Italy)	1952	6
10=	Juan Manuel Fangio (Argentina)	1954	6
10=	Jim Clark (UK)	1965	6
10=	Jackie Stewart (UK)	1969	6
10=	Jackie Stewart (UK)	1971	6
10=	James Hunt (UK)	1976	6
10=	Mario Andretti (US)	1978	6
10=	Nigel Mansell (UK)	1987	6*
10=	Ayrton Senna (Brazil)	1990	6
10=	Damon Hill (UK)	1994	6*

* Did not win the world title that year

In 1988 the Marlboro-McLaren pair of Ayrton Senna and Alain Prost completely dominated the Grand Prix scene by winning 15 of the 16 rounds between them.

T O P 1 0

MANUFACTURERS WITH THE MOST WORLD TITLES

	Manufacturer	Titles
1	Ferrari	8
2=	Lotus	7
2=	Williams	7
4	McLaren	6
5=	Brabham	2
5=	Cooper	2
7=	BRM	1
7=	Matra	1
7=	Tyrrell	1
7=	Vanwall	1
7=	Benetton	1

McLaren, who shares the most wins with Ferrari, had their 104th win in 1993 when Ayrton Senna won at Monaco. The McLaren team was first formed in 1963 by New Zealander Bruce McLaren and ventured into Formula One in 1966. McLaren's first Grand Prix did not come until the 1968 Belgian Grand Prix with McLaren himself driving. The team suffered a great loss in 1970 when McLaren was killed during a training session at Goodwood, but with a host of designers behind them it has remained at the forefront of Formula One.

T O P 1 0

MANUFACTURERS WITH THE MOST GRAND PRIX WINS

	Manufacturer	Years	Wins
1	Ferrari	1951–95	105
2	McLaren	1968–93	104
3	Williams	1979–95	83
4	Lotus	1960–87	79
5	Brabham	1964–85	35
6	Benetton	1986–95	25
7	Tyrrell	1971–83	23
8	BRM	1959–72	17
9	Cooper	1958–67	16
10	Renault	1979–83	15

CAR RACING – US

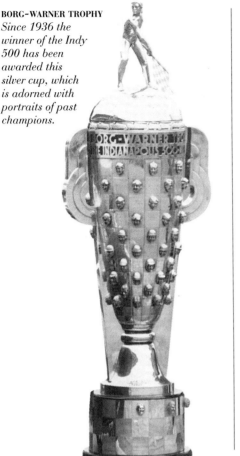

BORG-WARNER TROPHY
Since 1936 the winner of the Indy 500 has been awarded this silver cup, which is adorned with portraits of past champions.

TOP 10

FASTEST WINNING SPEEDS OF THE INDIANAPOLIS 500

	Driver*	Car	Year	Speed km/h	mph
1	Arie Luyendyk (Netherlands)	Lola-Chevrolet	1990	299.307	185.984
2	Rick Mears	Chevrolet-Lumina	1991	283.980	176.457
3	Bobby Rahal	March-Cosworth	1986	274.750	170.722
4	Emerson Fittipaldi (Brazil)	Penske-Chevrolet	1989	269.695	167.581
5	Rick Mears	March-Cosworth	1984	263.308	163.612
6	Mark Donohue	McLaren-Offenhauser	1972	262.619	162.962
7	Al Unser, Jr.	March-Cosworth	1987	260.995	162.175
8	Tom Sneva	March-Cosworth	1983	260.902	162.117
9	Gordon Johncock	Wildcat-Cosworth	1982	260.760	162.029
10	Al Unser	Lola-Cosworth	1978	259.689	161.363

*All US drivers unless otherwise stated

The first Indianapolis 500, known affectionately as the "Indy," was held on Memorial Day, May 30, 1911, and was won by Ray Harroun driving a bright yellow 447-cubic inch six-cylinder Marmon Wasp at an average speed of 74.59 mph/120.04 km/h. The race takes place over 200 laps of the 2½-mile Indianapolis Raceway, which from 1927 to 1945 was owned by the World War I flying ace Eddie Rickenbacker. Over the years, the speed has steadily increased: Harroun's race took 6 hours 42 minutes 6 seconds to complete, while Arie Luyendyk's record-breaking win was achieved in just 2 hours 18 minutes 18.248 seconds.

TOP 10

MONEY-WINNERS AT THE INDIANAPOLIS 500 IN 1995

	Driver	Chassis	Total prizes ($)
1	Jacques Villeneuve	Reynard/Ford Cosworth	1,312,019
2	Christian Fittipaldi	Reynard/Ford Cosworth	594,668
3	Bobby Rahal	Lola/Mercedes Benz	373,267
4	Eliseo Salazar	Lola/Ford Cosworth	302,417
5	Robby Gordon	Reynard/Ford Cosworth	247,917
6	Mauricio Gugelmin	Reynard/Ford Cosworth	284,667
7	Arie Luyendyk	Lola/Menard V6	247,417
8	Teo Fabi	Reynard/Ford Cosworth	206,853
9	Danny Sullivan	Reynard/Ford Cosworth	193,453
10	Hiro Matsushita	Reynard/Ford Cosworth	196,053

Drivers are ranked here according to their finishing order, but as the list indicates, prize money – which in 1995 totaled $8,063,550 – does not follow precisely, varying according to such designations as first using a particular brand of tire. Even losers can be high earners in the Indy: Carlos Guerrero, who finished in 33rd and last position, earned $172,853. The only woman in the race, Lyn St. James, was placed 32nd in the money-winners with $157,803.

TOP 10

WINNERS OF THE INDIANAPOLIS 500 WITH THE HIGHEST STARTING POSITIONS

	Driver	Year	Starting position
1=	Ray Harroun	1911	28
1=	Louis Meyer	1936	28
3	Fred Frame	1932	27
4	Johnny Rutherford	1974	25
5=	Kelly Petillo	1935	22
5=	George Souders	1927	22
7	L.L. Corum and Joe Boyer	1924	21
8=	Frank Lockart	1926	20
8=	Tommy Milton	1921	20
8=	Al Unser, Jr.	1987	20

Of the 75 winners of the Indianapolis 500, 44 have started from a position between 1 and 5 on the starting grid. This Top 10 is of those winners who started from farthest back in the starting lineup.

DRIVERS WITH THE MOST WINSTON CUP TITLES

	Driver	Years	Titles
1=	Richard Petty	1964–79	7
1=	Dale Earnhardt*	1980–94	7
3=	Lee Petty	1954–59	3
3=	David Pearson	1966–69	3
3=	Cale Yarborough	1976–78	3
3=	Darrell Waltrip*	1981–85	3
7=	Herb Thomas	1951–53	2
7=	Tim Flock	1952–55	2
7=	Buck Baker	1956–57	2
7=	Ned Jarrett	1961–65	2
7=	Joe Weatherly	1962–63	2

* Still driving at the end of the 1995 season

The Winston Cup is a season-long series of races organized by the National Association of Stock Car Auto Racing, Inc. (NASCAR). Races, which take place over enclosed circuits such as Daytona speedway, are among the most popular car races in the US. The series started in 1949 (when it was won by Red Byron) as the Grand National series, but changed its style to the Winston Cup in 1970 when sponsored by the R. J. Reynolds tobacco company, manufacturers of Winston cigarettes. Cale (William Caleb) Yarborough, who also won the Daytona 500 on four occasions, is the only driver to win three successive titles. He, and all the other drivers in this Top 10, are all from the US.

NASCAR* MONEY-WINNERS OF ALL TIME

	Driver	Total prizes ($)
1	Dale Earnhardt	25,948,545
2	Bill Elliott	15,540,479
3	Darrell Waltrip	14,441,866
4	Rusty Wallace	12,754,720
5	Terry Labonte	10,454,755
6	Mark Martin	10,030,812
7	Rickey Rudd	10,023,314
8	Geoff Bodine	9,412,788
9	Harry Gant	8,438,094
10	Richard Petty	7,757,964

* National Association for Stock Car Auto Racing, Inc.

CART* DRIVERS WITH THE MOST RACE WINS

	Driver	Wins
1	A.J. Foyt, Jr.	67
2	Mario Andretti	52
3	Al Unser	39
4	Bobby Unser	35
5	Al Unser, Jr.	31
6	Michael Andretti	30
7	Rick Mears	29
8	Johnny Rutherford	27
9	Roger Ward	26
10	Gordon Johncock	25

* Championship Auto Racing Teams

FASTEST WINNING SPEEDS OF THE DAYTONA 500

	Driver*	Car	Year	Speed km/h	mph
1	Buddy Baker	Oldsmobile	1980	285.823	177.602
2	Bill Elliott	Ford	1987	283.668	176.263
3	Bill Elliott	Ford	1985	277.234	172.265
4	Richard Petty	Buick	1981	273.027	169.651
5	Derrike Cope	Chevrolet	1990	266.766	165.761
6	A.J. Foyt, Jr.	Mercury	1972	259.990	161.550
7	Richard Petty	Plymouth	1966	258.504	160.627
8	Davey Allison	Ford	1992	257.913	160.260 #
9	Bobby Allison	Ford	1978	257.060	159.730
10	LeeRoy Yarborough	Ford	1967	254.196	157.950

* All drivers from the US
 # Race reduced to 495 miles/797 km

RACING INTO HISTORY
Ray Harroun, in his Marmon Wasp, speeds down the home stretch in 1911 to win the very first Indianapolis 500.

ICE HOCKEY

TEAMS WITH THE MOST STANLEY CUP WINS

	Team	Wins
1	Montreal Canadiens	24
2	Toronto Maple Leafs	13
3	Detroit Red Wings	7
4	Ottawa Senators	6
5=	Boston Bruins	5
5=	Edmonton Oilers	5
7=	Montreal Victorias	4
7=	Montreal Wanderers	4
7=	New York Islanders	4
7=	New York Rangers	4

During his time as Governor General of Canada from 1888 to 1893, Sir Frederick Arthur Stanley (Lord Stanley of Preston and 16th Earl of Derby) became interested in what is called hockey in the United States, and ice hockey elsewhere, and in 1893 presented a trophy to be contested by the best amateur teams in Canada. The first trophy went to the Montreal Amateur Athletic Association who won it without a challenge from any other team.

POINT-SCORERS IN STANLEY CUP PLAY-OFF MATCHES

	Player	Total points
1	Wayne Gretzky*	346
2	Mark Messier*	272
3	Jari Kurri*	222
4	Glenn Anderson	209
5	Bryan Trottier	184
6	Jean Beliveau	176
7	Paul Coffey*	172
8	Denis Savard*	170
9	Denis Potvin	164
10=	Mike Bossy	160
10=	Gordie Howe	160
10=	Bobby Smith	160

* Still active at end of 1994–95 season

BIGGEST NHL ARENAS

	Stadium	Location	Home team	Capacity
1	Thunderdome	Tampa	Tampa Bay Lightning	26,000
2	Forum	Montreal*	Montreal Canadiens	21,401
3	United Center	Chicago	Chicago Blackhawks	20,500
4	Canadian Airlines Saddledrome	Calgary	Calgary Flames	20,200
5	Joe Louis Sports Arena	Detroit	Detroit Red Wings	19,275
6	Kiel Center	St. Louis	St. Louis Blues	19,260
7	General Motors Place	Vancouver*	Vancouver Canucks	19,056
8	Meadowlands Arena	East Rutherford	New Jersey Devils	19,040
9	Paladium	Ottawa*	Ottawa Senators	18,500
10	Madison Square Garden	New York	New York Rangers	18,200

* New venue opened for the 1995–96 season

WINNERS OF THE HART TROPHY

	Player	Years	Wins		Player	Years	Wins
1	Wayne Gretzky	1980–89	9	**7=**	Phil Esposito	1969–74	2
2	Gordie Howe	1952–63	6	**7=**	Bobby Hull	1965–66	2
3	Eddie Shore	1933–38	4	**7=**	Mario Lemieux	1988–93	2
4=	Bobby Clarke	1973–76	3	**7=**	Guy Lafleur	1977–78	2
4=	Howie Morenz	1928–32	3	**7=**	Mark Messier	1990–92	2
4=	Bobby Orr	1970–72	3	**7=**	Stan Mikita	1967–68	2
7=	Jean Beliveau	1956–64	2	**7=**	Nels Stewart	1926–30	2
7=	Bill Cowley	1941–43	2				

The Hart Trophy has been awarded annually since 1924 and is presented to the player "adjudged to be the most valuable to his team during the season." The winner is selected by the Profesional Hockey Writers' Association and the trophy is named after Cecil Hart, the former manager/coach of the Montreal Canadiens. The first winner of the trophy was Frank Nighbor of Ottawa, and the first man to win it three years in succession was Bobby Orr.

"THE GREAT ONE"

Of the 50 Individual Career Records categories sanctioned by the NHL, Wayne Gretzky holds no fewer than 20. His records for Most Goals, Most Assists, Most Points, Most Consecutive 100-or-More Point Seasons, and Most Three-or-More Goal Matches are all achievements that are unlikely to be surpassed. In addition, Gretzky reached the 1,000 points pinnacle after just 424 games, 89 games fewer than Mario Lemieux. His Hart Trophy and Art Ross Trophy consecutive awards from 1981 to 1987 truly earn him his nickname, "The Great One."

TOP 10

BEST PAID PLAYERS IN THE NHL, 1995–96

	Player/team	Salary ($)
1	Wayne Gretzky, Los Angeles Kings*	6,545,363
2=	Mark Messier, New York Rangers	6,000,000
2=	Keith Tkachuk, Winnipeg Jets	6,000,000
4	Mario Lemieux, Pittsburgh Penguins	4,571,429
5	Pavel Bure, Vancouver Canucks	4,500,000
6	Pat Lafontaine, Buffalo Sabres	4,300,000
7	Eric Lindros, Philadelphia Flyers	4,182,000
8	Serge Fedorov, Detroit Red Wings	4,162,033
9	Brett Hull, St. Louis Blues	3,800,000
10	Steve Yzerman, Detroit Red Wings	3,703,803

* Traded to the St. Louis Blues during the 1995–96 season

Salaries take into account base salary and deferred payments. Signing bonuses are not included.

TOP 10

GOALS IN AN NHL CAREER*

	Player	Season	Goals
1	Wayne Gretzky#	16	814
2	Gordie Howe	26	801
3	Marcel Dionne	18	731
4	Phil Esposito	18	717
5	Mike Gartner#	16	629
6	Bobby Hull	16	610
7	Mike Bossy	10	573
8	Jari Kurri#	14	565
9	Guy Lafleur	16	560
10	John Bucyk	23	556

* Regular season only
 # Still active at end of 1994–95 season

TOP 10

ASSISTS IN AN NHL CAREER*

	Player	Season	Assists
1	Wayne Gretzky#	17	1,692
2	Gordie Howe	26	1,049
3	Marcel Dionne	18	1,040
4	Paul Coffey#	15	978
5	Stan Mikita	22	926
6	Ray Bourque#	16	908
7	Bryan Trottier	18	901
8	Mark Messier#	16	877
9	Phil Esposito	18	873
10	Bobby Clarke	15	852

* Regular season only
 # Still active at end of 1994–95 season

TOP 10

GOALTENDERS IN AN NHL CAREER*

	Goaltender	Season	Wins		Goaltender	Season	Wins
1	Terry Sawchuk	21	447	6	Gump Worsley	21	335
2	Jacques Plante	18	434	7	Harry Lumley	16	333
3	Tony Esposito	16	423	8	Andy Moog#	15	313
4	Glenn Hall	18	407	9	Billy Smith	18	305
5	Rogie Vachon	16	355	10	Turk Broda	14	302

* Regular season only   # Still active at end of 1994–95 season

TOP 10

POINTS-SCORERS IN AN NHL CAREER*

	Player	Season	Goals	Assists	Points
1	Wayne Gretzky*	16	814	1,692	2,506
2	Gordie Howe	26	801	1,049	1,850
3	Marcel Dionne	18	731	1,040	1,771
4	Phil Esposito	18	717	873	1,590
5	Stan Mikita	22	541	926	1,467
6	Bryan Trottier	18	524	901	1,425
7=	John Bucyk	23	556	813	1,369
7=	Mark Messier#	16	492	877	1,369
9	Guy Lafleur	17	560	793	1,353
10	Paul Coffey#	15	358	978	1,336

* Regular season only   # Still active at end of 1994–95 season

TOP 10

GOAL-SCORERS IN AN NHL CAREER*

	Player	Team	Season	Goals
1	Wayne Gretzky	Edmonton Oilers	1981–82	92
2	Wayne Gretzky	Edmonton Oilers	1983–84	87
3	Brett Hull	St. Louis Blues	1990–91	86
4	Mario Lemieux	Pittsburgh Penguins	1988–89	85
5=	Phil Esposito	Boston Bruins	1970–71	76
5=	Alexander Mogilny	Buffalo Sabres	1992–93	76
5=	Teemu Selanne	Winnipeg Jets	1992–93	76
8	Wayne Gretzky	Edmonton Oilers	1984–85	73
9	Brett Hull	St. Louis Blues	1989–90	72
10=	Wayne Gretzky	Edmonton Oilers	1982–83	71
10=	Jari Kurri	Edmonton Oilers	1984–85	71

SOCCER – THE TOP TEAMS

COUNTRIES IN THE WORLD CUP*

	Country	Win	R/u	3rd	4th	Total
1	Germany/ West Germany	3	3	2	1	26
2	Brazil	4	1	2	1	24
3	Italy	3	2	1	1	21
4	Argentina	2	2	-	-	14
5	Uruguay	2	-	-	2	10
6	Sweden	-	1	2	1	8
7=	Czechoslovakia	-	2	-	-	6
7=	Holland	-	2	-	-	6
7=	Hungary	-	2	-	-	6
10=	England	1	-	-	1	5
10=	France	-	-	2	1	5

* Based on 4 pts for winning the tournament, 3 pts for runner-up, 2 pts for 3rd place, and 1 pt for 4th, up to and including 1994 World Cup

TEAMS IN THE THREE MAJOR EUROPEAN CLUB COMPETITIONS

	Club/country	EC*	ECWC#	UEFA+	Total
1	Real Madrid (Spain)	6	0	2	8
2=	AC Milan (Italy)	5	2	0	7
2=	Barcelona (Spain)	1	3	3	7
4=	Ajax Amsterdam (Holland)	4	1	1	6
4=	Liverpool (England)	4	0	2	6
6	Juventus (Italy)	1	2	2	5
7=	Bayern Munich (Germany)	3	1	0	4
7=	Inter Milan (Italy)	2	0	2	4
9=	Anderlecht (Belgium)	0	2	1	3
9=	Tottenham Hotspur (England)	0	1	2	3
9=	Valencia (Spain)	0	1	2	3

* EC = European Champions' Cup
 # ECWC = European Cup-winners' Cup   + UEFA = UEFA/Fairs Cup

BRAZILIAN CHAMPIONS
Mazinho holds the FIFA World Cup aloft as Brazil become the first team to win the tournament for a 4th time, although the way they beat Italy in 1994 – after a penalty shoot-out – remains controversial.

EUROPEAN CLUBS WITH THE MOST DOMESTIC LEAGUE TITLES

	Club/country	Titles
1	Glasgow Rangers (Scotland)	45
2	Linfield (Northern Ireland)	42
3	Benfica (Portugal)	30
4	Rapid Vienna (Austria)	29
5	CSKA Sofia (Bulgaria)	28
6	Real Madrid (Spain)	26
7=	Floriana (Malta)	25
7=	Ajax Amsterdam (Holland)	25
7=	Olympiakos (Greece)	25
10=	Anderlecht (Belgium)	24
10=	Ferencvaros (Hungary)	24

The top English club is Liverpool with 18 League titles. Glasgow Rangers has won seven consecutive League titles. Aberdeen has finished runners-up to them in five of the last seven seasons. Rangers won its first title in the Scottish League's first season (1890–91) and has won at least one title every decade since then.

OLDEST UK SOCCER LEAGUE CLUBS

	Club	Year formed
1	Notts County	1862
2	Stoke City	1863
3	Nottingham Forest	1865
4	Chesterfield	1866
5	Sheffield Wednesday	1867
6	Reading	1871
7	Wrexham	1873
8=	Aston Villa	1874
8=	Bolton Wanderers	1874
10=	Birmingham City	1875
10=	Blackburn Rovers	1875

HIGHEST SCORES IN THE EUROPEAN CHAMPIONSHIP*

	Winners/losers	Score	Year#
1	Spain *vs.* Malta	12–1	1984
2	France *vs.* Azerbaijan	10–0	1996
3=	England *vs.* Luxembourg	9–0	1984
3=	Spain *vs.* Albania	9–0	1992
5=	Hungary *vs.* Luxembourg	8–1	1976
5=	Greece *vs.* Finland	8–1	1980
7=	Holland *vs.* Luxembourg+	8–0	1972
7=	West Germany *vs.* Malta	8–0	1976
7=	West Germany *vs.* Malta	8–0	1980
7=	Ireland *vs.* Malta	8–0	1984
7=	England *vs.* Turkey	8–0	1988
7=	Holland *vs.* Cyprus	8–0	1988
7=	Holland *vs.* Malta	8–0	1992
7=	Portugal *vs.* Liechtenstein	8–0	1996

* Achieved in the knockout stage
# Year the tournament finished;
 1996 tournament up to and including
 qualifying tournament only
+ Away win

CLUBS WITH THE MOST BRITISH TITLES

	Team	League Titles	FA Cup	League Cup	Total
1	Glasgow Rangers	45	26	19	90
2	Glasgow Celtic	35	30	9	74
3	Liverpool	18	4	5	27
4=	Arsenal	10	6	2	18
4=	Aston Villa	7	7	4	18
4=	Manchester United	9	8	1	18
7	Aberdeen	4	7	4	15
8	Everton	9	5	-	14
9	Heart of Midlothian	4	5	4	13
10	Tottenham Hotspur	2	8	2	12

COUNTRIES IN THE EUROPEAN CHAMPIONSHIP*

	Team	Winner	Runner-up	Semi-finalist	Points
1	Germany/West Germany	2	2	1	11
2	Former USSR	1	3	1	10
3=	Yugoslavia	0	2	1	5
3=	Spain	1	1	0	5
3=	Italy	1	0	2	5
3=	Czechoslovakia	1	0	2	5
3=	Holland	1	0	2	5
3=	Denmark	1	0	2	5
9	France	1	0	1	4
10	Belgium	0	1	1	3

* Based on 3 points for winning the title,
2 points for being runners-up, and 1 point
for being a beaten semifinalist

HIGHEST-SCORING SOCCER LEAGUE GAMES

	Match	Division	Season	Score	Goals
1	Tranmere Rovers *vs.* Oldham Athletic	3N	1935–36	13–4	17
2=	Aston Villa *vs.* Accrington	1	1891–92	12–2	14
2=	Manchester City *vs.* Lincoln City	2	1894–95	11–3	14
2=	Tottenham Hotspur *vs.* Everton	1	1958–59	10–4	14
5=	Stockport County *vs.* Halifax Town	3N	1933–34	13–0	13
5=	Newcastle United *vs.* Newport County	2	1946–47	13–0	13
5=	Barrow *vs.* Gateshead	3N	1933–34	12–1	13
5=	Sheffield United *vs.* Cardiff City	1	1925–26	11–2	13
5=	Oldham Athletic *vs.* Chester	3N	1951–52	11–2	13
5=	Hull City *vs.* Wolverhampton Wanderers	2	1919–20	10–3	13
5=	Middlesbrough *vs.* Sheffield United	1	1933–34	10–3	13
5=	Stoke City *vs.* West Bromwich Albion	1	1936–37	10–3	13
5=	Bristol City *vs.* Gillingham	3S	1926–27	9–4	13
5=	Gillingham *vs.* Exeter City	3S	1950–51	9–4	13
5=	Derby County *vs.* Blackburn Rovers	1	1890–91	8–5	13
5=	Burton Swifts *vs.* Walsall Town Swifts	2	1893–94	8–5	13
5=	Stockport County *vs.* Chester	3N	1932–33	8–5	13
5=	Charlton Athletic *vs.* Huddersfield Town	2	1957–58	7–6	13

WORLD TENNIS

WINNERS OF MEN'S GRAND SLAM SINGLES TITLES

	Player/country	A	F	W	US	Total
1	Roy Emerson (Australia)	6	2	2	2	12
2=	Björn Borg (Sweden)	0	6	5	0	11
2=	Rod Laver (Australia)	3	2	4	2	11
4=	Jimmy Connors (US)	1	0	2	5	8
4=	Ivan Lendl (Czechoslovakia)	2	3	0	3	8
4=	Fred Perry (UK)	1	1	3	3	8
4=	Ken Rosewall (Australia)	4	2	0	2	8
8=	René Lacoste (France)	0	3	2	2	7
8=	William Larned (US)	0	0	0	7	7
8=	John McEnroe (US)	0	0	3	4	7
8=	John Newcombe (Australia)	2	0	3	2	7
8=	William Renshaw (UK)	0	0	7	0	7
8=	Richard Sears (US)	0	0	0	7	7
8=	Mats Wilander (Sweden)	3	3	0	1	7

A = *Australian Open*; F = *French Open*; W = *Wimbledon*;
US = *US Open*

WINNERS OF WOMEN'S GRAND SLAM SINGLES TITLES

	Player/country	A	F	W	US	Total
1	Margaret Court (*née* Smith) (Australia)	11	5	3	5	24
2	Helen Wills-Moody (US)	0	4	8	7	19
3=	Chris Evert-Lloyd (US)	2	7	3	6	18
3=	Martina Navratilova (Czechoslovakia/US)	3	2	9	4	18
3=	Steffi Graf (Germany)	4	4	6	4	18
6	Billie Jean King (*née* Moffitt) (US)	1	1	6	4	12
7	Maureen Connolly (US)	1	2	3	3	9
8=	Suzanne Lenglen (France)	0	2	6	0	8
8=	Molla Mallory (*née* Bjurstedt) (US)	0	0	0	8	8
8=	Monica Seles (Yugoslavia)	3	3	0	2	8

A = *Australian Open*; F = *French Open*; W = *Wimbledon*;
US = *US Open*

PLAYERS WITH THE MOST FRENCH CHAMPIONSHIP SINGLES TITLES

	Player/country	Years	Titles
1	Chris Evert-Lloyd (US)	1974–86	7
2	Björn Borg (Sweden)	1974–81	6
3	Margaret Court (*née* Smith) (Australia)	1962–73	5
4=	Henri Cochet (France)	1926–32	4
4=	Helen Wills-Moody (US)	1928–32	4
4=	Steffi Graf (Germany)	1987–95	4
7=	René Lacoste (France)	1925–29	3
7=	Hilde Sperling (Germany)	1935–37	3
7=	Yvon Petra (France)	1943–45	3
7=	Ivan Lendl (Czechoslovakia)	1984–87	3
7=	Mats Wilander (Sweden)	1982–88	3
7=	Monica Seles (Yugoslavia)	1990–92	3

PLAYERS WITH THE MOST AUSTRALIAN CHAMPIONSHIP SINGLES TITLES

	Player*	Years	Titles
1	Margaret Court	1960–73	11
2=	Nancy Bolton	1937–51	6
2=	Roy Emerson	1961–67	6
4	Daphne Akhurst	1925–30	5
5=	Pat Wood	1914–23	4
5=	Jack Crawford	1931–35	4
5=	Ken Rosewall	1953–72	
5=	Evonne Cawley	1974–77	4
5=	Steffi Graf (Ger)	1988–94	4
5=	Monica Seles (Yug)	1991–96	4

* *Players are from Australia unless otherwise stated*

THE GREAT ROY EMERSON
Throughout the 1960s Roy Emerson and fellow Australian Rod Laver were the world's best tennis players. Along with Fred Perry, they remain the only men to win all four Grand Slam titles, with Emerson winning a record 12.

TOP 10
PLAYERS WITH THE MOST US SINGLES TITLES

	Player*	Years	Titles
1	Molla Mallory (*née* Bjurstedt)	1915–26	8
2=	Richard Sears	1881–87	7
2=	William Larned	1901–11	7
2=	Bill Tilden	1920–29	7
2=	Helen Wills-Moody	1923–31	7
2=	Margaret Court (Australia)	1962–70	7
7	Chris Evert-Lloyd	1975–82	6
8	Jimmy Connors	1974–83	5
9=	Robert Wrenn	1893–97	4
9=	Elisabeth Moore	1896–1905	4
9=	Hazel Wightman (*née* Hotchkiss)	1909–19	4
9=	Helen Jacobs	1932–35	4
9=	Alice Marble	1936–40	4
9=	Pauline Betz	1942–46	4
9=	Maria Bueno (Brazil)	1959–66	4
9=	Billie Jean King	1967–74	4
9=	John McEnroe	1979–84	4
9=	Martina Navratilova	1983–87	4

* Players are from the US unless otherwise stated

TOP 10
PLAYERS WITH THE MOST WIMBLEDON TITLES

	Player/country	Years	Singles	Doubles	Mixed	Total
1	Billie Jean King (*née* Moffitt) (US)	1961–79	6	10	4	20
2	Elizabeth Ryan (US)	1914–34	0	12	7	19
3	Martina Navratilova (Czechoslovakia/US)	1976–95	9	7	2	18
4	Suzanne Lenglen (France)	1919–25	6	6	3	15
5	William Renshaw (UK)	1880–89	7	7	0	14
6=	Louise Brough (US)	1946–55	4	5	4	13
6=	Lawrence Doherty (UK)	1897–1905	5	8	0	13
8=	Helen Wills-Moody (US)	1927–38	8	3	1	12
8=	Reginald Doherty (UK)	1897–1905	4	8	0	12
10=	Margaret Court (*née* Smith) (Australia)	1953–75	3	2	5	10
10=	Doris Hart (US)	1947–55	1	4	5	10

Billie Jean King's first and last Wimbledon titles were in the ladies' doubles. The first, in 1961, as Billie Jean Moffitt, was with Karen Hantze when they beat Jan Lehane and Margaret Smith 6–3, 6–4. When Billie Jean won her record-breaking 20th title in 1979, she partnered Martina Navratilova to victory over Betty Stove and Wendy Turnbull. Billie Jean could have increased her total in 1983 but was defeated in the mixed doubles. The foremost male player, William Renshaw, won two of his titles in the doubles in 1880 and 1881. These matches were then known as the Oxford University Doubles Championship but are now regarded as having full Wimbledon Championship status. William and his twin brother Ernest won 22 titles between them. The Doherty brothers' dominance of world tennis began with Reginald, known as "Big Do," winning the 1897 Wimbledon singles title. For the next eight years they reigned supreme, winning a total of 25 titles.

WIMBLEDON RECORD-HOLDER
Martina Navratilova's nine singles wins between 1978 and 1990 make her Wimbledon's undisputed singles champion.

TOP 10
FEMALE PLAYERS*

	Player	Country
1=	Steffi Graf	Germany
1=	Monica Seles	US
3	Conchita Martinez	Spain
4	Arantxa Sanchez Vicario	Spain
5	Iva Majoli	Croatia
6	Anke Huber	Germany
7	Gabriella Sabatini	Argentina
8	Magdalena Maleeva	Bulgaria
9	Kimiko Date	Japan
10	Mary Jo Fernandez	US

* As ranked by the ATP and the WTA

TOP 10
MALE PLAYERS*

	Player	Country
1	Thomas Muster	Austria
2	Pete Sampras	US
3	Andre Agassi	US
4	Boris Becker	Germany
5	Michael Chang	US
6	Yevgeny Kafelnikov	Russia
7	Thomas Enqvist	Sweden
8	Jim Courier	US
9	Goran Ivanisevic	Croatia
10	Wayne Ferreira	South Africa

* As ranked by the ATP and the WTA

WINTER SPORTS

WINNERS OF WORLD ICE DANCE TITLES

Skater/country	Years	Titles
1= Alexsandr Gorshkov (USSR)	1970–76	6
1= Lyudmila Pakhomova (USSR)	1970–76	6
3= Lawrence Demmy (GB)	1951–55	5
3= Jean Westwood (GB)	1951–55	5
5= Courtney Jones (GB)	1957–60	4
5= Eva Romanova (Cze)	1962–65	4
5= Pavel Roman (Cze)	1963–65	4
5= Diane Towler (GB)	1966–69	4
5= Bernard Ford (GB)	1966–69	4
5= Jane Torvill (GB)	1981–84	4
5= Christopher Dean (GB)	1981–84	4
5= Natalya Bestemianova (USSR)	1985–88	4
5= Andrei Bukin (USSR)	1985–88	4

COOL RUNNINGS
The four-man bobsled has been an Olympic event since 1924.

ICE DANCE CHAMPIONS
British ice-skaters Jane Torvill and Christopher Dean dominated the sport in the 1980s, winning four World titles and the 1984 Olympic Ice Dance gold medal, with a maximum score of nine sixes for artistic impression.

OLYMPIC BOBSLEDDING NATIONS

	Country	G	S	B	Total
1	Switzerland	9	8	8	25
2	Germany/ West Germany	4	5	6	15
3	US	5	4	5	14
4	East Germany	5	6	2	13
5	Italy	3	4	3	10
6=	Austria	1	2	0	3
6=	UK	1	1	1	3
6=	Former USSR	1	0	2	3
9	Belgium	0	1	1	2
10=	Canada	1	0	0	1
10=	Romania	0	0	1	1

G = Gold medal
S = Silver medal
B = Bronze medal

WORLD AND OLYMPIC FIGURE SKATING TITLES – MEN

Skater/country	Years	Titles
1 Ulrich Salchow (Sweden)	1901–11	11
2 Karl Schäfer (Austria)	1930–36	9
3 Dick Button (US)	1948–52	7
4 Gillis Grafstrom (Sweden)	1920–29	6
5= Hayes Jenkins (US)	1953–56	5
5= Scott Hamilton (US)	1981–84	5
7= Willy Bockl (Austria)	1925–28	4
7= David Jenkins (US)	1957–60	4
7= Ondrej Nepela (Czechoslovakia)	1971–73	4
7= Kurt Browning (Canada)	1989–93	4

WORLD AND OLYMPIC FIGURE SKATING TITLES – WOMEN

Skater/country	Years	Titles
1 Sonja Henie (Norway)	1927–36	13
2= Carol Heiss (US)	1956–60	6
2= Herma Planck Szabo (Austria)	1922–26	6
2= Katarina Witt (East Germany)	1984–88	6
5= Lily Kronberger (Hungary)	1908–11	4
5= Sjoukje Dijkstra (Netherlands)	1962–64	4
5= Peggy Fleming (US)	1966–68	4
8= Meray Horvath (Hungary)	1912–14	3
8= Tenley Albright (US)	1953–56	3
8= Annett Poetzsch (East Gemany)	1978–80	3
8= Beatrix Schuba (Austria)	1971–72	3
8= Barbara Ann Scott (Canada)	1947–48	3
8= Kristi Yamaguchi (US)	1991–92	3
8= Madge Sayers (UK)	1906–08	3

DOWNHILL RACER
Ski races have been held since the last century, but have developed as major Olympic and World events in the 20th along with the international growth of interest in the sport.

T O P 1 0

ALPINE SKIING WORLD CUP TITLES – WOMEN

	Name/country	Years	Titles
1	Annemarie Moser-Pröll (Austria)	1971–79	6
2=	Vreni Schneider (Switzerland)	1989–95	3
2=	Petra Kronberger (Austria)	1990–92	3
4=	Nancy Greene (Canada)	1967–68	2
4=	Hanni Wenzel (Liechtenstein)	1978–80	2
4=	Erika Hess (Switzerland)	1982–84	2
4=	Michela Figini (Switzerland)	1985–88	2
4=	Maria Walliser (Switzerland)	1986–87	2
9=	Gertrude Gabl (Austria)	1969	1
9=	Michèle Jacot (France)	1970	1
9=	Rosi Mittermeier (West Germany)	1976	1
9=	Lise-Marie Morerod (Switzerland)	1977	1
9=	Marie-Thérèse Nadig (Switzerland)	1981	1
9=	Tamara McKinney (US)	1983	1
9=	Anita Wachter (Austria)	1993	1

T O P 1 0

ALPINE SKIING WORLD CUP TITLES – MEN

	Name	Country	Years	Titles
1	Marc Girardelli	Luxembourg	1985–93	5
2=	Gustavo Thoeni	Italy	1971–75	4
2=	Pirmin Zurbriggen	Switzerland	1984–90	4
4=	Ingemar Stenmark	Sweden	1976–78	3
4=	Phil Mahre	US	1981–83	3
6=	Jean Claude Killy	France	1967–68	2
6=	Karl Schranz	Austria	1969–70	2
8=	Piero Gross	Italy	1974	1
8=	Peter Lüscher	Switzerland	1979	1
8=	Andreas Wenzel	Liechtenstein	1980	1
8=	Paul Accola	Switzerland	1992	1
8=	Kjetil-Andre Aamodt	Norway	1994	1
8=	Alberto Tomba	Italy	1995	1

T O P 1 0

WINTER OLYMPIC MEDAL-WINNING NATIONS

	Country	Gold	Silver	Bronze	Total
1	Russia/Former USSR	99	71	71	241
2	Norway	73	77	64	214
3	US	53	55	39	147
4	Austria	36	48	44	128
5	West Germany/Germany	45	43	37	125
6	Finland	36	45	42	123
7	East Germany	39	36	35	110
8	Sweden	39	26	34	99
9	Switzerland	27	29	29	85
10	Italy	25	21	21	67

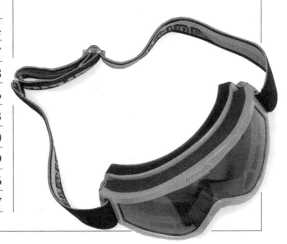

OTHER SPORTS

MOST COMMON
SPORTS INJURIES

	Common name	Medical term
1	Bruise	Soft tissue contusion
2	Sprained ankle	Sprain of the lateral ligament
3	Sprained knee	Sprain of the medial collateral ligament
4	Low back strain	Lumbar joint dysfunction
5	Hamstring tear	Muscle tear of the hamstrings
6	Jumper's knee	Patellar tendinitis
7	Achilles tendinitis	Tendinitis of the Achilles tendon
8	Shin splints	Medial periostitis of the tibia
9	Tennis elbow	Lateral epicondylitis
10	Shoulder strain	Rotator cuff tendinitis

WORST DISASTERS AT SPORTS VENUES*

	Location	Disaster	Date	No. killed
1	Hong Kong Jockey Club	Stand collapse and fire	Feb 26, 1918	604
2	Lenin Stadium, Moscow, Russia	Crush in soccer stadium	Oct 20, 1982	340
3	Lima, Peru	Soccer stadium riot	May 24, 1964	320
4	Sinceljo, Colombia	Bullring stand collapse	Jan 20, 1980	222
5	Hillsborough, Sheffield, UK	Crush in soccer stadium	Apr 15, 1989	96
6	Le Mans, France	Racing car crash	Jun 11, 1955	82
7	Katmandu, Nepal	Stampede in soccer stadium	Mar 12, 1988	80
8	Buenos Aires, Argentina	Riot in soccer stadium	May 2, 1968	73
9	Ibrox Park, Glasgow, UK	Barrier collapse in soccer stadium	Jan 2, 1971	66
10	Bradford Stadium, UK	Fire in soccer stadium	May 11, 1985	56

* 20th Century only

Before the Ibrox Park disaster, the worst accident at a British stadium was caused by the collapse of a stand at Burnden Park, Bolton, on March 9, 1946, which left 33 dead and 400 injured. Such tragedies are not an exclusively modern phenomenon: during the reign of Roman Emperor Antoninus Pius (AD 138–161), a stand at the Circus Maximus collapsed during a gladiatorial spectacle, and 1,162 spectators were killed.

MOVIES WITH
SPORTS THEMES

	Movie/year	Sport
1	*Rocky IV* (1985)	Boxing
2	*Rocky III* (1982)	Boxing
3	*Rocky* (1976)	Boxing
4	*A League of Their Own* (1992)	Women's baseball
5	*Rocky II* (1979)	Boxing
6=	*Days of Thunder* (1990)	Stock car racing
6=	*White Men Can't Jump* (1992)	Basketball
8	*Chariots of Fire* (1973)	Track
9	*Field of Dreams* (1989)	Baseball
10	*The Main Event* (1979)	Boxing

The boxing ring, a natural source of drama and thrills, dominates Hollywood's most successful sports-based epics.

TV AUDIENCES OF ALL TIME FOR
SPORTS EVENTS IN THE US

	Program	Date	TV households total	%
1	Super Bowl XVI (San Francisco *vs.* Cincinnati)	Jan 24, 1982	40,020,000	49.1
2	Super Bowl XVII (Washington *vs.* Miami)	Jan 30, 1983	40,500,000	48.6
3	XVII Winter Olympics	Feb 23, 1994	45,690,000	48.5
4	Super Bowl XX (Chicago *vs.* New England)	Jan 26, 1986	41,490,000	48.3
5	Super Bowl XII (Dallas *vs.* Denver)	Jan 15, 1978	34,410,000	47.2
6	Super Bowl XIII (Dallas *vs.* Pittsburgh)	Jan 21, 1979	35,090,000	47.1
7=	Super Bowl XVIII (LA Raiders *vs.* Washington)	Jan 22, 1984	38,800,000	46.4
7=	Super Bowl XIX (San Francisco *vs.* Miami)	Jan 20, 1985	39,390,000	46.4
9	Super Bowl XIV (LA Rams *vs.* Pittsburgh)	Jan 20, 1980	35,330,000	46.3
10	Super Bowl XXI (Giants *vs.* Denver)	Jan 25, 1987	40,030,000	45.8

Copyright © 1994 Nielsen Media Research

"TV households" indicates the number of households with TV sets: population growth and the acquisition of sets steadily increase this figure, so recent events attract higher audiences. Super Bowl XXX on January 28, 1996 attracted the greatest number of individual viewers of any US TV program ever, but a rating of only 41.3 keeps it outside this Top 10.

T O P 1 0

HIGHEST-EARNING SPORTSMEN IN THE WORLD IN 1995

	Name*	Sport	Income ($) Salary/ winnings	Other#	Total
1	Michael Jordan	Basketball	3,900,000	40,000,000	43,900,000
2	Mike Tyson	Boxing	40,000,000	-	40,000,000
3	Deion Sanders	Football/ Baseball	16,500,000	6,000,000	22,500,000
4	Riddick Bowe	Boxing	22,000,000	200,000	22,200,000
5	Shaquille O'Neal	Basketball	4,900,000	17,000,000	21,900,000
6	George Foreman	Boxing	10,000,000	8,000,000	18,000,000
7	Andre Agassi	Tennis	3,000,000	13,000,000	16,000,000
8	Jack Nicklaus	Golf	600,000	14,500,000	15,100,000
9	Michael Schumacher (Germany)	Motor racing	10,000,000	5,000,000	15,000,000
10	Wayne Gretzky (Canada)	Ice hockey	8,500,000	6,000,000	14,500,000

* All sportsmen are from the US, unless otherwise stated
# Sponsorship and royalty income from endorsed sporting products
Used by permission of Forbes Magazine

Michael Jordan's return to basketball not only increased his sports earnings from a meager $100,000 to $3,900,000, but also elevated his endorsements from $30,000,000 to $40,000,000. *Forbes's* analysis of highest-earning athletes lists 40 with total incomes of more than $6,200,000, up from $4,800,000 last year. Among them, baseball is the best-represented sport, with eight individuals in the chart; followed by basketball and football, both with seven; tennis and boxing with five; golf and motor racing with three; ice hockey with two; and one stock car racer.

T O P 1 0

MOST EFFECTIVE FITNESS ACTIVITIES

1	Swimming
2	Cycling
3	Rowing
4	Gymnastics
5	Judo
6	Dancing
7	Soccer
8	Jogging
9	Walking (briskly)
10	Squash

These are the Top 10 sports and activities recommended as the best means of acquiring a degree of all around fitness, building stamina and strength, and increasing flexibility.

T O P 1 0

PARTICIPATION SPORTS, GAMES, AND PHYSICAL ACTIVITIES IN THE US

	Activity	No. participating*
1	Exercise walking	70,800,000
2	Swimming	60,300,000
3	Cycling	49,800,000
4	Fishing	45,700,000
5	Exercising with equipment	43,800,000
6	Camping	42,900,000
7	Bowling	37,400,000
8	Billiards/pool	34,000,000
9	Basketball	28,200,000
10	Boating	26,400,000

* On more than one occasion
Source: National Sporting Goods Association

Perhaps surprisingly, the US National Sporting Goods Association survey indicated that the national game of baseball as a participation sport scored relatively low (15,100,000 followers), below such activities as golf (24,600,000), in-line roller-skating (19,500,000), and hunting with firearms (15,400,000). Soccer has greatly increased its following over the past decade – particularly following the country's hosting of the 1994 World Cup – and now has 12,500,000 adherents.

INDEX

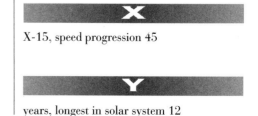

ACKNOWLEDGMENTS

I would like to thank Caroline Ash for her indispensable assistance in compiling *The Top 10 of Everything*, along with Luke Crampton, Barry Lazell, Ian Morrison, Dafydd Rees, and the following individuals and organizations who kindly supplied the information to enable me to prepare many of the lists:

Richard Braddish, Steve Butler, Shelly Cagner, Annette Combs, Jim Davie, Paul Dickson, Dr. Stephen Durham, Christopher Forbes, Darryl Francis, Max Hanna, Peter Harland, Duncan Hislop, Tony Hutson, Robert Lamb, Bernard Lavery, Dr. Benjamin Lucas, Rebecca McCloud, Hugh Meller, Dr. Jacqueline Mitton, Giles Moon, George Needham, Tim O'Brien, Adrian Room, Yoel Sand, Rocky Stockman, MBE, James Taylor, Steve van Dulken, Tony Waltham, Arthur H. Waltz

Academy of Motion Picture Arts and Sciences, AEA Technology, Airport Operators Council International, American Forestry Association, American Kennel Club, *Amusement Business*, *Animal World*, *Annual Abstract of Statistics*, Arbitron, Art Sales Index, Association of Comics Enthusiasts, Audit Bureau of Circulations, BAFTA, Bank of England, BBC Publicity, BBC Radio, BBC Worldwide Television, BBC Written Archives, Ben & Jerry's, Beverage Marketing Corporation, *Billboard*, BMI, BNIF, Bonhams, Bookwatch Ltd, *BP Statistical Review of World Energy*, Brad Shaw Promotion Consultants, British Astronomical Society, British Broadcasting Corporation, British Library, British Museum, British Rate & Data, Bureau of Engraving and Printing, Bureau of Federal Prisons, Bureau of Justice Statistics, Cadbury Schweppes Group, Cameron Mackintosh Ltd., Carbon Dioxide Information Analysis Center/ Greg Marland/Tom Boden, Carson Productions, Cat Fanciers' Association of the USA, Central Intelligence Agency, Central Statistical Office, Championship Auto Racing Teams (CART), Channel Four Television, Channel Swimming Association, Christie's East, Christie's London, Christie's South Kensington, Civil Aviation Authority, *Classical Music*, Coca-Cola, Coca-Cola Great Britain and Ireland, Council for the Care of Churches, Criminal Justice Reference Service, *Criminal Statistics England & Wales*, Curtis Management Group, Dateline, Death Penalty Information Center, Department of Health, Department of Trade and Industry, Department of Transport, Electoral Reform Society, Entertainment Data, Inc., Environmental Protection Agency, Euromonitor, The Fancy Dress Emporium, Federal Bureau of Investigation, Feste Catalogue Index Database/Alan Somerset, Food and Agriculture Organization of the United Nations, *Forbes Magazine*, Ford Motor Company Ltd, Generation AB, Geological Museum, London, George Foster Peabody Awards, Giga Information Group, Global Network Navigator, Inc., Governing Council of the Cat Fancy, Hamleys of Regent Street Ltd., Harley Medical Group, Health and Safety Executive, H.J. Heinz Co. Ltd., Higher Education Statistics Agency, Hollywood Foreign Press Association, Home Office, Indianapolis 500, Infoplan, Institute of Sports Medicine, International Civil Aviation Organization, International Cocoa Organization, International Coffee Organization, International Dairy Foods Association, International Monetary Fund, International Tea Committee, International Union of Geological Sciences Commission on Comparative Planetology, *International Water Power and Dam Construction Handbook*, ITV Network Centre, Jewish Board of Deputies, Jockey Club, Kellogg Company of Great Britain, Kennel Club, Library Association, Lloyds Register of Shipping, London Heathrow Airport, London Regional Transport, London Theatre Record, London Transport Lost Property, Magazine Publishers of America, Major League Baseball, MARC Europe, Mars, Inc., Mars UK Ltd., Meteorological Office, Metropolitan Museum of Art, New York, Metropolitan Opera House, New York, MORI, Motor Vehicle Manufacturers Association of the United States, MRIB, MTV, NASA, National Association for Stock Car Auto Racing (NASCAR), National Basketball Association (NBA), National Canine Defence League, National Center for Education Statistics, National Center for Health Statistics, National Climatic Data Center, National Criminal Justice Reference Service, National Dairy Council, National Football League (NFL), National Gallery of Art, Washington, DC, National Grid Company plc, National Hockey League (NHL), National Public Radio, National Railway Museum, National Safety Council, National Solid Waste Management Association, National Sporting Goods Association, NCAA, NCTA, New York Drama Desk, Niagara Falls Museum, A.C. Nielsen Co Ltd, Nielsen Media Research, Nobel Foundation, Office of Population Censuses and Surveys, The Pasta Information Centre, Patent and Trademark Depository Library, Patent Office, UK, Pet Industry Joint Advisory Council, PGA Tour, Inc., Phillips West Two, Phobics Society, Produktschap voor Gedistilleerde Dranken, Professional Golf Association (PGA), Public Library Association, *Publishers Weekly*, Pullman Power Products Corporation, *Railway Gazette International*, RAJAR, Really Useful Group, Registrar General, Relate National Marriage Guidance Council, Royal Aeronautical Society, Royal Mint, Royal Opera House, Royal Society for the Prevention of Cruelty to Animals, Royal Society for the Protection of Birds, Science Museum, London, *Screen Digest*, Shakespeare Birthplace Trust, Siemens AG, Society of Actuaries, Sotheby's London, Sotheby's New York, *Spaceflight*, Sports Council, *Statistical Abstract of the United States*, The Sugar Bureau, Tags & Etc., Tate Gallery, Taylors of Loughborough, Telecom Security, Theatre Museum, Theatre Record, Tidy Britain Group, *Time*, *The Times*, *The Times 1000*, Trebor Bassett, Tree Register of the British Isles, UNESCO, *Uniform Crime Statistics*, United Nations, University of Westminster, University Statistical Record, US Bureau of Labor Statistics, US Bureau of the Census, USCOLD, US Department of Agriculture, US Department of Agriculture Forest Service, US Department of Justice, US Department of Labor, US Department of the Interior, National Register of Historic Places, US Department of Transportation, Federal Aviation Administration, US Department of Transportation, Federal Highway Administration, US Department of Transportation, National Traffic Safety Administration, US Fish and Wildlife Service, US Geological Survey, US Immigration and Naturalization Service, US Mint, US Social Security Administration, *USA Today*, *Variety*, Victoria & Albert Museum, London, Videoscan, *Video Store Magazine*, *Waste Age*, *Wisden Cricket Monthly*, World Bank, World Health Organization, World Intellectual Property Organization, *World of Travel Shopping*, Zenith International.

PICTURE CREDITS

t=top c=center a=above b=below l=left r=right

© Academy of Motion Picture Arts & Sciences ® 156al;

Allsport 224bl, 224acr, 236bcl, 244bcr, 245br, 246tc /Dave Cannon 3br, 246bl;

© Bassano & Vandyk Portrait Studios 59tc;

Bridgeman Art Library 58tl /National Gallery 119br /Victoria & Albert Museum 111tl;

Camera Press 114tr;

J. Allan Cash 208tc;

Bruce Coleman 103tr;

Mary Evans Picture Library 15cb, 71tr, 216tl;

FLPA 11tl;

Giraudon/Bridgeman Art Library/Louvre, Paris 122bl;

Ronald Grant Archive 152bl /Columbia 169tr /MGM 168tr /Miramax Buena Vista 163bcr /Paramount 169tl /Twentieth Century Fox 168tl;

Robert Harding Picture Library: 84tl, 123tr, 178bl, 210–211bc / G. & P. Corrigan 42bl;

Hulton-Getty Collection 44bl, 56ac, 62bcl, 79tl, 221bcr /MSI 171tc;

Image Bank 11br /Steve Dunwell 208c /Guang Jui Xie: 86tr /Peter Hendrie 87tr /Bill Hickey 89tr /Michael Salas 209bcr;

Imperial War Museum 77tr;

Jurassic Park 1993/UIP/Universal/Amblin 151c;

Katz Pictures/Snap Photo 127tr;

Kellogg Company of Great Britain Ltd 197br;

David King Collection 112tl;

Magnum Photos Ltd/Burt Glinn 62tr;

Microscopix 46bcr;

The Military Picture Library/Julie Collins 4br, 79cb /John Peart: 81 br;

Tony Morrison/South American Pictures 43tr;

NASA 18bl, 26b, (front jacket bl) /Finley-Holiday Films 1bc, 19tr /Science Photo Library 45br;

Robert Opie 196bc, 197bl, 197tc;

Photostage 145tl, (front jacket cr) /Donald Cooper 142tl;

Pictor 235tcr;

Range/Bettmann UPI 238tl, 239bc /Reuter/Bettmann 83tr;

Redferns/John de Garis 176cb;

© 1996 Les Éditions Albert René/Goscinny-Uderzo 1br, 113tr;

Rex Features 1cr, 54cb, 57tl, 64bcl, 118bl, 124tr, 128acr, 129bl, 132tr, 133cr, 155br, 158bl, 159tr, 165tc, 167br / Fotex, R.Dreschsler 137tr /Fotos International 153cr /D.Hogan 134tl /Dave Lewis 1bl, 164bl /Brian Rasic 124bl /Crispin Rodwell 125bl /Jim Selby 172tl /Sipa 135tc;

Science Photo Library/US Naval Observatory 8tr, /Dr Fred Espenak 9c /J.Baum & N.Henbest 14bl /David Nunuk 14–15tc;

Sotheby's 3ct, 140bc;

Frank Spooner Pictures: 64tr /Clasos Press: 191bl / Simon Grosset 2cb, 62cr /A.Mohadir 144bl /Stills 148tl;

Sporting Pictures 230bl, 233bcr, 242bcl, 247tl;

Tony Stone Images/ Val Corbett 101br /Tony Garcia 72tl /Arnulf Husmo 187tl /Jon Riley 185tc /Terry Vine 105tc;

Syndication International 125bcr;

Text 100/Microsoft 193bcr;

World Pictures/Feature-Pix Colour Library 20tc;

Zefa Pictures 1cl, 2tr, 10bl, 25tr, 28br, 29tcl, 88tc, 104bc, 106cr, 212bl, 214tr, 215br.

Every effort has been made to trace the copyright holders and we apologize in advance for any unintentional omissions. We would be pleased to insert the appropriate acknowledgement in any subsequent edition of this publication.

ILLUSTRATIONS

Paul Collicutt, Angelika Elsebach, Nicholas Hewetson, Roger Hutchins, Kenneth Lilly, Janos Marffy, Robbie Polly, Eric Thomas, Halli Verrinder, Richard Ward, David Webb, Dan Wright.

PUBLISHER'S ACKNOWLEDGMENTS

Dorling Kindersley would like to thank the following people: For design, editorial, and DTP assistance: Zirrinia Austin, Austin Barlow, Collette Connolly, Penelope Cream, Katie John, Jason Little, Phil Ormerod, Ellen Woodward. For administrative assistance: Anna Youle.